OUR
UNFREE
PRESS

100 Years of Radical Media Criticism

OUR
UNFREE
PRESS

100 Years of Radical Media Criticism

Edited by Robert W. McChesney
and Ben Scott

THE NEW PRESS

NEW YORK
LONDON

Pages 437–38 constitute an extension of this copyright page

Published in the United States by The New Press, New York, 2004
Distributed by W. W. Norton & Company, Inc., New York

LIBRARY OF CONGRESS CATALOGING-IN-PUBLICATION DATA

Our unfree press : 100 years of media criticism / edited by Robert W. McChesney and
Ben Scott.
    p. cm.
    Includes bibliographical references.
    ISBN 1-56584-917-5 (hc) — ISBN 1-56584-855-1 (pbk.)
    1. Freedom of the press—United States. 2. Mass media—Ownership—United States.
I. Title: Our unfree press, one hundred years of media criticism. II. McChesney,
Robert Waterman, 1952- III. Scott, Ben, 1977-

PN4738.O94 2004
323.44'5'0973—dc22

2003061542

The New Press was established in 1990 as a not-for-profit alternative to the large, commercial publishing houses currently dominating the book publishing industry. The New Press operates in the public interest rather than for private gain, and is committed to publishing, in innovative ways, works of educational, cultural, and community value that are often deemed insufficiently profitable.

The New Press, 38 Greene Street, 4th floor, New York, NY 10013
www.thenewpress.com

In the United Kingdom: 6 Salem Road, London W2 4BU

Composition by Westchester Book Composition

Printed in Canada

2   4   6   8   10   9   7   5   3   1

CONTENTS

INTRODUCTION

Robert W. McChesney and Ben Scott

Almost three years ago, in 2001, a prominent European media scholar contacted us. He said that he was compiling a book of essays chronicling radical democratic criticism of commercial journalism from nations around the world. The book would emphasize a common theme—the problems a market-based media system poses for societies that wish to have a free press that serves democratic values. He said that he doubted he would include a chapter from the United States, because there was no such tradition of criticism to be found there. Oh yes, he acknowledged, Ben Bagdikian and Noam Chomsky and one or two other people had written some critical material in recent times, but for the most part Americans appeared satisfied with the journalism generated by the commercial media. After all, the United States is the birthplace of commercial journalism, and it is there that many of the world's dominant media corporations are based. He asked us if there might possibly be enough material from the United States to produce even a short chapter, because his book would benefit by having something, anything, from the United States.

Being critical media scholars ourselves, we were sobered by this European assessment of the lack of quality and breadth in the history of U.S. press criticism. But we were not surprised. The conventional view within the United States is that the history of American journalism chronicles the development of a trusted vehicle for democratic public debate and informed citizenship. The commercial press system is thought to be ordained by the Founding Fathers as the engine of participatory self-government. While individual editors or publishers along the way may be castigated for failing to do their jobs well, the system itself is beyond reproach. The image of fair and balanced public servants hounding politicians and exposing corruption has been a staple of our civics classes for generations—and for good reason. It is in the United States, and the United States alone, that press freedom is the centerpiece of the entire political project. It is meant to be the shining star of a democratic political economy. Moreover, it is an integral part of the vision of greatness the U.S. projects of itself in the global media system. In this frame, the bottom-line principle that our free press is the envy of the world is not even subject to critical analysis; it is an article of faith if one believes in America, in freedom, in democracy.

The conventional wisdom and our European friend are both totally wrong. What he saw as token critics of the free press, Bagdikian and Chomsky, are actually at the vanguard of a wave of media criticism taking place right now in the United States. The current notoriety of radical media criticism extends far beyond social critics of the left. In fact, U.S. journalism is in the midst of a full-blown crisis, and an expanding, diverse group of critics are talking about it all the time. The symptoms of the crisis—a decline in hard news, a lack of investigative and process stories, staff cuts, concentrating ownership structures, closure of independent papers, more advertising, more tabloid fare, trends toward info-tainment, and bias in the name of balance—have become common knowledge as they worsen. The deeper roots of why all this is happening—the near total elision of public service priorities by commercial imperatives—have also begun to come under investigation by key groups.

In academic circles, American scholars have produced some of the most important critical studies of the media system ever written in the last few years. Notable among them are Robert W. McChesney's *Rich Media, Poor Democracy* and C. Edwin Baker's *Media, Markets, and Democracy*. Moreover, updated editions of classic texts like Noam Chomksy and Ed Herman's *Manufacturing Consent* and Bagdikian's *The Media Monopoly* have recently been reissued. Far from being renegade studies, they have become the standard by which contemporary academic work in the field is judged.

Public interest groups have also begun to speak out about the problems they see in newsrooms and to organize their members to raise awareness and agitate for reform. For example, Fairness & Accuracy In Reporting, founded in the late 1980s, has become a center of sophisticated media criticism. FAIR's weekly radio show, *Counterspin*, and its bimonthly publication, *Extra!*, are a trusted antidote to commercial journalism for tens of thousands of citizens. Consumer advocacy groups like Consumers Union and the Consumers Federation of America have joined the media debate and have become very involved in the political fight over government regulation. Moreover, activist groups have sprung up across the country to organize and agitate for a better media system—Free Press, Prometheus Radio Project, Media Channel, Reclaim the Media, and the Center for Digital Democracy, to name just a few.

Perhaps most tellingly, this critical movement also includes many journalists who are increasingly aware that corporate ownership and commercial pressures have gone a long way toward destroying journalism as a democratic public service. The unions are at the forefront of the struggle. Linda Foley, president of the Newspaper Guild, the union of print journalists, often states that the number-one concern of her members, even ahead of salary, is the negative effect of commercial encroachment on quality journalism. It is a cancer that plagues not only the news and views we see in the paper every morning, but the lives of working editors and reporters.

Foley's is not a critique confined to the view of the rank and file of the Guild. Leonard Downie Jr. and Robert Kaiser, both senior editors at the *Washington Post*, present a scathing critique of contemporary journalism in their recent book, *The News About the News: American Journalism in Peril*. It chronicles a downward spiral in the industry in the last decade. These editors note the intensification of the crisis in the late nineties, the dozens of articles in the trade press decrying the steady decline of journalistic standards, and the hand-wringing among the elite cadre of newsmakers who have stood by, watching the bottom fall out. At base, according to Downie and Kaiser, the problem is the conflict that has risen to the surface with a startling frequency between private profit and public service. "Many news people were caught off guard by the way economic forces blew through their business. By the second half of the 1990s—even before another damaging round of cuts in staffs and coverage in 2001—a crisis of confidence was evident in American journalism."[1]

Downie and Kaiser's critique is not a shot in the dark. It is the latest broadside in a volley of insider whistle-blowing. The former editor of the *Chicago Tribune* James Squires wrote his account of the "corporate takeover" of journalism in 1993, shortly after he left the industry. He concluded: "[The corporate media] are primarily concerned then not with the preservation of the free press or the conduct of democracy but with development of the information business in its most profitable form, whatever that may be. Anything else, under the rules of their ownership, is a betrayal of their stockholders."[2] In 1997, a group of two dozen leading journalists led by Bill Kovach and Tom Rosenstiel gathered to address the collapsing standards in their profession and formed the Committee of Concerned Journalists (CCJ). They convened a meeting and issued a statement, which has been signed by scores of their colleagues, reaffirming and committing themselves to the public service mission of democratic journalism.[3] "They were there because they thought something was seriously wrong with their profession. They barely recognized what they considered journalism in much of the work of their colleagues. Instead of serving a larger public interest, they feared, their profession was damaging it."[4] The group undertook a massive study of the profession and issued numerous articles and books.

These books stand in good company with many others. Greg Palast's *The Best Democracy Money Can Buy*, Kristina Borjesson's edited volume *Into the Buzzsaw*, and Arthur Rowse's *Drive-By Journalism* provide the latest round of reports from the trenches, documenting the political corruption of the news media, the gaps in its vision and service, and the predatory backlash that it visits upon dissenters and internal critics. This torch is carried nearly every week by progressive opinion magazines like *The Nation, The Progressive*, and *The American Prospect*, which brim with critical articles on media and journalism to an extent unthinkable just two decades ago. Contrary to the assumption of our European friend, this may well be a golden age of radical media criticism in the United States.

But there is more, much more—the surge of activity we have witnessed in the last few years is the tip of the iceberg. The richness of this radical critique of the commercial system of news production by scholars, activists, and journalists has not just materialized out of thin air. Contemporary radical press criticism is part of a long historical tradition in the United States. It is not a recent phenomenon by any stretch of the imagination; in fact, it has a depth and richness that is unmatched by any equivalent analytical theme in media history. This is a body of criticism that stands on a central and recurrent argument—that commercial journalism in the United States has been at best a mixed blessing and at worst a complete failure for democracy. It has more often served the minority interests of dominant political, military, and business concerns than it has the majority interests of disadvantaged social classes. It has taken advantage of its power to advance the specific political and economic agendas of media owners and advertisers while depoliticizing or misinforming the citizenry. It has abdicated its responsibilities to democratic self-government in the pursuit of greater revenues and higher returns for investors. These disastrous trends are not a function of editors and reporters, who, indeed, often struggle mightily to resist these forces. Rather, the commercial system in which they operate demands compromises with an antipublic agenda. It doesn't happen every day, and it doesn't happen overnight, but it is an inexorable process.

These are radical criticisms precisely because they see the source of the problem not in the incompetence or selfish nature of individuals, but, rather, in the industrial structures and the logic of commerce that make such journalism their necessary product. Edward Ross, a sociologist and media critic in the Progressive Era, captured the heart of the matter in the early decades of the century. He considered it utter futility to push for internal reform of a commercial press system: "To urge the editor, under the thumb of the advertiser or of the owner, to be more independent, is to invite him to remove himself from his profession. As for the capitalist-owner, to exhort him to run his newspaper in the interest of truth and progress is about as reasonable as to exhort the mill-owner to work his property for the public good instead of for his private benefit."[5] That is to say, no matter how conscientious an editor may be, if the primary purpose of the organization is to make money, eventually public interest standards will have to be sacrificed to that end.

The core argument defines the structure of a privately controlled, for-profit media system as fundamentally at odds with democratic social goals. Market power is based on the idea of reducing competition, streamlining production, leveraging preexisting advantages, and selling for the maximum price what may be produced for the minimum cost. Free market governance of the media system tends to produce fewer and fewer voices over time as competition is eliminated to increase profits. Diversity gives way to homogenization as each competitor races to the bottom to find the least costly, most salable stories. Meanwhile, the few industrial players large enough to survive this kind of competition find themselves ideally situated to leverage their influence to advance a political agenda. The circumstances of trading in public information and debate naturally lead down the path toward lower quality, diversity, and integrity in the news. The market is simply a poor mechanism for arbitrating public debates and comprehensively reporting public information. The better analogy for the media system than the market would be the voting system. Nobody advocates subjecting the electoral system to commercial values, where voters can sell their votes to the highest bidder. Such an approach would undermine the ability of all the other citizens to enjoy democratic governance. Could it be that the market has a similar effect upon the fourth estate?

In this commercial system, no matter how free speech is protected, there will be many whose voices remain unheard for lack of media to express them. Jerome Barron's savage explanation is a handy blueprint for the critique: "There is inequality in the power to communicate ideas just as there is inequality in economic bargaining power; to recognize the latter and deny the former is quixotic. The 'marketplace of ideas' view has rested on the assumption that protecting the right of expression is equivalent to providing for it."[6] The failure of that assumption to deliver democratic outcomes is manifested in the continued depoliticization of modern society and the recurrent crises in journalism. As radical criticism, the point of the critique was and is always predicated on the notion that the solution to the problem is to change the structure of the media system so a better grade of journalism can rationally be expected.

This radical tradition of U.S. journalism criticism has roots that reach back to the origins of the modern commercial media system in the late nineteenth century, though this is not widely realized or understood. It is one of the great problems of contemporary media studies that this recurrent theme in journalism history has been all but forgotten for decades. Only now is it beginning to surface again. It is in order to resurrect this rich legacy, and to draw attention to it, that we have compiled this volume. Indeed, in conducting our research we were struck by the mountains of radical press criticism we encountered, especially from the first half of the twentieth century. Although we expected to find scintillating examples of this core critique as we combed through the libraries, we were astounded by the sheer magnitude of it, how central radical press criticism has been to U.S. political culture in the not-too-distant past. What is collected herein is but a drop in the bucket; we have attempted to collect a representative sample of some of the best criticism by some of the better-known writers. But for every George Seldes or

Upton Sinclair or John Dewey, there were hundreds, even thousands, of other pamphleteers and writers making a radical critique of commercial journalism down through the decades.

And, as you will see, despite the breadth of the selection of material in this book there are many areas we have not even touched upon, though they are deserving of attention. Criticism of nonprint media, radio and television, and the Internet has been largely excluded. Further, the press coverage of foreign affairs and comparison of the American system with other, alternative media systems are mostly absent. In light of the current, heated debates over the failure of the media to properly cover the war in Iraq, our neglect of the historical record on foreign news is a considerable gap in our record. However, our research indicates that virtually every foreign war in the twentieth century has been a time of enormous press criticism, as the mainstream media blend with patriotic propaganda and default to the reproduction of official information. This topic deserves its own book, and we could fill two volumes of this size with critically relevant material. The same is true of writers describing alternative media systems—the British, Canadian, German, and Australian models all warrant substantial comparative study and provide rich insight when placed in comparison with the American commercial press system. The same is true of writers critiquing the media in the context of struggles for social justice with regard to race, class, sex, and ethnicity. Once again, we felt it necessary to save these crucial discussions for another day. Indeed, there are a great many specific historical cases upon which this argument could be plotted, and we were obliged to present the most straightforward case for this volume. That such a rich body of critical writing exists outside the bounds of the current study strengthens the argument that we are making—the radical tradition of press criticism has historical presence and influence far beyond what the history books tell us. It is the central foundation upon which the widely recognized contemporary wave of media criticism is based.

We have focused on print journalism because it is the historical backbone of American journalism, the medium with the longest history and the greatest opportunity to provide a deep and lasting public service over the years. However, the central issues at play in the essays we have chosen are easily adapted to new technologies and the circumstances they bring. Moreover, these issues are the guiding principles in media criticism surrounding foreign affairs, movements for minority rights, and the merits of alternative media systems. Our point is that there are certain key themes that resonate across the decades and are as important today as ever before.

Midstream in the course of doing the research for this volume we discovered that the argument we set out to demonstrate was insufficient to express the nature of the evidence. We must now argue for much more than simply the existence of a rich tradition of radical press criticism in the United States, though this is a large claim in itself. We must also argue that this rich tradition, rather than being a marginal or fringe phenomenon in opposition to the dominant mainstream perspective, can make a legitimate claim to being *the* mainstream tradition of a free press in the United States. Let us repeat this point: the radical critique of commercial journalism arguably is the mainstream position in U.S. free press theory. Its rival—the celebration of the unwavering integrity of America's commercial media system—is not really a tradition so much as a set of assumptions that has migrated into conventional wisdom. But as common as this image has become, we should ask ourselves at what point in modern times has this rosy picture *not* been called into serious question by the conditions of social life in America. We should ask ourselves at what point in the last century a large chunk of the American people have not felt themselves badly underrepresented by the press. We should ask ourselves when the gatekeeper of democratic public debate was not legitimately criticized as the arbiter of commercial rather than civic values. The fact is there has never been such a time. The critique has been ever present.

Much of the power of this radical critique lies in its ability to show that the modern commercial press system operates in a manner that is antithetical to the democratic values embodied in the First Amendment. Freedom of the press, the radical press critics argue, is a social right shared equally by all citizens in a democracy. It is the right of all citizens to be exposed to a wide range of uncensored, informed analysis of social affairs. This public right was primary to the private right of individual speech. If the press system was actively structured to promote the common right to hear all voices, then by default, all private voices would have the right to speak. And, as the Founders understood well, it was appropriate and necessary for government policies to nurture and encourage the formation of such a press system. A review of U.S. history shows that there were intense public debates about the importance of huge government printing and postal subsidies to spawn and foster a diverse and independent press. James Madison, in 1792, argued that the government should subsidize totally the cost of mailing publications. Anything less, he asserted, would be a form of censorship against unpopular and dissident ideas. Likewise, postal subsidies were a major political concern of the abolitionist movement in the succeeding generations of the republic. Certainly the Founding Fathers did not intend for the structural control of the means of mass communication by dominant economic interests. They could never have foreseen it. The early republican press was firmly, and appropriately, understood as the province of public regulation.

The idea of the freedom of the press as a commercial right limited to those with enough capital to purchase media companies did not come about for generations after the founding of the republic. It was then, too, that public debates over media policy became much more sensitive, and powerful commercial media interests discouraged critical inquiry into the basic tenets relating media and democracy. Far better to leave people with the impression that elite control over the press was a direct edict from Thomas Jefferson and Abraham Lincoln, and in some cases from God. In some minds, this class-based vision of freedom of the press ("freedom of the press belongs to those who own one") is characterized as "libertarian." It is the libertarianism of billionaires, or of fools. In fairness to the commercial interpretation of the freedom of the press clause, its advocates can find some evidence to support their claim that the First Amendment is intended to protect commercial control over the media; what we would argue is that there is also considerable evidence to support a much more radical interpretation. At any rate, it is the radical press critics, not Viacom, Clear Channel, and General Electric, who stand on the shoulders of Tom Paine, Ben Franklin, James Madison, and Thomas Jefferson.

Parenthetically, we must point out that dominant commercial interests now loudly oppose government regulation of commercial media as singularly un-American despite its roots in the Founders' policies and the foundation of principled, republican self-government. And such opposition is meted out with little sense of irony. The existing commercial system is not the result of free markets in which the government has played no role. The dominant commercial media firms rest upon a series of government subsidies and regulations that granted them their immense market power. These include monopoly broadcast licenses and copyright protection, to mention but two. But because these government policies serve commercial media interests, they are not stigmatized as "regulation," or, worse yet, "censorship." To the extent these government policies were and are acknowledged, they are regarded, with no sense of irony, as creating the "free market." The definition of "free" that includes aggressive anticompetitive behavior, astronomic barriers to entry, and routine state intervention to protect oligarchic control of near-monopoly profits has rankled radical critics for decades, just as it does today.

Understood this way, our argument becomes much more than an academic exercise. The battle for freedom of the press is at the heart of all the struggles over the very nature of the type of social order being constructed in the United States. This rich tradition of radical press criticism decimates the ideological fig leaf that protects the existing corporate media system from public analysis and debate. Not only do Americans have a right to question the nature of their media system, they have a duty to do so, if they are concerned about laying the foundations for a self-governing society. Every issue of concern to the citizens in this society must eventually depend upon a full and fair hearing in the media in order for citizenship and self-government to function properly. If the media are failing us and have been failing us for decades, the reform of that system is mission critical for all of us.

If there is such an historical wealth of radical press criticism in the United States, how and why has it been ignored to the extent that it has been? To no small degree, this reflects the success of the commercial media system; in a concrete sense the system works sufficiently well to satisfy a significant portion of the population. But the public's complacency is not a coincidental by-product. It is imperative for the largest media firms to propagate the notion that the U.S. media system is a "natural" development, and that they are the worthy and appropriate overlords of the press. Control over the media system is a highly sensitive issue, much like control over the economy, and those who benefit by the status quo prefer that it be a topic left unexplored. You might say that economics produces a hollow form of journalism, and that politics sustains it for its own ends. James Carey eloquently summarizes this kind of media system: "It is a journalism of fact without regard to understanding through which the public is immobilized and demobilized and merely ratifies the judgments of experts delivered from on high. It is, above all, a journalism that justifies itself in the public's name but in which the public plays no role, except as an audience; it is a receptacle to be informed by experts and an excuse for the practice of publicity."[7] Journalism today has much more in common with the elites it supposedly regulates than with the public on whose behalf it supposedly speaks.

In this climate, opposition is difficult to mount. But radical media criticism has never been criticism for criticism's sake. It is a structural critique with the intent of changing the system so there will be better journalism. If there is little sense in the political culture that there is any hope for change, the radical critique seems irrelevant, or at least beside the point. In such an environment it will tend to wither. But the deep-seated problems of the journalism spawned by the modern commercial media system are such that radical democratic criticism never disappears, despite the entrenched nature of the commercial system. It ebbs and flows, tending to grow in periods of broad social turmoil, when all the leading institutions are subject to popular interrogation. And it is when there is a sense that the criticism might actually lead to a change in the media system for the better that the quantity and quality of radical media criticism positively blossoms.

The history of modern American press criticism begins at the pivotal moment in the late nineteenth century when U.S. journalism gradually switched from being primarily a political press system to being a full-fledged commercial press system. In the first few generations of the republic, the idea of objective, professional journalism aimed at a cross section of the polity was not yet born. Neither, significantly, was the notion that vast profits could be made selling advertising in large-circulation, industrially published newspapers. The point of journalism in the early nineteenth century was to persuade and inform citizens through highly partisan papers with modest audience reach. The First Amendment was seen as protection for dissident political viewpoints, as most newspapers were tied to political parties. If the party in power could prohibit competing publications, it would effectively have the power to curb political debate and badly damage the opposition's ability to mobilize popular support. Without a free press with viewpoints from across the spectrum, it was clear that democracy would die in its infancy. The government sought to prop up this enriched press system through postal and printing subsidies. This partisan press system worked quite well, but it was predicated on the maintenance of a large number of viable, competing voices in the news.

As the nineteenth century advanced, the press system began to take on the commercial aspects that would come to dominate it. Newspapers remained explicitly partisan throughout the century. But as production costs declined and advertising revenues picked up, publishers began to increase in size and circulation. The number of papers available in any given city began a slow and steady decline. Debate waned as partisanship was blunted to attract a larger and more diverse readership. Competition began to erode, near-monopoly profits rolled in, and commercialism trumped partisanship as the central modus operandi.

It is here in the history of the press, at the point of transition from a political instrument to a commercial enterprise, that we can begin to think of journalism as the linchpin of the political economy of American society. However, we should think of this not as a substitution but rather as a reversal of priorities. Mass-circulation newspapers were engineered for economic reasons, but the consequences were political—that is, mass media altered the way power operated in society. The person who owned the newspaper stood to make a lot of money but also stood in a position of enormous public influence. By industrializing the production of ideas and concentrating the marketplace of their distribution, a small group of elites came into possession of the reins of public discourse and with them the ability to shape the political fortunes of the nation. The relationship between economic gain and political control determined the basic nature of modern journalism and has oscillated around the media system ever since. Over time, these two forces have begun to blend together, gaining momentum and power through the decades with the advance of technology and the further consolidation of the marketplace.

We can see this process operating from the earliest years of the Gilded Age. It was the logic of industrial capitalism that created the modern mass media. In simple terms, the process began because of overproduction in the American manufacturing sector thanks to industrialization, in combination with oligopolistic market structures. A huge capacity to produce retail goods filled warehouses to the ceiling and then ran smack into a paucity of markets and consumers. The ability to produce outran the capacity to sell. What could not be sold quickly lay idle, a circumstance that backed up the production engine and left factories running at less than full steam—a very unprofitable state of affairs for owners.

The rapid response was the explosion of a consumer culture driven by advertising.[8] The mere availability of consumer goods did not spark public desire for them. People had to be persuaded that they wanted these goods. Moreover, in concentrated markets, explicit price competition to expand market share was counterproductive, as it cut into potential profits for all large players. To boost sales without slashing prices, more goods had to be sold. To sell more goods, as many people as possible had to be shown advertising as often as possible. Advertisers naturally wanted to place their ads in publications with the largest circulation. The result was the explosion of advertising revenues for the largest metropolitan dailies. With the influx of cash, these publishers expanded their operations, industrialized their printing facilities, and expanded their network of distribution to more points of sale. They also dropped their cover price, often down to a penny. Advertising now paid for the cost of publishing, providing much more revenue to publishers than did subscriptions or newsstand sales. Medium-sized papers that could not garner the ad rates of their larger competitors were driven out of business by the lower cover prices. Moreover, entrepreneurs and investors were dissuaded from establishing new papers because of the prohibitive start-up costs involved in purchasing industrial printing facilities. By 1900, it was conventional wisdom that a cool $1 million was the minimum investment needed to start a newspaper, even in mid-sized communities.[9] The barriers to entry into the media markets rose sharply, and competition fell off. The largest papers in the country bought other large papers, consolidated them into national chains, and established powerful print empires. The total number of American newspapers began a steady decline. It has never stopped. Indeed, despite the exceptional profitability of U.S. newspapers throughout the twentieth century and the dramatic growth in the population and the national income, not a single successful new daily newspaper has been launched in an existing market in nearly a century. That is a sure sign of major-league monopoly market power.

The media barons of the Gilded Age were just like other titans of early American monopoly capitalism. They were wealthy white men with shared interests, both economic and political. The fortunes of publishers were deeply intertwined with those of manufacturers. The newspaper business would collapse without advertising—the news itself was no longer a profitable commodity. Likewise the manufacturers needed newspapers and magazines to hawk their wares or risk overcapacity, lower prices, and smaller profits. Both were heavily dependent on the financial sector. The bankers sustained the upper echelon of the national economy. To stay in the marketplace with monopoly-seeking giants required constant acquisitions and expansion. This expansion required loans and credit. Consequently, the financiers led by J. P. Morgan moved vast sums of money around the economy, took their cut, and let everyone know who ran the show. The influence financial interests expected and received posed a serious problem for the newspaper industry. Corruption of the press became systemic in the political economy by the first decade of the new century. Legendary progressive senator Robert M. La Follette reflected on this fact in 1911 in a speech before a group of publishers: "The control comes through that community of interests, that interdependence of investments and credits which ties the publisher up to the banks, the advertisers, and the special interests."[10]

The politics of the economic elites were naturally conservative. They presided over the status quo and had no intention of allowing that favorable situation to change. The only alterations that interested them were those that increased their control over the wealth of the nation and their power over its political governance. It was not long before the political circumstances of mass-circulation newspapers were explicitly perceived as an asset just as valuable as the very profitable business venture of publishing. Newspapers were a powerful device for social control and public manipulation. With fewer papers left standing after a round of consolidation, and little chance of new ones being founded, the publishing chains of Hearst, Scripps, Howard, and Pulitzer had enormous potential to influence political governance. Newspapers had, of course, always had this ability, but never on the scale offered by concentrated markets with only a handful of large-circulation players. The economic inequalities of industrial expansion had permitted this concentration of political power through media control. Now that the marketplace of ideas had been substantially monopolized, these same inequalities would offer ripe ground to sow one political agenda while blocking others with virtual impunity. What politician could afford to actively work against the interests of business leaders who professed to control public opinion? These efforts were remarkably successful, so successful that they began to provoke a bitter backlash from those who had watched with growing alarm as this system had evolved and solidified. These were the first modern press critics.

In the early years of the Progressive Era, a handful of publishing magnates began to consciously exploit their operations for both economic and political gain. Their efforts were brazen and only crudely disguised. In response, the early critiques were fierce, if relatively powerless to stop what they decried. At a general level, critics argued that most large newspapers were conservative and carried the class biases of wealth and privilege. The press was outspoken against all forms of transformative social change. By and large, publishers opposed labor, civil rights, socialism, and any effort to redistribute wealth to help the disadvantaged. In political coverage, mainstream parties received reasonable treatment, but radical ideas were shunned and excoriated. The parameters of political debate acceptable to owners were the limits within which journalists were permitted write. The economic elites, for their part, received little coverage at all, unless it was to inform one another about the state of the economy, promote products and services, or praise a philanthropic deed. The affairs of the business class remained beyond the pale of common knowledge. There were, of course, exceptions, but these were the general rules of big business journalism in the Progressive Era. They remain largely unchanged to this day.

Meanwhile, the quest for greater profitability did not slow. On occasion it worked at cross-purposes with the political interests of the owners. The increased sales brought by an investigative report crusading to expose local corruption or to resolve social and economic problems were too tempting to hold back for political reasons. There was remarkable interest among the middle-class consumers in hard-hitting social criticism. Indeed, in the first decade of the twentieth century, the famous muckrakers established a cottage industry for exposé journalism with a left-leaning social conscience. But despite the fame of the damning social critiques offered in the reports of Ida Tarbell, Lincoln Steffens, and Ray Stannard Baker, these journalists were not political radicals. They wanted to reform the excesses of the system, not overturn it altogether. They spoke to the impressive left-wing movement of populists, socialists, and progressives that occupied a sizable chunk of the political spectrum, but they usually went no further than the policy solutions of the reformers. Publishers who disagreed in principle with the intent of the reporting could nonetheless be confident that no serious changes would come of them—except of course a more profitable newspaper. The handful of muckrakers who did harbor revolutionary fervor, notably Upton Sinclair and Charles Edward Russell, were quickly banished from the mainstream media shortly after their most famous work was published. The other muckrakers faded from view as conservative owners and advertisers cracked down on adventurous editors. The "muckraking" moment was short-lived. In a classic chicken-and-egg scenario, middle-class interest in muckraking material was not cultivated. This contributed to its waning, and publishers eventually could content themselves with the notion that there was little demand for such material.

The other economic consequence of big-business publishing in the Progressive Era was yellow journalism. Sensationalism was the hallmark of the low-price, metro-dailies. Then as now, disaster, crime, sex, scandal, and celebrity sold well. Higher circulation meant higher ad rates and higher profits. More and more papers joined the tabloid game, and it became a race to the bottom as each tried to outdo the other to grab more readers. Fabrication was commonplace. The exclusion of serious news stories to make room for scandal became routine. This pattern was profitable, but it was also politically useful. The more distracted and out of touch the polity became with the core concerns of governance, the less likely it became that they would attentively and aggressively oppose the policies of the elites, despite their direct contradiction to the best interests of the majority. Sensationalism thus combined with suppression, omission, and thinly veiled political advocacy to produce a commercial media system with a strong conservative political bias that also effectively depoliticized the citizenry.

This was the first great crisis of commercial journalism. The critics on the left, ranging from socialist labor agitators to progressive senators, saw through this facade of democratic journalism and blasted it unrelentingly for years. The political culture was radical enough and the dissident media still vibrant enough to support these efforts on a massive scale. We would do well to recall that socialism was a viable political movement during the Progressive Era. These decades, characterized by historian Richard Hofstadter as an "age of broad social speculation," witnessed oppositional politics with a role in government unthinkable today.[11] The Socialist Party presidential candidate Eugene V. Debs polled well in each of the first three elections of the new century, peaking at 6 percent of the electorate in 1912. In that year, two million Americans got their news from socialist newspapers. The *Appeal to Reason*, a national socialist newspaper printed in Kansas, had a circulation of over a million and featured work by well-known public figures like Debs and Sinclair. The systemic challenge to the political and economic order carried out in these years by the labor movement and crusading social reformers quite naturally extended to a savage critique of the press. Reformers saw very clearly that no issue could mobilize the public if the power of the press was turned against it. Will Irwin, writing in 1911, commented that "the American press has more influence than it ever had in any other time, in any other country. No other extrajudicial form, except religion, is half so powerful."[12]

It was not just the socialists. Across the political spectrum, writers spoke of a "crisis in journalism." Conservatives shunned what they considered the immorality propagated by tabloid newspapers and the dilution of proper social norms through exposure to indecent publications. Progressives writing in the magazine founded by Wisconsin senator Robert La Follette exposed the economic connections between the business community, the publishers, and corrupt politicians. Journalists like Will Irwin denounced the dominance of the profit motive and conservative politics over editorial integrity. Academics like sociologist Edward Ross pointed out the deep contradictions between commercialism and democracy in the press. Upton Sinclair, in his 1920 retrospective on press criticism in the Progressive Era, *The Brass Check*, covered all of these issues and called for a total transformation of the commercial system. It was common knowledge that the press was antilabor, antireform and probusiness. Public trust in the free press receded to a state of outright skepticism of most anything written in the newspapers. Sinclair commented: "One could take a map of America and a paint-brush, and make large smudges of color, representing journalistic ownership of whole districts, sometimes of whole states, by special interests."[13] In short, it was widely thought that journalism was corrupt and straightforward class propaganda.

Some publishers realized they had gone too far. Neither profits nor political control could benefit from a skeptical public disgusted by what they saw in the papers. People were less likely to buy a paper and more likely to ignore what they read in it, including the advertisements. Moreover, the tidal wave of press criticism in a progressive political environment held the implicit threat of generating calls for new government policies to reform the media system. Some suggested that newspapers be turned into nonprofit, municipally owned concerns with editors elected by a popular vote. In 1912 three of the four presidential candidates specifically lambasted the newspapers, all but the soon-to-be-defeated incumbent, President William Howard Taft. We do not wish to exaggerate the danger to the newspaper status quo. Commercial media lobbies posed a formidable barrier to popular participation in policy making. But to major publishers at the time, this was small consolation. They did not enjoy having their control over U.S. journalism in the public spotlight.

Savvy publishers like Joseph Pulitzer realized that journalism needed to have the trappings of neutrality and balance in order to regain its sullied credibility. The idea born to quell this crisis was professionalism. Many of these publishers probably truly wanted reform and a degree of objectivity in the news columns, as long as it stayed comfortably within the parameters of mainstream political opinion. Journalists should be professionals, autonomous from the business office and the politics of owners. They should be trusted by the public to serve faithfully the goals of truth and fairness. These were the new codes of the newsroom. It was a dramatic departure from the rules of nineteenth-century partisan journalism and a concession to the critics of twentieth-century commercial journalism. Formerly, papers from every partisan stripe had explicitly reported from an overt point of view. This was satisfactory so long as numerous papers existed in every town and the possibility of starting a new one was not impossible. But the concentrating trends of ownership in the Progressive Era meant that most towns were reduced to one or two dailies, both of which were often owned by large chains or wealthy families that shared elite political interests. Declining diversity and commercial sensationalism had sparked this crisis, and publishers hoped that establishing professionalism (rather than rebuilding diversity) would stabilize the system once again. All of the nation's major schools of journalism were consequently founded in the Progressive Era. With the formal declaration that a wall stood between the interests of the publisher (both commercial and political) and the integrity of the news columns, the press hoped to reenter the public's good graces.

The most sophisticated of the critics did not fall for this ruse. Sinclair was particularly derisive of the veil professionalism dropped over business as usual. He claimed with hostility: "A professional journalist may be defined as a man who holds himself ready at a day's notice to adjust his opinions to the pocket-book of a new owner."[14] Moreover, the time it took for reputations to be reconstituted was far more rapid than the time it would realistically take to populate newsrooms with trained, "professional" journalists. Nonetheless, the idea of professionalism was a powerful one in American journalism, and its legacy was to become a significant player in future crises. But to many reporters on the inside, it was the continued abuse of the public trust painted as objective neutrality and public service. One well-known journalist, John Swinton, concluded: "Our talents, our possibilities and our lives are all the property of other men. We are intellectual prostitutes."[15]

Professionalism emerged just in time to blend with another significant moment for the press in the Progressive Era: the First World War. It was during the two years of American military engagement in Europe (as well as a postwar campaign in Russia) that home-front war planners discovered the effectiveness of calculated propaganda. In 1917, the Committee on Public Information, or the Creel Commission (named after its leader, journalist George Creel), recruited some of the nation's brightest intellectuals, writers, and reporters. The goal was to reach every sector of American society with the wisdom of Washington's wartime policies. The Creel Commission issued over 6,000 press releases (more than ten a day while American forces were overseas) in addition to frequent "PR packets"—vividly written, ready-for-printing packages of interviews, news stories, features, photographs, and maps that were distributed to newspapers across the country.[16] Through a massive campaign of public information deployed through the press, pamphleteers, and public speakers, America was transformed from a nation reluctant to go to war into an anti-German, militarized society. The rhetoric bore the unmistakable, repetitive message that antiwar sentiments were anti-American. For their part, the press lords did not protest the use of their media for this purpose.

The manufacture of consent to fight a war had been achieved with relatively little effort by a staff of social elites who had never before attempted such a task. The implications were clear. From then on, the power of the press was recognized as an absolutely vital vehicle for social control. Walter Lippmann published his reflections on this period in his classic *Public Opinion*, concluding that the average person was simply too ignorant to function properly as an informed citizen in a self-governing society. Modern times had become too complex. The governing was better left to the handful of experts who understood it. They would govern in the interests of the public at large, which could in turn report to the polls every few years to ratify or reject the overall result of their rulers' efforts. In the meantime, the public was far too distracted by what Lippmann called the "pictures in their heads," their erroneous understandings of the social world. Since they were already distracted by these impressions, what better way to keep them distracted and out of the way than through the press? Yellow broadsheets could serve the masses while the papers of record provided the technocrats with the information they needed to run the country. This statement of elite democracy and the role of the mass media has been the underpinning for much of the rest of twentieth-century America's governing philosophy.

Professionalism, wartime propaganda, and an economic boom time all came together in the 1920s to close down the most strident press criticism of the Progressive Era. Whatever political threat there had been to the hegemony of the big newspaper publishers disappeared. The decade saw a reconfiguration of the news media system in which professionalism began to take root in a new climate of papers that opted for either muted sensationalism or sophisticated reporting. Most significantly, a new player emerged on the media scene, emboldened by the discoveries of the Creel Commission: public relations (PR). Many politicians, businesses, and interest groups hired PR firms. Often they doubled as advertising agents. The tools of propaganda now began to take advantage of the peculiar functionalities of professionalism. Professional journalists, prohibited from offering their own analysis or betraying a political bias, needed news pegs (an event on which to hang a story) and on-the-record comments from key public figures. If officials weren't talking and events took place behind the scenes, issues simply did not make the paper. Meanwhile, where reticent editors balked, PR agents stepped up. Public relations spat out press releases, arranged media events, packaged official information for reporters, and in so doing managed to dictate the agenda in much of U.S. journalism. The PR agent became a clandestine reporter, crafting stories that officials would then feed to journalists. In this way, the reporter sometimes became a tool of elite class interests through occupational dependency. Powerless to speak the truth unless it could be attributed to an official source, the journalist was reduced to a scribe. In large part, these years laid the groundwork for what we still see today in the pressrooms in the seats of power.[17]

Significantly, however, the life of the "professional" reporter turned out not to carry the standard of living promised by a higher class of occupation. Even as publishers earned higher and higher profits, journalists were held in the role of humble public servants. If they earned too much, would that not compromise their objectivity? If they had too much power, could that not corrupt them? The ethos of the reporter as watchdog, whistle-blower, and representative of the public blended with an ascetic obligation to work long hours for relatively low wages. These conditions were paradoxically treated at the institutional level as badges of honor. If the conditions of their labor precluded critical honesty and true objectivity, at least their lifestyle bore the mark of a public servant. Despite the similarities with the working class in terms of standard of living, the professionals in the newsroom held themselves up as though they stood beside lawyers and doctors in the social hierarchy. This disparity between material conditions and social status was encouraged by the publishers and would prove a critical flashpoint in the years to come.

The critiques of the Progressive Era were muted in the twenties, but they did not disappear. Sensationalism and class bias, the twin beasts spawned in the political economy of the commercial system, were alive and well. There remained a pervasive cynicism about the press. In this decade, Walter Lippmann and John

Dewey engaged in a heated and much-studied debate about the functionality of democracy. The argument between these men hinged in no small part on whether the press could be rehabilitated to serve its necessary role in self-governance. Meanwhile, critics like Silas Bent carried on the tradition of lambasting advertisers, the degradation of quality journalism into tabloid fare, and the lack of public interest reporting in the newspapers. However, the Roaring Twenties did not offer the social conflict that had and would trigger major outbursts from radical press critics.

When the stock market crashed in 1929 and the economy plunged into the Depression, the American press entered a period of profound and sustained criticism. The 1930s very nearly saw the media system transformed from within, so great was the pressure to remake the nation into a more democratic society. True to its connection with political economy, the critique of the media rose with the social upheaval of the Depression and was integrated into the solutions of the New Deal. In the early 1930s a heterogeneous movement arose to challenge the capitalist and commercial basis of radio broadcasting in the United States. This coalition of journalists, educators, labor and religious groups, and women's organizations argued that it was inimical to democracy to permit broadcasting to be the province of a handful of commercial interests.[18] Likewise, a feisty consumer movement arose, which questioned the role of advertising in American life and demanded strict regulation so that advertising would serve consumers rather than deceive them.[19] Although these movements failed for the most part, they brought to the surface the tensions commercial media were creating for democratic societies. We need only look at the alternative paths taken by Canada, Britain, and much of western Europe to see how powerful these clashes over public media systems were. A slightly different configuration of power between the public, government, and industry could easily have produced media giants more akin to the BBC and the CBC than to NBC and CBS.

The main challenge to the practice of commercial journalism in the 1930s came from within the profession. The early years of the Depression saw the life of the journalist begin to change for the worse. Many reporters were laid off. Unemployment forced them to realize that they were only one step removed from the working classes they now joined in poverty. Almost every journalist who kept his job endured a substantial pay cut—often down to the threshold of subsistence wages. The politics of the New Deal that appeared in the news columns took on a far more visceral importance. In the 1920s, journalists could look at politically motivated editorial decisions with an attitude of nose-holding cynicism but grudging acceptance. They were seldom personally affected. In the 1930s, the destructive attacks on the Roosevelt administration orchestrated in the majority of daily newspapers across the country struck a different chord. Suddenly the necessity of government delivering social welfare was a harsh reality for the workers in the newsroom.

Breadlines lengthened. Unemployment became epidemic. The country seemed to be descending into full-blown class conflict.

The newspapermen were watching all this unfold. They were reporting it. They were reproducing it for the American public to read, react to, and act upon. And they knew that the job they were doing often betrayed the responsibility and public obligation demanded of the press in a democratic society—particularly at such a moment of crisis. The public openly mistrusted the press as a matter of common sense. A liberal government was openly at odds with a conservative press. FDR famously bypassed their influence by using the radio to address the people. Many journalists on the inside told tales of suppression, distortion, intentional misrepresentation, and the intimidation of any reporter who felt inclined to challenge these editorial policies. The turmoil of the 1930s brought the publishers' abuses of the free press as a commercial vehicle and a narrow ideological platform under uncomfortable scrutiny. Many looked at the disparity of the 1932 and 1936 elections—near overwhelming rejection of FDR by the press and yet resounding victories at the polls—as a sure sign that the public's right to a representative and comprehensive free press had been woefully neglected. The protection and proliferation of privilege had assumed the mantle of social leadership and mercilessly turned against its public responsibilities. Given the awakening class politics of the moment, the underprivileged sectors of the public took little time to notice that they were the ones underreported, misrepresented, and ardently opposed by their erstwhile First Amendment trustees. How could the lion's share of the public's press be antilabor, anti–New Deal, and anti-FDR in direct contradiction to the vast majority of Americans?

Professionally, reporters' loyalties lay with the publishers and a libertarian conception of the First Amendment as a negative right of the owners of the press. Economically, and increasingly politically, their interests lay with the working classes. It was hard not to notice that the union machinists in the print shop earned more and had greater job security than the white-collar journalists in the newsroom. And if their path lay with the laboring classes, how could they reconcile those politics with their meek acceptance of abysmal working conditions, their pride-swallowing allegiance to their publishers' editorial policies, and an effectively antipublic use of the First Amendment that actively perpetuated monopolization in the news media and its attendant compression of diversity and representativeness? Reporters began to see their own circumstances as part of the problem of economic inequality. In their efforts to redress those problems for themselves, they realized more and more how they had contributed to their own oppression. It was not a giant leap to equate the politics of class with the politics of the press and realize that the solutions to these problems lay on the same path.

One clear result of FDR's New Deal was the explosion of union membership.

The working classes, their ranks swollen by widespread poverty, embraced new unionizing guarantees and set out to use them to change society. The leading businessmen who had dominated the country for decades were hardly vanquished, but they had lost their rubber stamp from Washington and had seen public power acting in step with an aroused and politicized public opinion. In short, America's peculiar blend of monopoly capitalism and plutocratic democracy was vulnerable and under attack. One of the most obvious symptoms was the credibility gap between the newspaper publishers and their readers. Journalism was experiencing another crisis, this time as a part of a reordering of the society.

In 1933, a group of journalists took an unexpected, and unprecedented, leap into the fray by founding the American Newspaper Guild. It began small with a handful of locals in Ohio, Pennsylvania, and New York. Most guildsmen started with modest aims of minimum wages and maximum hours, if possible mandated through New Deal codes. But within a few months, it became clear that to win even those meager ends they needed radical methods. As it turned out, radical methods brought more expansive aims. In the early years, when the stakes were highest and the odds were longest, the leaders of the Guild, notably New York columnist and national personality Heywood Broun, quickly saw that the first steps had to be big ones. Broun and his fellow guildsmen began by hooking their union train to savage media criticism. The need for the Guild and the resistance it met were represented as evidence that the free press was in tatters. In a talked-about *Harper's* article in 1935, Isabelle Keating reflected that reporters were coming around to the truth that "the romantic legend of the newspaper reporter's freedom is smashed now, smashed to bits. The truth is that this freedom has been a sham, a patent fraud for years. Only recently has the reporter awakened to the truth, and the American Newspaper Guild, the newswriters' union, is evidence of the fact."[20]

From 1934 to 1939, the Guild fought a series of battles against the publishers, the courts, and the government. They lost more often than they won. But somehow, despite getting much worse than they gave, they managed not only to survive but to expand and thrive. In large part, their success was due to the audaciousness of the leadership and their rapid transition from a white-collar union hesitant to associate with the AFL to a radical spearhead operating with a seat at the battle councils of the CIO. The journalists were instrumental in the effort to broaden craft unions, to link up white-collar and blue-collar labor, and to unify all working people in each industry. By 1938, the union had forty-seven signed contracts, including sixteen from the Scripps-Howard chain, and nearly 17,000 members from 300 papers around the country. This figure represented 48 percent of eligible journalists nationwide, with much higher proportions in metropolitan areas.[21] The newsmen were at the forefront of the social movement of industrial unionization, the gradual organization of all working people into an institution that might overturn the harsh inequalities of the American political economy. The journalists held a key position in this movement, as they were the only workers who could deliver the media. They were the men and women who saw that it was their labor that marked the nexus of democratic public debate and political economic power.

Also working in this tumultuous mix were the clouds of fascism building in Europe and the ominous implications they bore for free societies everywhere. Systemic critique of the political economy of journalism from within the profession often referenced what was happening in Italy and Germany. George Seldes in particular was conscious of the connection between European totalitarianism and plutocratic control over the media. He linked it together with the power of the business community in America—the advertisers and the circle of financial interests that used the media to advance political and economic agendas that ran counter to the public interest. Seldes saw the Guild as the most important development in the history of American journalism. Other notable figures shared his critique and his assessment of the moment. Among them were other journalists like Ferdinand Lundberg and Oswald Garrison Villard; the preeminent journalism scholar of his day, A. M. Lee; and FDR's secretary of the interior, Harold Ickes. Systemic critique coming from inside the industry arguing on behalf of the people might well have had the power to overturn the system for the better. It was undeniably a mainstream critique in ways it had never been before and has never been since. FDR himself got into the act in a letter to Joseph Pulitzer Jr. dated November 2, 1938: "I have always been firmly persuaded," he wrote, "that our newspapers cannot be edited in the interests of the general public, from the counting room." He called for a symposium on freedom of the press and its corruption by special interests.[22]

This crucial revolt of journalists, unique to the 1930s, shook up the very idea of journalism for the last time in the twentieth century. At this moment, there was a chance that it would take a profoundly different direction. The journalists determined that the socioeconomic interests of the depressed masses were directly related to the need for better journalism, stripped of the illusions of the old ideas of professionalism. The media system could not be democratic if the journalists aligned their interests with the publishers and not the readers. Fairness, representativeness, objectivity, and comprehensive pursuit of truth and justice would be redefined to more accurately fit the social circumstances. The union journalists would be the people reclaiming the newsrooms from the bottom up. If publishers could not be relied upon to put commercial and partisan biases aside in order to do the work constitutionally guaranteed to the public, the journalists would have to be entrusted with that right and protected in their efforts by union contract. The Guild movement mirrored the social upheaval of the decade, the leftward shift in politics, and the widespread assumption that liberal capitalism had failed and its institutions would have to be remade. The most militant wing of the newspaper Guild, represented by George Seldes, demanded that newspapers should be run by the journalists—that owners should have no control over the content. The Guild never adopted this radical position, and as the radical moment faded, the Guild fully accepted the status quo of the newspaper industry and came to see itself as a traditional union, working exclusively to improve its members' wages and benefits.

Much like in the Progressive Era, war intervened to radically halt this rapidly changing social reality in America. Retooling American industry for military production and mobilizing society for total war finally lifted the Depression and unified the country behind a common goal. In the media sector, the Office of War Information took up where the Creel Commission had left off. Its efforts were even more successful. The propaganda campaign was massive and integrated itself into the media system with an urgency that defied the battle lines that had been drawn between publishers, journalists, and readers in the 1930s. The war changed everything. A final battle of sorts took place in the immediate postwar years, but by the end of the decade, the union movement, the left, and liberalism were in full retreat. In the late 1940s, too, a last gasp of structural press criticism retreated into a tamer call for industry self-regulation as the only viable solution to media flaws. Perhaps no document better captures the emerging pattern of strong critiques with weak solutions than the Hutchins Commission report on the freedom of the press, sponsored by media magnate Henry Luce. In some of the most straightforward and intellectually sophisticated analysis of the press system ever performed, a handful of the leading intellectuals in the country laid out an honest portrayal of the problems with the American press. But the solutions they offered were ineffectual and largely dependent upon the good faith of publishers, as if simply identifying the problems would be enough to reverse them. In many ways, the blueprint of quality journalism, its difficulties, and its possibilities served as a reinvigoration of professionalism—a new code of ethics for journalists. The norms of objectivity, neutrality, and balance had taken a beating in the 1930s and been knocked loose from the foundations laid at the close of the Progressive Era. The late forties set them back in place with a degree of solemnity that masked the toothless reform of the policy prescriptions.

The elevated critique of the American political economy and its commercial journalism sunk back out of the mainstream. The United States was greatly changed as a nation in the wake of Yalta, with new concerns, ambitions, and priorities. Tumult over the democratic credentials of the media system lacked the momentum to oppose the new order taking shape over the politics and culture of a burgeoning superpower. The generations that followed the war experienced the "American century," an era of unprecedented economic growth and global dominance. It was an environment in which the commercial media system thrived as never before.

The three decades following the end of the war were the high-water mark for professional journalism in the United States. Budgets were relatively lavish, and journalists had more autonomy from the dictates of owners and advertisers than ever before or since. The Watergate scandal, where the *Washington Post* launched a wave of reporting that led to the resignation of President Richard Nixon, is the capstone of this era. But we should not exaggerate the independence of the journalism, nor its quality. Commercial pressures still existed both indirectly and directly; hence in local news media, powerful commercial interests as always tended to be off-limits to critical examination. And with its reliance on official sources as the basis for news stories, journalism had a very establishment cast. This was painfully apparent during the Vietnam War, when the news media parroted the range of official debate in Washington for years, despite substantial evidence that they were being fed lies and half-truths. Moreover, the end of the war was heralded as a triumph for critical media, rather than the failure of commercial journalism to perform its duty to democracy except in the final stage of the most desperate circumstances. The postwar generation provided some of the most insightful press criticism of the century, nevertheless, and we feature several essays from that era in this book. This was the era of C. Wright Mills, I. F. Stone, A. J. Liebling, and a young Ben Bagdikian. It was also the era of press reviews, publications formed by journalists to review the mainstream press out of their concern that the journalism being produced was deeply flawed. The same problems evident in the first half century still infected the media system. However, the strength of the embrace that patriotism and nationalism held on the image of American journalism made it that much more difficult to believe that the emperor wore no clothes.

Consequently, the press criticism of the 1950s through the 1970s was muted by historical standards, largely because the commercial system was politically inviolate. Much of the criticism was intended to jawbone journalists to do a better job at being professionals within the commercial environment, not about changing the overall structure. Even those many radicals who emerged with the civil rights movement, the antiwar movement, and the New Left in the 1960s did not share the same interest as Progressive Era and 1930s activists in changing the media system. That was almost unthinkable at the time; such was the power of the commercial media system. Beyond critique, energies went toward establishing alternative or "underground" media. This produced a bounty of exceptional media but, within the market environment, survival as viable institutions was difficult, except under commercial premises. The truth understood in the first century of U.S. history but forgotten in the 1960s was that creating viable independent and alternative media requires explicit policies that allow them to prosper, much like the dominant commercial system requires explicit policies (like copyright and the free gift of monopoly licenses to radio and TV channels) to exist.

The third great wave of radical press criticism began haltingly in the late 1970s, blossomed during the 1980s, and exploded by the end of the 1990s. At least three factors contributed to the emergence of this latest wave of media activism. First, there was the defeat of the New Left and the end of the wave of progressive political activism of the 1960s. In the ashes of this defeat, many activists began to look for

explanations for why they could not generate more popular support for their politics and, more broadly, why so many people were misinformed and depoliticized.
For some feminists, antiwar activists, and progressives, any viable answer had to
address the media system and the role it played in American life. Todd Gitlin's *The
Whole World Is Watching* (1980) is the classic work in this genre. Second, the news
coverage of the Vietnam War alerted activists to the deep flaws in U.S. media
coverage of the U.S. role in the world, especially when it involved U.S. military
interests. In the 1980s, the Reagan administration's tacit support for death squads
in Central America and its illegal efforts to overthrow the government of Nicaragua
appalled a generation of human-rights activists. Many of them were able to visit
the region. When they returned to see the distorted U.S press coverage, it fueled
interest in press criticism. Citizens needed to learn how to "decode" the news media
and understand the structural basis for its flaws, if for nothing more than intellectual self-defense. Much of the work of Edward S. Herman and Noam Chomsky,
including their 1988 masterpiece, *Manufacturing Consent: The Political Economy of the
News Media*, falls into this category.

Finally, the media industries themselves underwent significant structural transformation in the final two decades of the twentieth century. On the one hand,
within each sector—e.g., newspapers, magazines, book publishers, cable TV companies, music companies, etc.—there was a wave of consolidation leaving fewer
and fewer massive firms with more and more market share. Despite the explosion
in the raw numbers of media channels, the degree of ownership concentration had
never been higher. Such consolidated markets made it all but impossible for start-
up firms to have a chance to compete successfully. On the other hand, media
conglomeration became the rage of the times. The largest media firms, through a
wave of mergers and acquisitions, quickly assembled empires with major players
in numerous different media sectors. What these firms discovered was that the
profit whole of a media empire could exceed the sum of the profit parts. It meant
that the independent media firm that did only one thing—publish books, make
movies, produce music—was at a decided competitive disadvantage going up
against a larger conglomerate. This is why independent production has more or
less ceased to exist as a viable factor in the media system. By the end of the twentieth century the largest media firms were ten times larger than the biggest media
firms of the mid-1980s. All of the largest media firms ranked among the 400 largest
corporations in the world; a generation earlier it was rare to find more than one
or two such firms on the list. All of these developments held disastrous implications
for the practice of journalism, as concentrated markets and pressures for profit
combined with corporate domination to produce a sustained attack on the relative
autonomy of professional journalists. The work of Ben Bagdikian, in his six editions
of *The Media Monopoly* (first published in 1983), has chronicled this crisis in a most
compelling manner.

Throughout the 1990s, as we have explained, journalists from across the media system started speaking out against the corporate control of the press and the failure of quality public interest reporting to survive the pressure of the bottom line. Paradoxically, as the media giants proceed to launch new media channels in print, broadcast, and on the Internet, the diversity of viewpoints available for public attention seems to decline. Multiplicity has been confused with diversity in the digital age, and critics are beginning to realize the colossal implications of this mistake. A decade ago, technology enthusiasts predicted that media channels would all converge on the same platform. It would be the great innovation of the twentieth century. We are beginning to see the results for democracy by way of the further deterioration of public service journalism. Newsrooms have indeed converged. Newspaper reporters are now posting their stories to the Internet, reading them on TV newscasts, and taping for satellite syndication. Fewer companies and fewer journalists are covering fewer stories with fewer resources. Reporters are stretched thin and increasingly rely on the shortest path to an "objective" story, regurgitating official press releases from both sides of any given issue—thus "balance" but not always truth or even analysis.[23] The same stories are then distributed over an ever-expanding number of media channels. Production is centralized while advertising income is diversified. It is a dream scenario for the business office. It is a nightmare for journalists and the reading public. Nonetheless, only a handful of news organizations have not fallen into this trap.

Defenders of this development in the "marketplace of ideas" argue that never before has the public had access to so much information. The problem is that so much of this information in the heart of the media system is the same—and more importantly, it is presented from the same point of view. Christopher Lasch points out: "What democracy requires is vigorous public debate, not information. Of course, it needs information too, but the kind of information it needs can be generated only by debate. We do not know what we need to know until we ask the right questions, and we can identify the right questions only by subjecting our own ideas about the world to the test of public controversy."[24]

It is small wonder that the critique of the system is broadening. But these developments alone are insufficient to characterize this era as a great moment in radical media criticism. For such a moment to truly exist, there has to be a sense that the criticism can lead to a structural change in the system, to political activity. Otherwise it will peter out. Throughout the 1990s political organizing around media policy issues increased alongside the growth of radical journalism criticism, though it still remained below the public radar. In 2000, a fairly significant grassroots public campaign struggled to protect the creation of 1,000 low-power noncommercial FM radio stations that had been permitted by a program established by the Federal Communication Commission under the Clinton administration. The movement failed to stop the commercial media lobby from getting its way with

Congress, but it gave the corporate media lobby the strongest fight from the public it had experienced in decades.

The politicization of media ownership and control in the United States may well have crystallized in 2003 with the massive and unprecedented public campaign to overturn the FCC's relaxation of media ownership rules. The FCC is the government body commissioned to assign monopoly rights to broadcasters for the scarce number of radio and TV channels. As part of the deal for receiving these lucrative monopoly licenses, commercial broadcasters theoretically are supposed to serve the public interest; i.e., they are supposed to do something they would not do if they were strictly out to maximize their profits. In theory, if a broadcaster fails to serve the public interest, the FCC would not renew its monopoly license but instead give the license to another firm more likely to do something in the public interest. In the cash-saturated, special-interest climate of Washington agency politics, the FCC never exercised this form of regulation in the public interest. The commercial broadcasters were far too powerful to permit such regulation to occur, and the general public was almost entirely oblivious to these affairs. It was a classic case of corrupt, inside-the-Beltway politicking, where the ante for admission was a few hundred million dollars.

There was one form of regulation the FCC did enforce with some rigor. As a condition of granting (and enforcing) monopoly licenses to the scarce publicly owned spectrum, the FCC put limits on how many monopoly licenses a single firm could possess as well as how much other media a license holder could own. The principles involved were simple and not especially controversial. Because monopoly broadcast licenses generated exceptional profits for those lucky enough to hold them, it was not in the public interest to let license holders use the super-profits generated by these government-created monopoly licenses to gobble up all the other media channels. And it is a core premise of liberal democratic theory that, on balance, it is much better to have many distinct and viable voices in the media than it is to have a few enormous firms operating in noncompetitive markets. Indeed, in democratic theory it should clearly be established that society would benefit by media consolidation before it may be permitted. When in doubt, it is always better to have more rather than fewer owners and operators of public media channels. So it developed that there were strict limits on the number of radio or television stations a single company could own. Further, cross-media ownership, i.e., owning broadcast outlets and newspapers in the same community, was prohibited. The reason why the FCC established media ownership regulations may have been less principled: there were numerous and politically powerful small media owners who understood that if the media ownership rules were relaxed or eliminated, they would not be able to survive in the marketplace. And it was when the political strength of these independents diminished that the ravenous media giants were able to use their political muscle to force the FCC to relax the media ownership rules.

We will not go in detail into the background and nature of the 2003 fight over the FCC's relaxation of the media ownership rules. Details on that struggle may be found elsewhere.[25] What is important for the purpose of this introduction is to note that the public response, first to the FCC and later to Congress when it considered overturning the FCC's rules changes, was extraordinary. Some 3 million Americans registered their opposition to relaxing media ownership rules during the first nine months of 2003. They caught the FCC and Congress entirely by surprise. Members of Congress said the issue received more public feedback than any other issue they faced except for the war on Iraq. Organizations ranging from Common Cause to the National Rifle Association stated that this issue struck a chord with their membership like few others. Poll after poll showed that the vast majority of Americans opposed what the FCC did, and that the more people knew about the issue, the more they opposed relaxing media-ownership rules. For the first time in generations, radical press criticism of commercial media was connecting with political activism and resonating in the broader political culture. FCC Commissioner Michael J. Copps wrote in his dissenting opinion to the FCC's deregulatory ruling that the debate over media ownership in 2003 had awoken a "sleeping giant" in the American public. The demand for a better, more diverse, more representative media system resonated across the political spectrum. Copps concluded profoundly: "The media concentration debate will never be the same. This Commission faces a far more informed and involved citizenry. The obscurity of this issue that many have relied upon in the past, where only a few dozen inside-the-Beltway lobbyists understood this issue, is gone forever."[26] It remains to be seen whether this will be the foundation of a much more broad and sustained movement for media reform or whether this was a one-shot deal. But by any account, what happened in 2003 was extraordinary.

To conclude, the rediscovery and reinvigoration of this tradition of media criticism is important for today's debates precisely because of the misperception that has so long excised it from the history books. In broad terms, the existence of a widespread rejection of commercial journalism at its inception and throughout its development shifts the burden of proof in contemporary criticism. The status quo can no longer stand on the assumption of immaculate conception and a birthright of established authority. Not only was the merger of commerce and the democratic public sphere challenged at the turn of the century, it was flatly opposed. Seen in this light, the debate over the legitimacy of the commercial press demands an equal obligation from critics and proponents alike to make a persuasive case for historical validity. Rhetorically, it is no longer a criticism of a heretofore unchallenged system entrenched in the foundation of liberal democracy, but rather the most recent manifestation of a long-standing, ongoing debate about what that foundation was and should be.

Redrawing the lines of the debate in this way allows contemporary critics to match up current arguments with their historical antecedents to lend them the credibility of longevity. Moreover, arguments made in every decade across the century to criticize the commercial press have steadily amplified, lending them the power of a recurrent critique when applied in the context of twenty-first-century corporate media. That is to say, the problems identified at the beginning and traced through time are now worse than ever before. By tracing current claims back to their roots and building historical arguments into a modern frame of reference, scholars can draw upon the basic logic and continuity that carries this critical perspective through the decades. This is an important proposition, because it allows critics to offer an alternative, integrated history of the press to stand beside the myths of commercial media. Furthermore, it allows for a powerful comparative analogy. Because the capitalist media system was less complicated in its early days, the logic of the criticism is straightforward and difficult to dispute. Particular anti-democratic trends or abuses of power were subjected to an immediate critique based on a firsthand knowledge of life before the commercial press. In this sense, their validity is fairly simply demonstrated. Consequently, studying the structural press criticism across numerous eras amounts to locating the indisputable common denominators of the current crisis. It is a tool for greater understanding, more accurate critique, and stronger argumentation.

The potential gains for radical media critics—and indeed for citizens—through the study of their forebears are not only substantial but essential. It is important to recapture the truth about the past and rejuvenate the potency of the criticism offered in the early decades of the last century. It is important to develop an accurate and persuasive picture of the continuity of structural media criticism through U.S. history. Most important, however, is the potential of recapturing the political culture that sustained these radical positions in the mainstream of U.S. public thought. Only this type of resonance carries the promise of change. This collection of essays is a step in that direction.

Notes

1. Leonard Downie Jr. and Robert G. Kaiser, *the News About the News* (New York: Alfred A. Knopf, 2002), 252.

2. James D. Squires, *Read All About It! The Corporate Takeover of America's Newspapers* (New York: Times Books, 1993), 218.

3. Statement of the Committee of Concerned Journalists, http://www.journalism.org/ccj/about/statement.html.

4. Bill Kovach and Tom Rosenstiel, *Warp Speed* (New York: The Century Foundation Press, 1999), 10.

5. Edward Alsworth Ross, "The Suppression of Important News," *Atlantic Monthly* 105 (March 1910): 310.

6. Jerome Barron, "Access to the Press—A New First Amendment Right," *Harvard Law Review* 80, no. 8 (June 1967): 1647–48.

7. James Carey, "The Press, Public Opinion, and Public Discourse: On the Edge of the Postmodern," in *James Carey: A Critical Reader*, ed. Eve Stryker Munson and Catherine A. Warren (Minneapolis: University of Minnesota Press, 1997), 247.

8. See Richard Ohmann, *Selling Culture* (New York: Verso, 1996).

9. Frank Luther Mott, *American Journalism*, rev. ed.. (New York: Macmillan, 1950), 546.

10. Robert La Follette, *La Follette's Autobiography* (Madison: University of Wisconsin Press, 1963), 258–59.

11. Richard Hofstadter, *The Age of Reform* (New York: Alfred A. Knopf, 1955), 238.

12. Will Irwin, *The American Newspaper: A Series First Appearing in* Collier's, *January—July, 1911* (Ames, IA: Iowa State University Press, 1969), 8. This particular quote is from Irwin's first installment.

13. Upton Sinclair, *The Brass Check*, with an introduction by Robert W. McChesney and Ben Scott (Urbana: University of Illinois Press, 2003), 241.

14. Ibid., 248; see also Oswald Garrison Villard, "Some Weaknesses in Modern Journalism," in *The Coming Newspaper*, ed. Merle Thorpe (New York: Holt and Co., 1915), 77.

15. Quoted in Paul Greer, "The Confession of a Reporter," *Nonpartisan Leader* (May 13, 1918): 5.

16. See David M. Kennedy, *Over Here* (New York: Oxford University Press, 1980), 60–61; and Stanley Cooperman, *World War I and the American Novel* (Baltimore: Johns Hopkins Press, 1967), 15.

17. See, for example, Mark Hertsgaard, *On Bended Knee* (New York: Farrar, Straus and Giroux, 1988).

18. See Robert W. McChesney, *Telecommunications, Mass Media and Democracy: The Battle for the Control of U.S. Broadcasting, 1928–1935* (New York: Oxford University Press, 1993).

19. The work of Inger Stole is instructive in this regard.

20. Isabelle Keating, "Reporters Become of Age," *Harper's* (November 1935): 601.

21. Herbert Harris, *American Labor* (New Haven: Yale University Press, 1938), 173, 185.

22. Quoted in the frontispiece of Joseph Pulitzer Jr., ed., *St. Louis Post-Dispatch Symposium on Freedom of the Press* (St. Louis: St. Louis Post-Dispatch, 1938). This booklet is the symposium the president requested; it is a compilation of statements by notable public figures, editors, and publishers on the state of the freedom of the press.

23. See Brent Cunningham, "Rethinking Objective Journalism," *Columbia Journalism Review* (July/August 2003).

24. Christopher Lasch, *The Revolt of the Elite and the Betrayal of Democracy* (New York: W. W. Norton, 1995), 162–63.

25. The website www.mediareform.net provides the most comprehensive coverage of the issue.

26. Statement of Commissioner Michael J. Copps Dissenting, *2002 Biennial Regulatory Review—Review of the Commission's Broadcast Ownership Rules and Other Rules Adopted Pursuant to Section 202 of the Telecommunications Act of 1996*, 22, http://hraunfoss.fcc.gov/edocs_public/attachmatch/FCC-03-127A5.doc.

PART ONE
"Our Master's Voice"

Concentration of Ownership

GEORGE SELDES

The House of Lords
(1938)

Once every year the American Newspaper Publishers Association, the House of Lords of our press, meets in secret. No one cares to spy on it, no newspapermen are present, no photographers interrupt, no representatives of a yellow journal harass or intimidate the members. It would be useless. If a reporter found out what plans are discussed, what plots are made, what schemes proposed, no newspaper would publish the disclosures, sensational as they might be. Nothing is sacred to the American press but itself.

And yet these secret meetings of our organized publishers rank among the most important actions against the general welfare of the American people ever taken (legally) by any small national group in our time. But since the press publishes the news, true or false or half-way, about everything in the world except itself, the American public knows nothing about what the rulers of public opinion annually decide for it.

Only rarely do the millions learn or sense the truth about the activities of this group of leaders. In the repudiation of the press in the 1936 election there was a symptom of the universal suspicion and growing anger of the public, but this awakening was made possible by the fact that millions were already pledged to the party the majority of newspapers attacked, and the radio was used extensively, and there were other means of breaking the press offensive. In social, rather than political, issues there is no means by which the public can defeat the dictation of the press.

The publishers' meetings are secret because their actions cannot bear the light of publicity. Three hundred and sixty days in the year the publishers speak editorially for open covenants openly arrived at, whether in international relations or in the advertising business, but every April they lock the doors and make a hypocritical paradox out of their own ideals.

We know that in the open meetings they approve annually of "freedom of the press as the bulwark of our civilization," and that in the closed meetings they

From *Lords of the Press* (New York: Julian Messner, 1938), 3–19.

discuss ways and means of fighting labor and their own employees who demand
higher wages or perhaps better light or decent toilet arrangements. We do know
that in the open meetings they pledge themselves to honesty and truth and the
whole bagful of tricks in the ethical code of their profession, and they also discuss
the cost of paper, the ways to increase advertising and gain circulation, and other
purely materialistic subjects which are necessary if any press, free or kept, is to
survive. But it is somewhat of a shock to learn that in the closed sessions they
defend the employment of child labor, they take united action against a Congressional measure which would keep drugmakers from poisoning or cheating the
American people, and they gloat over their own strike-breaking department which
offers scabs not only to members but to anyone who wants to fight the unions.

One of the most recent secret meetings was devoted to nothing but war on the
American Newspaper Guild, the association of newspaper workers which offended
the publishers when it joined the American Federation of Labor and drove them
into hysterics when it later joined the Committee for Industrial Organization. In all
American business and industry today there is probably no instance of such bitter-
ness, such conflict, such hatred, such opposition, and such war to the throat as
between the newspaper workers and the newspaper owners. The amusing angle
to this story is that the publishers still print that cockeyed falsehood about the
interests of capital and labor being identical. It certainly isn't in their own line.

What conspiratorial plans are made to fight labor at the secret sessions we can
judge best by what happens. We have seen such united action as an attack on
Congress when it considered passing the Wagner Labor Act which is regarded as a
Magna Carta of the working people of America. We have watched the press of the
country condemn it after it passed. And, moreover, we have seen the publishers
openly defy the law, declare it unconstitutional, and, when the Guild took the test
case to the Supreme Court and the law was declared constitutional, we have seen
the publishers inaugurate a movement to repeal or alter or emasculate this law.

We have seen the publishers declare the National Labor Relations Board unconstitutional long before the Supreme Court declared it constitutional. We have
seen the publishers unite to fight any and every attempt to increase taxes on the
rich and alleviate the burdens of the poor. All sorts of transcendental humanitarian
poppycock has been invented by the highly paid editorial writers and rich columnists to hide this fundamental conflict of the Haves and Havenots in America. But
the fact is becoming known to the public that the press lords of America are the
champions of the former while still flying the pre-war flag of "service to the common people."

There are of course many men of the highest ideals in the membership. But so
far as can be learned they have not been able in the past to gain their points even
in the most flagrant cases of violation of journalistic ethics.

The La Follette Civil Liberties Investigation Committee has given documentary evidence that four of the biggest newspapers in the country had employed spies or thugs, but no action was taken by the publishers' association.

Some years ago one of its members was found guilty in a Federal court of theft. His news service had stolen the news from another service. But he was not fired from either the publishers' association or the service which he robbed and of which he is still a member.

Another newspaper was found guilty of blackmailing oil companies for a million dollars. And a third of suppressing the scandal for $92,000. There was some talk of taking action.

Twenty or more of the big newspapers of the country were found by a Congressional investigation to be secretly controlled by the power and paper trust. Colonel Robert Ewing, publisher of the *New Orleans States*, president of the Southern Newspaper Publisher Association, a component branch of the A. N. P. A., offered, at the convention of the latter, a resolution condemning the power and paper trust's activities. It was tabled. S. E. Thomason, then of the *Chicago Journal*, went Colonel Ewing one better with a resolution that all the great publishers in America make public all their connections with power and paper trusts, with all the banks, and with all the powerful financial institutions which control the country.

The resolution was defeated with a roar of laughter.

On the other hand, when a speaker for the National Electric Light Association— with its $25,000,000 a year fund for influencing newspapers—said at its convention that "There we are, brothers under the skin, utility and newspaper battling shoulder to shoulder. Our most important contact is . . . the American Newspaper Publishers Association," the latter accepted the remark as a compliment.

In fact every annual convention proves more fully than the last the statement made by William Allen White, now president of the editors' association, that the newspaper business is a business and nothing more. The code of ethics of the journalistic profession is no longer put into practice. But all the anti-social activities of big business have become the program of the A. N. P. A. In fact it is frequently difficult to distinguish its program from that of the National Association of Manufacturers and the United States Chamber of Commerce.

Heywood Broun, president of the Guild, who attended several open and secret sessions one year, said he was shocked by the smallness "of this collection of very small men so obviously drunk with a smug sense of power and self-righteousness," who "get themselves up as the full and all-sufficient judges of what the public should get in the way of news and of opinion." He listened for days. "The ghost of Thomas Jefferson was sent whirling along the flying trapeze as Bainbridge Colby, exhumed from heaven knows where, uttered dreary tory platitudes about big business and its sacred rights. I was struck by the fact that, with the mild exception of Glenn Frank, all the spokesmen and invited orators of the publishers were old men. And they did not talk of journalism but of the industry. If a man from Mars had happened in, I think he might have spent an hour and still remained puzzled as to whether he had happened in upon a convention of bankers, cotton-mill owners, or the makers of bathroom supplies. . . .

"The publishers decided that they would accept no sort of code of fair practice whatsoever. They decided not to disturb carrier boys between the ages of ten and twelve who are already on the job. They condemned the mild Copeland bill on foods and drugs. H. W. Flagg, of the Philadelphia *Public Ledger*, chairman of the Open Shop Committee, unofficially offered the services of his committee to all publishers, members and non-members, for strike-breaking purposes. And so you see once more the publishers have saved the freedom of the press."

When the National Electric Light Association was engaged in buying the good will of the American press, it also maintained a lobby in Washington for the purpose of using Congressmen for its own commercial purposes. This lobby was never exposed or mentioned.

Other lobbies, notably those which are not in any way affiliated with advertising, have from time to time been the subject of newspaper attacks. They have given the word "lobby" a sinister connotation, associated with such words as "propaganda" and "isms" and other things called "un-American."

But for years there has been a powerful lobby at work in Washington which up to now has been more successful than any except possibly the American Legion lobby. This is the publishers' lobby. It not only is active in making laws, amending laws, and preventing laws, but it has the unique distinction—can it be because of the power of the press?—of recommending that the publishers break the law.

Incidents and illustrations of this group's power are many and important. But before sampling those of New Deal time, I would like to mention an exposure of this lobby which can be found in "62nd Congress, 1st session, Senate Documents, Vol. 6, Reciprocity with Canada Hearings, Vol. 2," because this episode although belonging to another generation nevertheless illuminates not only the means the organization still employs, but also furnishes a clue to subjects of later chapters.

The United States, as many readers may remember, has from time to time been the scene of hefty debate over tariffs on foreign goods. The Republican press has been in favor, the Democratic press has been opposed to them, the industrialist North generally for protection, the agricultural South for free trade, the Republican newspaper propaganda insisting that prosperity and the full dinner pail—what memories these old-fashioned words bring up!—depended entirely upon the tariff wall keeping cheap foreign goods out and the American laborer contented in rich green pastures, the Democrat denying it all at every depression.

At the very time the Republican newspapers were publishing this drivel and propaganda they combined with the owners of Democratic newspapers in lobbying in Washington for the purpose of getting print paper and wood pulp exempt from a proposed severe tariff bill. The matter involved was a mere $5,000,000 per annum for the entire newspaper industry, no awe-inspiring sum in the face of a yearly advertising budget of one and a half to two billions, and the fact that more than one newspaper had net annual earnings of five millions or more. Yet for this sum at least half the entire press of the United States was willing to give up its editorial policies regarding tariff and join with its political enemies in a non-partisan bit of lobbying.

Among those who called on the Secretary of State to demand free wood pulp and free print paper was Frank B. Noyes, of the *Washington Star*, one of the founders of the Associated Press, and its president up to April, 1938. Within a few days after this visit the president of the A. N. P. A., Herman Ridder, sent a letter to every publisher, member or not, which after mentioning a saving of five millions added that the bill, if ratified, would also save our forests and remove "a tax upon knowledge"; therefore "will you promptly communicate with your Senators and representatives in Congress and urge favorable action."

So far the activities of the publishers' lobby had been both legal and ethical. But apparently the matter was not going through unopposed, for in the Congressional investigation there was introduced a copy of a confidential telegram which Ridder also sent, saying that "it is of vital importance to the newspapers that their Washington correspondents be instructed to treat favorably the Canadian reciprocity agreement. . . ." This request was a violation of every code of ethics in the history of journalism.

During the course of the debate it was proved that the "tax upon knowledge" was pure hypocrisy. It was purely a savings for publishers. The claim the reader would be benefited financially was proven false: it would take about thirty-three years for one average copy of a daily to consume a ton, and the duty of $3.75 meant ten cents a year more for each subscriber. And when farmers spoke against the tariff cut the Associated Press men took no notes, whereas those who spoke for it made the headlines. When Melville Stone, head of the A. P., said the press was fair although ninety percent of the publishers were against the tariff, it was proven statistically that the A. P. itself was sending out six times as much pro as anti news, and Mr. Stone was forced to admit that it was due "either to stupidity on the part of the people who were reporting . . . or ordinary weaknesses that attach to human beings."

These human weaknesses eventually rob a nation of a free press as great editors will testify. They are the weaknesses of egotism, of power seeking, of greed for profits, which men in other businesses often admit but which most publishers hide under beautiful words about public service. However, in the actions of the publishers' lobby against all reform legislation in more recent times we can see these motives a little more clearly than in the hypocritical past.

From the earliest days of the so-called New Deal, and immediately following the 1933 pro-Roosevelt parade in which the publishers marched under a friendly ban-

ner, their lobby has aimed at getting the press exempt from every law and regulation which affects other business and which might also affect their profits. The
story is told that Bernard Shaw, leaving an Albert Hall meeting which he had
addressed, was stopped by a beggar who held out a tin can. "Press!" said Mr. Shaw,
and moved on. Apocryphal as this story may be, it illustrates well the attitude of
the American newspaper publishers. In reply to every attempt to apply legislation
affecting unionization, child labor, hours, wages, sanitation, working conditions, or
other social reforms upon them, they have excused themselves with Mr. Shaw's
remark; they have not only whispered, but bellowed "Freedom of the Press!"

The President put them in their place in 1934 when the industrial codes, later
outlawed, were hailed as the salvation of the nation. The publishers' lobby favored
a code for every business except theirs. But since this could not be, they drew one
up which was "the most dishonest, weasel-worded and treacherous document"*
ever offered to General Johnson. The publishers' lobby code was so designed that
it would permit them to escape all the obligations (for promoting prosperity) which
they were urging upon all the rest of the nation.

When General Johnson threw the lobby code aside, the lobby replied by publishing a false statement that it had been accepted. When this intimidation failed,
the lobby demanded that Postmaster General Farley put pressure upon Johnson.
When this also failed, the attack was continued with other weapons, one tabloid
going so far as to publish an untrue story about the General and his party crashing
a speakeasy. General Johnson went speaking throughout the country. He was bitter
against the publishers, and especially the lobby. "They are few in number, but
ruthless in method," he declared. "Some of them control powerful newspapers and
they are using these papers to misrepresent every development of NRA. It is no
longer possible to get a square deal in truth and accuracy. . . ." But the betting in
newspaper offices was ten to one that "the big steamroller, as represented by the
American Newspaper Publishers Association, would crush General Johnson, the
President himself, and everyone connected with the NRA." This steamroller is still
crushing. In several instances, it is sad but true, the President has given in to the
publishers; and the latter repaid him by joining—Democrats and Independents with
Republicans—in the vast 1936 campaign against his second election.

In 1935 the publishers' lobby won four of its five campaigns in Washington,
and barely lost the last, an exemption from the provision of the Wagner Labor
Disputes Bill, where the Newspaper Guild was on the side of labor, as opposed to
the publishers who represented the employers. During the Senate hearings Elisha
Hanson, attorney for the A. N. P. A., attacked the bill as a whole, on the ground
that it would infringe freedom to print or fail to print what the publishers wished.
In the House, the publishers got Representative William P. Connery (Dem., Mass.)

*So reported by Washington Correspondent P. Y. Anderson.

to add a proviso which was nothing more than the old "Freedom of the Press" clause always trotted out when profits are at stake. The Guild spokesman, however, exposed this maneuver, and the amendment was out when the bill passed.

It is now well known that the publishers played the strongest hand in defeating the Tugwell Bill. Nevertheless, when the first Copeland Bill, its mild, emasculated successor, was produced in Congress, the publishers joined the Proprietary Association of Drug Manufacturers in defeating it also. The reason for this sanguinary attack on a bill already weakened to please the drugmakers, was the publishers' insistence on clauses putting all the blame for violations on the manufacturers and dealers, none on the advertising agencies and newspapers.

Along came the Agricultural Adjustment Act, and along came the publishers with amendments, one definitely stating that no marketing order could be issued "prohibiting, regulating or restricting" advertising, and providing that no processing tax can be fixed on material to be made into wood pulp, from which newsprint is manufactured.

The Black Thirty-Hour-Week Bill was kept in Representative Connery's labor committee until it emerged with exemptions for banks, newspapers and magazines.

Finally, there was the Eastman Bus and Truck Bill which was sent to the President for signature. It gives the Interstate Commerce Commission power to regulate motor carriers, but makes four commodity exemptions, the first three being livestock, fish and agricultural products, the last being newspapers.

When this list of 1935 achievements of the publishers' pressure lobby was announced the *Guild Reporter* said it was "overcome with admiration." Of course that provision in the last of the laws which sets maximum hours for truck drivers hauling papers in interstate commerce might well be interpreted as an attack on freedom of the press. Naturally, any attempt by Congress to tax wood pulp is a violation of the constitution which grants liberty to publishers. And of course if Congress insisted that the advertisers of worthless drugs tell the same truth in the newspapers which the 1906 law requires them to tell on the labels, that would curtail sales, curtail advertising, curtail profits for publishers and therefore become the most dastardly attack on the American public's inherent right to a free press which our history has ever known. So you see, the lobby has a lot of work.

It may not be ethical, or decent, or moral in the higher sense, but it is generally legal. The great publishers of America have never been afraid to defy legality when it was to their own benefit to do so. Openly the House of Lords has always stood for law and order so far as others were concerned. Generally speaking the big press of the nation has always accused labor of favoring and originating violence throughout the long and bloody history of the struggle of the working people for a better life. The exact opposite is true. After the daily newspaper has screamed its charge against the unions, the impartial historian has found, too late to be of any practical use, that in some ninety cases out of a hundred it is the employer or the police or the enemies of labor who are guilty of favoring and initiating violence.

And when it comes to lawbreaking or defiance of the law, actions which are generally charged only to criminals, the publishers have a great advantage when they do so because there can be no "public outcry" against them, no protest, no "vox populi," no "wave of indignation," nor any of the other movements they frequently invent, knowing they themselves are the only channel for such movements.

Here are, for example, two forces which affect the newspapers—and their profits. Despite publishers' opposition the Wagner Act was passed, the National Labor Relations Board came into being. Manufacturers did not like it but they obeyed it. Not so the publishers.

"If," said Elisha Hanson, chief counsel for the A. N. P. A., "the NLRB issues an order in this case, Mr. Hearst will not comply with it."

In October 1936 this same Hanson sent out a general statement to the publishers telling them not to obey the rulings of the same board because, he, Hanson, thought they were unconstitutional. "Publishers from now on," he ordered, "should flatly refuse to have anything to do with the National Labor Relations Board other than to notify it it is without power under the constitution to interfere with their business. . . . In so far as the newspaper business is concerned, I am convinced no order of the Board directed to a publisher requiring him to comply with a decision thereof will, if it is contested, be upheld in the courts."

The order under discussion (the Watson case) was upheld.

The NLRB law was upheld.

In other lines of business the government and its laws have also been challenged—but not defied. Government laws and regulations have been obeyed pending the institution of suits to test constitutionality, but in no important instance has there been defiance, as in the case of the publishers. Replying to Hanson's orders to the publishers the *Guild Reporter* called the lawyer an anarchist. Of his opinion it said (October 15, 1936): "All concern for the general welfare, all respect for the right of Congress to establish public policies which it deems to be essential for the country, have been abandoned in this document which its board sponsors. A law that most of the millions of workers of the country believe is needed to protect them in their right to earn a decent livelihood, treads to some extent on the interests of 1,200 publishers. Out with it! Ignore it!"

From the very first days of the New Deal—under which incidentally newspaper workers were first enabled to organize—until the present, the American Newspaper Guild has charged the publishers with violating not only the spirit of the law but the laws themselves. The publishers' proposed code was "treacherous and dishonest" but legal; but the subsequent "dark maneuverings," said the Guild editorially, proved that "the A. N. P. A. undertakes to set itself above Congress and the President." The Guild "questioned the sincerity of the publishers in their sanctimonious espousal of the freedom of the press. . . . The American Newspaper Guild has been the only organization in the country with the courage to bring the lawless spirit of this self-appointed oligarchy out into the open and denounce it. . . . A truly free and honest press is of more importance to the members of the American Newspaper Guild than any immediate economic interest."

Only one brave publisher agreed with the Guild. J. David Stern, of the *New York Post, Philadelphia Record, Camden Courier* and *Camden Post,* withdrew his membership in the House of Lords.

"We are resigning," he wrote the A. N. P. A., "because your association, founded to benefit and strengthen the daily newspapers of this country, has in the past few years so conducted itself as to lower American newspapers in popular esteem; to endanger the freedom of the press, and has even gone so far as to urge its members to breach the law. . . .

"I do not see how a law-abiding newspaper can consistently retain membership. . . .

"Your board recommended to its membership that no agreement be entered into with any group of employees. As we understand the Wagner Act it is obligatory upon employers to negotiate with representatives of a majority of employees. . . .

"Ever since the NRA code, the A. N. P. A. has been using the pretext of protecting the freedom of the press to gain special privilege in purely business obligations.

"That is why I say you are endangering the freedom of the press, and one of the most important essentials of democracy. . . ."

Mr. Stern's *Philadelphia Record* quit the A. N. P. A.; his *New York Post* had never been a member. Within a year from that date no less than twenty-nine charges of violation of the Wagner Act and other laws which not only the Supreme Court but even the publishers' association admit are legal, were made against as many publishers.

There were seventeen instances of intimidation, coercion and actual discharge of employees for utilizing the clauses in the Wagner Act which permit unionization; in six instances the publishers were accused of breaking the law by refusing to bargain with their employees; in two instances the publishers were accused of forming company unions, all these episodes forming a record which the official organ of the newspaper writers called "irresponsible, unscrupulous and contemptible."

Among the newspapers against which charges were filed were (Gannett's) *Knickerbocker Press* and *Albany News, Boston Herald, Boston Traveler,* (McCormick's) *Chicago Tribune, Detroit Times,* (Hearst's) *Los Angeles Examiner,* the Associated Press in New York, (Hearst's) *New York Daily Mirror, Seattle Post-Intelligencer, Seattle Star.*

With the exception of only a handful of liberal newspapers, the press of the country, which first failed to get a clause exempting itself from the Wagner Act, then defied the law, later in many instances violated the law, is today producing bitter and unfair editorials demanding that this measure—and in fact all measures which favor labor rather than capital—should be repealed.

Accused in numerous cases of discharging men for no reason but legal union activity, many publishers have sought to hide their prejudices by posting a "firing code" sent them by the A. N. P. A., and consisting of sixteen "grounds" for discharge, one of which is the failure to return a book to its proper place in the bookshelf before going home. Or leaving the electric bulb turned on over one's desk while going to the toilet. Or scratching the furniture.

The leader in the anti-labor movement of the A. N. P. A. has been its president, James G. Stahlman, publisher of the *Nashville Banner*. He is one of the minor press lords of America, and the story of his battle with the unions, his red-baiting, the sensationalizing of anti-C. I. O. news in his paper and the suppression of news favoring labor, will be found in a later chapter. The man chosen to lead the great publishers of America in their oft-announced fight for the freedom of the press is the same James G. Stahlman who, addressing the members of the Belle Meade Country Club, recently* said:

"If I had my way I would get me six husky policemen, take these labor organizers outside the city limits, and tell them it wouldn't be healthy for them to be seen in the vicinity again."

The foregoing are some of the subjects which the men who do a large part of the thinking, the leading or the misleading of the nation, discuss in their secret meetings. In the open meetings it is of course the welfare of the public, the freedom of the press, with only an occasional word about advertising money.

Strike breaking, the suppression of the labor movement, the maintenance of child labor, the mistakes of its counsel which sought to destroy the NLRB in the Watson case, and all general topics which are not concerned with public welfare, but with that of the pocketbook, make up most of the four days of the secret meetings which occur every year and the special Chicago meeting which was devoted to nothing but an attempt to destroy the Newspaper Guild. At that time an anonymous reporter wrote the "March of the Publishers":

> On to Chicago to fight for our freedom—
> Freedom to hire men, work 'em and bleed 'em—
> Freedom to chisel to heart's content—
> Freedom to make thirty-seven per cent.
> On to Chicago—but don't fail to stress—
> That our battle, of course, is for freedom of the press.

*Guild Reporter, August 30, 1937.

In the following chapters some of the individuals, all but one or two little known to the people of the country whose minds they rule, will be discussed at some length, and the common denominator of their power and their motives suggested. The reader may then judge whether or not the most powerful anonymous group of men in America can be classified as the friends or enemies of the American people.

It is the writer's intention to "let the facts speak for themselves," as Euripides suggested, and if there is criticism, expressed or implied, the reader will please remember that nothing that will be said can equal in severity that which has already come from within the ranks of the profession, from the very small minority, it is true, who still upholds the traditional journalistic liberalism of America. It is William Allen White, now president of the national editorial association, who first pointed out that the newspapers have degenerated from a noble profession to an eight percent investment, and who now states they are dominated by the "unconscious arrogance of conscious wealth," and it is J. Roscoe Drummond, executive editor of the *Christian Science Monitor*, who writes that freedom of the press "is not an end in itself. . . . A free press in the United States is not, I believe, in danger from without. It is always in danger from within. A truly free press requires . . . free men to give it life. Free men require free minds—minds intellectually honest, intellectually open, and intellectually eager. The press of the United States . . . needs . . . a leadership dedicated to the service of democracy."

The press lords of the United States in one year made this great record:

1. Fought all issues where their profits were involved.
2. Led the attack against a real pure food and drug law.
3. Opposed the Wagner Act, the Magna Carta of labor.
4. Urged amendment of proposed social insurance legislation putting newspapers in a special class.
5. Proposed compulsory arbitration of labor disputes with the outlawing of strikes.
6. Favored child labor.
7. Frowned at the Securities Act.

In its 1935 report which urged members to fight food, drug and cosmetics bills, the Wagner-Connery Law, the Thirty-Hour Bill, Social Insurance and laws "affecting the newspaper business," A. N. P. A. publishers were told to "be constantly alert and vigilant if their properties are not to be destroyed or irreparably injured."

Property, not public welfare, is the program of the A. N. P. A.

Their interests, says Alfred McK. Lee, historian of our present journalism, differ little from that of other industries; the A. N. P. A. "has sometimes been a powerful adjunct in legislative circles to the lobbies of the United States Chamber of Commerce, the National Association of Manufacturers and the trade associations of specific industries."

The press needs free men with free minds intellectually open; but its leadership consists of moral slaves whose minds are paralyzed by the specter of profits. The publishers are not leading the American people forward. They are not facing the social issues. Whether more often they are falsifying the social issues the reader may perhaps judge from the following documentation.

OSWALD GARRISON VILLARD

The Disappearing Daily
(1944)

The outstanding fact in any survey of the American press is the steady and alarming decrease in the number of dailies. Consolidation, suppression, and a strong drift toward monopoly are taking their toll. With an increase in population to more than 130,000,000, with world-shaking events of almost daily occurrence and the need for detailed, printed information greater than ever in the battle for human liberty, there are at this writing but 1,754 daily English-language journals in the great American nation as against 2,042 in 1920, and 1,933 in 1930. The decrease has been marked throughout this century. No less than 104 dailies died or were amalgamated between September 30, 1941 and March 31, 1943, although this period, except for the first two months, was distinguished by the attack on Pearl Harbor and the startling developments of our second World War. Not only were the factors making for the decrease of the dailies not offset by these thrilling events in all quarters of the globe, but there was almost no evidence of any desire to start new journals. Moreover, the war added to the difficulties of the weaker dailies through increasing costs, scarcity of labor, lack of paper, and a large decrease in advertising, such as automobile announcements, though others showed striking increases. Today there are no less than 1,103 towns and cities with only one newspaper, and in 159 large towns and cities having more than one daily there is complete ownership of the local press by one man or one group.

It is true that, according to figures compiled by *Editor and Publisher*, English-language daily newspaper circulations increased approximately four per cent during the period from Pearl Harbor to March 31, 1943, the total daily circulation for all the newspapers being 44,392,829 copies. This is the highest figure recorded in the history of the American press, and this despite the loss in the number of newspapers. But this gain in total sales by no means offsets the loss of many organs of public opinion. There are still 11,474 weekly papers (though here, too, there is a marked decrease), and some of these carry considerable weight in their commu-

From *The Disappearing Daily* (New York: Alfred A. Knopf, 1944), 3–18.

nities by trying to print more news, and in some cases even taking over standard features, such as the work of some of the columnists. In the weekly field there are few signs of vital growth if by that is meant the entrance into the business of vigorous young personalities with a message to impart. The case of the newspaper proprietor in the large towns and small cities also becomes more and more difficult because of those increasing costs of conducting the modern newspaper with its expensive machinery—the New York *Times*'s newest press is valued at more than $1,000,000—and its more and more elaborate means of acquiring and receiving its news. Only in periods of intense financial depression is there any slackening of the mounting costs of producing a daily, whose owners are often at the mercy of the inventor of a labor-saving or time-saving device, however expensive. Finally, in war-time the limitation of the supply of paper comes into the picture. Thus on a single day in October 1943 one of our largest newspapers was forced to omit 125 columns of advertising, and this was not even a Sunday issue.

Few laymen understand that in the smaller communities in particular there is a definite limitation of the possible support to be had for a daily. While there exists, of course, a large volume of what is known as "national advertising," paid for by concerns marketing goods or services in which all communities are more or less interested, the main support of a daily usually comes from the merchants of the place of publication. These sellers of goods not only do not oppose the newspaper trend to monopoly, but encourage it on the ground that if they advertise in only one daily they will save time and labor in the preparation of their announcements and have much less to pay out. What they and the proprietors of newspapers who seek monopolies overlook is that the newspaper business is unlike most others in that it is "affected by a public interest." It is a vital public need that the people in a democracy shall have the news and the opportunity to read all sides of political debates of the hour. As Thomas Jefferson put it, the best way to head off unsound opinion in a democracy is "to give them [the people] full information of their affairs thro' the channels of the public papers and to contrive that these papers should penetrate the whole mass of the people." To establish a press monopoly in a locality is to restrict the field of public information or to narrow its vision, or even perhaps to put an end to the presentation in the remaining dailies of anything but a partisan aspect of the national political or economic situation—and this despite the coming of the radio. Yet every successful publisher is beset by the temptation to increase his power and to make sure of financial profit by eliminating competitors.

From the point of view of economy and avoiding duplication of labor and editorial effort, a case can be made for the realization of the average newspaper publisher's dream of only one morning and one evening newspaper in each large city, and only one daily in all cities having 100,000 or fewer inhabitants. But aside from special influences in the newspaper business, there never was any reason to believe that the newspapers, having changed from a profession open to men of small means into a business requiring millions and therefore possible for only the very wealthy, could escape those economic tendencies which, notably in America, have more or less affected all other large industrial enterprises. Since no one would dream of starting a metropolitan newspaper with less than ten or even fifteen millions in the bank, the daily everywhere takes its place as an important industrial enterprise, a big business whose proprietors are entitled to rank among the foremost mercantile leaders of the community. Their tendency is naturally to think and act as do the members of the economic group to which they belong, and to drift steadily away from the plain people and especially from the workers. Just as the profession of journalism has changed into a business, so there is every temptation for the proprietor to consider all political and economic questions from the point of view of those who have very large economic stakes and to look with alarm upon all proposed social and political reforms. The newspaper owner feels that he belongs in the Chamber of Commerce and the merchants' associations more naturally, perhaps, than anybody else except the heads of the public utilities. His property ranks with those powerful business corporations which in every American community dominate its economic and financial life, whose officials and their wives set the "society" tone and too often control all social progress.

Other important changes in the evolution of the dailies are their increasing standardization, their continuing change from a purely informative and news-printing medium into an organ of entertainment as well, and their great loss of political and editorial influence. As for standardization, that is so obvious as to need no stressing. It is naturally increased by the existence of chains of dailies under one ownership. When one travels through the country on a fast train and buys successively the newspapers of larger cities, one is struck by their similarity. One finds the same comics, the same special features in almost all, the same Sunday magazine and financial section, and precisely the same Associated Press or United Press news. I have looked through the Sunday editions of nine large Eastern and Midwestern newspapers; a cursory examination of the Philadelphia *Inquirer* revealed twenty features that were also in the other eight newspapers. Today whenever a journal discovers a new feature, there is a widespread rush to copy it; the competition for a popular comic strip or its imitation is the clearest testimony on this point. There is no copyright to bar the adoption of new trade devices if they are dressed anew.

The newspaper of striking individuality has yielded to the desire to print everything offered by one's rivals. Almost nobody among present-day journalists sets any store by beauty of type and originality of appearance. There are still striking exceptions, like the *Herald Tribune*, the *Christian Science Monitor*, the Cincinnati *Enquirer*, and some Southern newspapers; but with the coming of mass production of dailies the desire for originality seemed to pass. Moreover, the columnists and the "canned editorials," the syndicated articles, and even the latest mechanical developments all make for similarity. When the teletypesetter came in, Frank Gannett, one of its backers, wrote that it would "work towards standardization," saying: "It will be necessary for newspapers that intend to go in a circuit to standardize their grammatical style, width of column, and the size of type used. It will also tend to standardize our news services." There are hundreds of newspapers that receive their editorials from one source, such as the Newspaper Enterprise Association. I have received as many as sixty clippings from as many small dailies all over the Union containing editorial comment upon some words of mine—all alike, all from the same source, the facts and opinions given being accepted by the editors receiving them without any critical examination whatever as to their correctness.

Indeed, nowhere is the drift toward standardization more marked than in the editorial pages, unless it be in the first pages, where, in the smaller cities particularly, one often finds slavish copying of the headlines and make-up of the large city dailies. Just as there is no longer any desire to make newspapers distinctive for individuality and for originality in the presentation of news, so many of the proprietors are influenced by this trend not to have striking personalities in charge of their editorial pages. The conservative owner does not want a powerful leader-writer to "ride hobbies or antagonize whole groups of readers," as one of them remarked to me. Curiously enough, he sticks to this although he is often aware of the lack of influence of his editorial page, for he frequently sees no inconsistency in spreading upon the first page of his daily editorials he specially wishes to have read. He even signs them himself in order to win the attention of politicians and public. At the same time he pays large sums to writers of distinction to take over his sports pages or contribute daily columns under their own signatures.

It has not been at all difficult for the dailies to swing over to the amusement side. Indeed, many have been compelled to do so and owe their continued existence to the comics, the illustrations, the puzzles, the fiction, the sports news, and the personal gossip they print. Thus, in order to keep alive, they enter fields of activity which seemed wholly outside of the scope of the newspaper until a few decades ago. Even when empty cupboards have not driven the owners along this road to success, many have realized the tremendous interest of the masses in the amusements which are their escape from their work and the routine of their lives, and, in war-time, from the nerve-racking strains to which most people are subjected. Some dailies, like the New York *Times*, to their infinite credit have refused to yield; but it has not been necessary for their financial welfare to do so. Here, as in so many other cases, we have a world-wide phenomenon.

Sir Philip Gibbs, for example, in discussing the sad plight of the British press, appealed for "less pandering to the gallery of human nature," in addition to his demand for more newspapers to offset the increasing monopolies, and for more responsibility and reliability because the press as a whole has lost its power, because "its word is no longer accepted as gospel." Few newspaper managers care for this loss of standing if they can add to their readership by printing pages and pages of comics, hints to the lovelorn, canned advice to parents, syndicated recipes for the housewife, widely marketed cuts of the coming fashions for women young and old. As long as such features make a popular appeal the modern proprietor does not care in how many other dailies they appear or how trivial and banal or vulgar they may be. He is competing with the movies, with the radio, with the legitimate stage. Hence he is sure that his greatest appeal to his readers is to be found in his "funnies" and his sensational pictures.

The commercial proprietor of this type is, therefore, little affected if he is told that he is not living up to his duty as the mentor and critic of our political and economic life. It is his income that is at stake. He is not worried when he reads a criticism like that of Irving Brant, the head of the editorial page of the St. Louis *Star-Times*, who has declared that: "Taken as a whole, the newspapers of America furnish no driving force for social reform. They are a positive handicap in economic reform. . . . It is impossible to point to one important constructive step in the last eight years which represents either the inventiveness, the initiative, or the supporting activity of the American press."* Mr. Brant, an ardent champion of the New Deal, says that for a few months in 1933 there was an emotional press response to the initiative and leadership of President Roosevelt, but that the metropolitan newspapers have been "substantially regimented against the New Deal" from the day "they were asked to limit the hours of their employees to forty per week and to pay reporters a minimum wage of $25, from the day they were told that the law guaranteed newspaper employees the right to organize for collective bargaining."

Largely because of this changed attitude of the press, it is a fact that its loss of prestige and influence is appalling and overshadows every other development except its decrease in numbers. The newspaper reader pays less and less attention to what the editors are saying and to their advice on the conduct of the nation's affairs. Here the outstanding proof is afforded by the results of the Presidential elections of 1936 and 1940. In both cases the vast bulk of the press opposed the re-election of the President. Indeed, the opposition was so overwhelming that the election of 1936 was called a vote against the newspapers, a "judgment day for America's daily press." The electorate went to the election booths under the strongest impression not only that the press was mainly Republican, but that it was fighting not for the country as a whole but for its own personal interests. They felt so keenly that it was a hostile force that in Chicago the crowds cheered attacks on their anti-Roosevelt dailies as the returns came in. In 1896 the press threw itself overwhelmingly into the fight against Bryan and stopped at nothing to accomplish its purpose. It showed its power and won. In 1936 and in 1940 it failed.

*"The Newspaper in Public Affairs," an address at the University of Colorado College of Journalism on May 8, 1937.

In an extraordinarily able article after the 1936 election, the editors of the *Christian Century* indicted the press for "its arrogance, its tyranny, its greed, its scorn of fairplay." They declared that every variety of political liberalism, in addition to organized labor and the organized farmer, had definitely come to the point where "they no longer hoped to be given just treatment" in the columns of the newspapers. Undoubtedly the intensity of this feeling, which still persists to a remarkable degree, was due to the opposition of the press to the NRA, and its long-continued refusal to accept a code for itself. Its challenging—and defeating—the child-labor constitutional amendment lest it be deprived of its newsboys, and its hostility to unions among its own workers, were both accepted as further proof that the press had cast aside all pretense that it was governed by devotion to the public welfare. Many a critic besides the *Christian Century* saw in this vote a branding of the press for its "social malfeasance," for its carrying on merely as the property of rich men, as a dangerous enemy in "the ultimate issue in a democracy, wealth versus commonwealth." Whatever the exact delinquency of the press in 1936, it cannot deny that Roosevelt carried the country by a 10,000,000 plurality, polling 27,000,000 votes.

The editors of the *New Republic* made a special study* of fifteen cities in connection with the 1936 Presidential election. Approximately 71 per cent of the total newspaper circulation of the fifteen cities, excepting those newspapers which were for neither Roosevelt nor Landon, was hostile to the Roosevelt candidacy, but in those cities only 31 per cent of the voters cast their ballots for the Republican candidate. In Boston, for example, there was a pro-Landon circulation of 1,158,352, yet there were only 96,418 votes cast for him. In Los Angeles the pro-Roosevelt newspapers sold only 74,252 copies, but there was a Democratic vote of 757,351, which was exactly 400,000 more than the Republican vote. In Detroit not a single newspaper advocated the reelection of Roosevelt, but he carried the city by 404,055 to a Republican vote of 190,732. The *New Republic*'s editors felt that the unfairness of some of the newspapers to Roosevelt's candidacy during the campaign showed that the press was getting worse and not better, and that the decay of the editorial page was more and more marked. They charged that the Chicago *Tribune* and the Hearst chain were the worst offenders because they "not only prevaricated editorially, but distorted and discolored news."

Were there any doubt as to the reactionary and selfish character of much of the press, it would be ended by a study of the policies of the American Newspaper Publishers' Association, which speaks largely for it. The Association not only opposed the NRA, the newspaper code, the coming of the newspaper guilds, and the child-labor amendment, but has also attacked the National Labor Relations Act, and stood against the advance of labor all along the line. If many of the individual

*Issue of March 17, 1937.

newspapers allow themselves to be controlled by the Association, then we have here a very grave threat to freedom of the press. As Mr. Brant has said, the objection to such control lies not in the fact that it is conservative, for it would be just as serious if it came from liberals on behalf of a liberal program. It lies in the truth that any attempt at a centralized control of newspaper opinion is an attack upon a fundamental freedom and "weakens the basis of our American democracy."

The loss of influence by the newspapers is also in large measure due to the belief that much of the local reporting is one-sided, biased, and inefficient. Every large community knows how many of its activities go unrecorded, and many of its citizens are aware by personal experience of the too frequent misrepresentation of what does happen. Often the public errs in its judgment of what should and could be reported of a city's life, even by the greatest newspapers. But those citizens who in every municipality are struggling to rectify misgovernment, to apply social curatives, and to improve civic methods know all too well how difficult it is to win and to hold the attention of the dailies. The reformers' programs are usually not sensational and are often not well presented, even when there is a "human interest" side to what they have to offer. When they are told that the lack of space makes it impossible to give room to their activities, yet see columns and columns given to gossip, scandal, and crime, they naturally believe that they have been deceived. They cannot understand it when the editor or publisher tells them he must print discussions of sports, crimes, fiction, "society" and club events, and so on, in order to hold the attention of so diversified a group as any aggregation of newspaper readers.

As one who has been on both sides of the fence, for many years on one side as a reporter and editor, and on the other as a lecturer, author, and protagonist of many causes, I can come to no other conclusion than that there has been a marked deterioration in the character and quality of the average reporting. There are brilliant exceptions—dailies earnestly seeking to be accurate—but in the main the reliability of news accounts is far below what it was years ago, and the chance of misrepresentation through unintentional misquotation as well as carelessness is so great that it is frequently necessary for speakers to safeguard themselves by preserving a copy of their statements, or by preparing in advance a "hand-out" for the reporters. Too often the reporter sent to interview the visitor in town knows nothing about the subject he asks his victim to discuss. Distinguished authors from overseas find themselves cross-examined by high-school graduates who have not the faintest idea of the background or the achievements of the men whom they are undertaking to report and to describe, or just what makes the visitors at that moment "good copy." "Where do you live and how many books have you written?" is hardly the best way to greet a man whose name is known all over the Anglo-Saxon world.

In my small sphere I have encountered reporters who admitted that they did not know whether I was an editor or a hardware merchant or a politician and had no conception of the purpose of their errand. Others could not understand the simplest developments in international affairs and showed their ignorance of outstanding men in American political life. Everyone who has traveled much and attracted the notice of the press will recall his unutterable relief on meeting a reporter who was intelligent, informed, and eager to be accurate. When one has the remarkable experience of having one's remarks recorded with stenographic accuracy and complete understanding, one naturally sends an immediate letter of thanks to the editor and the reporter. I am sure that many besides myself, so far from looking eagerly for the reproduction of an interview, have turned to it only with a wonder as to how bad the misrepresentation would be that time, or have felt relief if no interview was reported at all, or if what appeared was boiled down to a couple of "stickfuls."

On behalf of the reporters it should be said that they are as much sinned against as sinning. It is constantly dinned into their ears that when they go to public meetings or to interviews they must look for something "spicy," something to warrant a smart headline, something unexpectedly sensational or controversial. There must always be a bright, snappy "lead." So happenings of no real importance are constantly "played up" and really valuable statements or actions overlooked. A controversy between two speakers is particularly beloved, or an interruption from the audience. American assemblies and speakers in a joint debate are so unused to heckling and interrogations that when anyone does speak up, it becomes something extraordinary—to be "featured."* So the reporter is trained to look for the bizarre as all-important. If nothing exciting happens and the reporter does not bring out valuable points, or it is a crowded night at the office, his whole report is thrown on the floor. Indeed, what often puzzles the public is to see a group of reporters at a meeting and then to search in vain the next morning for one word of the happenings, or to find only a few skimpy lines. "Why was the reporters' time wasted?" the public asks. "Who called them off?"

One Washington meeting comes to mind, held during midsummer of 1942 to protest against conditions in India and to demand India's freedom. The hall was crowded to suffocation, despite dreadful heat, and hundreds were turned away, even from an overflowing meeting. The speakers were of good standing and reputation, one a national figure. The reporters' table was crowded, and the next day— not a word anywhere except a complete misrepresentation of the meeting in an evening newspaper! The speakers had been scrupulously polite to the British, but had any one of them made a violent attack upon Lord Halifax or Winston Churchill,

---

*Colonel Henry W. Nevinson, the great English journalist and war correspondent, once said to me, after a meeting in New York at which he had spoken, that he knew he had made a bad speech because no one had interrupted or heckled him!

or somebody else, the meeting would have made the front pages. I asked the owner of one of the Washington newspapers why his daily had suppressed the news of so large a meeting on so vitally important a war subject. He said he did not know why, but that he was sure that it was due to the shortage of paper and lack of space and not to any deliberate effort to suppress criticisms of English policy. To the question why, if there was so little space, the newspapers wasted time and money in sending reporters out to do nothing and print nothing, he had no reply.

In the case of this Washington meeting the reporters were obviously not responsible for the failure of their "stories" to appear. The night make-up editor holds the final say, unless overruled by superior authority. Indeed, the modern reporter is blamed frequently for the errors and the stupidities of the copy-readers. There can be no question that there has been a marked deterioration in the technical handling of "copy" and news dispatches. The newspapers of the 1890s and the first two decades of this century prided themselves upon the accuracy of their reports and were zealous in their efforts to catch blunders, bad English, and inaccurate descriptions. Today a veteran journalist writes me that "sloppiness in product is the outstanding phase of the Manhattan newspapers in 1943. Nobody seems to be concerned about the real meaning of words. The city and copy desks no longer care about blunders. The old zealot pride in Tiffany-grade craftsmanship seems moribund. Showmanship has replaced reportorial accuracy and ability. How can an eager cub develop into an ace when he lacks persistent coaching in the fundamentals of his profession? I have just read this morning's newspapers and gagged over their inexcusable sloppiness." The above cited ignorance of the average reporter as to recent history, political and other personalities, and current events is too often reflected on the copy-desk.

The readiness of the American daily to drop local happenings on any excuse affects not merely meetings and causes, but accounts of notable events. So marked has this been for some time that the late Frank Vanderlip once declared that if he were a younger man he would launch a new-type daily, one that would contain no news dispatches except those from Washington relating directly to the welfare of the city in which the paper was published. Everything else would be news of local affairs. Yet home coverage used to be the groundwork of every newspaper, and notably of the small country weeklies and dailies with their printing of "personal mentions" to take the place of local events of importance when those were not forthcoming. It will be regrettable indeed if after this war the press does not return to its prime duty of reporting the progress, or the retrogression, or the ambitions of its home communities.

One may well wonder if many proprietors and editors have seriously studied the exact division of their daily's space, or really sought to find out if the city's feelings, as indicated by the public's expression of its views, are adequately covered by their publications. Yet there are few things that have done so much to destroy faith in the press as inexact reporting. It is especially dangerous because persons present at events reported testify widely to the failure or the bias of the press. Here again it must be repeated that there are brilliant exceptions. This is, however, one of the many reasons why people no longer say: "I saw it in the newspapers, and so it must be true," but "Oh, you can't believe what you see in the dailies." Yet the former phrase was on the whole well earned by the press during the generations when the reporting—even in the 1850s—was far superior in detail and accuracy to that of the general run of today's. The New York *Herald*, for example, during the anti-slavery struggle, reported an Abolition meeting with stenographic fidelity even when it was entirely opposed to the purposes of the meeting, and, as in the case of one address by Wendell Phillips, had actually hired a mob to break up the meeting; its verbatim report was superior to that of the Abolition *Tribune*. It is true that in those days there was plenty of space and relatively little news. Today the demands on space are tremendous, but the selection of what is to go into it is too one-sided, too often, as said, guided by the search for sensation, by likes and dislikes.

When we turn to the field of labor it is not difficult to understand why the great body of workers believes the newspapers to be their most potent enemy. This is because of their ability, when strikes and other labor troubles occur, to judge newspaper accounts by their own experience and knowledge. Usually the press is against them and presents colored editorial opinions and misleading or false newspaper reports. However in the wrong and unjust the employers may be, or how partisan the conduct of the authorities and the police, it is rare indeed that a newspaper holds the scales even or leans to the labor side. Of late years the New York *Times* and some other strong newspapers have set an admirable example in appointing special labor reporters, like Louis Stark of the *Times*, and have given them free rein to report what is actually going on within the unions and to portray truthfully the labor point of view. But in the main the tendency to take sides with passion and hostility against labor, and particularly any such unpopular labor leader as John L. Lewis, renders any fair reporting out of the question in the bulk of the press or by the press associations.

Certainly no one would allege that the press as a whole has even began to do its duty in reporting the unfair practices of employers and public authorities such as have recently been brought out by Senator La Follette's inquiry into them through his special Committee to Civil Liberties in connection with labor troubles. The ordinary tendency is to uphold the police, however lawless and brutal its actions, however ghastly its slaughter of the workers, such as took place in Chicago during the great strike at the Republic Steel Company's works, when the police interfered with a murderous brutality surely not exceeded except by Hitler's S.S. Moving-picture films proved the scandalous conduct of the police, and some corrective measures were taken by the authorities. But if anybody should need further proof of how lawless the press and the police can be, he should turn to the trouble in San Francisco in 1934 which took on the character of a general strike. This is one of the very few cases in which the charge of a newspaper conspiracy can be brought against the dailies. The San Francisco newspapers formed the "Newspaper Publishers' Council" so that they could act together. Their first important effort was to prevent the declaration of martial law on the ground that if order was maintained—and therefore the strike was not illegally interfered with—"the announced objective of the general strike" would have been aided. They were successful in this, and next printed on their first pages editorials stating that radicals had got control of the unions and "that the general strike was a revolution against constituted authority," which it was not in the remotest degree.

Then General Hugh Johnson, the head of the NRA, arrived in San Francisco. Eager to "grant the request of the general strike committee that the longshoremen's demands for complete control of hiring halls be accepted as a condition before any discussion of arbitration should occur," he declared that the ship-owners were "anti-social," because "labor is inherently entitled to bargain collectively through leaders of its own choosing," and because "in the American shipping industry, including the loading and unloading of ships, this right has not been justly accorded." He went on to say that because of this the responsibility "for anything that may happen here" would be "on the head" of the shipping managers. Then the Publishers' Council got to work on him and kept at him until three a.m. When the next dawn came he announced that the workers whose cause he had just justified constituted "a threat to the community," planning "civil war," "bloody insurrection," "a blow at the flag of our common country." More than that, he declared that if the government did not act, the people would. This was immediately followed by the appearance of "vigilantes," who, with the police following and abetting them, were soon smashing private property, entering private premises without warrant, and destroying the contents of the headquarters of unions, Communists, and radical newspapers.

The police arrested hundreds of people—again without warrant—and, without the excuse that mob violence was going on, beat them up and threw them into jail. One San Francisco judge alone released eighty men against whom, he said, no shadow of a charge of lawless conduct could be brought. In all of this the newspapers, always with the admirable exception of the Scripps-Howard *News*—which was not in the Council—continued to play a despicable part, inciting by their headlines to public excitement and disorder. They pretended that union men made the raids, which was not true, for, according to reliable witnesses, the police themselves were the most lawless and the most guilty. What can be said of the mentality of those publishers who could not see that offenses by officials under oath to uphold and defend the laws and the rights of the individual constitute vastly more dangerous blows to our American institutions and our Constitution than could the activities of the few really "radical" leaders in San Francisco? Was it any wonder that thereupon the San Francisco unions voted to boycott all the newspapers except the *News*?

It is hardly surprising in the light of this, and any amount of similar evidence, that the workers have no faith whatever in the daily press, that in 1936 and 1940 they loved Mr. Roosevelt for his newspaper enemies. Whatever else may be said of Mr. Roosevelt—and I am entirely opposed to his continuance in office—the workers believed rightly that the New Deal gave them their only hope of the improvement of their social and economic position—until Mr. Roosevelt himself betrayed his creation. The public is buying more newspapers as the quoted figures show, partly, of course, because we are in the greatest of wars. The readers want their comics, they want their sports, they want news of Hollywood, and they want the news of our steady progress in the war. Especially they want the radio timetables that they may hear not only the entertainment features offered by the stations, but important public addresses and "flash" news bulletins. But the people buy the newspapers not for their counsel or their leadership, not for any inspiration, nor in any experience of finding them championing any far-reaching, fundamental reforms or leading them toward a better era.

Finally, in this survey of the trend of American journalism during the last twenty years, it must be stressed again that the tendencies cited are to be found not merely in the United States, but in other freedom-loving countries. They are part and parcel of the evolution of this capitalistic age, which, through its failure to head off the second World War, has invited its own destruction. In my judgment, the burden of guilt upon the press of the world for the coming of this war is second on the Allied side only to that which rests upon the shoulders of the statesmen of Belgium, of France, of England, for their refusal to see from 1920 on whither the Treaty of Versailles was leading us, their unwillingness to aid the German Republic and the democratic forces supporting it, their failure to prevent the rearming of that country by Hitler, their giving him the right to re-create a navy, and their appeasing of the German dictator.

That a very considerable portion of the press in both England and the United States foresaw what was coming and repeatedly warned against it and encouraged their foreign correspondents to portray what was actually happening, does not mitigate the dreadful failure of the newspapers as a whole to prevent the coming of the greatest catastrophe in human history. But the governments were too short-sighted, composed of men too small mentally or too stupid, too steeped in worn-out diplomatic and power-political conceptions, to heed. And the editors were neither sufficiently united nor powerful enough to arouse a compelling public opinion on their side. It unfortunately cannot be added that the press, both here and abroad, is redeeming itself by its presentation of the war news, or by its editorial leadership in this struggle. Indeed, it is constantly misleading by wrongful emphasis, notably in the headlines, in failure to hold the news-scales evenly and objectively. There seems to be as little statesmanship in the editorial offices as in the chancelleries here or abroad. All of this may be playing its part in the disappearance of the American daily.

Robert W. McChesney

U.S. Media at the Dawn of
the Twenty-first Century
(2000)

The United States is in the midst of an almost dizzying transformation of its media system. In this chapter I address the main trends, the real trends, in U.S. media at the dawn of the twenty-first century. These are corporate concentration, conglomeration, and hypercommercialism. I argue that the U.S. media system is an integral part of the capitalist political economy, and that this relationship has important and troubling implications for democracy. I then discuss the flip side of hypercommercialism, which is the decline, if not elimination, of notions of public service in our media culture. In particular, I concentrate upon the corruption and degradation of journalism, to the point where it is scarcely a democratic force. Moreover, I analyze the undemocratic and corrupt manner in which the core laws and codes regulating communication, most notably the Telecommunications Act of 1996, have been enacted. The system I describe does not exist as a result of popular will, nor is it by any means a "natural" occurrence. The media system exists as it does because powerful interests have constructed it so that citizens will not be involved in the key policy decisions that have shaped it.

The striking structural features of the U.S. media system in the 1990s are concentration and conglomeration. It may seem ironic that these are the dominant structural features when, to the casual observer, the truth can appear quite the opposite. We seem inundated in different media from magazines and radio stations to cable television channels and, now, websites. But, in fact, to no small extent, the astonishing degree of concentrated corporate control over the media is a response to the rapid increase in channels wrought by cable, satellite TV, and digital media. Media firms press to get larger to deal with the uncertainty of the changing terrain wrought by new media technologies. "If you look at the entire chain of entities—studios, networks, stations, cable channels, cable operations, international distribution—you want to be as strong in as many of those as you can," News Corporation president Peter Chernin stated in 1998. "That way, regardless of where

From *Rich Media, Poor Democracy* (New York: The New Press, 2000), 15–29.

the profits move to, you're in a position to gain."[1] Yet, any explanation of media concentration and conglomeration must go beyond media technologies. They also result from changes in laws and regulations that now permit greater concentration in media ownership. But the bottom line, so to speak, is that concentrated media markets tend to be vastly less risky and more profitable for the firms that dominate them.

In fact, media concentration is not a new phenomenon. Classically, it has assumed the form of *horizontal integration,* where a firm attempted to control as much of the output in its particular field as possible. The ultimate form of horizontal integration, therefore, is monopoly. Horizontal integration has two great benefits for firms. First, as firms get a bigger share of the market it permits them to have lower overhead and to have more bargaining power with suppliers. Seagram, for example, estimates cost savings of $300 million for its music division from its purchase of PolyGram in 1998.[2] Second, as a firm gets a larger share of a specific market, it gains more control over the prices it can charge for its products.[3] Firms operating in oligopolies—meaning markets dominated by a handful of firms each with significant market share—tend to do what monopolists do: they cut back on output so they can charge higher prices and earn greater profits. Hence, when Bertelsmann bought Random House for $1.4 billion in 1998 to become the dominant U.S. book publisher, fears of canceled authors' contracts spread throughout the literary community.[4] Stable oligopolies are very desirable for large firms, because despite their potential for profits, it can be quite difficult for a new player to enter an oligopolistic market. All of this not only drives the firms to use mergers and acquisitions to get bigger and more powerful but it also drives them to lobby for ownership deregulation and to generate new technologies that make concentration more feasible.

The U.S. mass media industries have been operated along noncompetitive oligopolistic lines for much of the twentieth century. In the 1940s, for example, broadcasting, film production, motion picture theaters, book publishing, newspaper publishing, magazine publishing, and recorded music were all distinct national oligopolistic markets, each of them dominated by anywhere from a few to a dozen or more firms. In general, these were *different* firms dominating each of these industries, with only a few exceptions. Throughout the twentieth century there have been pressing concerns that these concentrated markets would inhibit the flow and range of ideas necessary for a meaningful democracy.[5] For a variety of reasons, however, these concerns rarely spilled over into public debate.[6] In particular, the rise of the notion of professional journalism in the early twentieth century—which became widespread, even dominant, by mid-century—attempted to disconnect the editorial process from the explicit supervision of the owners and advertisers of the mass media, thus making the editorial product seem more credible as a "public service." To the extent that this process was seen as successful, the corporate commercial domination of the media seemed a less pressing, perhaps even insignificant, matter.[7]

Concentration has proceeded in specific media markets throughout the 1990s, with the proportion of the markets controlled by a small number of firms increasing, sometimes marginally and at other times dramatically. The U.S. film production industry has been a tight-knit club effectively controlled by six or seven studios since the 1930s. That remains the case today; the six largest U.S. firms accounted for over 90 percent of U.S. theater revenues in 1997.[8] All but sixteen of Hollywood's 148 widely distributed (six hundred or more theaters) films in 1997 were produced by these six firms, and many of those sixteen were produced by companies that had distribution deals with one of the six majors.[9] The newspaper industry underwent a spectacular consolidation from the 1960s to the 1980s, leaving a half-dozen major chains ruling the roost.[10] The emerging consolidation trend in the newspaper industry is that of "clustering," whereby metropolitan monopoly daily newspapers purchase or otherwise link up with all the smaller dailies in the suburbs and surrounding region.[11] Clustering permits newspapers to establish regional and/or broadly metropolitan newspaper monopolies and is quite lucrative. In 1997 it accounted for 25 percent of the record $6.2 billion in U.S. newspaper transactions.[12] Two major 1998 deals further concentrated U.S. book publishing and music production. With Bertelsmann's purchase of Random House, the U.S. book publishing industry is now dominated by seven firms.[13] And with Seagram's $10.4 billion purchase of PolyGram, the five largest music groups account for over 87 percent of the U.S. market.[14]

Media sectors that were once more competitive and open have seen the most dramatic consolidation in the past decade. In cable television systems, six firms now possess effective monopolistic control over more than 80 percent of the nation, and seven firms control nearly 75 percent of cable channels and programming.[15] As Time Warner's Ted Turner puts it, "We do have just a few people controlling all the cable companies in this country."[16] *Variety* notes that "mergers and consolidations have transformed the cable-network marketplace into a walled-off community controlled by a handful of media monoliths."[17] Radio station ownership, which I return to at the end of this chapter, has gone through a stunning transformation in the late 1990s, leaving four newly created giants with one-third of the industry's annual revenues of $13.6 billion.[18] With no small amount of irony, even the "alternative" weekly newspaper market—which was established to provide a dissident check on corporate media and journalism—has come to be dominated by a few chains.[19]

Concentration arguably has been most dramatic in the 1990s at the retail end of the media food chain. In motion picture theaters, for example, the era of the independent or even small chain theater company has gone the way of the passenger pigeon. In 1985 the twelve largest U.S. theater companies controlled 25 percent of the screens; by 1998 that figure was at 61 percent and climbing rapidly.[20] The largest chain, co-owned by the leveraged-buyout firms Kohlberg, Kravis, Roberts and Co. and Hicks, Muse, Tate and Furst, controls around 20 percent of the nation's movie screens.[21] U.S. book retailing has undergone a revolution to such a degree that more than 80 percent of books are sold by a few huge national chains like Borders and Barnes & Noble.[22] The share of books sold by independent book dealers fell from 42 percent to 20 percent from 1992 to 1998.[23]

But concentrating upon specific media sectors fails to convey the extent of concentrated corporate control. The dominant trend since the 1970s or 1980s, which has accelerated in the 1990s, is the conglomeration of media ownership. This is the process whereby media firms began to have major holdings in two or more distinct sectors of the media, such as book publishing, recorded music, and broadcasting. So it is that each of the six main Hollywood studios are the hubs of vast media conglomerates. Each of the six owns some combination of television networks, TV show production, television stations, music companies, cable channels, cable TV systems, magazines, newspapers, book publishing firms, and other media enterprises. The vast majority of the dominant firms in each of the major media sectors are owned outright or in part by a small handful of conglomerates. And this has all come about seemingly overnight. Published in 1983, Ben Bagdikian's seminal, even shocking, *The Media Monopoly* chronicled how some fifty media conglomerates dominated the entirety of U.S. mass media, ranging from newspapers, books, and magazines to film, radio, television, cable, and recorded music. Today that world appears to have been downright competitive, even populist. After the massive wave of media mergers and acquisitions since 1983, Bagdikian has reduced the number of dominant firms, until the most recent edition of *The Media Monopoly* in 1997 put the figure at around ten, with another dozen or so firms rounding out the system.[24]

The "first tier" of media conglomerates includes Time Warner, Disney, Viacom, Seagram, Rupert Murdoch's News Corporation, and Sony, all connected to the big six film studios. The remaining first-tier media giants include General Electric, owner of NBC, and AT&T, which in 1998 purchased TCI, the cable powerhouse with vast holdings in scores of other media enterprises.[25] GE (1998 sales: $100 billion), AT&T-TCI (1997 sales: $58 billion), and Sony (1997 sales: $51 billion) all are enormous firms, among the largest in the world. Their media holdings constitute a distinct minority of their assets.

These media empires have been constructed largely in the 1990s, with a rate of growth in annual revenues that is staggering. In 1988 Disney was a $2.9 billion per year amusement park and cartoon company; in 1998 Disney had $25 billion in sales. In 1988 Time was a $4.2 billion publishing company and Warner Communications was a $3.4 billion media conglomerate; in 1998 Time Warner did $28 billion in business. In 1988 Viacom was a measly $600 million syndication and cable outfit; in 1998 Viacom did $14.5 billion worth of business. The figures are similar for the other giants.[26] Consider the holdings of Viacom to get a sense of how one of these giants looks. Viacom owns Paramount Pictures, Simon and Schuster book publishers, Spelling Entertainment, MTV cable network, VH1 cable network, Nickelodeon cable network, TV Land cable network, Showtime cable network, eighteen U.S. television stations, the UPN network, the Blockbuster video rental chain, five theme parks, retail stores, and a vast movie theater empire outside of the United States.

The "second tier" of U.S. media giants includes the great newspaper-based conglomerates like Gannett, Knight-Ridder, and the New York Times Company, cable-based powerhouses like Comcast and Cox Enterprises, as well as broadcast-based powers like CBS. These fifteen or so "second-tier" firms are all conglomerates, but they are smaller than the first-tier firms, with annual sales ranging from $2 billion to $7 billion. They also all tend to lack the film, TV, and music production capacities of the first-tier giants. These second-tier firms have all grown quickly over the past decade and they, too, have been swallowing up smaller firms.

It is unclear how much more upheaval will occur in the U.S. media system, but there is no reason to think that more major mergers and acquisitions are not on the horizon. AT&T's purchase of TCI left its subsidiary Liberty Media in former TCI CEO John Malone's hands, with Malone in complete control and flush with up to $20 billion in liquidity. "When the smoke clears," Malone said when announcing the TCI sale to AT&T, "Liberty is going to have tons of cash."[27] By most accounts, Liberty Media will aggressively move to structure a new media empire in the near future.[28] At any rate, all of the media firms are actively juggling assets to improve market power, even if only a minority will engage in major mergers. As one media analyst puts it, "consolidation among distribution and content players rages on."[29] What is clear is that the option of being a small or middle-sized media firm barely exists any longer: a firm either gets larger through mergers and acquisitions or it gets swallowed by a more aggressive competitor.

Why is that the case? To some extent this trend has been fueled by a desire to create an extremely lucrative *vertical integration*, meaning that media firms would not only produce content but would also own the distribution channels that would guarantee places to display and market their wares. For decades U.S. laws and regulations forbade film studios from owning movie theaters and television networks from producing their own entertainment programs because it was well understood that this sort of vertical integration would effectively prohibit newcomers from entering the film or television production industries. Such restrictions have been relaxed or eliminated in these deregulatory times, and some of the merger pandemonium can be attributed to the race by producers and distribution networks to link up with each other formally rather than be squeezed out by their competitors. Hence Disney owns ABC while News Corp. owns Fox. Viacom and Time Warner have launched their own U.S. television networks as well, the UPN and

WB networks respectively. The vast majority of the fifty leading cable television channels, too, are owned outright or in part by the first-tier conglomerates, and the rest are all affiliated with a few of the second tier of media giants. Sony has moved aggressively into U.S. movie theater ownership while Viacom owns Blockbuster video rentals.[30]

These vertically integrated media conglomerates have not necessarily established exclusive arrangements such that their films only appear on their own TV stations and networks, or that their films get first crack in their movie theaters or movie rental stores. For the most part the largest conglomerates are increasingly interdependent, competing in some markets while they are customers for each other in other markets. But when vertical integration can be applied effectively, it is logical to expect media conglomerates to keep production directed to their own distribution outlets.

The first market where full vertical integration looks plausible is with the production of television shows for the TV networks. Television show production had already become increasingly concentrated in the hands of the big six Hollywood studios by the mid-1990s. According to one report, they accounted for thirty-seven of the forty-six new primetime shows on network TV in fall 1998. The four studios which also own TV networks produced twenty-nine of the programs.[31] Fox supplied over 40 percent of its 1998 programs whereas CBS had a stake in 57 percent of its prime-time lineup, a 20 percent increase over 1997.[32] What is new is the demand by the six TV networks—the four affiliated with Hollywood studios plus NBC and CBS—to own a piece of shows that appeared on their networks. "Each and every one of these networks," one studio executive stated in 1998, "are going to endeavor to own and control as much content as they possibly can." CBS, for example, produced or coproduced six of its seven new shows in 1998.[33]

Some expect that the logical trajectory will be for networks eventually to produce nearly all of their own programs, something that would have been illegal just a decade ago. Hence Viacom CEO Sumner Redstone fired an executive who did not mind seeing programs produced by Viacom's Spelling Entertainment (like *Frasier*) being sold to other networks if they paid more than UPN, although UPN was languishing in the ratings. "I think you are going to see a lot more Spelling shows on UPN," Redstone commented in 1998.[34] The exact same process is taking place with cable TV channels, where most of them are now owned wholly or in part with a major production studio.[35] If this process does continue at this pace, NBC and CBS logically would become part of deals to formally link up with production studios.

But the pressure to become a conglomerate is also due to something perhaps even more profound than the need for vertical integration. It was and is stimulated by the desire to increase market power by cross-promoting and cross-selling media properties or "brands" across numerous, different sectors of the media that are not linked in the manner suggested by vertical integration. "Cross-promotion offers incredible efficiencies, while cross-selling promises major opportunities," *Variety* notes, in explaining the drive to conglomeration.[36] Hence, if a media conglomerate had a successful motion picture, it could promote the film on its broadcast properties and then use the film to spin off television programs, musical CDs, books, merchandise, and much else. "When you can make a movie for an average cost of $10 million and then cross promote and sell it off of magazines, books, products, television shows out of your own company," Viacom's Redstone said, "the profit potential is enormous." (Viacom's) Paramount *Beavis and Butt-Head Do America* film, for example, based on Viacom's MTV cartoon series, cost $11 million but generated a *profit* of $70 million. When Viacom released its *Rugrats* movie—based on its Nickelodeon TV program—in December 1998, it provided extensive editorial programming to promote the movie on Nickelodeon, its VH-1 and Showtime cable networks, and the syndicated television program *Entertainment Tonight*, which is produced by Viacom's Paramount Television.[37] In the new world order of conglomerated media, as an MTV executive put it, "the sum is greater than the parts."[38] "These firms no longer make films or books," Paine Webber's media analyst Christopher Dixon observes, "they make brands."[39]

Disney, more than any media giant, is the master at figuring out "new synergistic ways to acquire, slice, dice and merchandise content."[40] Its 1994 animated film *The Lion King* generated over $1 billion in profit. It led to a lucrative Broadway show, a TV series, and all sorts of media spin-offs. It also led to 186 items of merchandising.[41] Wall Street analysts gush at the profit potential of animated films in the hands of media conglomerates; they estimate that such films on average generate *four times more profit* than their domestic box-office take.[42] A look at some of Disney's recent operations shows how it employs the logic of synergy to all of its endeavors. Its *Home Improvement* show is a big hit on its ABC television network. So Disney then has *Home Improvement* star Tim Allen take roles in Disney movies and write books for Disney's book-publishing firms. The other giant media conglomerates are increasingly emulating this pattern.[43] In another example, Disney takes its lucrative ESPN cable channel and uses the name to generate other properties, including an ESPN radio network.[44] In 1998 Disney launched *ESPN Magazine* to compete directly with Time Warner's *Sports Illustrated*.[45] Using incessant promotion on ESPN, the magazine exceeded initial estimates with a circulation approaching five hundred thousand after only a few months.[46] Likewise, Disney is launching a chain of ESPN Grill restaurants to appeal to those who wish to combine sports with dining out.[47]

Murdoch's News Corp. exploits its *X-Files* TV program in the same manner. It produces the show, airs it over its Fox network, and then shows reruns on its twenty-two Fox TV stations and its FX cable network. News Corp. has generated

X-Files books and extensive merchandising, and Twentieth Century Fox (owned by News Corp.) released a movie version of the *X-Files* in 1998.[48] News Corp. even has a traveling *X-Files* Expo that visited ten U.S. cities in March 1998 with active promotion through all other News Corp. media properties. Organized by the News Corp. licensing and merchandising division and sponsored by General Motors, the Expo is "part rock concert and part fan festival," with the avowed aim of "extending the life cycle" of the *X-Files* property.[49] (Not surprisingly, News Corp. also uses the *X-Files* on its worldwide television channels.) This is synergy indeed, and it works. Time Warner, too, is aggressively working to have the parts in its massive empire work more closely together. In 1998 it began promoting new releases from its music companies on the videotapes for Warner Bros. films.[50]

If synergy is the principle that makes becoming a media conglomerate more profitable and, indeed, mandatory, the other side of the coin is *branding*. All media firms are racing to give their media properties distinct brand identities. Although the media system has fewer and fewer owners, it nonetheless has a plethora of channels competing for attention. Branding is the primary means of attracting and keeping audiences while also offering new commercial possibilities. Cable channels and even broadcast networks each strive to be regarded as brands by the specific demographic groups desired by advertisers. Hence Viacom's Nickelodeon cable net-work battles its new competition from News Corp.'s Fox Kids Network and the Disney Channel by incessantly hammering home the Nickelodeon brand name on Nickelodeon and in its other film, television, and publishing holdings.[51] Take, for one fairly minor example of the rise of branding to preeminence as a business strategy, News Corp.'s HarperCollins book-publishing division. In the past few years, HarperCollins has developed *The Little House on the Prairie* from the 1930s and 1940s into a contemporary book series aimed at 8–12 year olds, and has added several new books to the series. HarperCollins has also generated ninety related products, ranging from paper dolls and cookbooks to picture books, all bearing the "Little House" logo.[52]

As this suggests, branding opens up for the media giants the entire world of selling retail products based on their branded properties, and it is a course they have been pursuing with a vengeance.[53] In 1997, $25 *billion* of Disney merchandise was sold, more than twice the global sales of Toys 'R' Us.[54] Disney's own licensing revenue in 1997 was $10 billion, while Time Warner's was more than $6 billion. In 1998, for one example of branded products, Disney introduced a "Mickey Un-limited" fragrance line for men and women in Germany, following the successful release of a "Mickey for Kids" perfume there in 1997. Disney plans to roll out the perfumes across Asia and into the United States.[55] Murdoch's News Corp. generated a paltry $1 billion in licensing revenue, leading to a major shakeup in the Fox hierarchy in early 1998.[56] Disney now has 660 retail stores to sell its branded products; Time Warner has 160 stores. Some of the other media giants are moving in the same direction.[57]

In sum, the logic and trajectory of the media market is such that firms that do not have the cross-selling and cross-promotional opportunities of the media giants are finding it ever more difficult to survive or prosper. As Diane Mermigas, one of the leading observers of the media industry, put it in 1998: "The bottom line is that a handful of sprawling giants like Time Warner and Disney have more options for building out their brands in many different ways across all their business lines that smaller players don't have. The options for generating additional earnings can make all the difference in difficult times that may prove even brand kings—like Disney—are vulnerable."[58]

One important qualification needs to be made concerning media conglomeration and synergy. Not all media sectors mesh equally well with all others. The major newspaper chains have almost all found it lucrative to extend their holdings to radio and television stations, and sometimes to magazine or book publishing. The core unifier for these synergies is news-oriented content and facility with advertisers. Television stations have also been made parts of conglomerates that include TV networks, cable channels, film studios, and music studios. The core unifier for this set of synergies is entertainment content production combined with distribution, cross-selling, and cross-promotion. But there is little evidence, as yet, that newspaper chains and film studios or newspaper chains and music studios offer each other significant "synergies." Hence Disney sold the newspaper interests it acquired as part of its 1995 purchase of ABC and ESPN. And in 1998 Viacom sold all aspects of its Simon and Schuster book publishing that pertained to the business and educational markets. It is worth noting that Viacom kept its general "trade"-book-publishing interests, so it can continue to publish odes to Beavis and Butt-Head. When giant firms sell off assets like these, some observers jump to the conclusion that this proves synergy does not work and that large firms are ultimately too large for their own competitive good. In fact, what it establishes is that smart firms get bigger and bigger, but they carefully assess their holdings to see that they complement each other well. And the trajectory of the 1990s is that the field of media assets that can complement each other for a media conglomerate is growing.

Nor is the media system entirely closed. Despite the ravages of concentration, independent record labels and book publishers have proliferated in recent years, albeit getting a minuscule share of the market. Some argue that the concentration in music and book retailing makes it easier for these independents to establish distribution networks and that this will lead to more competitive markets down the road.[59] That remains to be seen. What is clear right now is that small independent publishers and recording companies play an indispensable part in the overall system of providing content that is too risky for the giants to consider. Then, if the fare proves successful, the big firms can begin to produce it, or even buy up the independent. This is the case in the film industry, where independents account for only 5 percent of industry revenues but serve an important creative function for the giants.[60] By 1998 almost all of the Hollywood "indies" were either owned outright by a major studio or effectively affiliated with one otherwise. Independents have become a source of low-risk profit-making for the media giants, giving the latter near total control over the industry.[61] "Lone wolf production companies," *Variety* noted in 1998, "have become integral to the corporate studio filmmaking process."[62] The notion that independents might sprout up to challenge the existing giants is dead.

Will new first-tier media giants emerge from the woodwork? It is possible if some second-tier firms merge, or if a huge nonmedia firm elects to buy its way into the market, as General Electric, Sony, AT&T, and Seagram have done over the past decade. With the convergence of media with telecommunication and computering, this is an increasing prospect.

The one clear effort to establish a new media giant is DreamWorks, the new Hollywood studio formed by Steven Spielberg and David Geffen, among others, and backed with billions of dollars in investment capital from the Korean heiress Miky Lee and Microsoft co-founder Paul Allen. Can it succeed, becoming, for example, the first successful new Hollywood studio since the 1930s? The connection to Spielberg and Geffen may provide some hope, but otherwise the venture looks like an absurd deployment of capital. One look at animation, one of DreamWorks's main areas of development, shows why: whereas media giants Disney, Time Warner, Viacom, and News Corporation can generate profit from animated films that do lackluster box office by exploiting their numerous other revenue streams, DreamWorks must rely disproportionately on the film's theatrical success. DreamWorks also does not have an arsenal of other media on which to promote its animated films. In 1998 its first animated film, the critically acclaimed *Prince of Egypt*, struggled at the box office compared to concurrent animated films released by Viacom and Disney, each of which were heavily promoted on their various media aimed at children.[63] All of this puts DreamWorks at a distinct disadvantage. It suggests that DreamWorks will either become part of a larger media conglomerate or establish a close relationship with a media conglomerate, making it a de facto subsidiary at some point down the road.[64] This is what the independent computer animation firm Pixar did in 1996, when it formally allied with Disney.[65]

This is not to say that the media market is at all stable. In just three years in the late 1990s the leveraged buyout specialists Hicks Muse spent billions of dollars to build up an empire in radio stations, sports teams, television stations, book publishing, billboards, and movie theaters.[66] According to a *Forbes* profile of Hicks Muse, its goal "is to blanket entire areas for advertisers, with radio, TV and billboards—one-stop advertising."[67] Hicks Muse is now a multibillion-dollar second-tier media conglomerate, having quickly exploited the opportunities for entering media markets that presented themselves with deregulation following the 1996 Telecommunications Act. Whether those opportunities remain in place for others is questionable, unless they want to pay a prohibitive price. But the experience with Hicks Muse underlines the overall logic of the media market: it only makes sense to be a player if you are a very, very big player with a broad stable of media assets to exploit.

Market concentration and conglomeration are necessary for profitability, but they do not assure it. The creation of these empires brought considerable debt to may of these firms, and it was only in the late 1990s that Viacom, Time Warner, and News Corp. returned to profitability. Gordon Crawford, who manages the $400 billion Capital Research mutual fund that has large holdings in all of the media giants, believes the short-term profit difficulties were and are exaggerated, especially if the problem is due to increased corporate debt to finance acquisitions.[68] "Most of these decisions make sense long term, and 20 years down the road, they're going to be all right."[69] Moreover, not all mergers and acquisitions pan out, so benefits accrue to the shrewder and/or more fortunate media giants. But the overarching trajectory for the media system is rapid growth for the largest firms well into the next century. Ironically, in the eyes of investors, the main problem with the existing media system is that there is *too much* competition. "The problem is that too many players are at the table," *Business Week* concludes in its analysis of the media industry, "and it's ruining everyone's hand."[70] Gordon Crawford forecasts that the eventual outcome will be a global media oligopoly dominated by six firms: Time Warner, Disney, Viacom, News Corporation, Sony, and Seagram. Crawford is more than a silent investor; he works quietly but persistently to coordinate deals among the media giants to increase profitability for all of them.[71]

Despite the seeming excess of "competition," the media system is anything but competitive in the traditional economic sense of the term. Not only are all of the markets oligopolies, where almost all of the main players are owned by a handful of firms, the media giants also tend to work quite closely together. The CEOs of Crawford's select six—together with all the other media giant CEOs (and now computer industry CEOs like Bill Gates and Andy Grove)—meet annually at a by-invitation-only retreat in Idaho to discuss the future of their industry.[72] Regardless of what actually happens in Idaho, these interactions bear many of the earmarks of a cartel, or at least a "gentleman's club."

And this barely begins to indicate how noncompetitive the media market is becoming. In addition to their oligopolistic market structure and overlapping ownership, the media giants each employ equity joint ventures with their "competitors" to an extraordinary extent. These are media projects where two or more media giants share the ownership between them. They are ideal because they spread the risk of a venture and eliminate the threat of competition by teaming up with potential adversaries.[73] Each of the eight largest U.S. media firms have, on average, joint ventures (often more than one) with five of the other seven media giants.[74] Rupert Murdoch's News Corp. has at least one joint venture with every single one of them. While competition can be fierce in specific markets, the same firms are often the best customers for each other's products, and the overall effect is to reduce competition and carve up the media pie to the benefit of the handful of giants. According to most theories of market performance, this degree of collaboration can only have negative consequences for consumers.

Finally, when one looks at the membership on the U.S. media giants' boards of directors—the people who legally represent the shareholders and therefore run the companies—the notion that this is a collaborative industry is even more justified. Crawford's select six, less the Japanese Sony and Seagram and adding CBS and GE, have eighty-one directors on their boards. These eighty-one hold 104 additional directorships on the boards of Fortune 1000 corporations. Indeed, the boards for these six firms plus the five largest newspaper corporations (New York Times, Washington Post, Times-Mirror, Gannett, and Knight-Ridder) have directors who also serve on 144 of the Fortune 1000 firms. The eleven media giants also have thirty-six *direct* links, meaning two people who serve on different media firm boards of directors and also serve on the same board for another Fortune 1000 corporation. Each of the eleven media giants has at least two such interlocks. GE has seventeen direct links to nine of the other ten media giants; Time Warner has direct links to seven of them. In combination, this suggests that the corporate media are very closely linked to each other, and to the highest echelons of the corporate community. The point is not that the corporate media are necessarily more intertwined with other large firms than any other industrial sector but, rather, that the media are full participants in the corporate community. As the most recent study of this issue concluded, "The media in the United States effectively represent the interests of corporate America."[75]

Finally, for what it is worth, many of the very wealthiest Americans generated their bounty through their holdings in media properties. Some 17 percent of the Forbes 400 list of the richest Americans derived their wealth primarily from media, entertainment, or computer software. Exactly 20 percent of the fifty largest family fortunes were derived therefrom.[76] Nor are the owners the only beneficiaries of media prosperity. The average compensation in 1997 for the CEOs of General Electric, Viacom, Disney, Time Warner, Universal Studios, the New York Times, CBS, Times-Mirror, Comcast, Cox, TCI, AT&T, Tribune Company, the Washington Post, and Gannett was approximately $4,500,000.[77] In short, those that sit atop our media empires are at the very pinnacle of success as it is measured in a capitalist society.

Notes

1. Marc Gunther, "The Rules according to Rupert," *Fortune*, Oct. 26, 1998, p. 104.

2. Diane Mermigas, "Seagram Co. to Shed Parts of PolyGram," *Electronic Media*, May 25, 1998, p. 32.

3. "Bertelsmann Purchase Set to Open a Whole New Chapter," *Financial Times*, Mar. 25, 1998, p. 18.

4. Martin Arnold, "Nervous Twitch in the Wallet," *New York Times*, July 2, 1998, p. B3.

5. From the 1940s see, for example, Morris Ernst, *The First Freedom* (New York: Macmillan Company, 1946); Commission on Freedom of the Press, *A Free and Responsible Press* (Chicago: University of Chicago Press, 1947).

6. For one of the few moments it did, see McChesney, *Telecommunications, Mass Media, and Democracy.*

7. See Robert A. Hackett and Yeuzhi Zhao, *Sustaining Democracy: Journalism and the Politics of Objectivity* (Toronto: Garamond Press, 1998).

8. "How the Studios Stack Up in '97," *Variety*, Jan. 5–11, 1998, p. 96.

9. "Basic Movie Statistics," *Cowen Perspectives*, May 14, 1998, p. 1.

10. For a clear discussion of chain newspapers and one-newspaper towns, see Ben H. Bagdikian, *The Media Monopoly*, 5th ed. (Boston: Beacon Press, 1997).

11. Iver Peterson, "California Draws Newspaper Chains Eager to Cluster," *New York Times*, Sept. 1, 1997, pp. B1, B4.

12. Dorianne Perrucci, "Papering the Town," *Adweek*, Apr. 20, 1998, p. 8.

13. I. Jeanne Dugan, "Boldly Going Where Others Are Bailing Out," *Business Week*, Apr. 6, 1998, p. 46.

14. Alice Rawsthorn, "The Perils of Artistic Growth," *Financial Times*, May 26, 1998, p. 15; "Birth of a Giant," *Variety*, June 22–28, 1998, p. 22; "Sony Music Spins the Hits," *Wall Street Journal*, Feb. 23, 1998, p. B4.

15. Les Brown, "Market Forces Killed the Media Dream," *Television Business International*, Apr. 1998, p. 10.

16. "All Together Now," *Electronic Media*, Dec. 15, 1997, p. 14.

17. John Dempsey, "Cable Ops Caught in the Nets," *Variety*, Feb. 17–23, 1997, p. 1.

18. Matthew Schifrin, "Radio-active Men," *Forbes*, June 1, 1998, p. 131.

19. Eric Bates, "Chaining the Alternatives: What Started as a Movement Has Become an Industry," *Nation*, June 29, 1998, pp. 11–18.

20. "Kohlberg Kravis Said to Seek Deal for Regal Cinemas Chain,"*New York Times*, Jan. 17, 1998, p. B4.

21. Steven Lipin and Bruce Orwall, "KKR, Hicks Muse to Buy Regal Cinemas,"*Wall Street Journal*, Jan. 20, 1998, pp. A3, A8; Allen R. Myerson and Geraldine Fabrikant, "2 Buyout Firms Make Deal to Acquire Regal Cinemas," *New York Times*, Jan. 21, 1998, p. C2.

22. Hardy Green, "Superstores, Megabooks—and Humongous Headaches," *Business Week*, Apr. 14, 1997, p. 93.

23. "Random Thoughts," *Economist*, Mar. 28, 1998, p. 58.

24. Bagdikian, *Media Monopoly.*

25. Eben Shapiro, "John Malone Prepares for a New Life as Pa Bell," *Wall Street Journal*, June 25, 1998, p. B1.

26. Robert La Franco, "Rupert's on a Roll," *Forbes*, July 6, 1998, p. 186; Frank Rose, "There's No Business like Show Business," *Fortune*, June 22, 1998, pp. 86–104, esp. p. 88.

27. Jim McConville, "Liberty Has Money to Spend," *Electronic Media*, June 29, 1998, p. 1A.

28. Martin Peers, "Liberty Ends Up Home Malone," *Variety*, June 29–July 12, 1998, pp. 1, 52; Diane Mermigas, "Malone's New Fun House," *Electronic Media*, July 6, 1998, p. 10.

29. Diane Mermigas, "TCI Headed in the Right Direction,"*Electronic Media*, Sept. 1, 1997, p. 20.

30. Bruce Orwall, "Cineplex Odeon–Loews Merger Is Backed by Regulators, with Sales of Theaters," *Wall Street Journal*, Apr. 17, 1998, p. B3.

31. "Series for Sale," *Variety*, May 25–31, 1998, p. 40.

32. Dominic Schreiber, "Murdoch Re-Groups Businesses," *Television Business International*, July/Aug. 1998, p. 11; Michael Stroud, "Programmers Clash over Ownership," *Broadcasting and Cable*, Sept. 28, 1998, p. 34.

33. Michael Schneider, "Studios Feel Networks' Strong-arm," *Electronic Media*, May 25, 1998, p. 26.

34. John Gapper, "Star of His Own Show," *Financial Times*, June 22, 1998, p. 8.

35. Michael Schneider, "Independent Producers Left Out," *Electronic Media*, Apr. 6, 1998, p. 20.

36. Richard Morgan, "Radio Biz Stirs in Cross-Promo Fizz," *Variety*, June 22–28, 1998, p. 25.

37. Henry Goldblatt, "Viacom's Itty-Bitty, Synergistic, Billion-Dollar Franchise," *Fortune*, Nov. 23, 1998, p. 223.

38. Diane Mermigas, "Surf and Groove," *Electronic Media*, May 4, 1998, pp. 16, 20.

39. "Size Does Matter," *Economist*, May 23, 1998, p. 57.

40. Frank Rich, "Tina and Disney Elope," *New York Times*, July 11, 1998, p. A19.

41. Tim Carvell, "How Sony Created a Monster," *Fortune*, June 8, 1998, p. 162.

42. Bruce Orwall, " 'Armageddon,' Missing Disney Targets, Draws Less Than Astronomical Numbers," *Wall Street Journal*, July 6, 1998, p. A20.

43. Bruce Orwall and John Lippmann, "Lawsuit Casts Tim Allen TV Series as Victim of Synergy," *Wall Street Journal*, Mar. 17, 1997, p. B1.

44. Mira Schwirtz, "ESPN Expands Push in Radio," *Mediaweek*, Aug. 29, 1998, p. 8.

45. Robin Pogrebin, "ESPN Rivals Set for Fight as Magazine Debut Nears," *New York Times*, Jan. 19, 1998, pp. C1, C6; "Promo Muscle of Cable Net Will Back 'ESPN Magazine,' " *Advertising Age*, Oct. 13, 1997, p. 6.

46. Lisa Granatstein, "*ESPN* Shoots, Scores," *Mediaweek*, June 15, 1998, p. 23.

47. Bruce Orwall, "Disney to Enter Restaurant Business, and Chain Will Sport an ESPN Theme," *Wall Street Journal*, Oct. 15, 1997, p. B6.

48. Henry Goldblatt, "TV's Most Lucrative Franchise: It's a Mystery," *Fortune*, Jan. 12, 1998, p. 114.

49. Jeff Jensen, "Fox Lands Intrigue for Big 'X-Files' Push," *Advertising Age*, Jan. 12, 1998, p. 8.

50. Adam Sandler, "WB to Promote Its Music on Vids," *Variety*, June 1–7, 1998, p. 11.

51. Jeff Jensen, "Nickelodeon Channels into Retail with 3 Stores," *Advertising Age*, Nov. 24, 1997, p. 45.

52. Ann Marie Kerwin, "Branding Is the Buzzword at Murdoch's Print Group," *Advertising Age*, Jan. 12, 1998, pp. 6, 39.

53. Dominic Schreiber, "Tie-ins That Bind," *Television Business International*, Sept. 1997, pp. 29–30.

54. *Economist*, May 23, 1998, p. 57.

55. Dagmar Mussey, "Disney Sniffs Out Profit," *Advertising Age International*, July 13, 1998, p. 8.

56. Jeff Jensen, "New Fox Unit to Revitalize 'Simpsons' Merchandise," *Advertising Age*, May 11, 1998, p. 65.

57. Eben Shapiro, "Can the Rugrats Take on Mickey Mouse?" *Wall Street Journal*, May 22, 1997, pp. B1, B5; De'Ann Weimer, "Hardly a Household Name," *Business Week*, Dec. 22, 1997, p. 42.

58. Diane Mermigas, "Comparing Survival Strategies," *Electronic Media*, Oct. 12, 1998, p. 22.

59. Rawsthorn, "Perils of Artistic Growth."

60. Jennifer Nix, "Indies Make Big Book Mark," *Variety*, May 18–24, 1998, pp. 1, 89.

61. Monica Roman and Benedict Carver, "Ya Gotta Have Art," *Variety*, May 4–10, 1998, pp. 1, 103.

62. Dan Cox, "Studios Woo New Indies," *Variety*, Jan. 19–25, 1998, p. 1.

63. Geraldine Fabrikant, " 'Prince of Egypt' Is No King at the Box Office," *New York Times*, Dec. 28, 1998, pp. C1, C4.

64. Geraldine Fabrikant, "Dreamworks' Lackluster Start Is Putting Pressure on the Company to Perform," *New York Times*, Mar. 2, 1998, p. C7. DreamWorks is a bit of an anomaly, however, as its founders, including Steven Spielberg and David Geffen, have unusual market power. Without the likes of a Spielberg or a Geffen the idea of establishing an independent major Hollywood studio would seem far-fetched, to say the least. It has not been done since the 1930s.

65. See Peter Burrows and Ronald Grover, "Steve Jobs, Movie Mogul: Can He Build Pixar into a Major Studio?" *Business Week*, Nov. 23, 1998, pp. 140–54.

66. Christopher Parkes, "Chancellor to Acquire Martin Media," *Financial Times*, June 23, 1998, p. 22.

67. Schifrin, "Radio-active Men," p. 132.

68. John M. Higgins, "Capital Research's Gordon Crawford," *Broadcasting and Cable*, Aug. 17, 1998, p. 30.

69. *Business Week*, Feb. 16, 1998, p. 95.

70. Elizabeth Lesly Stevens and Ronald Grover, "The Entertainment Glut," *Business Week*, Feb. 15, 1998, p. 95.

71. Alan Deutschmann, "The Ted and Jerry Show," *Gentleman's Quarterly*, Dec. 1997, pp. 131–32; Eben Shapiro, "Viacom Considers Selling All or Part of Its Simon & Schuster Publishing Unit," *Wall Street Journal*, Dec. 30, 1997, p. A2.

72. Mark Landler, "From Gurus to Sitting Ducks," *New York Times*, Jan. 11, 1998, sec. 3, pp. 1, 9.

73. Geraldine Fabrikant, "Cooperation Counts," *New York Times*, Dec. 15, 1997, p. C12.

74. Frank Rose, "There's No Business like Show Business," pp. 90–91.

75. Peter Phillips, with the research assistance of Bob Klose, Nikki Mazumdar, and Alix Jestron, "Self Censorship and the Homogeneity of the Media Elite," in *Censored 1998*, ed. Peter Phillips (New York: Seven Stories Press, 1998), chap. 5.

76. "The Forbes 400," *Forbes*, Oct. 12, 1998, pp. 414–28.

77. "Salary Survey," *Advertising Age*, Dec. 7, 1998, pp. s18, s20.

Interlocking Web

of Business Interests

Promote, then, as an object of primary importance, institutions for the general diffusion of knowledge. In proportion as the structure of Government gives force to public opinion, it is essential that public opinion should be enlightened.

—WASHINGTON: *Farewell Address*

Dick Turpin is blamed—suppose—by some plain-minded person, for consuming the means of other people's living. "Nay," says Dick to the plain-minded person, "observe how beneficently and pleasantly I spend whatever I get!"

"Yes, Dick," persists the plain-minded person, "but how did you get it?"

"That question," says Dick, "is insidious and irrelevant."

—RUSKIN: *Fors Clavigera*, Letter LX

HENRY GEORGE JR.

Bondage of the Press
(1906)

Imagine two of our Princes of Privilege laying out a campaign for the acquisition of a fresh franchise grant. If they had to deal with a political boss, the course would be simple: merely to name the consideration and receive the grant. In the absence of a boss, the process must be different.

"Who would have charge of the matter?" asks one.

"Mr. M, the superintendent of our system," is the reply.

"How many votes could he count in the Board of Aldermen?"

"With no talk or fuss, two thirds; with friction, a few less."

"Could he be sure that the majority would see how the public would benefit by the grant?"

"He says he could."

"Of course there should be no bribery or scandal, but would he have ample funds for 'attorney fees,' 'clerk hire,' and the like?"

"Ample."

"And suppose the newspapers should cry out?"

"We must take care of that. I own an influence in *The Dart*. I think the management would be unprejudiced enough to print what we should be pleased to have said. Mr. Y's bank has lent considerable money to *The Bow*, as I happen to know. We could take him in with us and have him observe to *The Bow's* management that our enterprise will mean more money to be spent in wages and more railroad facilities for the general public; that it therefore should be supported; that, at any rate, it should not be antagonized. And then there is *The Quiver:* you know it is mainly owned by the Z estate. The executor is a conservative man. We can give enough time to be civil and friendly with him and let him understand how all the conservative interests ought to support us in this matter; that if any of us abandons the others and gives the least countenance to such a thing as public ownership and operation of railroads, there is no saying where the public might

From *The Menace of Privilege* (New York: The Macmillan Company, 1906), 267–85.

let itself be led by unprincipled, self-seeking agitators. If he would not listen to reason, then we could influence some of his larger advertisers to object to a paper expressing the sentiments of socialists and anarchists and to say that to continue to advertise in it would hurt their trade. This would hit the purse and get the paper. But such a plan would have to be well executed to be altogether successful, and the possibility of a misfire makes it an extremity measure."

"But *The Fly* and *The Sparrow*—what of them? They would bother us."

"Granted, but they always were against us. Are they important enough to hurt? Besides, it would look better not to have the press unanimous. The charge of 'owning' and 'subsidizing' would not appear as apt. With the three largest papers presenting our argument in our way, and ignoring or belittling that opposed to us, we could put the deal through."

"But the job is a big one—bigger than any before."

"Bigger, because we're bigger."

"Such a privilege in the streets capitalized means fifty millions, at least."

"Which makes the weightier motive for capturing politics, the politicians and the press."

This may serve to illustrate the broader conditions. Acquiring through the exercise of their privileges vast wealth, and striving to conserve and extend those privileges through the corruption of politics and by control of the legal and military arms of the government, our princes try at the same time to shape public thought on such matters through the press, the university and the pulpit. And of the three means of guiding the minds of the multitude, the first and most obvious is the press. A privilege is in violation of equal rights. No sooner does it appear under a popular government than popular attack upon it begins. The natural mouthpiece for this attack is the press. It expresses the consensus of opinion. Privilege at once stealthily moves to get control of that mouthpiece. Getting control, it achieves a double purpose if, without general realization, it offers Esau's hands, but Jacob's voice—that is, if it makes the popular mouthpiece appear to speak for equal rights, but in reality speak for privilege.

At first it might seem the cheaper and easier course to control the press by putting restrictions upon it. This would appear not to be a difficult matter for the power that manipulates our politics. But such a course would stir the American people to a quick resentment. "The liberty of the press is essential to the security of freedom of a state," says the Massachusetts Bill of Rights of 1780. "It ought not, therefore, to be restrained in this Commonwealth." This has been the sentiment of the whole country. From colonial days the press has had a liberty of utterance which to Europeans has appeared to be no less than a wild license, especially as it presents and discusses personal matters. It might be called the public gossip. All manner of questions, public and private, important and trivial, are offered to public view in this forum. If our best judgment does not approve of the excesses committed under this freedom, it prizes the free utterance. The body of the people have accepted the words of Thomas Jefferson, that such things must be set down as "a part of the price we pay for our liberty, which cannot be guarded but by the freedom of the press, nor that be limited without danger of losing it."[1] Politicians learned a stern lesson from the attempt of President John Adams to use shackles. He procured the passage of the "Sedition Act," empowering him to punish political criticism in the newspapers. It became one of the main causes of the overwhelming defeat of Adams for reëlection in the "civil revolution of 1800." The century since passed has seen no change in the popular attitude.

The great Federation of Labor, with its one and three quarter million trade unionists, signalized this in its twenty-fourth annual convention, held in San Francisco in the fall of 1904. The labor council of New Orleans had boycotted a newspaper, not on the ground that it was nonunion, but because it had criticised some of the actions of the council. The National Convention of the Federation condemned the boycott in these positive terms: "The untrammeled freedom of the press is so important to the well-being, not only of organized labor, but to human civilized life, that no conceivable circumstance can arise that can warrant trade unionists in their organized capacity to place a publication upon a boycott list for the expression of opinion."

And so, aside from Adams's "Sedition Act," we might say, as De Tocqueville wrote fifty years ago: "Not a single individual of the millions who inhabit the United States has, as yet, dared to propose any restrictions on the liberty of the press." Of course there have been repressive acts under military rule, as during the Civil War; and under hostile acts of mob, as with the mob of mine owners and militia in Colorado during the strike struggle in 1903–1904. But these were only isolated cases. We are considering the attitude of the people at large toward the press in general. That attitude has been one of the jealous preservation of freedom of expression even to frequent wanton abuse. Privilege, in consequence, has been constrained to guide what it could not muzzle.

For purposes here being considered the press may be divided into two general classes: the monthly and weekly publications belonging to one, the dailies to the other. Putting apart those publications that rarely or never trench upon political or economic subjects, and aside from trade union and propagandist organs, most of the monthlies and weeklies until recently have been in general respects on the monopoly side. Their owners or readers were there. Their sentiments have been boldly or qualifiedly exclusive. They have appealed to the comparatively small privileged class and to those of easy circumstances who uphold that class through a mistaken idea of the nature of monopoly and confusion of it with what is properly wealth. These periodicals have been high of price and small of circulation.

It must be admitted that periodicals of less exclusive and more general sentiments touching monopolies would not before the present time have flourished.

The monopoly issue was not ripe. Except in singular instances, the general public took no particular interest in it. A magazine devoted to it and aiming to be popular would have died. But the rapacious march of monopoly within the past decade has awakened lively popular interest, and latterly a number of low-priced, well-printed, well-illustrated magazines, containing, besides, generally attractive features, have offered exposures of the more flagrant superficial aspects of Privilege, and, in consequence, have sprung into phenomenal vogue.

Yet so long and so many are the arms of Privilege, and so slow are the masses of men to overcome the inertia of habit, especially the habit of thinking, that, save in particular and superficial aspects, Privilege is for the present, at least, safe against general periodical discussion. However searching the examination and cogent the argument of any of these monthlies and weeklies as to this or that phase of Privilege, not one of the flourishing ones will dare arraign the larger and wider aspects for fear of hurting its business credit, which Privilege gives; or of losing advertising, which Privilege closely or remotely controls; or of offending a considerable body of readers, some of whom, belonging to the privileged class, might set it down for a "socialist" or "anarchist" organ, and others of whom, being of the general mass of the population, but advancing by only slow degrees in thought, might dub it a "crank" publication. Its attacks are really not against even a particular phase of monopoly, but rather a particular kind of transgressing individual. It seeks out the distinct person, as if he and only he by his own moral turpitude were the transgressor; as if the monopoly powers he possesses do not exist elsewhere and in other hands would not produce similar results.

In this way Privilege, by the hurt it can do or by the prejudice it inspires, puts limitations upon even those monthlies and weeklies that attack its outposts. As Privilege grows stronger, the attacking power of such publications weakens, unless, indeed, the body of the people themselves become thoroughly roused. Then all individual wills must succumb to the collective will, if that collective will be well directed. But short of these conditions, Privilege, as it gathers strength, gathers sway over this division of the press.

And what is to be said of the monthlies and weeklies is to be said of the dailies, which it has far more need to control, since the daily papers reach the mass of the population more intimately and more often.

The increasing cost of making a newspaper has helped this, since it has put restrictions upon competition. A legend of newspaperdom is that Mr. James Gordon Bennett, the elder, started the *New York Herald* on a dry-goods box. His means were undoubtedly meager. At that time much was not needed. Energy in getting local news and attractiveness of presentation were the chief requisites of newspaper making. But competition for readers in order to attract advertisers has within the past three or four decades added enormously to the cost. While the quantity of local news has been greatly increased and a remarkable era of effective and varied illustration has been opened and developed, there has been a still more remarkable, an almost bewildering, advancement in telegraphic news. This was the least part of our dailies of three generations ago. It now vies with local news in importance, for it offers the daily doings of the globe.

But telegraphic news is, as may be judged, very expensive. The first cause of this is that the telegraphic service in this country is not made a part of our efficient, accessible and same-rate-to-everybody post-office system, as it is in most of the countries of Europe, but is in the hands of private companies and subject to their high and discriminating rates. That is to say, the telegraphic highways in this country are in private hands. The high rates charged make a larger capital necessary to establish a newspaper than would be required if the rates were low. It discourages easy newspaper rivalry. It tends to concentrate the newspaper business in the hands of the comparatively few persons who, knowing its requirements, can afford to pay the telegraph charges. The principle is the same as a high liquor license, which prevents the starting of rival saloons that would come into existence did no such tax exist. It is also like a Federal internal revenue tax on, say, alcohol or matches, which adds so materially to the outlay necessary to engage in that line of enterprise as to shut out such as would be glad to enter the field against those already there. In this way the newspapers that now exist have to pay a heavier telegraph toll than they would were the telegraph lines a department of the postal service. But they are willing to pay it, and they make no general demand for a postal telegraph, because they are now free of competitors which then would embarrass them.

And if high rates operate to discourage the weak and consequently help the strong, discriminating rates do so still more. Discrimination occurs through secret rebates. If not so open as formerly, yet it is done. And it goes to the benefit of those papers which can bear the requisite influence upon the telegraph companies, just as railroad rate discrimination favors those on the inside who can exert the "pull."

Still another circumstance that works to the advantage of the big and the disadvantage of the small paper is the leased wire between the greater centers. This is a cheap way for the larger papers to handle a considerable part of its special telegraphic news. It is beyond reach of a paper having only a small amount of such special matter.

In this way it is seen that in the telegraphic field the strong papers have great advantages over the weak ones. All these advantages stand against the starting of new papers, and to them must be added still another element, a combination of the stronger papers into telegraphic news-sharing associations.

While the general wire service of an American newspaper is very costly, a joining together of a great many papers throughout the country in an Associated Press reduces the cost to each for news which they may share in common. None but members can get this service, and new members, except in new news centers, are not admitted. The purpose is not only to reduce the cost of such service to the

lowest point, but to make a monopoly of it to those included within the combination. In the course of time outside weaklings and bantlings must needs combine
to establish a common "wire service" for themselves. They in turn shut out papers
yet to be born. In this way the news associations contribute materially to prevent
the birth of daily newspapers.

Nor is it probable that the old "cribbing" channel will much longer be left open
for the free-lance newspaper. It is a habit among newspapers to appropriate or
"crib" local news from each other. Out of this habit, and impelled by the adverse
circumstances which have just been specified, the weaklings and bantlings came to
"crib" skeletons of wire news from any available source. That is to say, discouraged
from getting news in the legitimate ways, the smaller papers resorted to ways that
were illegitimate. These skeletons were "padded" into extended reports. This came
to be called "grapevine telegraph" service. Many of the proudest dailies of to-day
used "grapevine" at the start. But the Associated Press and the great newspapers
individually are now invoking the copyright law against it.

Not that Congress has made the copyright act broad enough to fit the case, for
it has not. In some of the British colonies legislative acts have in recent years been
passed to conserve news rights; but in this country Congress, for whatever reason,
has refrained from taking any such step, nor does it seem likely soon to do so. Still,
in cases where the legislative branch of the Government has failed or refused to
act, our courts have been found to be accommodating; and the Federal courts are
now reading things into the copyright act of which Congress obviously never
dreamed. This belongs to the body of "judge-made" law, many instances of which
we have seen in the labor injunction cases.[2]

One of the judicial extensions of the copyright act occurred in the case bearing
title of American Press Association, Appellant, *vs.* Daily Story Publishing Company.[3]
Another case was that of the National Telegraph News, F. E. Crawford and A. K.
Brown, Appellants, *vs.* The Western Union Telegraph Company.[4] Circuit Judges
Jenkins and Grosscup and District Judge Bunn sat in the latter case, and affirmed
exclusive right of the Western Union Company to news transmitted by its "ticker"
instruments in advance of others. That the principles involved, or evolved, had
very much wider application than this case, however, was demonstrated by Judge
Grosscup, who read the opinion of the unanimous court. The judge said, toward
the end of his opinion:—

> Is the enterprise of the great news agencies, or the independent enterprise of
> the great newspapers, or of the great telegraph and cable lines, to be denied
> appeal to the courts, against the inroads of the parasite, for no other reason
> than that the law, fashioned hitherto to fit the relations of authors and the
> public, cannot be made to fit the relations of the public and this dissimilar
> class of servants? Are we to fail in our plain duty for mere lack of precedent?

We choose rather, to make precedent—one from which is eliminated, as immaterial, the law grown up around authorship—and we see no better way to start this precedent upon a career than by affirming the order appealed from.

That is to say, these three Federal judges, by "making a precedent" through an enjoining order, make into law what Congress has not seen fit to enact! And here again it will be observed that, like the injunction issued by Judge Grosscup in the Pullman strike, this order was not issued in behalf of the humble citizen. Nor apparently did the court have the parties in the case chiefly in mind. It was thinking more particularly of, to quote its language, "the great news agencies," of "the great newspapers," and of "the great telegraph and cable lines"—always of the great interest, not at all of the small, struggling one.

By virtue of such construction of the copyright act, the Associated Press and the larger newspapers individually, which regularly "crib" from the European papers, will be able to prevent all "cribbing" from themselves by the weaker papers at home. If such a principle can apply to telegraphic news, it can apply to local news as well. Incidentally it carries with it a power to harry and kill a weak or new paper with litigation over trumped-up charges.

This, of course, is not to say that stealing should not be stopped. But if it is to be stopped in one instance, it should be stopped in all. If the weak papers steal news, it is largely because the opportunities to transmit news are practically stolen from them—being closed or made difficult for them. The abolition of stealing should apply to both cases. But the courts, so ready to construe the law to conserve the interests of the great, have no thought of the others. And this, as we have seen, is but a part of what confronts the lesser paper. The whole telegraphic news practice, which now is such an essential part of our newspapers, from first to last piles up advantages for the strong and refuses them to the weak.

Further advantage accrues to the larger newspapers from the constraint all are under to use high-priced, patented machinery—type-setting, stereotyping and printing. A peculiarly heavy burden for the small journal has arisen from the formation of a monopoly combination of the white paper manufacturers. Controlling the easily available supply of wood pulp, from which the newspaper webs and sheets are made, most of these manufacturers have entered into "a community of interest," by which the output is limited and the price put up. This advance has been considerable even for the newspaper which is a large user and can place a very large order. For the small paper, which can order only a little at a time, the advance has proved exorbitant.[5]

It is true that in the villages and smaller towns it is now possible to buy a daily service of "plate matter," made in New York, Boston, Chicago, Washington and other centers. This matter offers variety—from editorials and fashion gossip, to useful household hints and telegraphic brevities. It is made into thin type-plates, and shipped in small wooden boxes. The plates are ready to be fastened on metal blocks in a "form," and within a few minutes after they are received the press can be started.

But the railroad facilities that make the shipping of these plates to points within a radius of one, two, or three hundred miles of a plate-making center offer like facilities to the metropolitan dailies, which accordingly have wonderfully extended their circulations. The "bulldog" Sunday morning edition of some of the New York papers, for instance, goes to press on Saturday afternoon as early as four o'clock. This edition is sold on the news stands on Sunday morning in some of the Southern States. The large papers in Washington, Atlanta, Cincinnati, Louisville, St. Louis and New Orleans also have early train editions which circulate over the Southern States, so that small local papers have poor chance against these great rivals.

And, then, too, since advertising in any considerable volume will go only to the large or influential circulation, and since advertising is the staff of life to the newspaper, the weakling has no chance, and all things join to discourage the starting of daily papers, at least in the main centers, unless such new enterprises be heavily backed.

Thus we see the march of concentration in the newspaper field. Other centralizing processes have been at work, but thus far have not proved successful. From time to time efforts have been made to draw the newspapers of a given locality into close business relations. In Philadelphia, for instance, an agreement was mutually entered into to accept no death notices for an individual paper, but only on the understanding that they appear in all, a rate for the combined publication being fixed. The plan was short-lived, however. It did not work smoothly and was abandoned.

On the other hand, the coercive principle was tried in Milwaukee. Had it been successful, it might have proved a formidable weapon in the hands of monopoly. But it was too plainly in violation of personal and property rights, and the higher courts fell foul of it. The *News*, the *Sentinel* and the *Evening Wisconsin*, all published in Milwaukee, entered into a business agreement to force advertising away from a newspaper rival, the *Journal*, which was a very successful publication and which had raised its advertising rates. The allied papers announced that if any person should agree to pay the increased advertising rate charged by the *Journal*, he should not be permitted to advertise in any of the three other newspapers except at a corresponding increase of rate, but that should he refuse to pay the *Journal* the increased rate, then he should be allowed to advertise in any of the other three papers at the rate previously charged.

One of the statutes of 1898 of the State of Wisconsin imposed imprisonment and fine on "any two or more persons who shall combine . . . for the purpose of willfully or maliciously injuring another in his reputation, trade, business or profession by any means whatever." Under this statute the publishers of the leagued papers were convicted and sentenced. The Supreme Court of Wisconsin upheld the action of the lower court. Their case was then appealed to the United States Supreme Court on the ground that the proceedings violated the rights of the plaintiffs under the Fourteen Amendment of the Constitution of the United States. Presumably the passage was in section one of that amendment, reading: "No State shall make or enforce any law which shall abridge the privileges or immunities of citizens of the United States." But the appeal was of no avail. With but one dissenting voice, the Federal Supreme Court affirmed the decision of the State Supreme Court. Justice Holmes read the opinion of the Federal Court and said:—

> There is no anomaly in a statute which punishes a combination such as is charged here. It has been held that even the free use of land by a single owner for purely malevolent purposes may be restricted constitutionally, although the only immediate injury is to a neighboring land owner. Whether this decision was right or not, when it comes to the freedom of the individual, malicious mischief is a familiar and proper subject for legislative repression. Still more are combinations for the purpose of inflicting it.
>
> It would be impossible to hold that the liberty to combine to inflict such mischief, even upon such intangibles as business or reputation, was among the rights which the Fourteenth Amendment was intended to preserve.

But if these centralizing moves have failed, other attempts will come under the régime of Privilege—attempts that will be successful. For do not all these things make for the triumph of Privilege? The general interest is best served by a fair field and no favor for newspapers, where the cost of production is at the minimum and there is open invitation to competition. Privilege, on the contrary, asks a restricted field, the least competition; so that, obtaining the ownership or influence over existing newspapers, it will dominate. Our newspaper field *is* now to a great extent restricted; competition, relatively speaking, *is* limited; Privilege *does* own or influence most of the newspapers, if in differing lines, and to that degree it *now* rules.

Yet the public is not altogether deceived. It sees the livery. It reads this or that paper and makes allowance for bias. This is a habit of the people. It began with the free utterances of the press. Every citizen exercised the same freedom to judge as the editor did to write. And thus it was that De Tocqueville wrote half a century ago that "the personal opinions of the editors have no weight in the eyes of the public: what they seek in a newspaper is knowledge of facts, and it is only by altering or distorting those facts, that a journalist can contribute to the support of his own views."

Who will say that, speaking for the press at large, this is not so in this country to-day? How common is the remark: "I read the *Star Spangled Banner* for its bright and reliable news reports. I care nothing for its editorials, because I know the editor has political or other axes to grind"! This is one way in which the public shows independence, and that independence now and again becomes marked when the polls are carried for some measure despite the combined opposition of the press. But on the whole, Privilege, as it grows stronger, strives to strengthen its hold on the channel of news, whether of the newspaper or of the higher periodical press.

This is not to say that the entire press is actually in bondage to-day. Some of the greatest newspapers and periodicals are free in all respects. But the large majority of the dailies, weeklies and monthlies turn pleader and champion for Privilege in this, that or the other respect, each in its own way, some all the time, others only on rare occasions. And if Privilege shall wax in power, it must certainly increase its influence over the press, for that is the means of informing the public mind. Unless the informing be in favor of Privilege, it must be against Privilege. In the nature of things, the press in the United States must as a whole be for or against Privilege. Privilege is busy every hour binding it to itself. "From the control of the markets to the control of the minds of the people—this is the line of march," says Mr. Henry D. Lloyd. But the case is yet broader. It is: From the possession of or the desire for privileges to the control of the minds of the people.

Nor can any appreciable change in these relations reasonably be expected to follow the college rearing of the working newspaper man. That would give him a more varied stock of knowledge and a more finished technical skill. But would it enable him to see the workings of monopoly any better than he can see them now, or release him from any of the restraints in his newspaper attitude toward monopoly that check him now?

The distinguished journalist and public spirited citizen, Mr. Joseph Pulitzer, the owner and editor of the *New York World*, who has given a million dollars for the founding of a college of journalism in Columbia University, would develop an *esprit de corps* in the profession akin to that with which the military academy endeavors to imbue its graduates. Says he:—

> If such a class spirit existed, no editor who had degraded himself by becoming the hireling of any Wall Street king or ring would dare to face his colleagues. He would be too conscious of having been false to his better nature, and equally false to the traditions of his college and of his profession. . . . The knowledge that a reputable journalist would refuse to edit any paper that represented private interest against the public good, would be enough of itself to discourage such an enterprise. Such a refusal would be as severe a blow to public confidence in the newspaper as the rejection of a brief by a high-minded lawyer is to the standing of a case in court.[6]

Would that this could be so, but Mr. Pulitzer must realize that no amount of such "class spirit" will change the conduct of working newspaper men as a body, if the papers on which they must work are not impelled by similar principles. It is not necessary to suppose all editors to be like the one of which Mr. Walter S. Logan, ex-President of the New York Bar Association, wrote in congratulating Congressman Robert Baker of New York for introducing an anti-railroad pass bill into Congress. "I rode the other day with the editor of a leading daily," said Mr. Logan. "He pulled out a bunch of 'annuals' that would take him half over the country. He always had them in his pocket when he was writing editorials on the relation between the people and these railroads giving him the passes." Railroad passes are undoubtedly persuasive with a great many small papers, just as they are with a great many legislators and other public officials. Such editors are usually the owners of the papers they edit. Passes constitute part of their valued perquisites, which they are unwilling to lose. They therefore keep the peace with the railroads of the neighborhood. But in the large cities railroad passes do not often buy editors. That would be trivial compared to the value of a metropolitan newspaper's advocacy. But a better reason is that the railroads own or, through others, exercise a direct or indirect influence over the papers; and that ownership or influence the editor must heed or get out.

"The policy of this paper is devoid of principle," protested an aroused editorial writer to his employer. "I know this speech means insubordination, and so with the declaration goes my resignation." The resignation was not accepted because the proprietor really wished his newspaper to adopt a principle, and because he valued the honest, outspoken words. But of how many newspaper proprietors of the first magnitude may this be said? Just as the vacant chair and the walking stick of the dead and gone Peter Stuyvesant were potent in the council of the New Amsterdam Fathers, so in the editorial councils of most of the great dailies the spirit of privilege is present. There are steam railroad, pipe line, street railroad, telegraph, telephone and gas privileges; there are electric lighting, heating and power privileges; there are mineral, oil, timber, agricultural, grazing, urban and suburban land privileges; there are incorporating, patent and tariff privileges, and a brood of lesser privileges growing out of these and belonging to legislative enactment, judicial favoritism and political graft. These vast, immensely powerful, ramifying and, for offensive and defensive purposes, coördinating powers of privilege, want the voice of the press to influence the people. And when they cannot purchase it, they try any of a thousand other expedients at their command.

Picture a session of the editorial council of a great morning daily. The departmental heads are gathered about a large table, and each in turn reports the important news features in sight for the next day's issue. In this way all the news and comment departments act with full knowledge and in harmony. The city or local editor generally has the heaviest budget, and in this instance he has at the head of his long-written list what he calls "a first-class sensation and scoop."

"Well?" says the chief editor, expectantly.

"Smithson, our City Hall man," observes the city editor, "has got under the lid of the gridiron railroad grant—names, dates, places, amounts, affidavits—everything. Good for two pages, straight running. Not another paper has a peep at it. Will give the town the biggest shake-up it has had in a year!"

"Any important people involved?" asks the chief, with easy self-command.

"Traced almost up to the door of old Croesus himself, and inferentially to a lot of highly respectable—"

"Hump!" breaks in the chief; "it reminds me of an epoch in New Orleans history. The city had descended to the depths, perhaps owing to the post-bellum 'black-and-tan' politics. Some of the best and most substantial men of the town got together and resolved to make a change. They needed a newspaper to help them in the task. They bought the *Picayune*. The difficult thing was to find a suitable editor—some man whose name would stand for honesty, ability and fearlessness. Colonel Daniel Dennett of the parish of St. Mary's seemed ideal. His character was unimpeachable. He had a brilliant, fearless, pungent pen. He was known and honored far and wide in the planter region as the publisher of the *Planter's Banner*. A committee waited upon the colonel and formally invited him to come to New Orleans and accept the editorship of the *Picayune*. 'Strike with a free hand,' said the committee. 'Clean up the town.' Colonel Dennett accepted, took a little time to fit himself in his place and size up things, and then, with an avalanche of eloquence and a blaze of indignation, fell upon the great Louisiana Lottery as the first evil for extermination.

"The Lottery was at that time in the heyday of its power. Colonel Dennett's intrepid onslaught spellbound the town. The *Picayune's* board of directors met hastily, and Colonel Dennett was requested to attend. 'How is it, Colonel,' asked the chairman, 'that you waylay in this astonishing fashion one of the great institutions of the State?' The doughty colonel replied: 'You said: "Strike with a free hand. Clean up the town." I struck the Lottery, which appeared to me to be good for a start.'—'But,' rejoined the chairman, 'I neglected to tell you that President Charles Howard of the Lottery Company contributed $100,000 toward our purchase of this paper. It hardly befits us to use the paper in which he owns a large interest to torpedo the company of which he is president.'—'Then your injunction to me,' observed Colonel Dennett, 'is not to be to strike with a free hand; clean up the town?'—'Oh, yes,' answered the chairman of the board; 'strike anything, barring the Lottery.'—'Ah!' said the colonel, 'you mean, clean the town, but leave the corruption. I decline the task. Gentlemen, I resign.' And he went back to the parish of St. Mary's and the *Planter's Banner*."

A pause falls upon the council when the chief finishes his anecdote. The city editor is the first to speak. "I suppose that means that the gridiron sensation is not to be; that it's dangerous; that it may reach somebody at court. Well, it breaks my heart; but I'll kill it. A wink is as good as a nod to a blind ass."

"This council," adds the editorial writer, "being said ass." Nobody disputes the assertion, and the council resumes its routine.

Notes

1. To John Jay, he wrote (Paris, Jan. 25, 1786, Jefferson's Writings, Ford Edition, Vol. IV, p. 186): "It is really to be lamented that after a public servant has passed a life in important and faithful services, after having given the most plenary satisfaction in every station, it should be in the power of every individual to disturb his quiet by arraigning him in a gazette, and by obliging him to act as if he needed a defense, an obligation imposed on him by unthinking minds, which never give themselves the trouble of seeking a reflection unless it be presented to them. However, it is a part of the price we pay for our liberty, which cannot be guarded but by the freedom of the press, nor that be limited without danger of losing it. To the loss of time, of labor, of money, then must be added that of quiet, to which those must suffer themselves who are capable of serving the public, and all this is better than European bondage."

2. Book V, Chaps. I and II.

3. United States Circuit Court of Appeals, Seventh Circuit, No. 864, October term, 1901; May session, 1902.

4. United States Circuit Court of Appeals, Seventh District, No. 789. October term, 1901.

5. See testimony of Mr. Don C. Seitz, representing the *New York World*, and Mr. John Norris, representing the *New York Times*, before the House Judiciary Committee, Washington, D.C., commencing April 5, 1904.

6. *North American Review*, May, 1904.

CHARLES EDWARD RUSSELL

These Days in American Journalism
(1911)

There may be such things somewhere in this world as free government and free institutions without a free press, but I do not know how one can conceive of them. Certainly, so far in human experience, the right of free expression of opinion has been the absolute and indispensable foundation of all other rights. When free opinion has been threatened the whole structure of human liberty, reared so slowly and with so much sacrifice, has been shaken with it.

From this, I think, there will be no dissent by any person of whatsoever faith that has read any history or considered human affairs.

Whether free institutions are now held by the American people to be of vital importance to them is another question. Some persons of a cynical order of mind answer it promptly in the negative. If they are wrong, then the most stupendous fact now before the country is that in the main we no longer have anything that can be called a free press. Sometimes this assertion is made by those that only believe it. I happen to know it because I have sat on the inside of the machine and seen the strings at work that pull it, knowing perfectly well whither those strings led.

The daily newspapers of the United States may be divided into these classes:

1. Those that are owned outright by the public service corporations of the cities wherein they are published.

In one place the leading newspaper is owned by the street railroad company; in another by the electric light company; in a third by the gas company. These ownerships are always carefully concealed by the use of dummies, or still more effectually through the device of pretended loans. The public next to never knows anything about it; reading the news over the breakfast table the average man never suspects that it is news prepared in the interest of the street railroad company, for instance. The editor is a man well-known in the community, a man of standing

From *The International Socialist Review* 12, no. 4 (1911): 210–16.

and character. Who shall perceive that he is a mere dummy and figure-head for franchise grabbers?

Few persons outside of the business have any conception of the extent of this kind of secret ownership. Yet it is a fact that in every considerable city in the United States the public service corporations either own outright or absolutely control at least one newspaper. Sometimes they have their grasp upon more than one, but one they always have; purchased perhaps when the original franchise was obtained by bribery from a corrupt city council, perhaps purchased since as schemes and conditions indicted the necessity for a local organ. But once bought they have in almost every case been retained. Hundreds of newspapers are so owned; if the public could have a list of them it would be provided with a sensation much greater than any newspaper is likely to furnish this year or the next.

When now you consider that the ownership of all these public utilities, traction, gas and electric light, all about the country, drifts steadily into the hands of one small group of financiers, and that this group sits in New York and dictates both street railroad and newspaper policies in cities two thousand miles away, you begin to grasp something of the abnormal and colossal power placed in these few hands.

And yet only a small part of it; because this is only the faintest beginning of their story.

2. Newspapers that are swayed and controlled through the business investments and connections of their owners.

This is a very subtle but powerful influence that we almost never suspect. Mr. Pulitzer, owner of the New York World, began life as an extreme and probably sincere radical. When he was a reporter in St. Louis it was his favorite doctrine (which he preached with singular vehemence and tireless energy), that no man could possibly accumulate by honest means a great fortune; that necessarily the makers of millions were thieves; and he advocated a system by which no man should be allowed to possess more than $25,000 of wealth. For some years in his newspapers he championed the cause of the people, fought on the side of labor, denounced plutocracy and showed daily and very forcibly the disasters it would bring upon the country.

All the time he was making money, and as he made it he invested it, and as he invested it his sympathies were drawn away from the people to the side of the exploiters. The transformation was one of the most interesting it has ever been my fortune to observe, and kept exact pace with Mr. Pulitzer's prosperity. Every dollar he put away became an influence for conservatism. He is now a very rich man and very conservative and his newspapers are the chief and ablest of all champions of existing conditions—the ablest and the meanest, the most adroit, persistent, tireless and unscrupulous.

Mr. Pulitzer, when I knew him, would have leaped upon and torn with his two hands anybody that offered to bribe him.

But all the time he was bribing himself. Now he is as completely and heartily in the camp of the public enemy as any kept newspaper prostitute in the land. With all the force of his ability he is fighting on the side that he was wont in the old days to attack—bribed by his own money.

There are others like him, but he happens to be the most conspicuous illustration. The thing is perfectly natural. More and more newspapers become purely commercial enterprises; they are conducted for profits and for nothing else. Well, what are you going to do with the profits? You can't dig holes in your celler and bury them. Naturally you invest them in good sound lines of securities representing solid business. Yes. And all the good sound lines of business in the country are either owned or controlled or dominated by the one group of the Central Interests that control the government and prey upon the people. If you combat them you combat your own investments. Want to do that? I think not.

You see the thing is both inevitable and irresistible. You can hardly find an investment in these days that has any promise of returns and will not bring you into contact and sympathy with the Central Interests. Therefore, it is either one thing or the other. If your newspaper makes money the profits sweep you into line, and if it doesn't then you are swept the same direction in the manner to be told next.

3. Newspapers that are financed by the Interests.

Every year newspaper publishing becomes more and more expensive. You may have noticed that in the last fifteen or twenty years very few daily newspapers have been started in our great cities. Although the population of those cities may have doubled or more the number of newspapers tends to decrease and not to increase. Well, here is the explanation for this singular fact. No one but a multi-millionaire can start a daily paper now and even a multi-millionaire cannot keep one afloat without the assistance of the money power. Take any newspaper in the dull months of summer. The receipts from advertising and sales fall far short of the expenses; the paper must go on, it cannot stop; it cannot materially curtail those daily expenses that tend constantly to become greater. To get through the slack season it must have accommodations, which means ready money; it can get those accommodations from but one source, for the Central Interests control the banks and the money supply. It is therefore thrown into their power; they have their clutch upon its very heart; conduct your newspaper upon safe, sane and conservative grounds or you get no money and go to the wall. The editorial gentlemen may rave and the public imagine a vain thing; in the business office, where the paper really lives, there is no hallucination about it and before long the whole establishment is sailing along on a course laid down by the Interests.

Just how this works in practice was shown recently in the case of Hampton's Magazine, in New York. It was warned not to publish an article attacking Mr. Morgan and the New York, New Haven & Hartford Railroad. It disregarded the warning and went ahead with the article. Immediately afterward it found that it could not borrow a dollar at any bank in New York upon any security whatsoever. It was in reality prosperous and making a profit, but to navigate it must have accommodations; for these it must go to the banks; and after the word had been given out from headquarters there was not a bank in the country that would accept any of its paper no matter how endorsed nor how backed with unquestionable securities. The result was that the magazine could not go on and its owners were obliged to dispose of it. The explicit threat had been made to them that they would be ruined; this was the manner in which the threat was carried out. What a tremendous power is here! How absurd to speak of a free press when over the head of every publisher is held such a coercion! Print what we want you to print or down you go. The censorship in Russia was never more autocratic nor absolute. I have known cases where the presidents of banks have directly notified newspaper managers that they must not print certain lines of news if they expected to get any money at the banks, and the injunction has always been obeyed. There was nothing else to do; the bank had the whip hand over the newspapers just as the Central Interests had the whip hand over the bank.

Some of the newspapers are permanently financed and kept by the Central Interests; some are mortgaged, some are secretly owned. You must understand that a great many daily newspapers in this country are published at a loss; I suppose that taking the country this is true of a majority of them. Since the days of Jay Gould and C. P. Huntington it has been customary for the Interests to secure their control over some of these needy publications by practically assuming the annual loss. The curious may find exact information as to the manner of this in the celebrated Colton letters of C. P. Huntington, but persons on the inside of newspaper secrets will need no such revalation; the thing is too common.

Where this is not the plan the mortgage is a handy and useful disguise for the control that is the real object of the Interests. Two of the foremost daily newspapers of New York city are held hard and fast by this secure tenure. One of them is the out and out, willing, zealous and faithful drudge of the Interests. It is a harlot and likes the business; it will sit for company all night and then go upon the street and joyously flaunt all the scarlet signs of its calling while it looks for more custom. The other is demure and practices its vocation under the guise of respectability. It favors all public reforms that do not interfere with the profits of its masters. It is strong for morality and all that sort of thing, including what is vaguely but conveniently known as good government. It sternly rebukes Tammany Hall and all the low-brows and rough-necks whenever it happens that these elements are not engaged in carrying an election for Mr. Ryan and the traction Interests. It is the professed champions of the "better classes" but all the time it is nothing but a harlot—kept through a mortgage.

There are more of these sheets scattered about the country than the uninitiated ever suspect. If you want to know who really owns the newspaper that with such avidity you peruse over your breakfast table and whose are the opinions that you daily imbibe therefrom you must look over the mortgage lists in your county. You would probably be much amazed if you could understand the purport of some of them.

4. The newspapers that are dominated through their advertising accounts.

This is the most potent influence of all, the commonest and the most constant. It is always present; no newspaper can possibly escape it. It supplements all the other influences; it works efficiently where the other influences have been evaded. It is always at work and everywhere. It is intangible, indomitable and irresistible, and it is steadily dragging the entire American press at the heels of the corporation chariot. Let the newspaper proprietor or editor be, in purpose and conviction, as independent as he will, this thing will get him at last. No resolution and no endeavor can avail against it, and its strength is not the strength of men's wills or minds but the strength of vast and uncontrollable evolutions and conditions.

With very few exceptions the American newspaper is manufactured at a loss. Its sales price does not cover the cost of the white paper it is printed upon, to say nothing of press work, ink, rent, insurance, taxes, editorial labor and other items. Every copy is sold at a loss on the cost of manufacture, and the greater the circulation the greater the loss.

Therefore it is thrown wholly upon its advertising, not merely for its profits, if there are to be any, but for its existence from day to day. The necessity is sheer and absolutely imperative. Life and death are involved; it must have the advertising or it will cease to exist.

In these days the bulk of display advertising comes from the department stores.

The ownership of the department stores, like the ownership of the street railroads, and of the other public utilities, is steadily narrowing. Year by year the process of evolution that brought the department store into being is unifying its ownership. Year by year the "chain" store stretches over the country, and always the chain comes eventually into the same hands.

Where the department store is not owned outright by the Central Interests it is strictly under their control. It likewise must have money; it likewise can get money from but the one source. When years ago the control of the money supply of this nation was allowed to pass into the hands of a small coterie of financiers there was erected a power greater than was ever swayed by any conqueror or emperor in the world's history. This coterie, now composed of the same identical men that control the railroad interests and most of the productive industry of the United States, can refuse money supplies to any department store that advertises in any newspaper inimical to their acts or profits. They not only can refuse it but innumerable times they have refused it until now the department stores have come to act instinctively as the Interests desire. They will not advertise in any newspapers except those that are good and go along with the game.

Whenever they put forth that power the newspaper involved has nothing to do but to surrender and make the best terms it can. The Interests have the strangle hold upon it.

This accounts for the dailies. As for the weeklies, they are easily kept in line by their local banks and their local business men, who are also tied up to the banks.

So stands the circle complete. I do not overlook the small and diminishing number of good newspaper men that being in charge of journals see the sure drift of the times and strive conscientiously against it; men like Fremont Older of the San Francisco Bulletin and the managing editors of the Scripps combination. These men have respect for their profession; they revolt against its pollution. Yet even they can do next to nothing to stem the tide. The newspapers they guide are also more or less at the mercy of conditions; they too must have money and can get it only at the one source; they too must have advertising and can get it only from enterprises that are strung up to the Central Interests. Soon or late they must be driven down with the rest; not because of anybody's will or design but because conditions are so framed that nothing else is possible.

It was necessary first to get the methods of newspaper control clearly stated before we could come to the results of that control, which is the most important matter we have to consider here.

Every one of these kept and controlled newspapers has what is called its "news policy"—which means its attitude toward daily events and the scheme according to which its columns are colored.

If you ever heard of such a thing you probably thought it a merely technical device pertaining only to the newspaper office, a thing like a press or a counter. As a matter of fact the whole subject hinges here and nothing else about your newspaper is of so much importance to you.

Every day you are accustomed to read in your favorite journal elaborate reports purporting to be of current events. There is noting to warn you, nothing to arouse your suspicions; you read that this event or that occurred yesterday; and as you read you get a certain impression of that event upon which you form your opinion.

You believe that impression to be created by the event. In ninety-nine cases in one hundred the impression is not created from any such source but by the manner in which the event is described.

You could read another account of it from another source and receive a totally different impression leading to quite another opinion. You seldom do read any other account; hence your mind is, as a matter of fact, completely at the mercy of the man that writes that one account, and he in turn is directed by the "news policy" of his journal, which is arranged to suit the exigencies of the business office, which must keep close to the advertisers, who are tied through the banks to the Central Interests. And by this declension, lo! the predatory forces that you probably fear and abhor and regard as your country's enemies are daily in direct and subtle contact with your mind and busily at work forming your opinions.

Or to put it in another way, attached to that reporter's pencil is a string that leads a thousand miles hither and thither but ends in the hands of men that have an object in creating a certain impression. Someone gives a pull on this string and the next day you are reading tainted news and never know it.

That is the "news policy." Usually it consists of a definite understanding in the newspaper office that reports of events are to be so handled that certain interests or persons shall not be offended. "We don't print anything that would give them the worst of it," said a city editor, referring to a piece of news about the Metropolitan Street Railroad that he had conscientiously suppressed. He said it in perfect good faith and with a kind of naïve astonishment that anybody should think the matter important. It was perfectly well known in his office that this course was to be steered; it was part of the "news policy"; it had always been part of that policy; long familiarity had made him regard it as not only reasonable but absolutely right. That was what his journal wanted and he was there to give it its desire; so he discharged a reporter that wrote something of a disagreeable nature about the traction thieves. His business was to protect them.

In precisely the same way it is the "news policy" of the papers of New York not to allow anything of an unpleasant nature to appear regarding banks or the condition of business. You can no more get an accurate impression about the real condition of business from a New York paper than you can from one in Siam. It is part of the game to make everybody think that all is well in the markets, although, as a matter of fact, the bottom may be dropping out of everything. Consequently, the newspapers play the game. That is what is required of them by the Interests that hold the strings and exercise the American censorship.

The vast extent of this evil cannot be imagined by anyone that has not industriously followed it. Let me give one or two illustrations. They can afford no gauge of the practice but they may indicate its nature.

Most of the telegraphic and nine-tenths of the cabled news printed in American newspapers is furnished by an institution called the Associated Press. Its function is to gather news and send it in identical form to all the journals that belong to the association. Through it millions of readers can be reached every day with the same matter.

An engine of such almost inconceivable power for influencing public opinion would not be likely long to escape the attention of the Interests. They early in the game laid hands upon it and now it is conducted in part for the benefit and largely at the direction of Mr. Morgan and his associates.

It is held by the gentlemen exercising this control that there should not be printed anything that tends to show a spirit of revolt among the people anywhere, and it is also held to be desirable that the Catholic church should be upheld and strengthened. These are points in their own "news policy."

Now observe: The execution of Francesco Ferrer was as cold-blooded a judicial murder as ever occurred in this world. It was a pure piece of mediaevalism, a revival of the Spanish Inquisition, a savage cruelty without palliation. If it had happened in the sixteenth century we should shudder as we read of it in our Motley and abhorring the fiends capable of such an atrocity, give thanks that such times had passed away.

So long as it possibly could the Associated Press ignored the story. When it could no longer suppress the news it sent out an account that was manifestly, and, to any one acquainted with the facts, grossly unfair to Ferrer. Its "news policy" was to give the best of it to royalty and the church.

This perverted and poisoned despatch was sent all about the country and read by millions, the vast majority of whom had no other knowledge of the affair.

It came to the office of one of the greatest and most famous of New York dailies which also had a "news policy" covering such things. And someone in that office took that despatch and injected into it about five or six sentences of pure venom, and when that was done no one unfamiliar with the facts could read the story without feeling that the execution was a just and proper thing and the earth was rid of a dreadful beast when Ferrer was put to death.

The result of these perversions was to create such a false impression about the matter that there never was any adequate protest from America against an outrage that stirred all the rest of the world to indignant outcries.

Here was a case where deliberately tainted news gave to practically an entire people a false impression that no amount of protest has ever been able to remove. Is not this a tremendous power? Where in the history of the world has there existed its like? What compared to this was the power of Napoleon at the height of his glory? What empire that ever was erected in this world was the equal of the empire over the minds, thoughts, opinions and actions of the hundreds of millions of Christendom?

This is an illustration from international affairs. If you wish another you need only refer to the well-known case of the Boer war, wherein a great and powerful nation was allowed to suppress a small and weak country for the sole benefit of certain mine owners and stock speculators and the world submitted to the infamy because it was persistently and successfully lied to about the nature and origin of the trouble. Perhaps you believe that enlightened opinion is the true safeguard against war and the true protection of the weak against the strong. Then let me tell you that if you will consider well of the history of the Boer war you will perceive that the men that sway this colossal power of tainting the world's news are able to make war at any time in any part of the world, and are able to distort and misrepresent the facts that they can make you too believe in a war and shout for it. What a power is this to lie in the hands of men whose only concern in humanity is to prey upon it!

Let me show you next a case more recent and nearer home. On the 25th of last January occurred the most deplorable tragedy that removed the brightest of young American novelists, David Graham Phillips. It was the work of a madman; of that there is no more doubt than there is of the revolution of the earth; without fault on poor Phillips' part and without origin in anybody's belief or doctrine, a lunatic's reasonless deed and nothing else. It is part of the "news policy" of one of the New York newspapers to give the Socialists and Socialism what is known as "the worst of it" upon every possible occasion. This newspaper got up a wild-eyed story, without foundation in any fact, that Phillips had been murdered by a Socialist because he had declined to ally himself with the Socialist cause. Its attention was called to this most bare faced and preposterous fake; it persistently refused to correct it. So in the minds of its readers the story stands today, and so strong are first impressions that from the average mind among those readers it would be found almost impossible to dislodge the belief. Socialism got "the worst of it," for such was the "news policy" of the paper. But how many of the readers thereof will ever suspect that every day they are being stuffed with similar lies as the result of the "policy"?

It is the deliberate manufacture of what goes for news that does the harm. Nobody is influenced now by editorials. There used to be such an influence in the days of "old Greeley" and "old Raymond" but now that is all dead and gone. What influences the American people today is the news column; they make up their minds from what they regard as events. If these events are described to them in a way that practically compels them to come to a certain conclusion and that conclusion is for the benefit of the gentlemen that profit from existing condition, how tremendous is the task of ever dislodging this gang!

Two years ago we were holding the first national conference in behalf of the negro. One of the New York newspapers had a "news policy" inimical to the purpose of the conference. It put into the mouth of one of the speakers, Bishop Walters, a remark that he never dreamed of making and could not possibly make, a disgusting and revolting remark, that could not fail to prejudice the mind of any reader against any conference that would listen in silence to such a thing. An indignant protest was sent to the editor of the journal that perpetrated this infamy, with a demand for a correction. He never printed the letter, nor acknowledged it in any way, nor did his paper ever afford us the shadow of a correction. Its "news policy" was to give the worst of it to any such conference, and it proceeded to follow its policy by manufacturing remarks and putting them into the mouths of speakers. We were two years recovering from the injury wrought by that one simple fake.

There is no cause that cannot similarly be disgraced and defeated. Imagine then what show any cause will have that threatens the supremacy of the Interests by whom all these newspapers are absolutely controlled! It is no longer wonderful that the American people submit to the tyranny of their corporations. The wonder is that any persons are aware of the facts and prepared to make revolt.

Because such adept work in the use of poisons as I have indicated in these few examples is going on all the time. There is no item that you read in any copy of any newspaper conducted for profits that may not be similarly dosed and for similar results upon your minds. Howsoever innocent it may appear, how much a matter of routine, how plain or how ordinary, make no difference. The simplest item is probably cooked in accordance with the recipes of the "news policy" for the purpose of protecting some Interest or furthering some game. Of all this you would have ample and visible proof if by any chance you could get hold of one of the lists of things forbidden that is now a part of the outfit of every metropolitan newspaper office; persons, corporations, enterprises and movement that are not to be mentioned, schemes and men that are to be boosted at every opportunity. If you could see one of these you would understand how difficult and intricate has become the work of steering by the "news policy" and how important to the gentlemen that hold the ends of the strings.

By this time I think all the old glamor and romance must be out of this business. There is no longer an idea of getting news for public consumption, of serving a constituency, of giving to readers the truthful and accurate picture of a veritable event. The romance is all gone. What is left is nothing but the sordid manufacture of something for profits. The newspaper is the most thoroughly commercial of modern enterprises. It exists for the balance sheet and for no other purpose. It manufacturers a certain product. To get rid of that product and make money therefrom it must shape the product to suite the taste of the gentlemen that control the advertising and hold the money bag. Consequently it is so shaped regardless of facts or warrant.

What then is the average man to do about his newspaper reading if he does not really care to be forever fooled and misled and lied to?

To this question I know of but two answers. He can keep on reading the profit mongering press, bearing himself constantly on his guard and disbelieving all he reads; or he can restrict his newspaper reading to journals like the Socialist dailies that are published for other purposes than to make money. In the former case he will be obliged to say to himself a hundred times a day, "I don't know whether there is any truth in this or not, and I shall not allow myself to accept it nor to form any opinion upon it." In the latter case his reading will be somewhat small in amount if good in quality. But in that latter case he can also comfort himself that what he is missing is something of not the slightest value to him. For how shall it profit a man to regale himself daily with the trivialities and scandals with which the kept press seasons the service it renders to the men that pay its board?

UPTON SINCLAIR

Owning the Owners
(1920)

The second of the methods by which our Journalism is controlled is by far the most important of all the four. I do not mean merely that the owners are owned by mortgages, and such crude financial ties. They are owned by ambition, by pressure upon their families, by club associations, by gentlemen's agreements, by the thousand subtle understandings which make the solidarity of the capitalist class. I have written elsewhere of labor-leaders, otherwise incorruptible, who have accepted "the dress-suit bribe." These same bribes are passed in the business-world, and are the biggest bribes of all. When you have your shoes shined, you pay the boot-black ten cents; but can you figure what you are paid for having your shoes shined? When you buy a new suit of clothes, you pay the dealer, say, one hundred dollars; but can you figure what you are paid for being immaculately dressed, for having just the right kind of tie, just the right kind of accent, just the right manner of asserting your own importance and securing your own place at the banquet-table of Big Business?

If you are the publisher of a great newspaper or magazine, you belong to the ruling-class of your community. You are invited to a place of prominence on all public occasions; your voice is heard whenever you choose to lift it. You may become a senator like Medill McCormick or Capper of Kansas, who owns eight newspapers and six magazines; a cabinet-member like Daniels, or an ambassador like Whitelaw Reid or Walter Page. You will float upon a wave of prosperity, and in this prosperity all your family will share; your sons will have careers open to them, your wife and your daughters will move in the "best society." All this, of course, provided that you stand in with the powers that be, and play the game according to their rules. If by any chance you interfere with them, if you break their rules, then instantly in a thousand forms you feel the pressure of their displeasure. You are "cut" at the clubs, your sons and daughters are not invited to parties—you find your domestic happiness has become dependent upon your

From *The Brass Check* (Urbana: University of Illinois Press, 2003 [1920]), 258–62.

converting the whole family to your strange new revolutionary whim! And what if your youngest daughter does not share your enthusiasm for the "great un-washed"? What if your wife takes the side of her darling?

It is such hidden forces as this which account for much of the snobbery in American newspapers; the fact that in every department and in every feature they favor the rich and powerful, and reveal themselves as priests of the cult of Mam-mon. I have watched the great metropolitan dailies, and those in many smaller cities and towns; I have yet to see an American newspaper which does not hold money for its god, and the local masters of money for demi-gods at the least. The interests of these Olympian beings, their sports, their social doings, their political opinions, their comings and goings, are assumed by the newspapers to be the object of the absorbed interest of every American who knows how to read.

On every page and in every column of every page the American newspaper preaches the lesson: "Get money, and all things else shall be added unto you—especially newspaper attention." When Mr. John P. Gavit, managing editor of the "New York Evening Post," wrote to Mr. Melville E. Stone, general manager of the Associated Press, that I had a reputation "as an insatiable hunter of personal pub-licity," what Mr. Gavit meant was that I was accustomed to demand and obtain more space in newspapers than the amount of my worldly possessions entitled me to. Some years ago my wife went for a visit to her home in the far South, after the unusual adventure of marrying a Socialist; she met one of her girlhood friends, who exclaimed:

"My, but your husband must be a rich man!"

"My husband is a poor man," said M. C. S.

Whereat the girl-friend laughed at her. "I know better," said she.

"But it's true," said M. C. S. "He has no money at all; he never had any."

"Well," said the other, skeptically, "then what are the papers all the time talking about him for?"

A large part of what is called "conservatism" in our Journalism is this instinctive reverence for wealth, as deeply rooted in every American as respect for a duke in an English butler. So the average American newspaper editor is a horse that stands without hitching, and travels without a whip. But emergencies arise, a fork in the road, a sudden turn, a race with another vehicle; and then a driver is needed—and perhaps also a whip! I showed you Mr. Ochs pulling the "Metropolis" story off the front page of the "New York Times" at one o'clock in the morning. Every Hearst editor has stories to tell of one-o'clock-in-the-morning visits from the owner, re-sulting in the whole policy of the paper being shifted. And where the owner is owned, maybe somebody will call *him* up and lay down the law; maybe an agent will be set to keep watch over his doings, and to become the real master of his paper. I could name more than one famous editor and publisher who has been thus turned out of his job, and remains nothing but a name.

For great "interests" have a way of being wide-awake even at the late hour when the forms of newspapers close; they have a way of knowing what they want, and of getting it. "I am a great clamorer for dividends," testified old Rockefeller; and imagine, if you can, a publishing enterprise controlled by old Rockefeller—how closely the policy of that enterprise would be attended to! Imagine, if you can, one controlled by Pierpont Morgan!

It happens that I can tell you about one of these latter. The story has to do with one of the most famous publishing-houses in America, a house which is a national institution, known to every literate person—the ancient house of "Harper's," which now has the misfortune to have an eight hundred thousand dollar mortgage reposing in the vaults of J. P. Morgan & Company. Would you think me absurd if I should state that the publishing-business of Harper & Bros. is managed to the minutest detail by this mortgage?

First, recall to mind "The Money-changers," a novel dealing with the causes of the 1907 panic. The "villain" of this novel is a certain "Dan Waterman," a great financier who dominates the life of Wall Street, and who in his relations to women is an old wild boar. The veil of fiction was thin, and was meant to be. Every one who knew the great Metropolis of Mammon would recognize Pierpont Morgan, the elder, and would know that the picture was true both in detail and in spirit. Naturally old "J. P." himself would be furious, and his hired partisans would be looking for a chance to punish his assailant.

Very well. Five years passed, and I was editing an anthology of revolutionary literature. I was quoting authors from Homer to H. G. Wells, several hundred in all, and as part of the routine of the job, I addressed a long list of authors and publishing-houses, requesting permission to quote brief extracts from copyrighted books, due credit of course to be given. Such quotations are a valuable advertisement for any book, the more valuable because they are permanent; the request is a matter of form, and its granting a matter of course. It proved to be such in the case of all publishing-houses both in America and in England—all save one, the house of the eight hundred thousand dollar mortgage! This house informed me that no book of mine might contain a line from any book published by them. My reputation was such that I would injure the value of any book which I quoted!

I am interested in this capitalistic world, and try to find out as much about it as I can. So I took the trouble to visit the dingy old building in Franklin Square, and to interview the up-to-date gentleman who had rendered this unexpected decision. He was perfectly polite, and I was the same. I pointed out to him that some of the authors—"his" authors—were personal friends of mine, and that they themselves desired to be quoted in my anthology. Mr. Charles Rann Kennedy, for example, was a Socialist. Mr. William Dean Howells was one of Harper's own editors; he was in that very office, and I had in my hand a letter from him, giving cordial consent to the publication of two passages from "A Traveller from Altruria"! Also Mr. H. G.

Wells, an English Socialist, who had honored me with his friendship, had published "When the Sleeper Wakes" through "Harper's," and now requested that I be permitted to quote from this book in my anthology. Also Mark Twain had honored me with his friendship; he had visited my home in Bermuda, and had expressed appreciation of my writings. He was no longer where I could consult him in the matter, but I offered evidence to Messrs. Harper & Bros. proving that he had not regarded me as a social outcast. But no matter; the decision stood.

I took the question to the authors themselves, and I am sorry to have to record that neither Mr. William Dean Howells nor Mr. Charles Rann Kennedy cared to support a fellow-Socialist in this controversy with a great capitalist publishing-house. So it comes about that you will not find Mr. Kennedy or Mr. Howells quoted in "The Cry for Justice"; but you will find "When the Sleeper Wakes" quoted, the reason being that Mr. Wells did stand by me. Mr. Wells lives farther away, and is not so deeply influenced by an eight hundred thousand dollar mortgage in the vaults of a Wall Street banking-house!

The point of this story is the petty nature of the vengeance of this mortgage, the trouble it took, the minute detail into which it was willing to go. The moral for you is just this: that when you pick up your morning or evening newspaper, and think you are reading the news of the world, what you are really reading is a propaganda which has been selected, revised, and doctored by some power which has a financial interest in you; and which, for the protecting of that financial interest, has been willing to take trouble, and to go into the most minute detail!

You will miss the point of this book if you fail to get clear that the perversion of news and the betrayal of public opinion is no haphazard and accidental thing; for twenty-five years—that is, since the day of Mark Hanna—it has been a thing deliberately planned and systematically carried out, a science and a technique. High-priced experts devote their lives to it, they sit in counsel with the masters of industry, and report on the condition of the public mind, and determine precisely how this shall be presented and how that shall be suppressed. They create a public psychology, a force in the grip of which you, their victim, are as helpless as a moth in the glare of an arc-light. And what is the purpose of it all? One thing, and one only—that the wage-slaves of America shall continue to believe in and support the system whereby their bones are picked bare and thrown upon the scrap-heap of the profit-system.

P. S. to ninth edition: There have been changes on the staff of Harper & Bros., and I am pleased to record that the decision against me has been rescinded, and you will find the quotations in the new edition of "The Cry for Justice."

GEORGE SELDES

Big Business and the Press
(1935)

There would be no reason for this chapter if the newspapers of the world admitted, as William Allen White of the *Emporia Gazette* recently did, that journalism was once a profession, "a noble calling; now it is an 8 per cent investment and an industry."

Not even the seven corrupt newspapers of my Pittsburgh years, however, would admit they were purely business propositions. My own *Leader* was the People's Friend; the *Press* was the clarion of the masses, the conservative papers owned by Banker Given and Senator Oliver and Colonel Rook proclaimed their public service every day, and without exception they published the news as the Pittsburgh bankers, coal, iron and steel interests and politicians affiliated with these interests, dictated.

If these seven newspapers had not pretended to be newspapers, observing a code of ethics, maintaining the honesty and integrity which belonging to a profession connotes—if they had published, as house organs do, an announcement that they represented the Union Trust Company (Mellon) interests, or Farmers National Bank (Given) interests, or the Pennsylvania Railroad and the U.S. Steel Corporation, affiliated with these banks—there could be no reason for criticism.

But there are still many other angles for viewing this problem of the commercialization of the press, the interrelationship between publishing and stockholding, the multimillionaire publisher who may not own stock in any corporation but his own, and the economic system of which he is a part and which he is pledged to preserve.

The present economic trends, the merger of commercial interests, when they include newspapers, according to William Allen White, can be summed up in the word "bad." In the last thirty years, he says, newspapers

From *Freedom of the Press* (Garden City, NY: Garden City Publishing Company, 1935), 110–26.

have veered from their traditional position as leaders of public opinion into mere peddlers and purveyors of news. . . . The newspapers have become commercial enterprises and hence fall into the current which is merging commercial enterprises along mercantile lines.

As the newspaper's interest has become a mercantile or industrial proposition, the dangers of commercial corruption of the press become greater and greater. The power trust of course is buying the newspapers in order to control the old vestige of leadership, the remaining fragment of professional status that still remains in the newspaper business.

As a commercial enterprise the newspaper is yielding good returns for investment.

But as a political weapon it is worth to self-seeking service corporations hundreds of dollars in under-cover influence where it is worth dollars in direct returns. If this country turns from a democracy into a Hamiltonian plutocracy, it will be because the moral sense, moral intelligence, and moral courage of the American people are sapped at the roots by insidiously corrupt plutocratic influence undermining the sources of courage and intelligence which has been so ably represented by the American press in other generations. Unless democracy is indignant at the encroachments of plutocracy, democracy cannot fight. When plutocracy destroys the sources of information which should make indignation, plutocracy has paralyzed democracy. But it is no sudden thing. It is a part of the tendency of the times. I do not know the answer.

Without giving a definite answer, let us continue the documentation of the influence of big business on the press which we have already seen in department-store advertising, food and drug activities, oil interests, and the utility propaganda system. The railroads, the packers, the coal and steel corporations and the bankers have left behind them a trail just as interesting if not as open.

When Lee M. Russell was elected governor of Mississippi it was on the inevitable Democratic platform; never has he been accused of being a liberal, let alone a radical. Here is what Governor Russell during his incumbency wrote on the subject of this chapter heading:

I have noticed throughout the nation for many years the unmistakable signs that the money power of this government was controlling the policy of the press. It is rare indeed to see a journal with any circulation and with any standing that would dare to speak out in behalf of the great masses of the people. From the first along to the last there is unmistakable evidence that these papers are subsidized. They speak the language of their masters, the predatory interests.

In our own State we haven't a daily paper that would dare to champion the cause of the common people upon any question, and they follow the wishes of the "big interests" always. . . .

The fight in this State now and in the years to come is against this sort of octopus and others of this kind, and if we had an honest and fearless press we would run these criminals out of the State at once, but unfortunately we have but few editors that will take up the fight against this common enemy. The small country paper has come under the same criminal influence of these predatory interests as have the larger papers, until now our State has only a very small percentage of honest-to-goodness newspapers. These are making a valiant fight, but the common enemy is continually closing in on them, and unless a revolution takes place it will not be long before they are all silenced—I pray this revolution may come soon.

How much does big business pay and how many papers does it influence? In the case of the government versus the New Haven railroad, Attorney (now Supreme Court Justice) Louis D. Brandeis insisted that the investigation include the publicity department whose pay vouchers he demanded be seized and made public. The New Haven president, Mr. Mellen, testified as follows (Court Record, page 1350):

Mr. Folk—Was not something paid practically to every newspaper in New England?

Mr. Mellen—I do not know as to that.

Mr. Folk—The records show that more than 1,000 newspapers got something.

Mr. Mellen—Well, I have no doubt that is correct.

Then there is the testimony regarding amounts. (Court Record, page 1363):

Mr. Folk—The New York, New Haven & Hartford Railroad paid about $400,000 a year, it appears from this document, for publicity purposes. For instance, to the *Boston Republic* you paid about $3,000 a year, it seems. . . . Why did you pay so much to that paper?

Mr. Byrnes—Well, because I thought it was worth it.

Mr. Folk—Why did you think it was worth it?

Mr. Byrnes—Do you mean the *Boston Republic*?

Mr. Folk—Yes.

Mr. Byrnes—Well, that is Mayor Fitzgerald's paper.

In the hearings of the New Haven the fact was established that the four hundred thousand dollars a year was "relatively less than was paid by any other large railroad in the country."

In the Mulhall investigation in the Senate it was shown that the National Association of Manufacturers and the Merchant Marine League were using enormous sums to influence newspapers. By spending two million dollars a year various marine corporations were able to drum up opposition to La Follette's seamen's law.

In the insurance companies' scandals, many newspapers paid by the corporations' publicity bureau for favorable articles were named.

These are matters of record. They happened not so long ago. And they show the same method of big-business procedure which the public utilities employed later.

Here is the testimony of Senator George W. Norris, of Nebraska, in 1921, regarding another big-business enterprise, the packers. He calls it "one of the most remarkable attempts to control the public sentiment through the instrumentality of the public press"; he writes that

the packers are not the only corporations engaged in this great undertaking. There are many other great corporations that are equally guilty. It is a nationwide campaign to build up a reactionary sentiment in favor of the great corporations of the country. But in this article we are dealing only with the packers and I confine myself in my comments to the part which they have taken in this colossal undertaking. I do not want to be understood as claiming that all of this advertising was unnecessary or subject to criticism. Neither do I argue that because a newspaper accepts advertising it is necessarily controlled in its editorial policy. The assertion is made, however, that the advertising of the packers is far beyond any legitimate, fair, or even liberal allowance for that purpose, and neither can there be any doubt but that some newspapers are controlled in their editorial policy by the advertising end of the business. Many others remain silent in their editorial columns when they would otherwise condemn, if it were not for the oiling of the business machinery through advertising.

There can be no doubt, but that one of the objects of this campaign was to mold public sentiment, and to close up the criticism that their acts would otherwise receive at the hands of newspapers. There was evidence developed upon the investigation to show that this was the real intent and purpose of a large portion of the advertising. The packers carry large page and half-page advertisements in all the newspapers of the United States. No country paper was too small to be taken into consideration by them. Large display advertisements appeared in newspapers that had only two or three hundred sub-scribers. Moreover, the greatest of this advertising took place at a time when there was a shortage of production, when they were positively unable to supply the hungry with the food desired. . . .

To illustrate his charges Senator Norris tells the story of what happened in Fort Worth, Texas, where both Armour and Swift have packing plants. Both loaned money to a man named Armstrong to buy up an unfriendly paper and convert it into a packer's paper. Three packers, Swift, Armour and the Stock Yards Company lent five thousand dollars to Armstrong's rival, Senator Norris adds, thus controlling public opinion in the town.

When big business in the form of coal comes up for discussion there are docu-ments made public by the Senate Committee on Manufacturers which was consid-ering a fuel control bill. Senator La Follette, writing in 1923, said it was an "amazing indictment of certain of the newspapers of the United States." The tran-script of the meeting of the National Coal Association "contains indisputable evi-dence that the coal operators set out . . . to subsidize the press and use it as a medium to create 'shortage' scares, and to induce the people to buy coal at high prices. The object of the National Coal Association was not merely to use the ad-vertising columns of the newspapers but to obtain the publication of inspired news stories and editorials. The record shows that in this object the association was em-inently successful."

The evidence made public by the Senate committee showed that the coal cor-porations assessed themselves one mill a ton, raising between three hundred thousand dollars and four hundred thousand dollars for their "educational cam-paign . . . safeguarding influence against the enactment of harmful and expensive legislation in coal-mining districts and in the nation at large. . . ." The verbatim transcript of the National Coal Association meeting as published in the hearings of the Senate Committee on Manufacturers, contains the statement from one coal operator that he obtained the assistance of Melville Stone of the Associated Press who agreed to send between three hundred and four hundred words of coal cor-poration propaganda daily.

Senator Kenyon read a statement charging the publicity department of the Na-tional Coal Association with supplying certain propaganda to the Associated Press: "Over telegraph wires that night the Associated Press carried a news report of over 1,000 words to its 3,500 or more newspaper plants, written by its Cleveland man-ager after consultation with the (coal) publicity director."

"In other words," commented Senator La Follette, "at the time the newspa-pers of the country were publishing the 'shortage' advertisements and news stories prepared by the National Coal Association (and while receiving hundreds of thousands of dollars from the Association in advertising contracts) the actual facts as to coal were entirely at variance with the information 'fed' to the people through the press.

"A coal operator appearing before the Calder committee admitted that the extortionate prices charged the American people for coal in 1920 may have reached $600,000,000 in excessive profits.

"This is an operator's estimate of what the 'educational campaign' of the National Coal Association in 1920—conducted through the columns of the daily press—cost the people of the United States."

Something more recent and perhaps more important? Here is an item of December 14, 1934. It concerns the House of Morgan.

If the reader is curious enough to look up the sayings and writings of certain persons opposed to the entry of the United States in the World War—and they range all the way from William Randolph Hearst to Eugene V. Debs—he will find that they alone among other issues raised the cry of commercialism. Money, they said, was taking us to war. Big business, they declared, wanted our entry. The international bankers, especially the fiscal agent of the Allies, John Pierpont Morgan, wanted us to join the Allies.

Such statements became sedition after April 6, 1917.

In 1919, September fifth to be exact, it was not Eugene Debs but Woodrow Wilson who confessed that commercialism, money, big business, was responsible for the war. The President of the United States admitted exactly what the pacifists said two years earlier. But the President did not name the bankers.

From 1917 on, newspaper men have from time to time heard the report that the American Ambassador to Great Britain cabled to Woodrow Wilson to come into the war to save the Morgan investment. The Germans were the original authors of this charge. They supplied no evidence.

Very recently part of the text of Ambassador Page's cable to President Wilson was being reported by many persons, notably Father Coughlin in one of his radio speeches in 1933. Father Coughlin told millions of Americans this was the absolute proof we entered the war to save the House of Morgan.

On December 14, 1934, the Nye Committee investigating the munitions industry, gave to the world the text of Ambassador Page's cable to President Wilson, the most important paragraphs of which are:

The pressure of this approaching crisis, I am certain, has gone beyond the ability of the Morgan financial agency for the British and French Governments. . . . It is not improbable that the only way of maintaining our present pre-eminent trade position and averting a panic is by declaring war on Germany.

. . . pressing danger that the Franco-American and Anglo-American exchange will be greatly disturbed; the inevitable consequences will be that orders by all the Allied governments will be reduced to the lowest possible amount, and that transatlantic trade will practically come to an end.

The result of such a stoppage will be a panic in the United States. . . . We shall soon reach this condition unless we take quick action to prevent it. Great Britain and France must have a credit in the United States which will be large enough to prevent the collapse of world trade and the whole financial structure of Europe.

If the United States declares war against Germany, the greatest help we could give Great Britain and the Allies would be such a credit. If we should adopt this policy, an excellent plan would be for our Government to make a large investment in a Franco-British loan. Another plan would be to guarantee such a loan. A great advantage would be that all the money would be kept in the United States.

We could keep on with our trade and increase it, till the war ends, and after the war Europe would purchase food and an enormous supply of materials with which to re-equip her peace industries. We should thus reap the profit of an uninterrupted and perhaps an enlarging trade over a number of years, and we should hold their securities in payment.

Nothing that has come out of all the secret archives of the world is so illuminating as the foregoing appeal. It shows up the political leadership of the world as dealing with investments and profits, not with human suffering and human lives. It incidentally and forever removes the American diplomats from the category of naïve children, where Europeans usually place them, and puts them first in realism, in *Realpolitik*.

This appeal to arms was dated March 5, 1917; the United States declared war on April 6, 1917. The Morgan millions were saved.

The Nye Committee has been clever in its publicity campaign. Knowing as it did that there would be opposition from certain War, Navy and State Department officials, from all the corrupt businesses in the nation, from all the merchants of death and from the press controlled by all the interests opposed to international peace, Senators Nye and Vandenberg timed some of their sensations to make the headlines of the morning and evening press. But events ran away from them. There were not merely two daily sensations, there was a torrent of them.

Certainly by every rule or custom in the newspaper game the publication of one of the most guarded documents of the World War was a news item. But what happened to it? A member of the staff of the *New Republic* immediately made an investigation, and this is his report:

The full text of this [the Page] cablegram was released to the public by the Nye Committee on December 14, 1934. The United Press put the text of the cable into its munitions story of that day. So far as we can learn the Associated Press, International News Service and Universal Service did not. We have examined some twenty leading papers of the country, both in New York City and elsewhere, and find the following interesting facts: Only four of these papers carried the text of the cable. The *New York Post*, the *New York World-Telegram*, the *Louisville Courier-Journal* and the *Pittsburgh Press* did so. The *Cleveland Plain Dealer* carried the U. P. munitions story, but, in the edition that we examined, cut out all mention of the Page message. The *New York Tribune* printed a denial that the Nye Committee would investigate the cable but did not print the cable itself. A number of other papers printed a denial of an investigation of Morgan's, but were careful, even in the denial, not to mention the existence of the cable. Is this the freedom of the press about which the publishers have lately been so solicitous?

At my request the writer of the foregoing editorial, Lawrence Brown, has supplied additional information. He talked to the Associated Press but received an evasive answer, and finally a statement that the committee had not given out the text at all; he then asked the telegraph editor of the *Herald Tribune* who said he had received the United Press story and telegraphed his Washington bureau about it, but the correspondent had apparently not been interested. The *Times* does not receive the United Press service.

The *New York Post* not only printed the cable, but reprinted it the night of December seventeenth with the editorial suggestion that fifty thousand doughboys died to make the world safe for profits. "The same newspapers which ignored or buried the Page revelations," continued the *Post*, "will spread propaganda for our entrance into the [next] war because our entrance into the war will safeguard those investments and those profits."

From a world war and the Morgans to California and the state brewers is a far leap, but it reaches another angle of the same subject. Again, as with almost every example which is mentioned here, the thanks of the reader are due to the one or two papers which always refuse to go along with the rest. Testimony is from Stephen F. O'Donnell, publisher of the *Huntington Park Signal*, who alleges:

The California Newspaper Publishers' Association accepted money from the California Brewers' Association to pay for the authorship, printing and preparation of matrices, of articles ostensibly designed to encourage the citizens to vote, and actually designed to encourage them to vote Republican [meaning, of course, against Sinclair]. . . .

I think all honest newspaper men will agree with me that it is not a proper function for an agency such as the California Newspaper Publishers' Association to circulate brewers' propaganda by means of such a flimsy device as the re-christening of the brewers by some such flossy title as "Steadfast Californians, Associated."

Anyone familiar with the current campaign in California can see that these editorials were conceived by some one interested in the preservation of the *status quo* and hostile to both the New Deal and to Upton Sinclair's EPIC program. Regardless of the merit of the political theories advocated in these articles, the fact remains that many people and even some newspaper publishers are not in favor of them. Thus the effort to get propaganda of the type contained in the "Stand Fast—America" series into the columns of all member publishers of the California Newspaper Publishers' Association in California, at a very nominal fee, intended only to defray mechanical costs, has every mark of an effort to give away the support of the country press in this state to one party. . . .

Editor O'Donnell wrote to the publishers' association that the eight matrices they sent the newspapers to arouse Americans to the fact "their liberty and peace" were being "attacked on all sides by strong outside forces" was "unmitigated bilge"; to which John B. Long, general manager, replied that the "publicity campaign, which I have read clear through, is non-political and is based upon the anti-communism campaign of the Elks, Junior Chambers of Commerce and the American Legion," which should make it holy in California.

Of California journalism and big business there is much more to be said. According to Guy Emery Shipler, editor of the *Churchman*, the *Los Angeles Times* is not only reactionary but a social menace. He contrasts two trends, the way it dealt with the electrocution of Sacco and Vanzetti, and its relation to big-business interests of the city. Regarding the former he quotes from "The Lancer" column signed by Harry Carr, as follows:

Executions of murderers usually hold a melancholy but negative value for the public. The execution of Sacco and Vanzetti has been of sad but positive value. It has brought into the revealing light an amazing number of vicious fools who have been, until now, secret enemies of the United States. As usual, the outcry over this murder case comes from three classes of people—parlor socialists of the Greenwich Village variety, who are seeking cheap excitement; dangerous Reds, who are against everybody on the general principles of a mad dog; and small-bore writers. All of these vermin would be making trouble about something else if Sacco and Vanzetti had never existed.

But while radicals are mad dogs, public utilities are sacred cows. Writes Mr. Shipler:

> During the same period the *Times* has continued its campaign of vilification
> and misrepresentation against the Bureau of Power and Light of the city of
> Los Angeles, representing one of the most successful public ownership en-
> terprises in America. The explanation lies in the fact that the ownership of
> the *Times* is heavily interested financially in the Southern California Edison
> Company, the private competitor of the Bureau of Power and Light. The
> municipal group has no newspaper through which to reach the taxpayers in
> order to offset the campaign of the *Times*, and is forced to resort to circular-
> ization by mail.

Every newspaper man can add to these examples of big business editing or
making the news. There are even newspaper owners who admit it. Lord Northcliffe,
for example. He is the author of a pamphlet, *Newspapers and their Millionaires*, in
which he says, "Some of the provincial papers, like some of the London newspapers, are maintained by wealthy men for the purpose of political and social advancement. There is nothing wrong in that. . . . The *Westminster Gazette* . . . was
always a 'kept' paper. For years it passed from one millionaire to another." Sir
Robert Donald, editor of the *Daily Chronicle*, said to the Institute of Journalists that
"during the last twenty years the press has been commercialized. Under syndicate
ownership the main concern of shareholders was their dividend, and dividends
must be earned even if principle had to suffer." Sir Willmott Lewis, of the London
Times, deplored the fact that "in my country by reason of national circulations and
the passing of control of newspapers to men who are primarily millionaires and
not journalists, we have the immediate and pressing danger of the view that the
press should make its will prevail."

In America the same thought was expressed by Dean Ackerman, of Columbia,
who holds "the great basic fault of the press is its ownership. The press cannot be
an impartial and true advocate of public service as long as its owners are engaged
or involved in other businesses." Professor E. A. Ross, of the department of political economy, University of Wisconsin, who believes that the aspiration of the
press has been upward, that venality has waned, makes "the one deadly, damning count against the daily newspaper as it is coming to be, namely, *It doesn't give
the news*." This apostasy of the daily press, Professor Ross believes, is due to three
economic developments in our time: the capitalist-owner instead of editor-owner;
advertisers censoring the news; and the newspaper organ becoming an organ of
special interest.

The majority of sacred cows are the big-business corporations. The packers, the
medicine men, the coal companies, the railroads, the public-service corporations,

the traction companies have always been sacred cows in a great many newspapers. If one may "point with pride" to the fact that the street-car companies, the railroads and the packers no longer bribe newspapers, one may in turn "view with alarm" the activities of the medicine men and the public utilities.

In all these specific instances there have been outright conspiracies, propaganda—or enlightenment campaigns for those who prefer milder and more euphemistic terms—by organized big business. In all these specific instances they were caught and brought before the humbugged public by congressional investigations.

Yet every intelligent reader of the newspapers knows that there are stronger but unseen ties which make a great number of the most powerful organs of public opinion part of the big-business set up. Take for example the case of Whitelaw Reid and his widow, Mrs. Elizabeth Mills Reid. They owned the old *New York Tribune*. May 26, 1934, the will of the late Mrs. Reid showed the estate held securities valued at $16,210,809. Among them were:

2093	shares	American and Foreign Power.
2000	"	American Car and Foundry.
1200	"	American Smelting and Refining.
1780	"	Bethlehem Steel 7% prf.
2120	"	Commonwealth Edison.
1000	"	Consolidated Gas prf.
7000	"	Standard Oil of N. J.
10,761	"	International Paper & Power.

and so on through the list of railroads, mines, public utilities worth three or four million dollars, Mexican and Cuban stocks and bonds, etc.

Every move the American Government made toward intervention in Cuba and Mexico affected Whitelaw Reid's and Mrs. Reid's Mexican and Cuban investments. Every adverse policy of the public utility commissions or President F. D. Roosevelt is a blow to the utility portfolio of the Reid estate.

A Republican *Herald Tribune* would naturally attack a Democratic administration, and poke editorial fun at Democrats, as well as Republicans aligned with them, who would have the state and nation control the utilities, as for example:

What is a reforming Administration without a whipping boy? The bankers served Mr. Roosevelt admirably in this capacity from inauguration day, when he lashed them out of the temple, to the late love feast in Washington. Mr. Walsh's report is just one more sign that the wicked utility companies are to be promoted from relative obscurity to this new and important post as the Administration's principal devil.

And here is a cavalry charge against the committee which is providing the nation with sensational disclosures of the war traffic (*Herald Tribune*, lead editorial, December 15, 1934):

A BLUNDERBUSS ATTACK

The Nye Committee started out to investigate the munitions traffic. It has already reached the point of publishing lists of all who made a million dollars or more during the war, regardless of whether their income had the slightest connection with munitions or not. . . . Many of those whose names are thus being mentioned feel, not unreasonably, that this is going pretty far afield and that they are being unjustly pilloried as munitions makers and profiteers of death when they were nothing of the kind. Their resentment is warranted, for the Nye Committee has manifested a cheerful carelessness about letting its inferences fall where they may.

. . . . the "munitions maker" is largely a myth. Or, to put it a little differently, he is all of us . . . the war wealth did not go merely to manufacturers of powder or shell casings; it went to everybody; farmers, shipyard mechanics, workers in mines and every kind of factory . . . every sort of business industry.

One more illustration of the relations of big business and the press: the Montana copper companies, according to Mr. Villard, owned outright the following newspapers:

Montana Standard of Butte
Daily Post of Butte
Anaconda Standard
Helena Independent
Record-Herald of Helena
Missoulian
Sentinal of Missoula
Billings Gazette
Livingston Enterprise

The press of the state of Montana was heavily subsidized by the copper industry and many papers were run at a loss. The biggest and most powerful daily, the *Tribune* in Great Falls, was published by friends of the owners of the Anaconda Copper Company. In 1928 W. A. Clark, Jr., son of the copper Senator, established the fearless independent *Montana Free Press* at Butte. A whispering campaign and an advertisers' boycott caused the loss of thirty thousand dollars a month, and

eventually the paper was sold to the *Anaconda*. Villard believes it would have succeeded if young Clark had held out a little longer. But even if it had paid for itself
it is doubtful if it could have broken the monopoly of public information which
the copper interests maintained. Of course the fact that Montana makes it a habit
to elect enemies of copper to Congress is one of the many proofs that big business
although controlling a large part of the press sometimes drives the electorate, grown
suspicious of the newspapers, to defeat both the corporations and their political
manikins.

The establishment of a lone paper in a journalistically corporation-owned state
is not the answer to the problem, nor do I feel that I could solve it when Mr.
White, one of the notable leaders of the free press, refrains from trying. But we do
know this, that when a president appoints certain important officials they dispose
of their commercial bonds, literally and figuratively. This may not solve the problem
but it helps. Mr. Mellon of course remained a business man although he sold his
holdings. The law already requires newspapers to file a statement of all bondhold-
ers. We know that the position of editors and publishers of important newspapers
is, to say the least, the equivalent of a place in the Senate, if not in the White
House. Unless we can assure ourselves that all the editors and publishers of our
powerful newspapers are not bound to big business by millions of dollars in stocks
and bonds, in mortgages on their plants, in common business enterprises, or in
directorates in outside corporations, we cannot be sure that their protestations of
serving the reader, published daily, have any meaning.

Perhaps the best solution of the problem of business and the press would be to
let real newspaper men run the newspapers. But that is a subject for a later chapter.

Advertising

WILL IRWIN

The Advertising Influence
(1911)

From these last ten years of so-called muckraking we have evolved a phrase—"the system." Like most new phrases, it has behind it meaning and history. In the complex organization of modern society grow large and rooted injustices, often the fault of no one man, at worst the fault of only a few. The agents of these systems may be above the ordinary in private virtue. They are but operatives, each tending, oiling, and repairing one little wheel in a great machine. Or, if they work directly and personally for evil, as does the ward boss in a political system, they may do it without any searing of the inner soul. They found the system at their birth into affairs; they absorbed it with their business education; they have never seen it through virginal eyes. The modern specialization of industry beats souls into tortured forms, as it does minds and bodies.

The main handicap on American journalism in its search for truth, in its presentation of that truth to its times, is precisely such a system. And, curiously, this one—unlike the Wall Street system, the Standard Oil system, or the system of ward politics—did not owe its inception to moral turpitude on the part of its founders. No Rockefeller or Gould, Quay or Croker, built it up; on the contrary, it grew from the editorial and business policy not only of the ruthless Bennett and Hearst, but of the conscientious Greeley and Medill. It arose with the growth of the times; but it is no less a perplexity and a danger.

The Advertiser Pays

The "system" in the American newspaper proceeds from the fact that the subscriber, who buys the newspaper that it may teach him about his times and fight his battles

From *The American Newspaper*, with comments by Clifford F. Weigle and David G. Clark (Ames: Iowa State University Press, 1969). A series first appearing in *Collier's*, January–July 1911.

against privilege, is not paying for that newspaper. *The advertisers are paying*—about one per cent of the population, and often the very one per cent united, in the present condition of American society, with the powers most dangerous to the common weal.

That, however, is not quite the taproot of the trouble. The American newspaper has become a great commercial enterprise. A million dollars—yardstick of big business—seems like a pauper's purse beside the fictitious or actual value of many metropolitan journals. The possibilities of profit and loss vary between the Chicago *News'* net earnings of $800,000 per annum and the $400,000 dropped in one year to establish a new kind of journalism in Boston. Men and companies controlling such funds look at business in the business way. It has followed inevitably that the controlling head of most newspapers, the so-called publisher, is not an editor with the professional point of view, but a business man. When the American Newspaper Publishers Association meets in the national convention, it does not discuss methods of news-gathering nor editorial problems. The addresses treat of the price of white paper, of new machinery, of organization for extending circulation, of the advertising rate.

The old "sixpenny" newspaper, which flourished before the time of Bennett, took advertisements, though it did not really need them. Its editorial running expenses were low; it could make profits on its sales alone. From the moment when the New York *Sun* and *Herald*—now, it happens, two- and three-cent papers—entered the field at a price of one cent, advertising became a vital necessity. Hudson, the old newspaper historian, stops for a moment his consideration of evaporated issues to record that Bennett systematized advertising, put it on a cash basis, and established a regular corps of solicitors. He had to do it in order to live. So did the old editors of high purpose who followed him. For after Day and Bennett cheapened the price on the street, the six-cent metropolitan newspaper departed this life. Only New Orleans and the Pacific Coast held to a price even as high as five cents—New Orleans because it proceeds in everything by ways of its own, the Pacific Coast because it would not recognize a coin smaller than a nickel. The Cincinnati *Enquirer* is the one subexception to this rule. One or two cents became the law; and the drift was toward the smaller price. Within six months all the Chicago newspapers have dropped to one cent. True, a few publications with special clienteles hold out to this day for a higher price. The New York *Herald*, for example, circulates mainly among the wealthy, easy-spending class of the lavish metropolis; so is it able to charge three cents. Yet many experts believe that greater circulation and advertising receipts, and in the end greater profits, would follow a lower sales rate. Reduction from two cents to one was the beginning of its present prosperity for the New York *Times*. The New York *Evening Post* and the Boston *Transcript*, three-cent newspapers, have their confessedly limited circulation among readers who do not weigh pennies. The Springfield *Republican* has been able to keep the three-cent rate because of its excellence and its place in the affection of western Massachusetts. Nevertheless, its one-cent rival across the street makes claim to nearly double its circulation.

A Change of Base

The newspaper whose subscribers paid for it died with the birth of the news. In the period between 1850 and 1880, if the advertiser's money did not do the paying a baser influence did. For we have lost along the way one excrescence of journalism. Time was when many newspapers "took their graft" from politics, and accepted regular subsidies from candidates or central committees. Generally, though not wholly, that passed. The business became systematized. The advertiser paid. Following the law of commerce, the newspapers organized their salesmen of advertising, and sent them forth to cajole business away from their rivals. The department store arrived with its enormous contracts—sometimes $50,000 a year to one publication—and its news-advertising, liked by housewives and therefore a builder of circulation. He who got most advertising was the most successful business manager. The rush for this kind of revenue became a craze. Many merely com- mercial publishers seemed to forget circulation, the product which they were selling to advertisers, in the rush for customers, as though a weaver should neglect his factory and his wool-supply and look only to his sales-agency. In the eighties all were issuing such proclamations as this: "Circulation 73,000, 20 per cent above that of our nearest morning rival." By the early years of this century newspapers were bawling: "We published 554,000 inches of advertising in this period against 448,000 by our nearest rival."

Slowly at first, then with increasing momentum, advertisers learned their power. Indeed, in certain quarters, the advertising solicitors helped to teach them. For the less conscientious and solidly-run newspapers began offering comforts and im- munities as a bonus to attract customers. Advertisers got into the way of asking for these special privileges; often, in communities where the newspapers were timid and mushy, for every privilege, even to dictating policies. The extent of their de- mands varied with the local custom of their communities. But finally, in cities like Philadelphia and Boston, an impossible state of affairs confronted even that pub- lisher who cared more to be an editor than a money-maker. The system had grown so set that he must make concession or fail. For if he did not, his rival would get "the business." And without "the business" he could not pay the high editorial salaries, the press bureau fees, the telegraph tolls, the heavy wages to mechanics, which first-class journalism demands. So must he cheapen product, lose circulation, and fade away.

Hardly can one blame the advertiser. His is the business view. Modern business demands mutual favors. With whom do department stores spend more of the earnings than with the publishers? Have they not, as business men, a right to ask not only slight favors but also policies favorable to their interests? And indeed we can not blame the publisher, if we concede that he is merely manufacturing a commodity, that a newspaper is just a commercial institution. In the strictest business ethics, the manufacturer holds to nothing beyond making the product which will honestly please and satisfy his purchasers. And the chief purchaser of newspaper wares is, after all, not the reader, but the advertiser. This consideration, if no other, reduces to an absurdity the business attitude toward journalism: "I am manufacturing a commodity. I am responsible for turning out a sound article—no more."

The Proportion of Ad Revenue

How much the advertiser pays, how little the subscriber, is shown by one unit of measurement employed in the business offices. The publishers of one-cent newspapers try to make the revenue derived from subscriptions and street sales pay for the white paper on which they print. If they achieve that result, they consider that they are doing exceptionally well; if, in addition, they pay for the cost of circulation—paper-wagons and carriers—they call themselves marvels. All other expenses, as rent, the upkeep of a great mechanical plant, salaries and wages to one, two, or three hundred employees, ink, power, and incidentals, the advertiser pays. More pertinently, he pays interest and profits.

Estimating from what exact knowledge we have, I should say that the advertiser turns about three and a half to four dollars into the average metropolitan newspaper to one dollar paid by subscription and street sales. The proportion varies greatly; practically, it is always on the side of the advertiser. One New York newspaper confesses that the proportion is 9 to 1. The Scripps League has an important member which makes a profit at 2 to 1. But Scripps is a genius at newspaper economies. In New Orleans alone is the balance on the other scale. Until recently the *Times-Democrat* got nearly two dollars from sales to one from advertisers. But New Orleans is a "five-cent town," and the *Times-Democrat* charges nine dollars a year to its regular subscribers, where a one-cent Northern newspaper with a five-cent Sunday edition charges six dollars or less. Besides, New Orleans, as I have said, is a law unto herself. And the *Item*, which has entered the city with new methods, more nearly approaches the Northern ratio.

News Suppression

What does the advertiser ask as bonus in return for his business favor? Sometimes a whole change of editorial policy—as when the Pittsburgh newspapers were forced to support a candidate for the bench chosen by the department stores; more often the insertion of personal matter of no news value in itself; most often the suppression of news harmful to himself, his family, or his business associates.

Taking one small and general example, I have never seen a story about a shoplifting case in which the name of the store was mentioned. It has occurred, I believe, in certain favored corners of the country, but not in my horizon. Usually the item reads: "In an uptown department store," "In a Fourteenth Street emporium." The department store exists for and by women; they like respectability and safety; news that criminals are at large among its counters may frighten them away. So reasons the store manager, and doubtless he is right. 'Tis but a small favor to a customer, the denaturing of such news. Publishers who show considerable backbone concerning advertising control of larger policies generally grant this favor to the department stores.

Carried further, the advertiser asks, and often gets, suppression of scandals and disgraces affecting his family, or disasters injurious to his business. Here the harm begins; for if the justification for newspaper publication of scandal and disaster is the extra-judicial justice which it evokes, this is class discrimination and special privilege.

For example—and a type-example at that—an elevator in Henry Siegel's Boston store came down to the first floor, behaving curiously. The operator investigated. He found the mangled and dead body of a woman—Jeanne Goulet of Marlboro, Massachusetts. How it happened no one exactly knew; it is only certain that Miss Goulet's death was an accident, not a crime. There was a good sensation. The Boston newspapers ignored the event—just as they had ignored an escalator accident in the same store a few years before. It is true that the Goulet case happened at the time of the Chelsea fire, when the newspapers were "cutting everything to the bone." But on that same day several of them carried a story about a little boy killed by a log at Dexter, Maine.

In fact, if one looks for a large general example, he can do no better than consider the present state of the Boston press. Like any one who is about to say something detrimental, I begin by stating the virtues of Boston journalism. For decency in drawing the line between silence and invasion of privacy, it is quite satisfactory. Much of it has a kind of intellectual cast which squares with Boston's best old ideals. The *Globe* satisfies the New England liking for small and pleasant personal gossip, and does it smoothly and sanely. The *Post* has taken the *Globe*'s policy and supplemented it with a large view—if a somewhat sensational one—on the larger world. It has achieved the miracle of appealing to both the Back Bay and the gashouse district. The *Transcript* justly regards itself as a beacon-light of journalism. Not even the New York *Evening Post* gives more real education on the "higher life," publishes such a mass of well-written advices concerning social and intellectual movements. The *American* is least yellow, and probably most truthful, of all the Hearst evening organs.

Yet Boston has all but universally fallen into an attitude of subserviency toward the advertiser. From his first cub assignment, the typical Boston journalist has been taught that the price of journalistic silence is a two-inch advertisement. Here and there throughout the country are newspapers just as respectful to their source of revenue; but in no other city is this system so frankly accepted as a necessary part of the business. Let us see how it works in practise.

The Beer Cases

Hearst had entered Boston in 1905; was struggling, Hearst-fashion, for circulation, and he began with the best device of yellow journalism, the war on special privilege. Later, he used that sword more sparingly. At about this time Dr. Charles Harrington, an admirable health officer, turned his attention to the Massachusetts breweries. He found by analysis that much of the beer and ale sold in his State was adulterated, contrary to law, with salicylic or fluoric acid. In the course of six weeks the grand jury indicted a dozen brewery companies and many bottling-houses for this offense. It was important news, as any newspaper man knows; Hearst used it for one of his loud campaigns. But did the *Transcript* or the *Globe* or the *Post* publish the fact? They did not. Red Fox Ale, made by the Massachusetts Breweries, was on the list of indictments. Red Fox Ale had a small advertisement in the *Transcript*. When the grand jury returned its finding in that case the *Transcript* published a list of the day's indictments, but omitted this highly important one. The grind of justice reached Harvard Beer, a heavy advertiser on billboards and in newspapers. Most of the other brands changed their names after the expos; Harvard Beer decided to give up adulteration and to go on with its name and advertising.

What the *Transcript* Published

The Harvard Brewing Company was indicted on Saturday, April 8. Most of the evening papers, including the *Transcript*, ignored this important piece of news. The *Transcript* published in its issue of April 8 the fact that a workman had fallen from a tree, that an aged pauper had been found dead in bed, that the Harvard Shooting Club was about to hold a meet, but not the fact that Harvard Beer, known to every consumer of malt liquors in Massachusetts, was in peril of the law for adulteration.

Neither was the fact noted on Monday, April 10. But on Tuesday, April 11, "Harvard Beer, 1,000 Pure," appeared in the pages of the *Transcript*—as a half page advertisement. This advertisement shrunk in the issue of April 13 to three columns, in which form it continued through ten issues. But for the *American* and the *Traveler* the adulteration of Harvard Beer would have escaped the Boston public. If any other newspaper noted the fact, it concealed it in a far corner of an obscure page. I regret that this special and glaring instance, so useful in proving the rule of Boston journalism, hits the *Transcript* so hard. For in a great many instances it has been the one Boston newspaper which has shown a disposition to sacrifice advertising for news. It fell in this case, however; and this is not the only case.

The *Transcript*'s Independence

The *Transcript*, indeed, has just given striking proof of its general independence. The Jordan Marsh department store is perhaps the heaviest single advertiser in Boston. In the spring of 1910 they built an annex across Avon Street from their main building; and they wanted permission for an overhead bridge connecting the two structures. By the law of Massachusetts, a municipal permit was not enough in this case; it was necessary to get a bill through the Legislature. This was not in itself a harmful measure; the bridge would have been a real convenience to the public. But the precedent was rather dangerous. Jordan Marsh, apparently, feared opposition; and they "requested" the newspapers to keep silence. The bill came up for hearing before the regular committee. The *Transcript* noticed this hearing, thereby making itself offensive to Jordan Marsh. The committee passed the bill over to the Attorney-General for an opinion on its constitutionality. He reported on March 31 that it was undoubtedly unconstitutional. Now that decision was news—first, because it denied to Boston a public convenience, and second, because it was a precedent for other firms which wished special favors in the use of the streets. As a matter of fact, it was the most important piece of State House news on that day. The *Transcript* printed it at its news value—three-quarters of a column. One or two of the others guarded themselves by brief mention. Silence from the rest. I do not know what contracts or arrangements the *Transcript* has with Jordan Marsh Company; but I do notice that Jordan Marsh has not advertised in the *Transcript* since early in April. Apparently the "Boston Bible" is paying for its impious presumption.

Boston went through several fights with the gas company before it got a fair rate. The company, realizing on what side its bread is buttered, is an advertiser—and it is allied with other advertisers. And the reformers, in successive battles, had to fight not only against the company and its allied interest, but against the thick, heavy silence of the newspapers—though Hearst, it is true, took their side in the last battle.

A Dollar a Line!

It was in one of the early skirmishes that the attorneys for the people and the company introduced their arguments on the same day. Next morning most of the newspapers printed the company's argument in full, and the argument of Louis Brandeis, attorney-at-large for the people, in brief synopsis. That night a reformer, himself an advertiser and therefore a privileged person, approached a Boston publisher.

"Why don't you give us a fair shake?" he asked. "Here's seven columns of gas argument and only a half a column of Brandeis's reply."

"Well, sir," replied the publisher, "I'd really like to accommodate you. But we're publishing a newspaper, and we can't make it all gas fight. The company paid a dollar a line in good money for that speech, so we just had to publish it in full; and we were forced to cut down on Mr. Brandeis."

The instances are too many for mention in detail. The following, rightly understood, are just funny:

A. Shuman, clothing dealer and philanthropist, is a liberal advertiser. He is also a director of the City Hospital. The Boston City Hospital is rather better than most; but in the best of such institutions arise from time to time cases of carelessness in diagnosis or treatment. When the "station man" reports such a case to a Boston newspaper, it goes into the wastebasket—automatically. I can not find that Mr. Shuman ever asked this favor. The trained mind of the Boston copy-reader says: "City Hospital—Shuman—Shuman—Advertiser—out with this." There was a divorce in a department store family. The proceedings occurred in open court. All the reporters had access to the records, and the family did not ask to have the fact suppressed. Perhaps they reasoned, as many do in like cases, that if a marriage be made public so should its dissolution. Nevertheless, the *Traveler* alone published the fact. That month the other newspapers had dozens of divorce stories, each affecting persons of lower social position, and therefore of smaller news value, than these. Again: the process was automatic, instinctive, in the mind of the Boston journalist.

Two excellent examples came out in 1910. Mrs. Minnie M. Akers entered Houghton & Dutton's department store in the Christmas rush of 1907. She was in a delicate condition. A store detective mistook her for a shoplifter; had her detained and searched. He made a great mistake; not only did he discover no evidence, but he gave her such a shock that she all but died. She and her husband brought a suit, which came to trial on May 16, 1910, and obtained a verdict of $8,400. Now note: there were seven jury sessions going on at the time; this was in the "fourth session." It was the most important case tried in all seven sessions on that date. The *Herald* and the *Advertiser* run a court column for the benefit of lawyers—a brief synopsis of all cases. The *Advertiser* gave a three-line, colorless record of the verdict;

the *Herald* dropped the case out of its record. It reported sessions one, two, three, five, six, and seven, but not session four—while that case was on! When, next day, a small personal damage case came up in four, the *Herald* resumed its full report. The *Herald* was then near bankruptcy, and was inclined to eat out of every hand that dipped into gold. At this period, indeed, it put forth for the benefit of its editors a "keep-out book," listing those persons and firms who must be "extended every courtesy." But the other papers were just as subservient. For this unusual case, this heavy verdict, was fair news matter in the general columns, outside of the legal department. Had the defendant been a saloon-keeper, for example, it would have been good for an item anywhere.

Publicity and the Department Store

The Boston *Traveler* changed management last year, after the episode of *Fahey vs. The National Shawmut Bank*, to be mentioned later. Cleveland capital bought it; Cleveland newspaper men took the management. And the Cleveland newspapers in general are fairly free from advertising control. The new editors started, apparently, with the same "square-deal-to-all" rule which Hearst followed when he invaded Boston. An ammonia tank blew up in the basement of Henry Siegel's department store at about four o'clock one afternoon last July. The *Traveler* and the *American* are the only Boston evening newspapers which publish a late "baseball extra." All the others had sent their last edition to press by four o'clock. The Hearst *American* ignored it. The *Traveler* sent a reporter. He found the condition of affairs picturesque, though not dangerous. The fumes had rolled up into the store, driving the shoppers and store-girls before them. A few of the girls had gone back for their hats; fumes had overcome them. When the *Traveler* reporter arrived, men employees were assisting them out.

The *Traveler* published this story on the front page. The morning newspapers passed it over without a line. The Associated Press sent it out. The New York newspapers proved their appreciation of its absolute value by giving it space—many on the front page. The Boston *Transcript* next afternoon showed better backbone than it did in the Harvard Beer case by printing the Associated Press story. And that was all the publicity which this "live news matter" got in Boston. In the same summer a hot bolt dropped into a barrel of tar at the Charleston Navy Yard. The barrel blazed, and the workmen heaved it overboard: whereupon the episode was closed. But that made space in all the Boston newspapers—the *American* gave it a "five-column display" on the front page. The navy does not advertise.

Another Influence

Another and more subtle influence spreads from the advertiser to asphyxiate free journalism in Boston. Before I attack that point I must digress to lay before the newspaper reader a distinction which every newspaper maker understands. If your journal is to preserve even the appearance of frankness, it must make some physical distinction between voluntary statement of the truth and paid matter. Generally, the distinction is set by the character and "face" of the type. The reader should know it at a glance, usually does know, whether this or that item is paid matter, or genuine news written untrammeled from the point of view of the reporter. The advertiser pays his tribute to the power of the press by his eagerness to get a "type-display" identical with that of the news columns. So appears the so-called "reading notice," whose price is from two to ten times that of corresponding space in advertising type. Fair newspapers generally accept such matter, but state its purpose by printing at the end "Advt." or the three stars (***), which have come, in the perception of most readers, to mean the same thing. Between those three stars and blank space lies the difference between truth and falsehood. When he makes a "reader" appear like news, the editor adulterates his product. It may be quite harmless adulteration, as when he gives news of a millinery opening in a department store. It may be poisonous adulteration, as when newspapers here and there throughout the country publish "dollar-a-line" Smith's paid dispatches lying about the situation in the corrupt insurance companies. It is always, in greater or smaller degree, a violation of the newspaper's tacit contract with its readers.

Reading Notices as a Bonus

Now "reading notices" published without star or distinguishing mark, have been a constant source of revenue to most Boston newspapers. Boston has recently improved a little in this respect; a new law is at the bottom of the reformation. By common consent, however, the department stores still expect reading notices as a bonus. "How many readers will you give us?" asks the store advertising manager of the solicitor. Unless he desire something contrary to obvious public morals or to the newspaper's policy, any one, until recently, could insert nearly anything in most Boston newspapers at a dollar a line. The Boston Elevated, for example, wishes to make an example of conductors convicted of "knocking-down" fares. These cases are merely petty larceny; the amount of the theft is seldom more than ten or fifteen dollars; they are hardly worth the attention of a metropolitan newspaper. But until recently the Elevated Company has paid certain newspapers a dollar a line to publish these items as news. Go back and compare these ten-dollar larcenies, published in full, with the $8,400 Houghton & Dutton verdict, absolutely suppressed! If the conductors also were advertisers, doubtless their crimes would not be published—not though they stole a whole railroad.

Much more "stuff," crowding out more valuable matter, gets into the Boston newspapers through this cringing attitude. If the management ask favors, so may the chiefs of departments. The sister-in-law of a head buyer belongs to the Little Busy Bees of the Tenth Unitarian Church, which is about to give a lawn party. The head buyer is likely to ask, and the newspaper to grant, extended advance notice of this mildly thrilling event. So, in preferred position, occupying three columns with pictures, we find the lawn party noticed, not as news, but merely as something about to happen. How much padding and "fluff' has appeared concerning the Boston Opera House only the Boston news editors know. For the department story family of Jordan is heavily interested in this philanthropic enterprise; and much of this matter comes from the press agency, not of the opera-house but of the Jordan Marsh Company. The process is harmless adulteration—not poison, only a little water. But when it becomes too common it distorts the picture of this world which the newspaper presents its readers.

The Effect of Boston Journalism

Decent of speech, cowardly of heart, a prophet when the cause does not touch its own pocket, a dumb thing when it does—by such journalism is Boston served. Has its half-hearted policy affected the public intelligence of its city? I believe that it has. For the social and intellectual caste of Boston is curious. The ancient New England spirit of stern virtue remains; the second generation from the fiery Abolitionists have kept their idealism, if not their fire. Boston orders its saloons closed on Sundays, and sees that they remain closed; it enforces strict decency of public conduct; it is the last American word on good taste in municipal architecture. And notice this parallel: on conventional personal morals, on merely physical municipal improvements, its newspapers are strong. In no other American city is so great a proportion of people who want to do the right thing. But they wobble ineffectually, while the gang and allied interests go straight to what they want. For in few other American cities do the people so dimly understand what is the right thing socially and politically. That the moral face of the world has changed in this generation; that the great issues are no longer political but economic; that new conditions have brought new sins—Boston as an entity knows not these things. And I for one believe that Boston is so not because she is Boston, but because her newspapers have withheld the light that never was in university or college—the light of a sane, broad, truthful point of view on the daily flow of the times.

JAMES RORTY

The Business Nobody Knows
(1934)

The title of this chapter was chosen, not so much to parody the title of Mr. Bruce Barton's widely-read volume of New Testament exegesis, as to suggest that, in the lack of serious critical study, we really know very little about advertising: how the phenomenon happened to achieve its uniquely huge and grotesque dimensions in America; how it has affected our individual and social psychology as a people; what its rôle is likely to be in the present rapidly changing pattern of social and economic forces.

The advertising business is quite literally the business nobody knows; nobody, including, or perhaps more especially, advertising men. As evidence of this general ignorance, one has only to cite a few of the misapprehensions which have confused the very few contemporary economists, sociologists and publicists who have attempted to treat the subject.

Perhaps the chief of these misapprehensions is that of regarding advertising as merely the business of preparing and placing advertisements in the various advertising media: the daily and periodical press, the mails, the radio, motion picture, car cards, posters, etc. The error here is that of mistaking a function of the thing for the thing itself. It would be much more accurate to say that our daily and periodical press, plus the radio and other lesser media, *are* the advertising business. The commercial press is supported primarily by advertising—roughly the ratio as between advertising income and subscription and news-stand sales income averages about two to one. It is quite natural, therefore, that the publishers of newspapers and magazines should regard their enterprises as *advertising businesses*. As a matter of fact, every advertising man knows that they do so regard them and so conduct them. These publishers are business men, responsible to their stockholders, and their proper and necessary concern is to make a maximum of profit out of these business properties. They do this by using our major instruments of social communication, whose free and disinterested functioning is embodied in the con-

From *Our Master's Voice* (New York: The John Day Company, 1934), 13–20.

cept of a democracy, to serve the profit interests of the advertisers who employ and pay them. Within certain limits they give their readers and listeners the sort of editorial content which experience proves to be effective in building circulations and audiences, these to be sold in turn at so much a head to advertisers. The limits are that regardless of the readers' or listeners' true interests, nothing can be given them which seriously conflicts with the profit-interests of the advertisers, or of the vested industrial and financial powers back of these; also nothing can be given them which seriously conflicts with the use and wont, embodied in law and custom, of the competitive capitalist economy and culture.

In defining the advertising business it must be remembered also that newspapers and magazines use paper and ink: a huge bulk of materials, a ramified complex of services by printers, lithographers, photographers, etc. Radio uses other categories of materials and services—the whole art of radio was originally conceived of as a sales device to market radio transmitters and receiving sets. All these services are necessary to advertising and advertising is necessary to them. These are also the advertising business. Surely it is only by examining this business as a whole that we can expect to understand anything about it.

The second misapprehension is that invidious moral value judgments are useful in appraising the phenomena. Advertising is merely an instrument of sales promotion. Good advertising is efficient advertising—advertising which promotes a maximum of sales for a minimum of expenditure. Bad advertising is inefficient advertising, advertising which accomplishes its purpose wastefully or not at all. All advertising is obviously special pleading. Why should it be considered pertinent or useful to express surprise and indignation because special pleading, whether in a court of law, or in the public prints, is habitually disingenuous, and frequently unscrupulous and deceptive? Yet liberal social critics, economists and sociologists, have wasted much time complaining that advertising has "elevated mendacity to the status of a profession." The pressure of competition forces advertisers and the advertising agencies who serve them to become more efficient; to advertise more efficiently frequently means to advertise more mendaciously. Do these liberal critics want advertising to be less efficient? Do they want advertisers to observe standards of ethics, morals and taste which would, under our existing institutional setup, result either in depriving stockholders of dividends, or in loading still heavier costs on the consumer?

There is, of course, a third alternative, which is neither good advertising nor bad advertising, but no advertising. But that is outside the present institutional setup. It should be obvious that in the present (surplus economy) phase of American capitalism, advertising is an industry no less essential than steel, coal, or electric power. If one defines advertising as the total apparatus of American publishing and broadcasting, it is in fact among the twelve greatest industries in the country. It is, moreover, one of the most strategically placed industries. Realization of this fact should restrain us from loose talk about "deflating the advertising business." How would one go about organizing "public opinion" for such an enterprise when the instruments of social communication by which public opinion must be shaped and organized are themselves the advertising business?

As should be apparent from the foregoing, the writer has only a qualified interest in "reforming" advertising. Obviously it cannot be reformed without transforming the whole institutional context of our civilization. The bias of the writer is frankly in favor of such a transformation. But the immediate task in this book is one of description and analysis. Although advertising is forever in the public's eye—and in its ear too, now that we have radio—the average layman confines himself either to applauding the tricks of the ad-man, or to railing at what he considers to be more or less of a public nuisance. In neither case does he bother to understand what is being done to him, who is doing it, and why.

The typical view of an advertisement is that it is a selling presentation of a product or service, to be judged as "good" or "bad" depending upon whether the presentation is accurate or inaccurate, fair or deceptive. But to an advertising man, this seems a very shallow view of the matter.

Advertising has to do with the shaping of the economic, social, moral and ethical patterns of the community into serviceable conformity with the profit-making interests of advertisers and of the advertising business. Advertising thus becomes a body of doctrine. Velben defined advertisements as "doctrinal memoranda," and the phrase is none the less precise because of its content of irony. It is particularly applicable to that steadily increasing proportion of advertising classified as "inter-industrial advertising": that is to say, advertising competition between industries for the consumer's dollar. What such advertising boils down to is special pleading, directed at the consumer by vested property interests, concerning the material, moral and spiritual content of the Good Life. In this special pleading the editorial contents of the daily and periodical press, and the sustaining programs of the broadcasters, are called upon to do their bit, no less manfully, though less directly than the advertising columns or the sponsor's sales talk. Such advertising, as Veblen pointed out, is a lineal descendant of the "Propaganda of the Faith." It is a less unified effort, and less efficient because of the conflicting pressure groups involved; also because of the disruptive stresses of the underlying economic forces of our time. Yet it is very similar in purpose and method.

An important point which the writer develops in detail in later chapters is that advertising is an effect resulting from the unfolding of the economic processes of modern capitalism, but becomes in turn a cause of sequential economic and social phenomena. The earlier causal chain is of course apparent. Mass production necessitated mass distribution which necessitated mass literacy, mass communication and mass advertising. But the achieved result, mass advertising, becomes in turn a generating cause of another sequence. Mass advertising perverts the integrity of the editor-reader relationship essential to the concept of a democracy. Advertising doctrine—always remembering that the separation of the editorial and advertising contents of a modern publication is for the most part formal rather than actual— is a doctrine of material emulation, keeping up with the Joneses, conspicuous waste. Mass advertising plus, of course, the government mail subsidy, makes possible the five-cent price for national weeklies, the ten- to thirty-five-cent price for national monthlies. Because of this low price and because of the large appropriations for circulation-promotion made possible by advertising income, the number of mass publications and the volume of their circulation has hugely increased. These huge circulations are maintained by editorial policies dictated by the requirements of the advertisers. Such policies vary widely but have certain elements in common. Articles, fiction, verse, etc., are conceived of as "entertainment." This means that controversial subjects are avoided. The contemporary social fact is not adequately reported, interpreted, or criticized; in fact the run of commercial magazines and newspapers are extraordinarily empty of social content. On the positive side, their content, whether fiction, articles or criticism, is definitely shaped toward the promotion and fixation of mental and emotional patterns which predispose the reader to an acceptance of the advertiser's doctrinal message.

This secondary causal chain therefore runs as follows: Mass advertising entails the perversion of the editor-reader relationship; it entails reader-exploitation, cultural malnutrition and stultification.

This situation came to fruition during the period just before, during and after the war; a period of rapid technical, economic and social change culminating in the depression of 1929. At precisely the moment in our history when we needed a maximum of open-minded mobility in public opinion, we found a maximum of inertia embodied in our instruments of social communication. Since these have become advertising businesses, and competition is the life of advertising, they have a vested interest in maintaining and promoting the competitive acquisitive economy and the competitive acquisitive social psychology. Both are essential to advertising, but both are becoming obsolete in the modern world. In contemporary sociological writing we find only vague and passing reference to this crucial fact, which is of incalculable influence in determining the present and future movement of social forces in America.

In later chapters the writer will be found dealing coincidentally with advertising, propaganda and education. Contemporary liberal criticism tends to regard these as separate categories, to be separately studied and evaluated. But in the realm of contemporary fact, no such separation exists. All three are *instruments of rule*. Our ruling class, representing the vested interests of business and finance, has primary access to and control over all these instruments. One supplements the other and they are frequently used coordinately. Liberal sociologists would attempt to set up the concept of education, defined as a disinterested objective effort to release capacity, as a contrasting opposite to propaganda and advertising. In practice no such clear apposition obtains, or can obtain, as is in fact acknowledged by some of our most distinguished contemporary educators.

There is nothing unique, isolate or adventitious about the contemporary phenomena of advertising. Your ad-man is merely the particular kind of eccentric cog which the machinery of a competitive acquisitive society required at a particular moment of its evolution. He is, on the average, much more intelligent than the average business man, much more sophisticated, even much more socially minded. But in moving day after day the little cams and gears that he has to move, he inevitably empties himself of human qualities. His daily traffic in half-truths and outright deceptions is subtly and cumulatively degrading. No man can give his days to barbarous frivolity and live. And ad-men don't live. They become dull, resigned, hopeless. Or they become dæmonic fantasts and sadists. They are, in a sense, the intellectuals, the male hetæræ of our American commercial culture. Merciful nature makes some of them into hale, pink-fleshed, speech-making morons. Others become gray-faced cynics and are burned out at forty. Some "unlearn hope" and jump out of high windows. Others become extreme political and social radicals, either secretly while they are in the business, or openly, after they have left it.

This, then, is the advertising business. The present volume is merely a reconnaissance study. In addition to what is indicated by the foregoing, some technical material is included on the organization and practices of the various branches of the business. Some attempt is made to answer the questions: how did it happen that America offered a uniquely favorable culture-bed for the development of the phenomena described? What are the foreign equivalents of our American rule-by-advertising? How will advertising be affected by the present trend toward state capitalism, organized in the corporative forms of fascism, and how will the social inertias nourished and defended by advertising condition that trend?

The writer also attempts tentative measurements of the mental levels of various sections of the American population, using the criteria provided by our mass and class publications. Advertising men are obliged to make such measurements as a part of their business; they are frequently wrong, but since their conclusions are the basis of more or less successful business practice they are worthy of consideration.

The one conclusion which the writer offers in all seriousness is that the advertising business is in fact the Business Nobody Knows. The trails marked out in this volume are brief and crude. It is hoped that some of our contemporary sociologists may be tempted to clear them a little further. Although, of course, there is always the chance that the swift movement of events may eliminate or rather transform that particular social dilemma, making all such studies academic, even archaic. In that case it might happen that ad-men would be preserved chiefly as museum specimens, to an appreciation of which this book might then serve as a moderately useful guide.

GEORGE SELDES

The Power of Advertising
(1935)

. . . good advertising [is] an economic and social force of vital importance.

—PRESIDENT F. D. ROOSEVELT

Advertising is one of the vital organs of our entire economic and social system.

—PRESIDENT HOOVER

Advertising (rather than competition) is the life of trade. Advertising ministers to the spiritual side of trade.

—PRESIDENT COOLIDGE

(The annual advertising budget in the United States is $1,500,000,000.)

The publication of fraudulent advertising costs the American public about $500,000,000 annually.

—W. E. HUMPHREY,
Federal Trade Commissioner

As a reporter my first hate was the advertiser. Every reporter hates the business office with its sacred cows, its son-of-a-bitch list, its business-office-musts. Every newspaper man in America, it is safe to say, hates the advertisers.

The advertisers supply the money with which the newspapers are run. Our bread comes from them. But we daily bite the hand that feeds us, and we hate, as the German war hymn had it, with a hate that shall never die. It is a hate to be proud of.

What is the reason for it? The newspaper advertiser, in the eyes of the honest

From *Freedom of the Press* (Garden City, NY: Garden City Publishing Company, 1935), 41–61.

newspaper man, stands for everything that is low and filthy and degraded in this world. Everything that is wrong with newspapers is usually laid on the golden doorstep of advertising. "If we could only do without advertising we could have a free press." So say we all.

How true is this expression? Is it largely emotional, or is it a reasonable statement of fact? Let the reader judge for himself. Herewith, and in the following chapters of this section, will be presented the following subjects with documentary evidence:

The part advertising plays in suppressing news.

How advertising in the newspapers corrupts the public, social, economic and political action.

How many patent-medicine advertisers sell vicious worthless products.

The activities of governments and big interests in influencing the public through the press.

How the propaganda machinery works with the cooperation of the press.

In the first part of the evidence I will give briefly a number of instances of suppression of news by advertisers. The range is many years. For those who think that things have changed for the better, examples during 1933 to 1935, the time of the writing of this book, are included. In addition to considering the influence of the advertiser on the news there is also considered the viewpoint of the advertiser, and still more important, the attitude of editors and publishers toward the utility corporations, the patent-medicine men, the department-store owners, toward big business—in short, toward the sources of their money.

Is news suppressed by the advertisers? Here is a mild statement from a questionnaire about the newspaper business which Marlen E. Pew recently published in the house organ of the American press, *Editor & Publisher*:

Q.—There is a belief that much news is colored or suppressed on order from the business office. Is this true? Can you recall incidents in support of your belief?

A.—It happens once in a while in many offices. The publisher is a weakling, or is out playing golf while some narrow-minded henchman is riding the staff. An advertiser calls up demanding that some scandal story be suppressed and invariably contacts with the business office, for obvious reasons. Some editors are independent enough to throw ink-wells at publishers' assistants or tell even the boss he doesn't know the butter side of his own bread and sometimes convince him of the fact. Other editors compromise or wiggle out of unpleasant situations of this sort.

"It happens once in a while in many offices" seems to me too half-hearted a confession from an editor who while engaged in daily newspaper work was known as a fearless fighter against the corrupting influences of the advertisers. Mr. Pew knows as well as I do that every newspaper man he has talked to in his whole lifetime has had some evidence of advertisers suppressing news.

The case of the entire press of Pittsburgh suppressing the news of a rape case in which the son of a department-store owner was the defendant is not unique. The entire press of Philadelphia suppressed the news of a charge of immorality against one of its leading department-store officials and the suicide of the accused. The New York papers published the story.

But the *New York World* went to a ludicrous extreme when it rejected O. Henry's famous *The Unfinished Story* because it dealt with a department-store girl who got seven dollars a week and who planned to sacrifice what in those days was euphemistically known as "her virtue." This story, the supposedly fearless *World* thought, might harm its relations with all department stores.

Suppression of news by the department stores is the most frequent and flagrant story. The department stores are the largest local advertisers; almost all newspapers live on this sort of advertising, and a boycott by the stores is frequently fatal to the publisher. Department-store owners are no better or worse than other business men. The fact to be noted is that they insist that their peccadilloes and their crimes, their divorces, their minor scandals and their violations of the law, be suppressed. Usually their insistence wins.

The *New York Times* reported that United States Commissioner Manley issued warrants for the arrest of members of the firm of a department store in Philadelphia, in violation of the Lever Act. The government accused this store of charging unreasonable prices for sausage, tea, cocoa. But the morning after the *Times* brought this information, there was no mention of the facts in the *Philadelphia Public Ledger*.

When an alumnae committee of Bryn Mawr accused the same store of failure to conform to the fire laws, the papers were silent; when the fire marshal filed suit against the store, the *Ledger*, according to Oswald Garrison Villard, could not see that there was any news value in the fact. But when the store denied the charge which the *Ledger* had never printed, the *Ledger* had space for it.

Then there were strikes of clothing workers, upholstery workers, and the picketing of department stores. The *Ledger* remained anti-union to the extent of refusing paid advertisements merely setting forth the claims of the workers. An indictment of the United Gas Improvement Company was either suppressed or hidden on inside pages by several Philadelphia papers. The lapses of the *Ledger*, which Curtis once said he would make the *Manchester Guardian* of America, Mr. Villard concludes, "are utterly unworthy of it and are a treachery of journalism itself."

With great frequency persons are caught shoplifting in department stores. According to a recent report this happens almost every day at Klein's in New York.

Usually such arrests are not news. But when the *New York Times* reports the arrest of two fashionably dressed persons who lived at the Hotel Vanderbilt and who posed as members of upper society, it is apparently news. It is news for many papers. But the *Times* mentions the store as James McCreery & Company, the *American* reports a "Thirty-fourth street department store," and the *Tribune* does not mention the episode.

In Chicago the vice-president of a department store is indicted for bribing city aldermen to obtain passage of an ordinance permitting him to bridge his two buildings. The press of Chicago obliges. For five days the trial goes on sensationally; for five days the newspapers of Chicago are silent. One German language newspaper brings the story.

The big sensation in all the Boston newspapers one day was the collapse of two hundred employees just after the noon hour. All had been poisoned by the food in their box lunches. Not a single paper mentions the name of the purveying restaurant; it is "a local chain restaurant."

In Boston a board fixes the minimum wage in the women's clothing industry at fourteen dollars a week, but is powerless to enforce it. It is authorized, however, to advertise the names of those who refuse to pay. The *Globe* runs the board's advertisement with an offending firm's name, but the *Transcript* refuses, although the law imposes a fine of one hundred dollars for such refusal.

Keith's Theater is a Boston advertiser. For ten weeks, at practically every performance, a maniac throws missiles, severely injuring persons in the audience. Every Boston paper knows of this but not until the maniac is caught is there any mention of his activities. "And," comments the *Springfield Republican*, "there are still journalists to declare that Upton Sinclair's strictures on the press were exaggerated and there are still innocent souls who believe that the Boston dailies are faithfully serving the city that supports them."

When the press in Ohio attacked the Standard Oil Company and the Rockefellers, their so-called "fixer," Dan O'Day, made out a series of new advertising contracts for a Standard by-product, Mica Axle Grease, which Ohio papers accepted. Perhaps it was a mere coincidence that the attacks ceased the same day.

Not alone is Will Rogers among newspaper critics to call humorous attention to the way California papers play up Florida hurricanes and the way Florida papers play up California earthquakes, each paper playing down the local lamentable acts of God. The situation is not alarming. Exaggerations and vice versa will not do much harm to the general public.

But there is the subject of disease and plagues. They affect life and death. Has it always been the role of the newspapers to suppress such unfortunate news? I have been much amused by the following quotation from the "Latrobe Journal" of 1819 which Ruth Boyd has so kindly sent me. The subject is yellow fever. "By the beginning of August," wrote the contemporary historian, "it was a matter of no-

toriety that the disease did exist. Every notice, however, of the calamity was carefully kept out of the newspapers. I asked one of the editors from what motive this
omission arose; his answer was that, the principal profit of a newspaper arising
from advertisements, the merchants, their principal customers, had absolutely forbade the least notice of fever, under a threat that their custom should otherwise
be withdrawn; thus sacrificing to commercial policy the lives of all those who believed from the silence of the public papers that no danger might come to the city.
From the beginning of August to the 19th of September the deaths increased from
10 to 12 a day to 46. . . . But no exact register is anywhere kept of deaths and
burials."

About a century later, when the bubonic plague reached San Francisco, the big-
business advertisers of that city asked the newspapers not to publish the fact. There
was a midnight conference of editors, publishers and business men. With the exception of the Hearst representative all agreed to suppress all mention of the plague.
Government experts announced it was spreading and causing death. The newspapers attacked the government experts and did everything to hamper their work.
The quarantine was made ineffective. The plague lasted until 1911, ten years. Lives
were lost, millions of dollars were lost. "In this case," says Will Irwin, "no one
directly threatened the withdrawal of advertising; the fact that the financial powers,
including department stores, were strongly on one side was enough for publishers
and managing editors trained in the modern commercial school."

Then in 1933 there was an epidemic of amoebic dysentery in Chicago. It was
the height of the World's Fair season and not a word appeared in the press. The
newspapers, accused later of suppressing the news, laid the blame on the Department of Health.

In March, 1934, the scandal at last was aired. The Chicago Medical Society
adopted a committee report censuring Dr. Herman N. Bundesen, the health commissioner. In reply he showed that on August 16, 1933, he traced two cases of
amoebic dysentery to the Congress Hotel and discovered fifteen clinical cases
among three hundred and sixty-four persons who handled food. In October he
submitted a report to the American Public Health Association convened in near-by
Indianapolis, and the *Indianapolis Times* (Talcott Powell, editor) scooped the country. With the aid of the local Health Department the *Times* traced eight cases which
originated in the Congress Hotel, Chicago. The other Indianapolis newspapers took
up the sensational story. These papers are for sale in Chicago. But not a word in
the Chicago papers. Doctor Bundesen heard of these reports in the Indianapolis
newspapers although no Chicago newspaper did. October nineteenth he made a
new investigation, finding one hundred eighteen additional infections among hotel
workers. In November he sent out sixteen thousand questionnaires to persons who
had been guests in the hotel and by November eighth he received thirty-five replies
indicating infections. He then issued a general warning through the press. The first

item to appear in a Chicago paper was under a three-line head November ninth saying the situation was "entirely under control, and there is no need for any alarm whatsoever." The Fair was to close in three days.

"The wool trust suppresses opinion by the force of its advertisements," said *Collier's,* and quoted from a letter of Wood, Putnam and Wood to *Collier's* agent, Brockholst Mathewson: "It is up to the advertiser, in a way, to decide whether to use *Collier's* or not. . . . I don't want to cancel the American Woolen Company's order. . . . I am very much inclined to say we will run a half page with you in March rather than a quarter page. Mr. [William M.] Wood of the American Woolen Company is particularly sensitive. . . . It would be a great source of gratitude to me if I could learn through you just how far Mr. Mark Sullivan proposes going in this matter. . . ."

The matter was Sullivan's exposure of the influences in Washington on Schedule K of the tariff. "Mark Sullivan," *Collier's* replied editorially, "has achieved a hitherto unaccomplished feat. The city of Washington reeks with society glamour, money prestige, special favors, ignorance of common life, and indifference to the common man. The journalist who can tell the whole truth about congress must be above the lure of gold and the glitter of social favor. He must see the hidden springs and obtain the inside news without paying with his soul. Mark Sullivan's mind is beyond the contagion of wealth or flattery. . . .

"Mr. Wood wishes us to practice the principle of deference to a powerful advertiser. . . . This attempt of the wool manufacturers to prevent the press from telling the truth about a necessity of daily life, affecting the struggles and the happiness of the poorest citizen, is a wide and calculated policy with especial bearing on the congress soon in session. . . . The time may come when the Wool Trust, or some other trust, is able to put *Collier's* out of business, but the time has not come yet."

William Winter was "forced to resign" by the *New York Tribune* for unfavorable criticism of plays presented by an advertiser.

Walter Pritchard Eaton, of the *New York Sun,* attacked dirty plays and the theater syndicate withdrew its advertising. Eaton was discharged within six months and the advertising came back.

Contrast the cases of William E. Corey and C. W. Post. Corey, a multimillionaire, wanted to divorce his wife and marry Mabelle Gilman. The press grew sentimental in powerful support of the abused wife.

Post divorced his wife and married his stenographer. Almost no newspaper in the country mentioned the case. Post was not only a large advertiser but the author of full-page paid ads attacking the labor unions. He is also the author of an article boasting of how he wrote letters to newspapers threatening to withdraw his advertising if they continued their attacks on big business, and how the newspapers complied.

In *My Own Story,* Fremont Older says, "The [San Francisco] *Bulletin* was on the payroll of the Southern Pacific Railroad for $125 a month. This was paid not for any definite service, but merely for 'friendliness.' . . .

"Crothers [owner] felt that the influence of the *Bulletin* was worth more than the Southern Pacific had been paying. He insisted that I go to Mills [W. H. Mills, 'who handled the newspapers of California for the railroad company'] and demand $25,000 from the railroad for supporting Gage. . . . the railroad paid Crothers $7,500. . . ."

After Upton Sinclair had exposed the horrors of the Jungle in Chicago, it was testified before the committee on agriculture and forestry of the Senate that "Frank Heney showed that to defeat a bill regulating the packing industry now before Congress, Swift and Company alone are spending a million dollars a month upon newspaper advertising. Heney testified that he has had an examination made of every newspaper in California, and every one has published the full-page advertisements of this firm. Senator Norris testified that he had an examination made in New York state, and has been unable to find a single paper without the Swift advertisements—which, it is pointed out, are not in any way calculated to sell the products of Swift & Company but solely to defeat government regulation of the industry. Armour & Company were paying over two thousand dollars a page to all the farm publications of the country—and this not for advertisements, but for 'special articles'!"

Again, thanks to William Randolph Hearst, the venality of a part of the press was indisputably proved in the publication of the Archbold letters. Planned as a bomb against Hearst's political enemies, the series showed how Standard Oil certificates of deposit and enormous sums of money in the form of subscriptions were sent to editors so that public opinion could be bought.

In mid-summer 1934, the New York regional labor board informs me, a decision was handed down against a bread company. No mention of this fact appeared in a majority of the newspapers.

The *Editor & Publisher* of February 11, 1933, exposed a campaign of the Bond Bread Company to enlist the newspapers in Connecticut. Ten kinds of co-operation were asked in a contest to which advertising was attached: "To receive all entries, to handle judging in the local contests, and to appoint judges; to announce the contest and later to announce the winners, in the news columns; to have the subject of Vitamin D discussed by food experts without special reference to Bond Bread or to the contest; to furnish reprints of advertisements for grocery stores; to have merchandising displays in the newspaper office; to write the grocers announcing the contest; and to offer further support through other individual ideas of the papers."

In reply to a question from *Editor & Publisher*, George R. Gould, director of advertising, *New Haven Register*, said "the same work has been done by many newspapers time and time again. . . . Here in New Haven we want more newspaper advertising and we feel that if we make a success of the contest advertising we will be aiding other newspapers in securing the campaign. . . ."

In July, 1932, Proctor & Gamble, soap manufacturers, canceled their advertising contracts with all newspapers which had used a syndicated article telling women how to make soap cheaply at home.

There are sins of commission and sins of omission. Has the press as a whole ever given any information to the American public about cigarette smoking?

When I was in Berlin I interviewed the greatest authority on that subject, Prof. Dr. Johan Plesch of the University of Berlin. Doctor Plesch is not an anti-nicotine fanatic. He is a smoker. But he has studied nicotine, written an exhaustive book on the subject, and is well acquainted with its dangers. He gave me a list of the deadly poisons contained in tobacco. He did not argue against cigarettes but he laid down this law: inasmuch as all tobaccos contain poisons, the continued use of certain brands of cigarettes is dangerous. We all know that temperance in tobacco as well as in alcohol is to be desired. But to escape danger to one's health the tobacco user must continually change the kind of tobacco he uses, so that the minute amount of poisons the different varieties contain may not affect him. American tobacco contains more of certain kinds of poison than Turkish, and vice versa. One should change kinds, not brands, frequently.

This mail article was sent to my paper which syndicates to more than thirty others, but no clipping ever came back showing that a single one had published it. This, of course, is not documentary proof. But the wager can safely be made that not more than ten per cent of the press of American publishing cigarette advertising will use an article of this kind.

In the midst of the Lucky Strike campaign, "Reach for a Lucky instead of a sweet," my friend Dr. Ben Jablons, authorized by the Medical Association of New York, made a public statement that "excessive use of tobacco to kill the appetite is a double-edged sword, for nicotine poisoning and starvation both leave dire results in their train." This, apparently, was not news.

In 1934 the Camel Company advertised that its cigarettes gave one a "lift." The New York Academy of Medicine, the *Journal* of the American Medical Association and medical meetings discussed this new stunt. Was it news or not? The newspapers thought not. But *Time,* which also runs Camel advertising, thought yes. It quoted doctors saying "the evidence seems to indicate that nicotine is at least one of the toxic factors in cigarette smoking," and "other toxic factors, ammonia, pyridine and pyridine derivatives, cyanides and sulphocyanides, arsenic," a list of poisons which tallies with that Doctor Plesch gave me several years ago.

In Europe the munitions makers frequently place full-page advertisements for guns or shrapnel or submarines in the press. The reader is not expected to buy a submarine. If he is intelligent, he understands that the ad is merely a bribe.

In the United States such advertising is confined to the technical press. It never reaches the lay reader. But this does not mean that the munitions makers of America do not influence the press by advertising. The Du Ponts, for instance, manufacture millions of dollars' worth of peacetime goods, including cloth for dresses, and advertise them extensively.

However, there have been, as there are at present, campaigns to take the profit out of war, to nationalize the war industry. At such times the power of the merchants of death makes itself felt.

On one occasion the Bethlehem Steel Company, faced with a public demand for a nationally owned armor plant, ran a series of full-page advertisements in 3,257 publications, at a cost of millions of dollars. It later issued them in pamphlets which the reader will find in the New York Public Library. Bethlehem was exceedingly pleased with the results its advertising money obtained. It reprints the favorable editorials and news items from the daily and weekly newspapers. Notable, it points out, is the two-column editorial published April 13, 1916, by Editor McLean in his *Washington Post*:

> Where private capital can and will serve the people well at reasonable and fair prices, the *Post* shall at all times oppose the entrance of the government into competition with such private enterprise.
>
> The Bethlehem Steel Company can serve the country well. No one doubts that. . . .
>
> Every patriotic American should be gratified that our country has secured such an offer . . . as proposed by the Bethlehem. . . .

The Bethlehem advertising helped defeat the project for a national armor-plate works. In the advertising the American public was told the company was prepared to make armor "at any price which the Federal Trade Commission may name as fair"; under the signature of Charles M. Schwab himself appeared the statement that "no representative of the Bethlehem Steel Company is seeking or has sought to influence legislation as to the size of naval or military expenditure." Under the signature of President E. R. Grace a letter to Senator Tillman, of the Naval Affairs Committee, stated: "It is said that a government plant should be built 'to take the profit out of war.' Our Company has no inclination to make capital out of the military necessities of the United States. In the event of war or threatened war, all the facilities we have for any purpose are at the disposal of the United States Government upon its own terms. . . ."

So much for advertising. Three congressional investigations have proved that the Bethlehem made hundreds of millions surplus profits out of the United States, that it set prices secretly in combination with its rivals, that it raised prices whenever it could, and that it was one of the three munitions companies which financed Shearer, who boasted of his lobbying in behalf of a large navy in Washington and was "credited" with defeating the Genoa conference to limit naval construction. The part the press played in the Shearer case is notorious.

Does advertising play a part in the political alignment of the press? We need not speak of the Communist Party, which is naturally anathema to about ninety-nine per cent of the American press, nor even the Socialist Party, which is merely tolerated as good-natured Christian political reform; the issue becomes clear when a "regular" party, that is, one which is not pledged to destroy the status quo, begins its campaign. Where is the press when a third party arrives? What does the press do to Progressive, Farmer-Labor Party, Non-partisan League and a hundred state and local independent party candidates?

The answer is that the press almost always helps destroy all but the Republican and Democratic Parties. The reason obviously is that the interests of the publishers of the majority of newspapers of the United States coincide with the interests which control the Republican and Democratic Parties.

Does advertising play a role? In New York, Chicago, Boston, Philadelphia, in fact the major cities of the nation, there is little or no political advertising, certainly not enough to buy up the editorial policy of the newspapers, but throughout the country the smaller press is fed this advertising by the Democratic and Republican machines.

Take the case of the *Pittsburgh Leader*, for example. We had the courage to support La Follette and Theodore Roosevelt. But our main campaign at every election was the office of sheriff. We usually elected our sheriff. In return we got the advertising of Allegheny County which this office controlled, many pages of official notices, paid at high rates.

But more important still: although nominally "Progressive," we maintained our link with the regular Republican organization, just as the other Pittsburgh newspapers which owed money to the Mellon banks remained tied to the Democratic organization. For us it meant that members of the Republican National Committee would visit Editor Moore once in a while to discuss mutually profitable market tips, also that bankers and brokers would let Moore and other owners in on the "ground floor" when new corporations were floated. No one can dispute the fact that it was profitable for the editor and publisher of the *Leader* and other publishers to remain linked to either the Republican or Democratic machine.

A large part of the small press, however, is bought outright. It was not until recently that some facts concerning the 1920 presidential campaign came to light showing how this is done. There was at that time a defunct advertising agency which was bought for a mere four hundred thousand dollars. Its specialty had been advertising in four hundred foreign-language newspapers which had a circulation of about four million and could be counted to influence some eight million voters.

Under the guise of the "Americanization" of these foreign-language paper readers, a committee was formed to purchase this agency. Among the members were

Secretary of the Treasury Mellon, John B. Farrell, William Boyce Thompson who had been vice-president of some of Harry Sinclair's oil companies and chairman of the Republican Finance Committee, John T. Pratt, New York capitalist now deceased, Francis Sisson of the Guaranty Trust Company, Senator T. Coleman du Pont, Samuel Insull, the Armour, Swift and Libby packing companies, the American Smelting & Refining Company, the Continental and Commercial National Bank of Chicago, the First National of Chicago, Don S. Momand, Mrs. Cabot Ward, Frank D. Gardner, and other business interests. Among the contributions received was thirty thousand dollars in Liberty bonds from Mr. Pratt who, it was later testified, had received fifty thousand dollars' worth of the Sinclair Liberty bonds from Will Hays.

This subsidized advertising bureau functioned from 1919, through the successful election of Harding, to 1924, when the equally reliable Coolidge was making the world safe for business. ("Profits and civilization go hand in hand"—Coolidge.) It then ceased operations. But, "where were the fearless Washington correspondents while this was going on?" asks a fearless Washington correspondent, referring to the Liberty-bond scandal and the confession from Mr. Mellon that he knew about the bonds, and once handled them. "Were they too dull and incompetent to obtain this important story, or was it the old familiar business of 'laying off' a secretary of the treasury who has been singularly generous in the matter of making tax refunds to influential newspapers? . . . What will such newspapers say when their editors read the foregoing list, and observe the cream of the 'lily whites' in the business world, including Mr. Mellon himself, deliberately engaged in an enterprise to control the editorial policies of 400 newspapers through their advertising—the ultimate goal being to accomplish the election of Warren G. Harding and the Ohio Gang?"

Is the situation better today than it was a score of years ago when the first pure food bill was passed, or ten years ago, or a hundred years ago? Many persons think so. F. P. A., famous columnist of the *New York Herald Tribune*, thinks so. To prove his contention he reprints the following address which Mrs. Dwight Morrow (Smith '96) made to the college alumnae:

> Our colleges have striven to prepare us for just this task by giving us inner resources of pleasure not dependent upon money or society. They have insisted, all of them, out of their own plain living, whether set down in cities or among the green hills of the country, that good clothes, fur coats, movies, orchids, champagne, fine houses, servants, theaters, fast motors, modern plumbing, gold mesh bags, all the magazines and strawberries in March are not necessary for happiness.

"Everything listed in Mrs. Morrow's speech," comments F. P. A., "is advertised in the issue of the paper that carried it, or is for sale by at least one advertiser. If

Mrs. Morrow, or somebody else, in 1896 had said those words, listing all those salable advertised articles, many newspapers—maybe all of them—would have been afraid to print them. This comment is made for the benefit of those cynical persons, like the *New Yorker*'s Mr. Clifton Fadiman, who think that newspapers are dominated by The Gate, or advertisers. . . . The old editorial disease, advertisophobia, does not exist in these parts. . . . Newspapers are honester and more fearless than they used to be."

To F. P. A. and Mr. Fadiman: On February 26, 1934, at a time material for this book was being collected, and at a time the Tugwell Bill for pure food and drugs was not yet dead, Mrs. Roosevelt, wife of the President, whose views as given at her press conferences are reported in the national press, made the following statement regarding the Tugwell Bill: "I think all goods sold to the public should be labeled as to their grade and quality. Without this the consumer cannot know what he is buying. This is the only way the consumer can intelligently have a hold on the market. I mean authentic government grades and standards."

Was this news? Was it news fit to print? All the newspaper women sent out Mrs. Roosevelt's statement. All of them said later they could find no trace of the statement ever having been printed.

Among those who leaped forward to attack the National Recovery Administration codes because they were producing restrictions on advertising, was Howard Davis, business manager of the *New York Herald Tribune*. The Associated Press sent to its more than one thousand newspapers the following excerpt from his address before the Inland Daily Press Association:

> Great changes are taking place. Whereas a few years ago business men were encouraged to advertise, now by governmental restrictions in many codes and marketing agreements they are being restrained in their efforts to acquaint the people through advertising with what they have to sell. If advertising is destroyed, a free press will be destroyed.

[But this last sentence was too much for the *New York Times*: It ran the item verbatim but cut these splendid words out.]

> Newspaper publishers do not want dishonest advertising, but the time has come when they should demand that no further restriction be placed on honest advertising. Those restrictions already placed should be removed at once.
>
> A tax on advertising was one of the favorite Old World methods of destroying a free press. In fact, the press of England did not become free until advertising taxes on newspapers were removed a half century ago.
>
> The United States is now threatened with such taxes in various States. If

taxes are to follow restrictions on advertising, the free press of this country will be a thing of the past.

Forward to battle the plumed knight of the free press, Elisha Hanson, counsel of the Publishers' Association, counsel of paper and power companies, bitterest enemy of the Newspaper Guild. In his attack on the NRA, he said:

Legislation and codes have had a really restricting effect on advertising.

If you don't believe that statement, take a look at your financial pages of the last year. The Securities Act nearly finished them. And as for codes, more than one hundred—the most important in so far as volume of sales is concerned—contain various restrictions on advertising. More are proposed in amendments now pending before the NRA.

The restrictions already accomplished, whether proper or improper—and many of them are improper—are nothing as compared with some which have been proposed but thus far defeated.

The Department of Agriculture, where Tugwell functions, was accused of making "the greatest drive against advertising of any agency in the history of the government" because it asked an amendment to the old Federal Pure Food Act which Hanson opposed.

The mind of the advertising man is a fearful and wonderful thing. Many ad-writers are merely newspaper men who, having grown tired of talking about "prostitution" at twenty-five dollars a week in the city room, go out for the big money that the profession of advertising pays, and remain immune, cynical and ironic. But that profession, like the oldest trade in the world, has its enthusiasts.

Here, for example, we look into the economic mind of Gilbert T. Hodges, chairman of the Advertising Federation of America. Before the American Home Economics Association convention he mentioned the charge that advertising is eighty-five per cent emotional and only fifteen per cent rational, and replied by saying that an emotional stimulus for buying is the only one that can promote the mass selling necessary for economic recovery in this country. Moreover:

The advertising industry will lead us out of this depression as surely as the automobile industry led us out of the panic of 1907. As for the claim that it is the consumer who pays for advertising, I can only say that advertising pays for itself.

Another leading economist and philosopher is Albert D. Lasker, chairman of the board of Lord & Thomas, advertising agents. To the *New York Times* he writes that there are low standard countries, like Mexico, where "consumers let their habits dictate their purchases," but America is different: "Largely through advertising we have created desire . . . stimulated production by stimulating consumption. It has done it on so vast a scale as to bring about a higher standard of living among the American people than could have possibly existed without advertising under any system of government."

(The date is September 27, 1934: on the front pages of the press is the announcement that one-sixth the population of the United States, twenty million persons, is living on money handed out by the government. There are more than ten million unemployed. But perhaps our economist refers to the standard of living on Park Avenue?)

Mr. Lasker takes the opportunity to discuss freedom of the press also. "No more vicious calumny has ever been put forth," he declares, "than the suspicion that the press, in any major or important way, can be influenced editorially by its advertising patrons." Mr. Lasker is herewith referred to the later chapter dealing with the public utilities.

There are also other types of advertising men. Lee H. Bristol, vice-president of a medicine company, sensing the public challenge to the entire profit system, believes that "advertising will be the focal point of the attack" upon it. And, he continues, "We've got to pledge ourselves to reform. We ourselves have been to blame for violations of good practices in the past. . . . They are a blot on all advertising. . . . What we have to do is clean house."

C. B. Larrabee, managing editor of *Printer's Ink*, one of the first to lead the attack on the Tugwell Bill, reminding the Advertising Federation of America that there has always been a good-natured skepticism toward advertising, adds that "today this skepticism is based on some pretty logical arguments by opponents of advertising. We must also face the rather unpleasant fact that a certain number of our advertisers are not ethically decent enough to conduct their business advertising fairly and honestly. . . . I think it is time to kick the crooks out. . . . John Public is gradually coming to believe in the faulty syllogism 'Crooks advertise. Therefore, all advertisers are crooks.' . . . Eliminate those shabby, shoddy, unethical gentlemen who do more by their unethical tactics to destroy advertising than Jim Rorty and the entire Communist Party."

But the most alarming statement about advertising does not come from Rorty or Communists, but from a colleague of Messrs. Lasker, Hodges and Larrabee. It is dated August, 1933, and refers to our own age, the golden age just ended:

1. Advertising played a deplorable part in the era of greed. It was the willing tool of avaricious business.

2. Advertising supinely submitted to practices and impositions that destroyed the foundations on which the theory of advertising is built.

3. Advertising catered to the violators of all the codes in the decalogue. It co-operated in its own pollution and prostitution. It descended to a racket.

4. Advertising was used for the purpose of establishing false value standards. Time-honored institutions, tried mediums, did not hesitate to lend themselves to schemes that were perhaps within the law, but far beyond the bounds of decency. A revelation of the facts would make our people gasp, inured to rackets as they are.

5. Advertising by its attitude indicated an absolute contempt for public intelligence. In the opinion of advertising, and we can only judge by its methods, tone, approach, and the character of its appeal, we are a nation of suckers and morons.

This outburst may be termed ill-tempered and ill-advised, but certainly not by those who are correctly informed. A revelation of the facts would be helpful and not harmful. Does anyone imagine that the suppression of the facts in the Harriman Bank helped this nation? Does the fact we were all guilty cover up the flagrant violations of public confidence?

The author of the foregoing is a highly placed advertising counselor, Louis Blumenstock by name, who speaks of "the black record of advertising," says his indictment cannot be challenged, who goes beyond his indictment when he mentions "crooked businesses, prosecuted and convicted, still buying space in publications; new crimes being hatched against readers; fraud written on the face of advertisements," and concludes with the statement that "advertising may also be blamed for most of our distress during the past four years." Could any advertising-hating newspaper man go further?

The attitude of the advertiser toward the editor was well expressed by George Frank Lord, when he directed the advertising of the Du Pont interests: to him editors and publishers were merely appendages of the advertising game. Said he:

Time was when publishers were editors who endeavored to mould the opinion of their readers along this line or that. Then the circulation and influence of the publication was in proportion to the popularity of the editor's ideas, but nowadays the *real publishers are the advertisers*, since their financial support of a publication is in most cases all that keeps it alive.

. . . they (advertisers, the *real* publishers) must see to it that the publication renders a real service, that it is constructive, sound and clean, rather than destructive, irrational and immoral.

The claim that the withdrawing of financial support from a destructive (i.e., in the opinion of the advertisers) publication is a mischievous use of advertising patronage to curb the power of the press, seems pure sophistry to me.

If he (the advertiser) stops demanding or using that kind of circulation (circulation gained by publishers who approve policies and measures that advertisers disagree with) it will quickly go out of existence.

Now let us see just what some big advertisers—the medicine men—have done to our free press.

MORRIS ERNST

Advertising
(1946)

Even in the uncertain middle period of the American newspaper, local advertising, or the lack of it, often determined whether or not a paper continued in existence. Ads made subscription prices lower. In time they were thought to be a necessary part of newspaper operation. Paid insertions grew in quantity as the effectiveness of reader response to newspaper advertising was apparent. This expansion made larger newspapers desirable.

Although circulation is important in so far as it permits raising of advertising rates, circulation in itself is carried at a loss. Circulation alone leaves publishers with deficits to be made up by advertising income.

Mr. Lee points out that the advertising of doubtful repute (patent medicines, lotteries and other fakes) was not reformed until after the Civil War. Before that time most of the pioneering was in the development of the copy and mechanics of all advertising. As late as 1912 the A.N.P.A. opposed laws which called for indicating which parts of the paper were paid advertising!

The Civil War, and the great interest engendered in its news, finally pushed paid insertions off the front page.

In the 1870's the invention of the thin stereotype plate guaranteed the advertiser advance knowledge of what his ad would look like, and gave great impetus to the development of advertising agencies which greatly aided in the standardization of advertising practices.

Newspapers were becoming economically stable. There was a growing tendency toward guaranteed circulation figures. Space charges were related to circulation. This movement culminated in 1914 in the Audit Bureau of Circulations, an organization to audit newspaper circulations, subsidized by publishers and advertisers. The American Newspaper Publishers Association in 1893 had already adopted the method of space measurement generally in use today, quoting rates on the basis

From *The First Freedom* (New York: The Macmillan Company, 1946), 95–102.

of cost per agate line (14 agate lines to the column inch). The milline rate is the cost of placing one agate line of advertising in 1,000,000 copies of a newspaper.

Newspaper advertising jumped into the saddle during the years of the development of big business and helped this development greatly by creating the volume demand which made mass production possible. Advertising was especially successful in the growth of the soap industry. One of these early effective ads read, "Do You Bathe?" With the turn of the century, half-tones and the development of the Ben Day engraving process made newspaper ads more attractive. Typesetting machines and the new large fast presses created larger newspapers and enabled more of them to be printed.

The increase in volume of advertising in the last years of the nineteenth century necessitated an increase in the percentage of space given to these paid insertions. The percentage of advertising space rose from about 25 in the 1870's to 30 or 35 at the end of the century. At the time of World War I there was a well established 50–50 ratio of paid advertising and editorial matter, but when the war made it necessary to economize on newsprint, news rather than advertisement was reduced in most papers.

The 1929 boom brought another peak in the advertising percentage but this dropped again in the early thirties. Thus in 1931 papers which in 1929 had given 65 to 75 per cent of their space to ads came down to about 50 per cent. Papers which formerly had about half their space taken up with advertising dropped to 30 or 35 per cent. Six New York papers in the summer of 1944 show an average of about 45 per cent advertising space.

Revenue from advertising over a period of years has been roughly two thirds of the entire revenue of the newspaper. The proportion of revenue from advertising to revenue from subscriptions and sales varies with individual papers, but in some cases the advertising revenue has gone more than 75 per cent. The following figures are from a publication of the Bureau of Advertising of the American Newspaper Publishers Association, *The Newspaper as an Advertising Medium*:

Year	Revenue from Subscriptions and Sales	Revenue from Advertising	Per cent of Revenue from Advertising
1909	$84,438,702	$148,554,392	65
1931	261,568,832	624,953,969	70
1933	239,147,402	428,672,688	65
1937	287,508,458	574,180,206	66

The Inland Press Association some years ago made a three-year survey recommending a newspaper budget of the following proportions:

Income	Per Cent	Expenses	Per Cent
Advertising	70	Editorial	15
Circulation	29	Circulation	11
Misc.	1	Advertising	7
	——	Paper and ink	12
	100	Other items	24
		Administration	19
			——
			88
		Profit	12
			——
			100

The trend of percentage of advertising revenue to total income for all newspapers *and* magazines is in keeping with such recommendation—1879, 44 per cent; 1904, 56 per cent; 1929, 71 per cent.

In 1929 the *average newspaper* looked to ads for 74 per cent of the income. Although the advertising income proportion declined between 1929 and 1939, it rose again during the war. We are still far from the great dream of Dana and Scripps of nearly half a century ago of a press primarily dependent on reader income. I am sure the answer is not ad-less papers. It lies in other directions.

The Bureau of Advertising gives the following breakdown of newspaper advertising figures for 1939: Retail advertising, $310,000,000; classified, $90,000,000; national, $152,000,000; total, $552,000,000. Thus in 1939, before the war with its mammoth "institutional" advertising campaigns by the national advertisers, which were invited by tax laws and encouraged by paper-rationing regulations, more than one quarter of the total advertising revenue received by newspaper publishers was from national as opposed to local advertisers. This is significant because it means that to that extent the newspaper is not being supported in any direct and traceable way by the local economy. Moreover, the mood and approach of the national advertising copy is created in a few offices located in a few of our big cities. The cost is buried in products sold in many other communities as well. Under this system it is impossible to determine how many papers the local economy could legitimately support. The final decision often rests with advertising agencies located a thousand miles away from the newspaper area of circulation.

In 1939, according to the Bureau of Advertising, there were only 646 national advertisers spending more than $25,000 each in our newspapers. That is a very small proportion of the total number of national business concerns which are potential advertisers. But the real shock is found in the concentration breakdown of this figure. Six per cent of these 646 advertisers, or thirty-nine concerns, account for nearly one half of the total expenditure for national advertising in the newspapers of the nation. In other words, in this field, as in radio, a handful of advertisers holds a dominant position in the total advertising in the press, which advertising income is the essential and often the vital income of daily papers.

Breaking down the expenditure for national advertising in 1939 by media, the newspapers received 32 per cent; magazines, 30 per cent, and radio, 26 per cent. The rest was outdoor, farm journals, etc. Newspapers have put up a stiff fight against competing media—billboards, car cards, magazines and finally radio. In many areas newspapers procured legislation banning the distribution from house to house of circulars printed by local merchants or mail-order houses. For a time the press associations put an embargo on their reports being sent over the air by radio to the people of the nation. This shabby attempt to restrain the market was ended only because the three press associations did not play fair with each other. The final weapon of the press against radio seems to be the old one of moving in and taking over—newspapers now have affiliations with or own one third of the total number of radio stations.

Dr. L. D. H. Weld, Director of Research for McCann-Erickson, Inc., in an article in *Printer's Ink*, has charted the relative changes of major media on the basis of advertising expenditures. In 1929, infant radio received only 1.6 per cent of the total advertising expenditure. This climbed to 5.2 per cent in 1933 and 7.7 per cent in 1937. By 1943 it reached 15.3 per cent, almost exactly half the newspaper advertising expenditure of that year. In the ten years between 1933 and 1943 the volume of radio advertising has tripled. Part of this radio gain has been the newspapers' loss. Magazines have about held their own.

The total advertising volume for all media in 1939, according to Dr. Weld, was $1,780,000,000. Since the war the total advertising bill of the nation has risen to $3,000,000,000, according to government figures, 67 per cent of which cost was borne by the government through tax deductions. War advertising, and its deductibility as allowed by the Treasury, has given a tremendous tax advantage to the large national industries, most of which are in the high-tax brackets. Thus, if X Company, which was in the 80 per cent tax bracket and had no product for sale during the war, wished to keep its name before the public, it ran advertising saying "Buy War Bonds Now And Buy Our Super-Swizzles After the War." The cost of such an ad was largely paid by the government in the form of a tax subsidy amounting to eighty cents on each dollar of advertising cost. This even though the advertising was political or inflationary. Thus X Company had the advertising spree of its life (for twenty cents on the dollar) in the name of patriotism.

There was probably no manpower wastage during the war as inexcusable as the waste of manpower in connection with "good will" institutional advertising. In forests, logging camps, manufacture and transportation we have expended enough man hours on turning trees into advertisements to have made unnecessary the draft of any married man for the armed services. In England percentage limits, 45 per cent and 55 per cent respectively, were put on advertising in newspapers and magazines. There was no loss of freedom to the press. Here, failing to adopt such pattern of paper control, we played farther into the hands of the large newspapers and the large advertisers in large cities.

There are two kinds of rates charged for advertising—the flat and the open rate. The flat rate, customarily charged national advertisers, is comparable to the luxury accommodations on a railroad as opposed to the freight charges. It is generally standard regardless of the amount of space used and runs to 75 per cent more than an open rate for the same ad. The only discount given to advertisements placed on a flat-rate basis is the 15 per cent allowed the agency. The open rate is a decreasing scale based on the volume of space used or the frequency of insertion. This is used for local advertising, especially that of retail stores, where insertions are frequent. The newspaper expects the national advertiser to pay more because his advertising is spasmodic, and this is the really profitable advertising. Where there is only one paper in a city, rates naturally do not decline as they might under the influence of competition.

A schedule of open rates for New York metropolitan papers during 1944, shows the degree of variation and the great advantage to the large advertiser. For example, the *New York Times* open rate of $1.10 (gross) drops to 43 cents for the purchaser of 250,000 lines. There is a comparable reduction for size in the rates of each of the papers listed. If the Robinson-Patman Act principle were applied to newspaper advertising, there could be no difference in price due exclusively to wholesale quantity or national versus local merchants. This would mean the application of a one-rate principle to all newspaper advertising save only for actual differences in cost of handling a big as compared to a small advertisement or a single insertion as compared to repeated insertions.

The advertising middlemen—the agencies and the publishers' representatives—fulfill a valuable and necessary function, that of placing ads in the papers for advertisers and handling all the attendant details, maintaining lists of papers for various types of campaigns and, in the case of publishers' representatives, soliciting advertising. However, in their selection and repetition of choice of papers for lists to receive ad campaigns, they tend to solidify and strengthen existing papers at the expense of small or new papers. There is also the indisputable fact that an advertiser prefers a large paper because of its circulation even if it costs more per reader. This operates further to the disadvantage of the smaller paper. Moreover, big companies have little understanding of or interest in small companies.

The advertisers, more particularly the agencies, have long encouraged the development of the one-paper town. In a fairly small community two papers often have overlapping circulations and it is obviously to the temporary business advantage of the advertiser not to have to pay two separate rates for reaching readers which in some cases are an identical group. There is a weird, ironic effect of this short-sighted policy. Advertisers encouraged the merger or consolidation of newspapers in many areas. They often forced the combination of newspapers into one ownership, only to find that the "combination" owner imposed "forced" duplicate advertising on them. After the purchase of a competing paper the new owner did not lower the advertising rates, or if he did there was slight benefit to the advertiser since the new owner invariably put through a policy of forced or compulsory block buying of advertising space. Thus advertisers desiring to buy space in only one paper had to buy it also in an additional paper. Thus a group of advertisers who have been prosecuted as in New York City for combining in a united front against the increased rates of a newspaper find themselves impotent in dealing with a combination of papers in a single ownership. Documentation of this subject matter is found in the Nixon article previously referred to in connection with the evaporation of the press.

There is another kind of advertising practice—the fault of the publishers alone—which kills off many small papers. If a more or less small paper with a low rate succeeded in getting a full-page advertisement from a local merchant, the competing, more successful paper refused to take an ad for the same merchant for less space. This kind of economic retaliation by the large papers represents a serious hold over the businessmen and is certainly a keen weapon against existing or future newspaper competition.

There is no area of our economy that needs an airing more than advertising—its impacts on our daily lives and its increasing indirect control over our mores. The large advertising agencies, realizing the power of boiler plating, have proposed to continue after the war their present practices of inserting as paid ads virtually identical copy in hundreds of dailies—the copy to deal with peacetime trends and problems instead of bond drives and the like. As one leading advertising agent said, "You can't expect 1,000 editors to comply with our request to write editorials on the same day with the same slant on a single selected national problem. Advertising can, however, carry on with an identic imprint to influence the thinking of the nation." Such a move would put thinking on a national belt and, if carried into action, will result in further abdication of the publishers and editors of the land.

GLORIA STEINEM

Sex, Lies & Advertising
(1990)

About three years ago, as *glasnost* was beginning and *Ms.* seemed to be ending, I was invited to a press lunch for a Soviet official. He entertained us with anecdotes about new problems of democracy in his country. Local Communist leaders were being criticized in their media for the first time, he explained, and they were angry.

"So I'll have to ask my American friends," he finished pointedly, "how more *subtly* to control the press." In the silence that followed, I said, "Advertising."

The reporters laughed, but later, one of them took me aside: How *dare* I suggest that freedom of the press was limited? How dare I imply that his newsweekly could be influenced by ads?

I explained that I was thinking of advertising's media-wide influence on most of what we read. Even newsmagazines use "soft" cover stories to sell ads, confuse readers with "advertorials," and occasionally self-censor on subjects known to be a problem with big advertisers.

But, I also explained, I was thinking especially of women's magazines. There, it isn't just a little content that's devoted to attracting ads, it's almost all of it. That's why advertisers—not readers—have always been the problem for *Ms.* As the only women's magazine that didn't supply what the ad world euphemistically describes as "supportive editorial atmosphere" or "complementary copy" (for instance, articles that praise food/fashion/beauty subjects to "support" and "complement" food/fashion/beauty ads), *Ms.* could never attract enough advertising to break even.

"Oh, *women's* magazines," the journalist said with contempt. "Everybody knows they're catalogs—but who cares? They have nothing to do with journalism."

I can't tell you how many times I've had this argument in 25 years of working for many kinds of publications. Except as moneymaking machines—"cash cows" as they are so elegantly called in the trade—women's magazines are rarely taken seriously. Though changes being made by women have been called more far-

From *Ms.*, July/August 1990, 18–28.

reaching than the industrial revolution—and though many editors try hard to reflect some of them in the few pages left to them after all the ad-related subjects have been covered—the magazines serving the female half of this country are still far below the journalistic and ethical standards of news and general interest publications. Most depressing of all, this doesn't even rate an exposé.

If *Time* and *Newsweek* had to lavish praise on cars in general and credit General Motors in particular to get GM ads, there would be a scandal—maybe a criminal investigation. When women's magazines from *Seventeen* to *Lear's* praise beauty products in general and credit Revlon in particular to get ads, it's just business as usual.

I.

When *Ms.* began, we didn't consider *not* taking ads. The most important reason was keeping the price of a feminist magazine low enough for most women to afford. But the second and almost equal reason was providing a forum where women and advertisers could talk to each other and improve advertising itself. After all, it was (and still is) as potent a source of information in this country as news or TV and movie dramas.

We decided to proceed in two stages. First, we would convince makers of "people products" used by both men and women but advertised mostly to men—cars, credit cards, insurance, sound equipment, financial services, and the like—that their ads should be placed in a women's magazine. Since they were accustomed to the division between editorial and advertising in news and general interest magazines, this would allow our editorial content to be free and diverse. Second, we would add the best ads for whatever traditional "women's products" (clothes, shampoo, fragrance, food, and so on) that surveys showed *Ms.* readers used. But we would ask them to come in *without* the usual quid pro quo of "complementary copy."

We knew the second step might be harder. Food advertisers have always demanded that women's magazines publish recipes and articles on entertaining (preferably ones that name their products) in return for their ads; clothing advertisers expect to be surrounded by fashion spreads (especially ones that credit their designers); and shampoo, fragrance, and beauty products in general usually insist on positive editorial coverage of beauty subjects, plus photo credits besides. That's why women's magazines look the way they do. But if we could break this link between ads and editorial content, then we wanted good ads for "women's products," too.

By playing their part in this unprecedented mix of *all* the things our readers need and use, advertisers also would be rewarded: ads for products like cars and mutual funds would find a new growth market; the best ads for women's products would no longer be lost in oceans of ads for the same category; and both would have access to a laboratory of smart and caring readers whose response would help create effective ads for other media as well.

I thought then that our main problem would be the imagery in ads themselves. Carmakers were still draping blondes in evening gowns over the hoods like ornaments. Authority figures were almost always male, even in ads for products that only women used. Sadistic, he-man campaigns even won industry praise. (For instance, *Advertising Age* had hailed the infamous Silva Thin cigarette theme, "How to Get a Woman's Attention: Ignore Her," as "brilliant.") Even in medical journals, tranquilizer ads showed depressed housewives standing beside piles of dirty dishes and promised to get them back to work.

Obviously, *Ms.* would have to avoid such ads and seek out the best ones—but this didn't seem impossible. *The New Yorker* had been selecting ads for aesthetic reasons for years, a practice that only seemed to make advertisers more eager to be in its pages. *Ebony* and *Essence* were asking for ads with positive black images, and though their struggle was hard, they weren't being called unreasonable.

Clearly, what *Ms.* needed was a very special publisher and ad sales staff. I could think of only one woman with experience on the business side of magazines—Patricia Carbine, who recently had become a vice president of *McCall's* as well as its editor in chief—and the reason I knew her name was a good omen. She had been managing editor at *Look* (really *the* editor, but its owner refused to put a female name at the top of his masthead) when I was writing a column there. After I did an early interview with Cesar Chavez, then just emerging as a leader of migrant labor, and the publisher turned it down because he was worried about ads from Sunkist, Pat was the one who intervened. As I learned later, she had told the publisher she would resign if the interview wasn't published. Mainly because *Look* couldn't afford to lose Pat, it *was* published (and the ads from Sunkist never arrived).

Though I barely knew this woman, she had done two things I always remembered: put her job on the line in a way that editors often talk about but rarely do, and been so loyal to her colleagues that she never told me or anyone outside *Look* that she had done so.

Fortunately, Pat did agree to leave *McCall's* and take a huge cut in salary to become publisher of *Ms.* She became responsible for training and inspiring generations of young women who joined the *Ms.* ad sales force, many of whom went on to become "firsts" at the top of publishing. When *Ms.* first started, however, there were so few women with experience selling space that Pat and I made the rounds of ad agencies ourselves. Later, the fact that *Ms.* was asking companies to do business in a different way meant our saleswomen had to make many times the usual number of calls—first to convince agencies and then client companies besides—and to present endless amounts of research. I was often asked to do a final ad presentation, or see some higher decision-maker, or speak to women employees so executives could see the interest of women they worked with. That's why I spent more time persuading advertisers than editing or writing for *Ms.* and why I ended up with an unsentimental education in the seamy underside of publishing that few writers see (and even fewer magazines can publish).

Let me take you with us through some experiences, just as they happened:

• Cheered on by early support from Volkswagen and one or two other car companies, we scrape together time and money to put on a major reception in Detroit. We know U.S. carmakers firmly believe that women choose the upholstery, not the car, but we are armed with statistics and reader mail to prove the contrary: a car is an important purchase for women, one that symbolizes mobility and freedom.

But almost nobody comes. We are left with many pounds of shrimp on the table, and quite a lot of egg on our face. We blame ourselves for not guessing that there would be a baseball pennant play-off on the same day, but executives go out of their way to explain they wouldn't have come anyway. Thus begins ten years of knocking on hostile doors, presenting endless documentation, and hiring a full-time saleswoman in Detroit; all necessary before *Ms.* gets any real results.

This long saga has a semihappy ending: foreign and, later, domestic carmakers eventually provided *Ms.* with enough advertising to make cars one of our top sources of ad revenue. Slowly, Detroit began to take the women's market seriously enough to put car ads in other women's magazines, too, thus freeing a few pages from the hothouse of fashion-beauty-food ads.

But long after figures showed a third, even a half, of many car models being bought by women, U.S. makers continued to be uncomfortable addressing women. Unlike foreign carmakers, Detroit never quite learned the secret of creating intelligent ads that exclude no one, and then placing them in women's magazines to overcome past exclusion. (*Ms.* readers were so grateful for a routine Honda ad featuring rack and pinion steering, for instance, that they sent fan mail.) Even now, Detroit continues to ask, "Should we make special ads for women?" Perhaps that's why some foreign cars still have a disproportionate share of the U.S. women's market.

• In the *Ms.* Gazette, we do a brief report on a congressional hearing into chemicals used in hair dyes that are absorbed through the skin and may be carcinogenic. Newspapers report this too, but Clairol, a Bristol-Myers subsidiary that makes dozens of products—a few of which have just begun to advertise in *Ms.*—is outraged. Not at newspapers or newsmagazines, just at us. It's bad enough that *Ms.* is the only women's magazine refusing to provide the usual "complementary" articles and beauty photos, but to criticize one of their categories—*that* is going too far.

We offer to publish a letter from Clairol telling its side of the story. In an excess of solicitousness, we even put this letter in the Gazette, not in Letters to the Editors

You may be surprised to learn, as I was, that in the ratio of advertising to editorial pages in women's magazines, the ads average only about 5 percent more than in *Time, Newsweek,* and *U.S. News.* That nothing-to-read feeling comes from editorial pages devoted to "complementary copy"; to text or photos that praise advertised categories, instruct in their use, or generally act as extensions of ads.

To find out what we're getting when we actually pay money for these catalogs, I picked random issues, counted the number of pages (even including letters to the editors, horoscopes, and so forth) that are not ads and/or copy complementary to ads, and then compared that number to the total pages. For instance:

Glamour, April 1990
339 pages total;
65 non-ad or ad-related

Vogue, May 1990
319 pages total;
38 non-ad or ad-related

Redbook, April 1990
173 pages total;
44 non-ad or ad-related

Family Circle, March 13, 1990
180 pages total;
33 non-ad or ad-related

Elle, May 1990
326 pages total;
39 non-ad or ad-related

Lear's, November 1989
173 pages total;
65 non-ad or ad-related

where it belongs. Nonetheless—and in spite of surveys that show *Ms.* readers are active women who use more of almost everything Clairol makes than do the readers of any other women's magazine—*Ms.* gets almost none of these ads for the rest of its natural life.

Meanwhile, Clairol changes its hair coloring formula, apparently in response to the hearings we reported.

• Our saleswomen set out early to attract ads for consumer electronics: sound equipment, calculators, computers, VCRs, and the like. We know that our readers are determined to be included in the technological revolution. We know from reader surveys that *Ms.* readers are buying this stuff in numbers as high as those of magazines like *Playboy;* or "men 18 to 34," the prime targets of the consumer electronics industry. Moreover, unlike traditional women's products that our readers buy but don't need to read articles about, these are subjects they want covered in our pages. There actually *is* a supportive editorial atmosphere.

"But women don't understand technology," say executives at the end of ad presentations. "Maybe not," we respond, "but neither do men—and we all buy it."

"If women *do* buy it," say the decision-makers, "they're asking their husbands and boyfriends what to buy first." We produce letters from *Ms.* readers saying how turned off they are when salesmen say things like "Let me know when your husband can come in."

After several years of this, we get a few ads for compact sound systems. Some of them come from JVC, whose vice president, Harry Elias, is trying to convince his Japanese bosses that there is something called a women's market. At his invitation, I find myself speaking at huge trade shows in Chicago and Las Vegas, trying to persuade JVC dealers that showrooms don't have to be locker rooms where women are made to feel unwelcome. But as it turns out, the shows themselves are part of the problem. In Las Vegas, the only women around the technology displays are seminude models serving champagne. In Chicago, the big attraction is Marilyn Chambers, who followed Linda Lovelace of *Deep Throat* fame as Chuck Traynor's captive and/or employee. VCRs are being demonstrated with her porn videos.

In the end, we get ads for a car stereo now and then, but no VCRs; some IBM personal computers, but no Apple or Japanese ones. We notice that office magazines like *Working Woman* and *Savvy* don't benefit as much as they should from office equipment ads either. In the electronics world, women and technology seem mutually exclusive. It remains a decade behind even Detroit.

• Because we get letters from little girls who love toy trains, and who ask our help in changing ads and box-top photos that feature little boys only, we try to get toy-train ads from Lionel. It turns out that Lionel executives *have* been concerned about little girls. They made a pink train, and were surprised when it didn't sell.

Lionel bows to consumer pressure with a photograph of a boy *and* a girl—but only on some of their boxes. They fear that, if trains are associated with girls, they will be devalued in the minds of boys. Needless to say, *Ms.* gets no train ads, and little girls remain a mostly unexplored market. By 1986, Lionel is put up for sale.

But for different reasons, we haven't had much luck with other kinds of toys either. In spite of many articles on child-rearing; an annual listing of nonsexist, multi-racial toys by Letty Cottin Pogrebin; Stories for Free Children, a regular feature also edited by Letty; and other prizewinning features for or about children, we get virtually no toy ads. Generations of *Ms.* saleswomen explain to toy manufacturers that a larger proportion of *Ms.* readers have preschool children than do the readers of other women's magazines, but this industry can't believe feminists have or care about children.

• When *Ms.* begins, the staff decides not to accept ads for feminine hygiene sprays or cigarettes: they are damaging and carry no appropriate health warnings. Though we don't think we should tell our readers what to do, we do think we should provide facts so they can decide for themselves. Since the antismoking lobby has been pressing for health warnings on cigarette ads, we decide to take them only as they comply.

Philip Morris is among the first to do so. One of its brands, Virginia Slims, is also sponsoring women's tennis and the first national polls of women's opinions. On the other hand, the Virginia Slims theme, "You've come a long way, baby," has more than a "baby" problem. It makes smoking a symbol of progress for women.

We explain to Philip Morris that this slogan won't do well in our pages, but they are convinced its success with some women means it will work with *all* women. Finally, we agree to publish an ad for a Virginia Slims calendar as a test. The letters from readers are critical—and smart. For instance: Would you show a black man picking cotton, the same man in a Cardin suit, and symbolize the antislavery and civil rights movements by smoking? Of course not. But instead of honoring the test results, the Philip Morris people seem angry to be proven wrong. They take away ads for *all* their many brands.

This costs *Ms.* about $250,000 the first year. After five years, we can no longer keep track. Occasionally, a new set of executives listens to *Ms.* saleswomen, but because we won't take Virginia Slims, not one Philip Morris product returns to our pages for the next 16 years.

Gradually, we also realize our naiveté in thinking we *could* decide against taking cigarette ads. They became a disproportionate support of magazines the moment they were banned on television, and few magazines could compete and survive without them; certainly not *Ms.*, which lacks so many other categories. By the time statistics in the 1980s showed that women's rate of lung cancer was approaching men's, the necessity of taking cigarette ads has become a kind of prison.

• General Mills, Pillsbury, Carnation, DelMonte, Dole, Kraft, Stouffer, Hormel, Nabisco: you name the food giant, we try it. But no matter how desirable the *Ms.* readership, our lack of recipes is lethal.

We explain to them that placing food ads *only* next to recipes associates food with work. For many women, it is a negative that works *against* the ads. Why not place food ads in diverse media without recipes (thus reaching more men, who are now a third of the shoppers in supermarkets anyway), and leave the recipes to specialty magazines like *Gourmet* (a third of whose readers are also men)?

These arguments elicit interest, but except for an occasional ad for a convenience food, instant coffee, diet drinks, yogurt, or such extras as avocados and almonds, this mainstay of the publishing industry stays closed to us. Period.

• Traditionally, wines and liquors didn't advertise to women: men were thought to make the brand decisions, even if women did the buying. But after endless presentations, we begin to make a dent in this category. Thanks to the unconventional Michel Roux of Carillon Importers (distributors of Grand Marnier, Absolut Vodka, and others), who assumes that food and drink have no gender, some ads are leaving their men's club.

Beermakers are still selling masculinity. It takes *Ms.* fully eight years to get its first beer ad (Michelob). In general, however, liquor ads are less stereotyped in their imagery—and far less controlling of the editorial content around them—than are women's products. But given the underrepresentation of other categories, these very facts tend to create a disproportionate number of alcohol ads in the pages of *Ms.* This in turn dismays readers worried about women and alcoholism.

• We hear in 1980 that women in the Soviet Union have been producing feminist *samizdat* (underground, self-published books) and circulating them throughout the country. As punishment, four of the leaders have been exiled. Though we are operating on our usual shoestring, we solicit individual contributions to send Robin Morgan to interview these women in Vienna.

The result is an exclusive cover story that includes the first news of a populist peace movement against the Afghanistan occupation, a prediction of *glasnost* to come, and a grass-roots, intimate view of Soviet women's lives. From the popular press to women's studies courses, the response is great. The story wins a Front Page award.

Nonetheless, this journalistic coup undoes years of efforts to get an ad schedule from Revlon. Why? Because the Soviet women on our cover *are not wearing makeup*.

• Four years of research and presentations go into convincing airlines that women now make travel choices and business trips. United, the first airline to advertise in *Ms.,* is so impressed with the response from our readers that one of its executives appears in a film for our ad presentations. As usual, good ads get great results.

But we have problems unrelated to such results. For instance: because American Airlines flight attendants include among their labor demands the stipulation that they could choose to have their last names preceded by "Ms." on their name tags—in a long-delayed revolt against the standard, "I am your pilot, Captain Rothgart, and this is your flight attendant, Cindy Sue"—American officials seem to hold the magazine responsible. We get no ads.

There is still a different problem at Eastern. A vice president cancels subscriptions for thousands of copies on Eastern flights. Why? Because he is offended by ads for lesbian poetry journals in the *Ms.* Classified. A "family airline," as he explains to me coldly on the phone, has to "draw the line somewhere."

It's obvious that *Ms.* can't exclude lesbians and serve women. We've been trying to make that point ever since our first issue included an article by and about lesbians, and both Suzanne Levine, our managing editor, and I were lectured by such heavy hitters as Ed Kosner, then editor of *Newsweek* (and now of *New York Magazine*), who insisted that *Ms.* should "position" itself *against* lesbians. But our advertisers have paid to reach a guaranteed number of readers, and soliciting new subscriptions to compensate for Eastern would cost $150,000, plus rebating money in the meantime.

Like almost everything ad-related, this presents an elaborate organizing problem. After days of searching for sympathetic members of the Eastern board, Frank Thomas, president of the Ford Foundation, kindly offers to call Roswell Gilpatrick, a director of Eastern. I talk with Mr. Gilpatrick, who calls Frank Borman, then the president of Eastern. Frank Borman calls me to say that his airline is not in the business of censoring magazines: *Ms.* will be returned to Eastern flights.

• Women's access to insurance and credit is vital, but with the exception of Equitable and a few other ad pioneers, such financial services address men. For almost a decade after the Equal Credit Opportunity Act passes in 1974, we try to convince American Express that women are a growth market—but nothing works.

Finally, a former professor of Russian named Jerry Welsh becomes head of marketing. He assumes that women should be cardholders, and persuades his colleagues to feature women in a campaign. Thanks to this 1980s series, the growth rate for female cardholders surpasses that for men.

For this article, I asked Jerry Welsh if he would explain why American Express waited so long. "Sure," he said, "they were afraid of having a 'pink' card."

• Women of color read *Ms.* in disproportionate numbers. This is a source of pride to *Ms.* staffers, who are also more racially representative than the editors of other women's magazines. But this reality is obscured by ads filled with enough white women to make a reader snowblind.

Pat Carbine remembers mostly "astonishment" when she requested African American, Hispanic, Asian, and other diverse images. Marcia Ann Gillespie, a *Ms.* editor who was previously the editor in chief of *Essence,* witnesses ad bias a second time: having tried for *Essence* to get white advertisers to use black images (Revlon did so eventually, but L'Oréal, Lauder, Chanel, and other companies never did), she sees similar problems getting integrated ads for an integrated magazine. Indeed, the ad world often creates black and Hispanic ads only for black and Hispanic media. In an exact parallel of the fear that marketing a product to women will endanger its appeal to men, the response is usually, "But your [white] readers won't identify."

In fact, those we are able to get—for instance, a Max Factor ad made for *Essence* that Linda Wachner gives us after she becomes president—are praised by white readers, too. But there are pathetically few such images.

• By the end of 1986, production and mailing costs have risen astronomically, ad income is flat, and competition for ads is stiffer than ever. The 60/40 preponderance of edit over ads that we promised to readers becomes 50/50; children's stories, most poetry, and some fiction are casualties of less space; in order to get variety into limited pages, the length (and sometimes the depth) of articles suffers; and, though we do refuse most of the ads that would look like a parody in our pages, we get so worn down that some slip through. Still, readers perform miracles. Though we haven't been able to afford a subscription mailing in two years, they maintain our guaranteed circulation of 450,000.

Nonetheless, media reports on *Ms.* often insist that our unprofitability must be due to reader disinterest. The myth that advertisers simply follow readers is very strong. Not one reporter notes that other comparable magazines our size (say, *Vanity Fair* or *The Atlantic*) have been losing more money in one year than *Ms.* has lost in 16 years. No matter how much never-to-be-recovered cash is poured into starting a magazine or keeping one going, appearances seem to be all that matter. (Which is why we haven't been able to explain our fragile state in public. Nothing causes ad-flight like the smell of nonsuccess.)

My healthy response is anger. My not-so-healthy response is constant worry. Also an obsession with finding one more rescue. There is hardly a night when I don't wake up with sweaty palms and pounding heart, scared that we won't be able to pay the printer or the post office; scared most of all that closing our doors will hurt the women's movement.

Out of chutzpah and desperation, I arrange a lunch with Leonard Lauder, president of Estée Lauder. With the exception of Clinique (the brainchild of Carol Phillips), none of Lauder's hundreds of products has been advertised in *Ms.* A year's schedule of ads for just three or four of them could save us. Indeed, as the scion of a family-owned company whose ad practices are followed by the beauty industry, he is one of the few men who could liberate many pages in all women's magazines just by changing his mind about "complementary copy."

Over a lunch that costs more than we can pay for some articles, I explain the need for his leadership. I also lay out the record of *Ms.:* more literary and journalistic prizes won, more new issues introduced into the mainstream, new writers discovered, and impact on society than any other magazine; more articles that became books, stories that became movies, ideas that became television series, and newly advertised products that became profitable; and, most important for him, a place for his ads to reach women who aren't reachable through any other women's magazine. Indeed, if there is one constant characteristic of the ever-changing *Ms.* readership, it is their impact as leaders. Whether it's waiting until later to have first babies, or pioneering PABA as sun protection in cosmetics, *whatever* they are doing today, a third to a half of American women will be doing three to five years from now. It's never failed.

But, he says, *Ms.* readers are not *our* women. They're not interested in things like fragrance and blush-on. If they were, *Ms.* would write articles about them.

On the contrary, I explain, surveys show they are more likely to buy such things than the readers of, say, *Cosmopolitan* or *Vogue*. They're good customers because they're out in the world enough to need several sets of everything: home, work, purse, travel, gym, and so on. They just don't need to read articles about these things. Would he ask a men's magazine to publish monthly columns on how to shave before he advertised Aramis products (his line for men)?

He concedes that beauty features are often concocted more for advertisers than readers. But *Ms.* isn't appropriate for his ads anyway, he explains. Why? Because Estée Lauder is selling "a kept-woman mentality."

I can't quite believe this. Sixty percent of the users of his products are salaried, and generally resemble *Ms.* readers. Besides, his company has the appeal of having been started by a creative and hardworking woman, his mother, Estée Lauder.

That doesn't matter, he says. He knows his customers, and they would *like* to be kept women. That's why he will never advertise in *Ms.*

In November 1987, by vote of the *Ms.* Foundation for Education and Communication (*Ms.*'s owner and publisher, the media subsidiary of the *Ms.* Foundation for Women), *Ms.* was sold to a company whose officers, Australian feminists Sandra Yates and Anne Summers, raised the investment money in their country that *Ms.* couldn't find in its own. They also started *Sassy* for teenage women.

In their two-year tenure, circulation was raised to 550,000 by investment in circulation mailings, and, to the dismay of some readers, editorial features on clothes and new products made a more traditional bid for ads. Nonetheless, ad pages fell below previous levels. In addition, *Sassy*, whose fresh voice and sexual frankness were an unprecedented success with young readers, was targeted by two mothers from Indiana who began, as one of them put it, "calling every Christian organization I could think of." In response to this controversy, several crucial advertisers pulled out.

Such links between ads and editorial content was a problem in Australia, too, but to a lesser degree. "Our readers pay two times more for their magazines," Anne explained, "so advertisers have less power to threaten a magazine's viability."

"I was shocked," said Sandra Yates with characteristic directness. "In Australia, we think you have freedom of the press—but you don't."

Since Anne and Sandra had not met their budget's projections for ad revenue, their investors forced a sale. In October 1989, *Ms.* and *Sassy* were bought by Dale Lang, owner of *Working Mother, Working Woman,* and one of the few independent publishing companies left among the conglomerates. In response to a request from the original *Ms.* staff—as well as to reader letters urging that *Ms.* continue, plus his own belief that *Ms.* would benefit his other magazines by blazing a trail—he agreed to try the ad-free, reader-supported *Ms.* you hold now and to give us complete editorial control.

II.

Do you think, as I once did, that advertisers make decisions based on solid research? Well, think again. "Broadly speaking," says Joseph Smith of Oxtoby-Smith, Inc., a consumer research firm, "there is no persuasive evidence that the editorial context of an ad matters."

Advertisers who demand such "complementary copy," even in the absence of respectable studies, clearly are operating under a double standard. The same food companies place ads in *People* with no recipes. Cosmetics companies support *The New Yorker* with no regular beauty columns. So where does this habit of controlling the content of women's magazines come from?

Tradition. Ever since *Ladies Magazine* debuted in Boston in 1828, editorial copy directed to women has been informed by something other than its readers' wishes. There were no ads then, but in an age when married women were legal minors with no right to their own money, there was another revenue source to be kept in mind: husbands. "Husbands may rest assured," wrote editor Sarah Josepha Hale, "that nothing found in these pages shall cause her [his wife] to be less assiduous in preparing for his reception or encourage her to 'usurp station' or encroach upon prerogatives of men."

Hale went on to become the editor of *Godey's Lady's Book*, a magazine featuring "fashion plates": engravings of dresses for readers to take to their seamstresses or copy themselves. Hale added "how to" articles, which set the tone for women's service magazines for years to come: how to write politely, avoid sunburn, and— in no fewer than 1,200 words—how to maintain a goose quill pen. She advocated education for women but avoided controversy. Just as most women's magazines now avoid politics, poll their readers on issues like abortion but rarely take a stand, and praise socially approved lifestyles, Hale saw to it that *Godey's* avoided the hot topics of its day: slavery, abolition, and women's suffrage.

What definitively turned women's magazines into catalogs, however, were two events: Ellen Butterick's invention of the clothing pattern in 1863 and the mass manufacture of patent medicines containing everything from colored water to cocaine. For the first time, readers could purchase what magazines encouraged them to want. As such magazines became more profitable, they also began to attract men as editors. (Most women's magazines continued to have men as top editors until the feminist 1970s.) Edward Bok, who became editor of *The Ladies' Home Journal* in 1889, discovered the power of advertisers when he rejected ads for patent medicines and found that other advertisers canceled in retribution. In the early 20th century, *Good Housekeeping* started its Institute to "test and approve" products. Its Seal of Approval became the grandfather of current "value added" programs that offer advertisers such bonuses as product sampling and department store promotions.

By the time suffragists finally won the vote in 1920, women's magazines had become too entrenched as catalogs to help women learn how to use it. The main function was to create a desire for products, teach how to use products, and make

products a crucial part of gaining social approval, pleasing a husband, and performing as a homemaker. Some unrelated articles and short stories were included to
persuade women to pay for these catalogs. But articles were neither consumerist
nor rebellious. Even fiction was usually subject to formula: if a woman had any
sexual life outside marriage, she was supposed to come to a bad end.

In 1965, Helen Gurley Brown began to change part of that formula by bringing
"the sexual revolution" to women's magazines—but in an ad-oriented way. Attracting multiple men required even more consumerism, as the Cosmo Girl made
clear, than finding one husband.

In response to the workplace revolution of the 1970s, traditional women's magazines—that is, "trade books" for women working at home—were joined by *Savvy,
Working Woman*, and other trade books for women working in offices. But by keeping the fashion/beauty/entertaining articles necessary to get traditional ads and
then adding career articles besides, they inadvertently produced the antifeminist
stereotype of Super Woman. The male-imitative, dress-for-success woman carrying
a briefcase became the media image of a woman worker, even though a blue-collar
woman's salary was often higher than her glorified secretarial sister's, and though
women at a real briefcase level are statistically rare. Needless to say, these dress-
for-success women were also thin, white, and beautiful.

In recent years, advertisers' control over the editorial content of women's magazines has become so institutionalized that it is written into "insertion orders" or
dictated to ad salespeople as official policy. The following are recent typical orders
to women's magazines:

• Dow's Cleaning Products stipulates that ads for its Vivid and Spray 'n Wash
products should be adjacent to "children or fashion editorial"; ads for Bathroom
Cleaner should be next to "home furnishing/family" features; and so on for other
brands. "If a magazine fails for 1/2 the brands or more," the Dow order warns, "it
will be omitted from further consideration."

• Bristol-Myers, the parent of Clairol, Windex, Drano, Bufferin, and much
more, stipulates that ads be placed next to "a full page of compatible editorial."

• S.C. Johnson & Son, makers of Johnson Wax, lawn and laundry products,
insect sprays, hair sprays, and so on, orders that its ads *"should not be opposite extremely controversial features or material antithetical to the nature/copy of the advertised
product."* (Italics theirs.)

• Maidenform, manufacturer of bras and other apparel, leaves a blank for the
particular product and states: "The creative concept of the campaign, and the very
nature of the product itself appeal to the positive emotions of the reader/consumer.
Therefore, it is imperative that all editorial adjacencies reflect that same positive
tone. The editorial must not be negative in content or lend itself contrary to the

product imagery/message (e.g. *editorial relating to illness, disillusionment, large size fashion, etc.*)." (Italics mine.)

• The De Beers diamond company, a big seller of engagement rings, prohibits magazines from placing its ads with "adjacencies to hard news or anti/love-romance themed editorial."

• Procter & Gamble, one of this country's most powerful and diversified advertisers, stands out in the memory of Anne Summers and Sandra Yates (no mean feat in this context): its products were not to be placed in *any* issue that included *any* material on gun control, abortion, the occult, cults, or the disparagement of religion. Caution was also demanded in any issue covering sex or drugs, even for educational purposes.

Those are the most obvious chains around women's magazines. There are also rules so clear they needn't be written down: for instance, an overall "look" compatible with beauty and fashion ads. Even "real" nonmodel women photographed for a woman's magazine are usually made up, dressed in credited clothes, and retouched out of all reality. When editors do include articles on less-than-cheerful subjects (for instance, domestic violence), they tend to keep them short and unillustrated. The point is to be "upbeat." Just as women in the street are asked, "Why don't you smile, honey?" women's magazines acquire an institutional smile.

Within the text itself, praise for advertisers' products has become so ritualized that fields like "beauty writing" have been invented. One of its frequent practitioners explained seriously that "It's a difficult art. How many new adjectives can you find? How much greater can you make a lipstick sound? The FDA restricts what companies can say on labels, but we create illusion. And ad agencies are on the phone all the time pushing you to get their product in. A lot of them keep the business based on how many editorial clippings they produce every month. The worst are products," like Lauder's as the writer confirmed, "with their own name involved. It's all ego."

Often, editorial becomes one giant ad. Last November, for instance, *Lear's* featured an elegant woman executive on the cover. On the contents page, we learned she was wearing Guerlain makeup and Samsara, a new fragrance by Guerlain. Inside were full-page ads for Samsara and Guerlain antiwrinkle cream. In the cover profile, we learned that this executive was responsible for launching Samsara and is Guerlain's director of public relations. When the *Columbia Journalism Review* did one of the few articles to include women's magazines in coverage of the influence of ads, editor Frances Lear was quoted as defending her magazine because "this kind of thing is done all the time."

Often, advertisers also plunge odd-shaped ads into the text, no matter what the cost to the readers. At *Woman's Day*, a magazine originally founded by a supermarket chain, editor in chief Ellen Levine said, "The day the copy had to rag around a chicken leg was not a happy one."

Advertisers are also adamant about where in a magazine their ads appear. When Revlon was not placed as the first beauty ad in one Hearst magazine, for instance, Revlon pulled its ads from *all* Hearst magazines. Ruth Whitney, editor in chief of *Glamour*, attributes some of these demands to "ad agencies wanting to prove to a client that they've squeezed the last drop of blood out of a magazine." She also is, she says, "sick and tired of hearing that women's magazines are controlled by cigarette ads." Relatively speaking, she's right. To be as censoring as are many advertisers for women's products, tobacco companies would have to demand articles in praise of smoking and expect glamorous photos of beautiful women smoking their brands.

I don't mean to imply that the editors I quote here share my objections to ads: most assume that women's magazines have to be the way they are. But it's also true that only former editors can be completely honest. "Most of the pressure came in the form of direct product mentions," explains Sey Chassler, who was editor in chief of *Redbook* from the sixties to the eighties. "We got threats from the big guys, the Revlons, blackmail threats. They wouldn't run ads unless we credited them.

"But it's not fair to single out the beauty advertisers because these pressures came from everybody. Advertisers want to know two things: What are you going to charge me? What *else* are you going to do for me? It's a holdup. For instance, management felt that fiction took up too much space. They couldn't put any advertising in that. For the last ten years, the number of fiction entries into the National Magazine Awards has declined.

"And pressures are getting worse. More magazines are more bottom-line oriented because they have been taken over by companies with no interest in publishing.

"I also think advertisers do this to women's magazines especially," he concluded, "because of the general disrespect they have for women."

Even media experts who don't give a damn about women's magazines are alarmed by the spread of this ad-edit linkage. In a climate *The Wall Street Journal* describes as an unacknowledged Depression for media, women's products are increasingly able to take their low standards wherever they go. For instance: newsweeklies publish uncritical stories on fashion and fitness. *The New York Times Magazine* recently ran an article on "firming creams," complete with mentions of advertisers. *Vanity Fair* published a profile of one major advertiser, Ralph Lauren, illustrated by the same photographer who does his ads, and turned the lifestyle of another, Calvin Klein, into a cover story. Even the outrageous *Spy* has toned down since it began to go after fashion ads.

And just to make us really worry, films and books, the last media that go directly to the public without having to attract ads first, are in danger, too. Producers are beginning to depend on payments for displaying products in movies, and books are now being commissioned by companies like Federal Express.

But the truth is that women's products—like women's magazines—have never been the subjects of much serious reporting anyway. News and general interest publications, including the "style" or "living" sections of newspapers, write about food and clothing as cooking and fashion, and almost never evaluate such products by brand name. Though chemical additives, pesticides, and animal fats are major health risks in the United States, and clothes, shoddy or not, absorb more consumer dollars than cars, this lack of information is serious. So is ignoring the contents of beauty products that are absorbed into our bodies through our skins, and that have profit margins so big they would make a loan shark blush.

III.

What could women's magazines be like if they were as free as books? as realistic as newspapers? as creative as films? as diverse as women's lives? We don't know.

But we'll only find out if we take women's magazines seriously. If readers were to act in a concerted way to change traditional practices of *all* women's magazines and the marketing of *all* women's products, we could do it. After all, they are operating on our consumer dollars; money that we now control. You and I could:

- write to editors and publishers (with copies to advertisers) that we're willing to pay *more* for magazines with editorial independence, but will *not* continue to pay for those that are just editorial extensions of ads;
- write to advertisers (with copies to editors and publishers) that we want fiction, political reporting, consumer reporting—whatever is, or is not, supported by their ads;
- put as much energy into breaking advertising's control over content as into changing the images in ads, or protesting ads for harmful products like cigarettes;
- support only those women's magazines and products that take *us* seriously as readers and consumers.

Those of us in the magazine world can also use the carrot-and-stick technique. For instance: pointing out that, if magazines were a regulated medium like television, the demands of advertisers would be against FCC rules. Payola and extortion could be punished. As it is, there are probably illegalities. A magazine's postal rates are determined by the ratio of ad to edit pages, and the former costs more than the latter. So much for the stick.

The carrot means appealing to enlightened self-interest. For instance: there are many studies showing that the greatest factor in determining an ad's effectiveness is the credibility of its surroundings. The "higher the rating of editorial believability," concluded a 1987 survey by the *Journal of Advertising Research*, "the higher the rating of the advertising." Thus, an impenetrable wall between edit and ads would also be in the best interest of advertisers.

Unfortunately, few agencies or clients hear such arguments. Editors often maintain the false purity of refusing to talk to them at all. Instead, they see ad salespeople who know little about editorial, are trained in business as usual, and are usually paid by commission. Editors might also band together to take on controversy. That happened once when all the major women's magazines did articles in the same month on the Equal Rights Amendment. It could happen again.

It's almost three years away from life between the grindstones of advertising pressures and readers' needs. I'm just beginning to realize how edges got smoothed down—in spite of all our resistance.

I remember feeling put upon when I changed "Porsche" to "car" in a piece about Nazi imagery in German pornography by Andrea Dworkin—feeling sure Andrea would understand that Volkswagen, the distributor of Porsche and one of our few supportive advertisers, asked only to be far away from Nazi subjects. It's taken me all this time to realize that Andrea was the one with a right to feel put upon.

Even as I write this, I get a call from a writer for *Elle*, who is doing a whole article on where women part their hair. Why, she wants to know, do I part mine in the middle?

It's all so familiar. A writer trying to make something of a nothing assignment; an editor laboring to think of new ways to attract ads; readers assuming that other women must want this ridiculous stuff; more women suffering for lack of information, insight, creativity, and laughter that could be on these same pages.

I ask you: Can't we do better than this?

PART TWO
Democratic Contradictions of Commercial Journalism

Profit and Partisan Politics

Undermine Public Service

EDWARD A. ROSS

The Suppression of Important News
(1912)

Most of the criticism launched at our daily newspapers hits the wrong party. Granted they sensationalize vice and crime, "play up" trivialities, exploit the private affairs of prominent people, embroider facts, and offend good taste with screech, blare, and color. But all this may be only the means of meeting the demand, of "giving the public what it wants." The newspaper cannot be expected to remain dignified and serious now that it caters to the common millions, instead of, as formerly, to the professional and business classes. To interest errand-boy and factory-girl and raw immigrant, it had to become spicy, amusing, emotional, and chromatic. For these, blame, then, the American people.

There is just one deadly, damning count against the daily newspaper as it is coming to be, namely, *It does not give the news*.

For all its pretensions, many a daily newspaper is not "giving the public what it wants." In spite of these widely trumpeted prodigies of costly journalistic "enterprise," these ferreting reporters and hurrying correspondents, these leased cables and special trains, news, good "live" news, "red-hot stuff," is deliberately being suppressed or distorted. This occurs oftener now than formerly, and bids fair to occur yet oftener in the future.

And this in spite of the fact that the aspiration of the press has been upward. Venality has waned. Better and better men have been drawn into journalism, and they have wrought under more self-restraint. The time when it could be said, as it was said of the Reverend Dr. Dodd, that one had "descended so low as to become editor of a newspaper," seems as remote as the Ice Age. The editor who uses his paper to air his prejudices, satisfy his grudges, and serve his private ambitions, is going out. Sobered by a growing realization of their social function, newspaper men have come under a sense of responsibility. Not long ago it seemed as if a professional spirit and a professional ethics were about to inspire the newspaper world; and to this end courses and schools of journalism were established, with

From *Changing America* (New York: The Century Co., 1912), 109–36.

high hopes. The arrest of this promising movement explains why nine out of ten newspaper men of fifteen years' experience are cynics.

As usual, no one is to blame. The apostasy of the daily press is caused by three economic developments in the field of newspaper publishing.

Capitalist-Owner Supplants Editor-Owner

In the first place, the great city daily has become a blanket sheet with elaborate presswork, printed in mammoth editions that must be turned out in the least time. The necessary plant is so costly, and the Associated Press franchise is so expensive, that the daily newspaper in the big city has become a capitalistic enterprise. To-day a million dollars will not begin to outfit a metropolitan newspaper. The editor is no longer the owner, for he has not, and cannot command, the capital needed to start it or buy it. The editor of the type of Greeley, Dana, Medill, Story, Halstead, and Raymond, who owns his paper and makes it his astral body, the projection of his character and ideals, is rare. Perhaps Mr. Watterson and Mr. Nelson are the best living representatives of the type.

More and more the owner of the big daily is a business man who finds it hard to see why he should run his property on different lines from the hotel proprietor, the vaudeville manager, or the owner of an amusement park. The editors are hired men, and they may put into the paper no more of their conscience and ideals than comports with getting the biggest return from the investment. Of course, the old-time editor who owned his paper tried to make money,—no sin that!—but just as to-day the author, the lecturer, or the scholar tries to make money, namely, within the limitations imposed by his principles and his professional standards. But, now that the provider of the newspaper capital hires the editor instead of the editor hiring the newspaper capital, the paper is likelier to be run as a money-maker pure and simple—a factory where ink and brains are so applied to white paper as to turn out the largest possible marketable product. The capitalist-owner means no harm, but he is not bothered by the standards that hamper the editor-owner. He follows a few simple maxims that work out well enough in selling shoes or cigars or sheet-music. "Give people what *they* want, not what *you* want." "Back nothing that will be unpopular." "Run the concern for all it is worth."

This drifting of ultimate control into the hands of men with business motives is what is known as "the commercialization of the press."

Advertising Censors the News

The significance of it is apparent when you consider the second economic development, namely, the growth of newspaper advertising. The dissemination of news and the purveyance of publicity are two essentially distinct functions which, for the sake of convenience, are carried on by the same agency. The one appeals to subscribers, the other to advertisers. The one calls for good faith, the other does not. The one is the corner-stone of liberty and democracy, the other a convenience of commerce. Now, the purveyance of publicity is becoming the main concern of the newspaper, and threatens to throw quite into the shade the communication of news or opinions. Every year the sale of advertising yields a larger proportion of the total receipts, and the subscribers furnish a smaller proportion. Thirty years ago, advertising yielded less than half of the earnings of the daily newspapers. To-day, it yields at least two-thirds. In the larger dailies the receipts from advertisers are several times the receipts from the readers, in some cases constituting ninety per cent of the total revenues. As the newspaper expands to eight, twelve, and sixteen pages, while the price sinks to three cents, two cents, one cent, the time comes when the advertisers support the newspaper. The readers are there to *read*, not to provide funds. "He who pays the piper calls the tune." When news-columns and editorial page are a mere incident in the profitable sale of mercantile publicity, it is strictly "business-like" to let the big advertisers censor both.

Of course, you must not let the cat out of the bag, or you will lose readers, and thereupon advertising. As the publicity expert, Deweese, frankly puts it, "The reader must be flim-flammed with the idea that the publisher is really publishing the newspaper or magazine for him." The wise owner will "maintain the beautiful and impressive bluff of running a journal to influence public opinion, to purify politics, to elevate public morals, etc." In the last analysis, then, the smothering of facts in deference to the advertiser finds a limit in the intelligence and alertness of the reading public. Handled as "a commercial proposition," the newspaper dares not suppress such news beyond a certain point, and it can always proudly point to the unsuppressed news as proof of its independence and public spirit.

The Lengthening Phalanx of Advertisers

The immunity enjoyed by the big advertiser becomes more serious as more kinds of business resort to advertising. Formerly, readers who understood why accidents and labor troubles never occur in department stores, why dramatic criticisms are so lenient, and the reviews of books from the publishers who advertise are so good-natured, could still expect from their journal an ungloved freedom in dealing with gas, electric, railroad, and banking companies. But now the gas people advertise,

"Cook with gas," the electric people urge you to put your sewing-machine on their current, and the railroads spill oceans of ink to attract settlers or tourists. The banks and trust companies are buyers of space, investment advertising has sprung up like Jonah's gourd, and telephone and traction companies are being drawn into the vortex of competitive publicity. Presently, in the news-columns of the sheet that steers by the cash-register, every concern that has favors to seek, duties to dodge, or regulations to evade, will be able to press the soft pedal.

The "Kept" Newspaper

A third development is the subordination of newspapers to other enterprises. After a newspaper becomes a piece of paying property, detachable from the editor's personality, which may be bought and sold like a hotel or mill, it may come into the hands of those who will hold it in bondage to other and bigger investments. The magnate-owner may find it to his advantage not to run it as a newspaper pure and simple, but to make it—on the sly—an instrument for coloring certain kinds of news, diffusing certain misinformation, or fostering certain impressions or prejudices in its clientèle. In a word, he may shape its policy by non-journalistic considerations. By making his paper help his other schemes, or further his political or social ambitions, he will hurt it as a money-maker, no doubt, but he may contrive to fool enough of the people enough of the time. Aside from such thraldom, newspapers are subject to the tendency of diverse businesses to become tied together by the cross-investments of their owners. But naturally, when the shares of a newspaper lie in the safe-deposit box cheek by jowl with gas, telephone, and pipe-line stock, a tenderness for these collateral interests is likely to affect the news-columns.

"Killing" Important News

That in consequence of its commercialization, and its frequent subjection to outside interests, the daily newspaper is constantly suppressing important news, will appear from the instances that follow. They are hardly a third of the material that has come to the writer's attention.

A prominent Philadelphia clothier visiting New York was caught perverting boys, and cut his throat. His firm being a heavy advertiser, not a single paper in his home city mentioned the tragedy. One New York paper took advantage of the situation by sending over an extra edition containing the story. The firm in question has a large branch in a Western city. There too the local press was silent, and the opening was seized by a Chicago paper.

In this same Western city the vice-president of this firm was indicted for bribing an alderman to secure the passage of an ordinance authorizing the firm to bridge an alley separating two of its buildings. Representatives of the firm requested the newspapers in which it advertised to ignore the trial. Accordingly the five English papers published no account of the trial, which lasted a week and disclosed highly sensational matter. Only the German papers sent reporters to the trial and published the proceedings.

In a great jobbing center, one of the most prominent cases of the United States District Attorney was the prosecution of certain firms for misbranding goods. The facts brought out appeared in the press of the smaller centers, but not a word was printed in the local papers. In another center, four firms were fined for selling potted cheese which had been treated with preservatives. The local newspapers stated the facts, but withheld the names of the firms, a consideration they are not likely to show to the ordinary culprit.

In a trial in a great city it was brought out by sworn testimony that, during a recent labor struggle which involved teamsters on the one hand and the department stores and the mail-order houses on the other, the employers had plotted to provoke the strikers to violence by sending a long line of strike-breaking wagons out of their way to pass a lot on which the strikers were meeting. These wagons were the bait to a trap, for a strong force of policemen was held in readiness in the vicinity, and the governor of the state was at the telephone ready to call out the militia if a riot broke out. Fortunately, the strikers restrained themselves, and the trap was not sprung. It is easy to imagine the headlines that would have been used if labor had been found in so diabolical a plot. Yet the newspapers unanimously refused to print this testimony.

In the same city, during a strike of the elevator men in the large stores, the business agent of the elevator-starters' union was beaten to death, in an alley behind a certain emporium, by a "strong-arm" man hired by that firm. The story, supported by affidavits, was given by a responsible lawyer to three newspaper men, each of whom accepted it as true and promised to print it. The account never appeared.

In another city the sales-girls in the big shops had to sign an exceedingly mean and oppressive contract which, if generally known, would have made the firms odious to the public. A prominent social worker brought these contracts, and evidence as to the bad conditions that had become established under them, to every newspaper in the city. Not one would print a line on the subject.

On the outbreak of a justifiable street-car strike the newspapers were disposed to treat it in a sympathetic way. Suddenly they veered, and became unanimously hostile to the strikers. Inquiry showed that the big merchants had threatened to withdraw their advertisements unless the newspapers changed their attitude.

In the summer of 1908 disastrous fires raged in the northern Lake country, and great areas of standing timber were destroyed. A prominent organ of the lumber industry belittled the losses and printed reassuring statements from lumbermen who were at the very moment calling upon the state for a fire patrol. When taxed with the deceit, the organ pleaded its obligation to support the market for the bonds which the lumber companies of the Lake region had been advertising in its columns.

On account of agitating for teachers' pensions, a teacher was summarily dismissed by a corrupt school-board, in violation of their own published rule regarding tenure. An influential newspaper published the facts of school-board grafting brought out in the teacher's suit for reinstatement until, through his club affiliations, a big merchant was induced to threaten the paper with the withdrawal of his advertising. No further reports of the revelations appeared.

During labor disputes the facts are usually distorted to the injury of labor. In one case, strikers held a meeting on a vacant lot enclosed by a newly-erected billboard. Forthwith appeared, in a yellow journal professing warm friendship for labor, a front-page cut of the billboard and a lurid story of how the strikers had built a "stockade," behind which they intended to bid defiance to the bluecoats. It is not surprising that when the van bringing these lying sheets appeared in their quarter of the city, the libeled men overturned it.

During the struggle of carriage-drivers for a six-day week, certain great dailies lent themselves to a concerted effort of the liverymen to win public sympathy by making it appear that the strikers were interfering with funerals. One paper falsely stated that a strong force of police was being held in reserve in case of "riots," and that policemen would ride beside the non-union drivers of hearses. Another, under the misleading headline, "Two Funerals Stopped by Striking Cab-men," described harmless colloquies between hearse-drivers and pickets. This was followed up with a solemn editorial, "May a Man go to his Long Rest in Peace?" although, as a matter of fact, the strikers had no intention of interfering with funerals.

The lying headline is a favorite device for misleading the reader. One sheet prints on its front page a huge "scare" headline, " 'Hang Haywood and a Million Men will March in Revenge,' says Darrow." The few readers whose glance fell from the incendiary headline to the dispatch below it found only the following: "Mr. Darrow, in closing the argument, said that 'if the jury hangs Bill Haywood, one million willing hands will seize the banner of liberty by the open grave, and bear it on to victory.' " In the same style, a dispatch telling of the death of an English policeman, from injuries received during a riot precipitated by suffragettes attempting to enter a hall during a political meeting, is headed, "Suffragettes kill Policeman!"

"Prosperity Dope"

The alacrity with which many dailies serve as mouthpieces of the financial powers came out very clearly during the recent industrial depression. The owner of one leading newspaper called his reporters together and said in effect, "Boys, the first of you who turns in a story of a lay-off or a shut-down, gets the sack." Early in the depression the newspapers teemed with glowing accounts of the resumption of steel mills and the revival of business, all baseless. After harvest time they began to cheep, "Prosperity," "Bumper Crops," "Farmers buying Automobiles." In cities where banks and employers offered clearing-house certificates instead of cash, the press usually printed fairy tales of the enthusiasm with which these makeshifts were taken by depositors and workingmen. The numbers and sufferings of the unemployed were ruthlessly concealed from the reading public. A mass meeting of men out of work was represented as "anarchistic" or "instigated by the socialists for political effect." In one daily appeared a dispatch under the heading. "Five Thousand Jobs Offered; only Ten apply." It stated that the Commissioner of Public Works of Detroit, misled by reports of dire distress, set afoot a public work which called for five thousand men. Only ten men applied for work, and all these expected to be bosses. Correspondence with the official established the fact that the number of jobs offered was five hundred, and that three thousand men applied for them!

"Sacred Cows"

On the desk of every editor and sub-editor of a newspaper run by a capitalist promoter now under prison sentence lay a list of sixteen corporations in which the owner was interested. This was to remind them not to print anything damaging to these concerns. In the office these corporations were jocularly referred to as "sacred cows."

Nearly every form of privilege is found in the herd of "sacred cows" venerated by the daily press.

The railroad company is a "sacred cow." At a hearing before a state railroad commission, the attorney of a shippers' association got an eminent magnate into the witness chair, with the intention of wringing from him the truth regarding the political expenditures of his railroad. At this point the commission, an abject creature of the railroads, arbitrarily excluded the daring attorney from the case. The memorable excoriation which that attorney gave the commission to its face was made to appear in the papers as the *cause* instead of the *consequence* of this exclusion. Subsequently, when the attorney filed charges with the governor against the commission, one editor wrote an editorial stating the facts and criticizing the commissioners. The editorial was suppressed after it was in type.

The public-service company is a "sacred cow." In a city of the Southwest, last summer, while houses were burning from lack of water for the fire hose, a lumber company offered to supply the firemen with water. The water company replied that they had "sufficient." Neither this nor other damaging information concerning the company's conduct got into the columns of the local press. A yellow journal conspicuous in the fight for cheaper gas by its ferocious onslaughts on the "gas trust," suddenly ceased its attack. Soon it began to carry a full-page "Cook with gas" advertisement. The cow had found the entrance to the sacred fold.

Traction is a "sacred cow." The truth about Cleveland's fight for the three-cent fare has been widely suppressed. For instance, while Mayor Johnson was super-intending the removal of the tracks of a defunct street railway, he was served with a court order enjoining him from tearing up the rails. As the injunction was not indorsed, as by law it should be, he thought it was an ordinary communication, and put it in his pocket to examine later. The next day he was summoned to show reason why he should not be found in contempt of court. When the facts came out, he was, of course, discharged. An examination of the seven leading dailies of the country shows that a dispatch was sent out from Cleveland stating that Mayor Johnson, after acknowledging service, pocketed the injunction, and ordered his men to proceed with their work. In the newspaper offices this dispatch was then embroidered. One paper said the mayor told his men to go ahead and ignore the injunction. Another had the mayor intimating in advance that he would not obey an order if one were issued. A third invented a conversation in which the mayor and his superintendent made merry over the injunction. Not one of the seven journals reported the mayor's complete excoriation later.

The tax system is a "sacred cow." During a banquet of two hundred single-taxers, at the conclusion of their state conference, a man fell in a fit. Reporters saw the trifling incident, yet the morning papers, under big headlines, "Many poisoned at Single-Tax Banquet," told in detail how a large number of banqueters had been ptomaine-poisoned. The conference had formulated a single-tax amendment to the state constitution, which they intended to present to the people for signature under the new Initiative Law. One paper gave a line and a half to this most significant action. No other paper noticed it.

The party system is a "sacred cow." When a county district court declared that the Initiative and Referendum amendment to the Oregon constitution was invalid, the item was spread broadcast. But when later the Supreme Court of Oregon re-versed that decision, the fact was too trivial to be put on the wires.

The "man higher up" is a "sacred cow." In reporting Prosecutor Heney's argu-ment in the Calhoun case, the leading San Francisco paper omitted everything on the guilt of Calhoun and made conspicuous certain statements of Mr. Heney with reference to himself, with intent to make it appear that his argument was but a vindication of himself, and that he made no points against the accused. The argument for the defense was printed in full, the "points" being neatly displayed in large type at proper intervals. At a crisis in this prosecution a Washington dispatch quoted the chairman of the Appropriations Committee as stating in the House that "Mr. Heney received during 1908 $23,000, for which he performed no service whatever for the Government." It was some hours before the report was corrected by adding Mr. Tawney's concluding words, "during that year."

In view of their suppression and misrepresentation of vital truth, the big daily papers, broadly speaking, must be counted as allies of those whom—as Editor Dana reverently put it—"God has endowed with a genius for saving, for getting rich, for bringing wealth together, for accumulating and concentrating money." In rallying to the side of the people they are slower than the weeklies, the magazines, the pulpit, the platform, the bar, the *literati*, the intellectuals, the social settlements, and the universities.

How a Vox Clamantis Becomes Property

Now and then, to be sure, in some betrayed and misgoverned city, a man of force takes some little sheet, prints all the news, ventilates the local situation, arouses the community, builds up a huge circulation, and proves that truth-telling still pays. But such exploits do not counteract the economic developments which have brought on the glacial epoch in journalism. Note what happens later to such a newspaper. It is now a valuable property, and as such it will be treated. The editor need not repeat the bold strokes that won public confidence; he has only to avoid anything that would forfeit it. Unconsciously he becomes, perhaps, less a newspaper man, more a business man. He may make investments which muzzle his paper here, form social connections which silence it there. He may tire of fighting and want to "cash in." In any case, when his newspaper falls into the hands of others, it will be run as a business, and not as a crusade.

Will News "Out"?

What can be done about the suppression of news? At least, we can refrain from arraigning and preaching. To urge the editor, under the thumb of the advertiser or of the owner, to be more independent, is to invite him to remove himself from his profession. As for the capitalist-owner, to exhort him to run his newspaper in the interests of truth and progress is about as reasonable as to exhort the mill-owner to work his property for the public good instead of for his private benefit.

What is needed is a broad new avenue to the public mind. Already smothered facts are cutting little channels for themselves. The immense vogue of the "muckraking" magazines is due to their being vehicles for suppressed news. Non-partizan leaders are meeting with cheering response when they found weeklies in order to reach their natural following. The Socialist Party supports two dailies, less to spread their ideas than to print what the capitalistic dailies would stifle. Civic associations, municipal voters' leagues, and legislative voters' leagues, are circulating tons of leaflets and bulletins full of suppressed facts. Within a year five cities have, with the taxpayers' money, started journals to acquaint the citizens with municipal happenings and affairs. In many cities have sprung up private non-partizan weeklies to report civic information. Moreover, the spoken word is once more a power. The demand for lecturers and speakers is insatiable, and the platform bids fair to recover its old prestige. The smotherers are dismayed by the growth of the Chautauqua circuit. Congressional speeches give vent to boycotted truth, and circulate widely under the franking privilege. City clubs and Saturday lunch clubs are formed to listen to facts and ideas tabooed by the daily press. More is made of public hearings before committees of councilmen or legislators.

When all is said, however, the defection of the daily press has been a staggering blow to democracy.

The Need of the Endowed Newspaper

Many insist that the public is able to recognize and pay for the truth. "Trust the public" and *in the end* merit will be rewarded. Time and again men have sunk money in starting an honest and outspoken sheet, confident that soon the public would rally to its support. But such hopes are doomed to disappointment. The editor who turns away bad advertising or defies his big patrons cannot lay his copy on the subscriber's doorstep for as little money as the editor who purveys publicity for all it is worth; and the masses will not pay three cents when another paper that "looks just as good" can be had for a cent. In a word, the art of simulating honesty and independence has outrun the insight of the average reader.

To conclude that the people are not able to recognize and pay for the truth about current happenings simply puts the dissemination of news in a class with other momentous social services. Because people fail to recognize and pay for good books, endowed libraries stud the land. Because they fail to recognize and pay for good instruction, education is provided free or at part cost. Just as the moment came when it was seen that private schools, loan libraries, commercial parks, baths, gymnasia, athletic grounds, and play-grounds would not answer, so the moment is here for recognizing that the commercial news medium does not adequately meet the needs of democratic citizenship.

Endowment is necessary, and, since we are not yet wise enough to run a public-owned daily newspaper, the funds must come from private sources. In view of the fact that in fifteen years large donations aggregating more than a thousand million of dollars have been made for public purposes in this country, it is safe to predict that, if the usefulness of a non-commercial newspaper be demonstrated, funds will be forthcoming. In the cities, where the secret control of the channels of publicity is easiest, there are likely to be founded financially independent newspapers, the gift of public-spirited men of wealth.

The Control of the Endowed Newspaper

The ultimate control of such a foundation constitutes a problem. A newspaper free to ignore the threats of big advertisers or powerful interests, one not to be bought, bullied, or bludgeoned, one that might at any moment blurt out the damning truth about police protection to vice, corporate tax-dodging, the grabbing of water front-age by railroads, or the non-enforcement of the factory laws, would be of such strategic importance in the struggle for wealth that desperate efforts would be made to chloroform it. If its governing board perpetuated itself by co-optation, it would eventually be packed with "safe" men, who would see to it that the newspaper was run in a "conservative" spirit; for, in the long run, those who can watch for an advantage *all* the time will beat the people, who can watch only *some* of the time.

Chloroformed the endowed newspaper will be, unless it be committed to the onward thought and conscience of the community. This could be done by letting vacancies on the governing board be filled in turn by the local bar association, the medical association, the ministers' union, the degree-granting faculties, the feder-ated teachers, the central labor union, the chamber of commerce, the associated charities, the public libraries, the non-partizan citizens' associations, the improve-ment leagues, and the social settlements. In this way the endowment would rest ultimately on the chief apexes of moral and intellectual worth in the city.

The Services of the Endowed Newspaper

While giving, with headline, cut, and cartoon, the interesting news,—forgeries and accidents, society and sports, as well as business and politics,—the endowed news-paper would not dramatize crime, or gossip of private affairs; above all, it would not "fake," "doctor," or sensationalize the news. Too self-respecting to use keyhole tactics, and too serious to chronicle the small beer of the wedding trousseau or the divorce court, such a newspaper could not begin to match the commercial press in circulation. But it would reach those who reach the public through the weeklies and monthlies, and would inform the teachers, preachers, lecturers, and public men, who speak to the people eye to eye.

What is more, it would be *a corrective newspaper*, giving a wholesome leverage for lifting up the commercial press. The big papers would not dare be caught smothering or "cooking" the news. The revelations of an independent journal that everybody believed, would be a terror to them, and, under the spur of a competitor not to be frightened, bought up, or tried out, they must needs, in sheer self-preservation, tell the truth much oftener than they do. The Erie Canal handles less than a twentieth of the traffic across the State of New York, yet, by its standing offer of cheap transportation, it exerts a regulative pressure on railway rates which is realized only when the canal opens in the spring. On the same principle, the endowed newspaper in a given city might print only a twentieth of the daily press output and yet exercise over the other nineteen-twentieths an influence great and salutary.

SILAS BENT

The Art of Ballyhoo
(1927)

I

It is common newspaper shoptalk that big news is bigger now than ever before. This depends, of course, on what one means by bigness. On any basis of authentic valuation the sinking of the *Titanic* was a bigger story than the Snyder-Gray murder trial in New York, the World War Armistice a bigger story than a trans-oceanic flight, yet neither got so big a "play" in the press. The news is no bigger now, but the headlines are, and the volume of space accorded to outstanding events, even though of minor consequence to society, is greater.

News standards, like conventions of morality, are subject to change. Styles as well as standards change. We have fashion in news. The saxophone of sex is as characteristic of the journalistic orchestra as the short skirt of feminine attire, and it is a jazz theme. Psychologists assert that sex should occupy the centre of attention only during adolescence. If that is so, the preoccupation of the American newspaper with this topic accounts in part for a sort of perpetual adolescence found charac- teristic of its readers. The trait is manifested not only in the avidity with which pornographic detail is devoured, but in the glorification of short-lived newspaper idols. The truth is that the press has developed this characteristic while developing a new technique of salesmanship and showmanship. It has evolved new methods of display. Just as a shop may devote its entire show window to a single enchanting fur, so the press concentrates public attention on a single thrilling news event, even at the expense of other more important happenings.

Not always is this discreditable. Every one must have observed during recent years an outcropping of stories dealing with the world's scientific advance. Tele- vision and osiso have supplied first-page material; a short while ago they would have been delegated to the weekly and monthly magazines. Radio telephony is but an extension of electrical principles and appliances with which the public has been

From *Ballyhoo* (New York: Boni and Liveright, 1927), 21–45.

made familiar, but the first transatlantic conversations got more newspaper space, easily by one-hundredfold, than the discovery of radium in 1898, although that discovery shook the scientific world, and upset forever the "law" that matter was inert. The circulation manager of one great New York newspaper has asserted with confidence that scientific news sells more papers than a good crime mystery.

The reason for this is not far to seek. The people of this country, having vanquished the last frontier and having achieved a commanding eminence as a world power, politically and financially, have turned in upon themselves. The extravert is manifesting some of the attributes of the introvert, if I may venture to employ what Dr. Ira S. Wile (himself a psychologist) has called "the transcendental nomenclature" of warring psychological sects. In the recognition of this change of base newspaper publishers have been far tardier than the publishers of books. Long before scientific news (excepting possibly eclipses of the sun) had a fair showing in our papers, the Homeric musings of Henri Fabre on the insect world were being translated and greedily enjoyed on this side of the water. Outlines of history, of literature and of philosophy; biographies, and popularized expositions of technical subjects, sold on a comparatively large scale long before the daily press awoke to this new appetite.

Even then the awakening was partly due to the skillful manœuvres of press agents, who enabled the man of science to meet the newspaper reporter on a common ground, without fear on one side of being made to look ridiculous, on the other side of having the heart cut out of any story submitted for a visé. The publicity man, familiar with news values and familiar from intensive study with the scientist's work, proved in this instance a valuable intermediary. Employed as a rule by a college, university or commercial research laboratory, he acted as a reportorial auxiliary. It is about the best thing that can be said for him. The practices of the guild as a whole have been of such doubtful character that a movement has been set afoot to professionalize it and establish a code of ethics: that is, to put upon a higher plane what newspaper men are wont to call space-grabbing, and to sanctify the ballyhoo of commercial commodities.

II

Never do the events, policies, possibilities and movements with which the press concerns itself represent a cross-section of existence at one moment, or for one day. William James has put before us in a vivid passage the disjointed order of the world. "While I talk and the flies buzz," he said, "a sea-gull catches a fish at the mouth of the Amazon, a tree falls in the Adirondack wilderness, a man sneezes in Germany, a horse dies in Tartary, and twins are born in France." He was making the point that mere contemporaneity of events forms no rational bond between them, and that we are forced to break them into definite sequences and tendencies: into histories, into arts, into sciences. Newspapers break them also, these chaotic happenings of the world, into certain patterns. None of the incidents James thought worth mentioning is newspaper news, excepting that the birth of twins might have been chronicled in a French provincial journal. If the twins had been born to the Queen of Spain, the news would have been put upon the cable. Evidently the newspaper man is governed by certain codes and standards which, although gradually variable, are potent and widely prevalent while they are in effect. Day after day one may note a certain sameness in the press: a sameness, not of content, but of effect. The effect is produced by a process of selection and emphasis. In this second quarter of the Twentieth Century ballyhoo is a noteworthy part of the process.

At the beginning of this century the Associated Press undertook to lay a measuring-stick along the commodity it was gathering and distributing. It attempted to instruct its correspondents by rule of thumb. Business failures were to be reported when in excess of $10,000; strikes, when the number of employés thrown out of work exceeded two hundred; accidents, when two or more lives were lost, and so on through a long list. The Associated Press has now ceased trying to grade news according to property values and loss of life. It no longer issues those instructions, presumably because the inflation of certain intangibles in the news has made such a gauge all but valueless.

Now, every layman knows what news is as it relates to him. It may be that an acquaintance has moved into an apartment around the corner, it may be a case of whooping cough, it may be the arrival of the first robin redbreast in Spring; it may be as negligible, from the newspaper standpoint, as any of the happenings William James noted. If we were asked to define this kind of news, we might say that it is fresh tidings touching our mental or social or emotional selves. Commonly it is called gossip. Dorothy Dix says that the stuff we read in the daily press is a sort of glorified gossip. It is glorified, if that is the word, by being selected with reference to mass and class, chiefly with reference to mass.

This has given rise to the paradox that, although the manipulation of news is a highly conventionalized craft, newspaper men are seldom able to define the commodity they handle. I think they are unable to define it because in selecting and presenting it they appeal to unconscious primary emotions and satisfy or stimulate primitive appetites. Thus they themselves function in part unconsciously. The elder Joseph Pulitzer, who thought more clearly about what he was doing, I suspect, than most of his successors, once dictated for a subordinate a memorandum which dealt acutely and comprehensively with the kind of news he thought a metropolitan daily should seek.

What is original [he wrote], distinctive, dramatic, romantic, thrilling, unique, curious, quaint, humorous, odd, apt to be talked about, without shocking good taste or lowering the general tone, good tone, and above all without impairing the confidence of the people in the truth of the stories or the character of the paper for reliability and scrupulous cleanness.

That was not all Pulitzer thought a newspaper should print. He was a great crusader. He told his men never to be satisfied with mere news, and he was capable of directing the preparation of a full-page editorial which in itself would be distinguished news. So far as routine news is concerned, the cat is now out of the bag. I beg you to note that nowhere in this memorandum did Pulitzer designate social importance or economic or historical magnitude as a factor. The paper which follows his prescription, and most of them do, need not instruct nor inform us.

The elder James Gordon Bennett, father of yellow journalism in this country (although his offspring was not christened until the Hearst-Pulitzer war gave it new vitality), was fond of saying that the newspaper's function was not to instruct but to startle. If he had added that a part of its function was to entertain, he would have covered his ground. The favorite Bennett-Pulitzer-Hearst brand of trivia has the quality of fire-crackers. It both surprises and amuses. It is pyrotechnic, and sometimes, like a Roman candle or a rocket, arouses naïve wonder and delight.

This is news in lighter vein. The heavier stuff must deal with sex, violence, conflict, mystery or suspense: one of these, or a combination of them. Metropolitan newspapers, according to this formula, need not contain a line of useful information. Only casually do they make us aware of the unseen world. A member of the Pulitzer staff, on the basis of a questionnaire sent to editors of national reputation, selected the ten biggest stories of 1926 (all of which fitted neatly into the Pulitzer formula), and noted the significant fact that only four of the ten stories were of any real social or historical consequence: the general strike in England, Mexico's attitude toward the Roman Catholic Church, and two transpolar flights. This gave an authentic informational value of forty per cent to the big news of a year. But observe, if you please, that the polar expeditions had the thrill of romance, suspense and danger; that the Mexican story involved religious strife, which is always good newspaper-selling stuff; and that the strike in England had to a high degree the dramatic quality of conflict. Readers of the daily press must jump for joy at such crumbs of significant information about their invisible environment as come their way.

III

We need not go here into the newspaper as an avenue of advertising ballyhoo. It is enough for the present to say that automobile manufacturers have gravely discussed the need of a "czar" for their industry, to set a mete and a bound on their claims. Sales managers, for instance, complained that the boasts of mounting production had caused prospective purchasers to pause, in the hope of heavy inventories and lower prices. Advertisements intended to convince the public that this or that car was becoming immensely popular tended to defeat themselves. Ballyhoo often has this boomerang reaction. Editorial soul-searchings take the form of doubts as to whether a current story has been overplayed, and downright despair at the protest of the Constant Reader.

Nor need we pause here for discussion of "feature" inflation, which has come about chiefly to lighten the load of advertisements the Sunday papers must carry. The very boastfulness of the press is a naïve ballyhoo. It prints unblushingly praiseful letters from its readers, who know that this is an easy way of getting their names before the public eye. It prints also its own pæans to itself. The Chicago *Tribune* avers that it is "the world's greatest newspaper," the St. Louis *Post-Dispatch* that it is "first in everything," the morning and afternoon *Sun* that Baltimoreans don't say "newspaper," they say "*Sun*-paper," the Detroit *News* that it is "the HOME newspaper," the *World* that it has "the best written feature page in American journalism." I am concerned at the moment not with these forms, but with the phenomenon as it is to be found in the news columns. Before we go further we may look for a moment at the reported "suicide wave" among school and college students. This did not run to such great lengths as were threatened before a damper was applied from an unexpected quarter; but while it ran the going was fine, from the newspaper standpoint. It will serve very well as an illustration of the origin and development of a fortuitous ballyhoo.

Two students, sons of men nationally known, destroyed themselves within a brief period. This was enough to set the press casting about for an epidemic of such suicides. Obscure cases at a distance, which would have been ignored in ordinary circumstances, suddenly assumed first-page importance. Each new instance was blazoned as an addition to the "suicide wave" among students.

"We have waves of news," says William Lewis Butcher of the New York State Crime Commission, "and we think we are having waves of crime." This passage of the report of his subcommission, which studied the relation of the daily press to crime and the administration of justice, is worth quoting more at length, as bearing on the wave of news about student suicides.

The average person is always unduly impressed by that which is prominently displayed and which has unusual attendant circumstances or which has been

brought vividly to his attention in some other way. Consequently, the average reader of newspapers is often-times led to the belief that a crime wave
is in progress because he has been reading an unusual amount of crime news.
This distributive tendency is largely the result of the exigencies of the newspaper business. Crime news is an ever present source of newspaper "copy."
It can be used when other sorts of news are not readily available. It is probable that if careful compilation should be made of the actual number of
crimes committed over a period of weeks and months, and if this should be
compared with the amount of crime news published during the same period,
it would be found that the amount of news bore no direct relation at all to
the actual amount of crime.

Such a comparison is precisely what was made in regard to the so-called "suicide
wave" among students. A statistician for a life insurance company stepped forward
coolly with the facts, showing that in truth the percentage of suicides among persons under twenty years of age had been falling off for sixteen years, the period
covered by his investigation. Instead of a "wave" there was a subsidence. No newspaper had the good grace to display this significant utterance as prominently as it
had displayed student suicides, so far as my extended observation went. Some of
them printed it as a "shirt-tail" to a current suicide. Meanwhile the editors of Sunday supplements had been interviewing psychoanalysts, preachers, deans of colleges, physicians and professors about the "wave." Was it a post-war neurosis? Was
the break-up of the home to blame? Was prohibition, mayhap, at the bottom of
it? If not, what have you? All this pother, mark you, about a phenomenon which
was no phenomenon because it did not exist, as any newspaper could have informed itself. The papers were less concerned with the truth than with preying
upon the fears of a multitude of parents, and suggesting self-destruction to an
extremely suggestible part of the population. A thirteen-year-old school boy hanged
himself at the height of this ballyhoo, and a physician who investigated the case
said that clearly it was imitative. The boy had succumbed to newspaper suggestion;
and a part of the press was so callous as to headline the tragedy as "imitative"
suicide.

The statistician's statement had the effect, at the height of the hysteria, of a
bucket of cold water. But the press could not with dignity, or would not, stop
discussion of student suicides. The more self-respecting newspapers stopped speaking of them as an epidemic or wave. Had the ballyhoo been permitted to continue,
there would indeed have been a wave. And it would have come as the result of a
circulation-building stunt.

The "suicide wave" was fortuitous, as I have said. Newspaper publishers count
such incidents as windfalls in their trafficking for mass attention. There are certain

kinds of news which are a stand-by of the circulation gogetters; sports rank in the forefront of these.

M. W. Bingay, managing editor of the Detroit *News*, once said that the editors created the Frankenstein monster of public interest in sports and then worshipped their handiwork. Will Owen Jones, editor of the Lincoln (Nebraska) *State Journal*, as chairman of a committee of the American Society of Newspaper Editors, reported in 1927 that a fair standard of pay for sport writers would do much to eliminate venality. His committee had investigated more than one hundred newspapers, showing that an average of ten columns daily was devoted to sports, with twice or thrice as much on Sundays. One-half of these papers were giving more than fifteen percent of their reader space to this sort of matter, and the percentages ran as high as forty and fifty.

> Some have "no limit" to the space devoted to sports [the report said] while the editors of other papers admit that they try to prevent their sporting departments from "going hog wild" but are quite worn out with the process.

The amazing efflorescence of free publicity for paid sports has come within the last fifteen years. The sporting editor has extended his domain from a column or two through whole pages and whole sections. I confess a weakness for prize-fights, baseball and racing *as spectacles*; as subjects of newspaper reading matter I can do without them. Yet in any catalogue of news this sort of stuff ranks second. Only business overtops it—and not even business in some papers. Business may be the first interest of the American people, but I venture to dispute that measurements of biceps and dope on selling platers is the second. This is quite obviously a cultivated, an artificial appetite. The newspapers have bred a sport fandom to build a circulation of dubious value. There are at least 166 morning dailies in this country, praise be, which do not print odds on horse races, nor guesses as to which will win this race or that. Those that continue to do so must pay a price in the loss of public respect. *Editor and Publisher*, a weekly paper about newspapers, has spoken its mind on this subject. Let me quote from an editorial:

> Is a newspaper in any wise justified in publishing "selections," which in effect means that a dopester in the employ of the paper is attempting to "sell" horses to readers?
>
> Is the circulation gained worth the expense of the wire service, composition and first-page displays, crowding legitimate news from the best editions of the evening papers?
>
> Is this good circulation? . . .

Is horse racing, as at present constituted in this country, a huge bunk of a gullible public? . . . Does race news pay?

This house organ of the press has been no less candid in its condemnation of the methods by which newspapers whip up interest in prize-fights, and give acres of free space to commercial enterprises of dubious character. I will wish to return in a later chapter to this topic. Dempsey the Mauler, never better than a second-rate pugilist because he never learned how to defend himself, is apotheosized in a *World* editorial as "a sort of legend with us, a superhuman colossus of brawn"; as "likable" and "picturesque," although he maintained his title for years chiefly by a studious avoidance of the prize ring. The *New York Times* asserts editorially that Babe Ruth "wears the laurel amid the deafening plaudits of the American nation" because he knocked three home runs in a World Series game.

For certain screen stars the ballyhoo has been almost as loud. Much comment was caused by the difference in space accorded by the press to the concurrent death and funeral of Rudolph Valentino and Dr. Charles W. Eliot. The President Emeritus of Harvard, commonly called our first citizen, got perhaps one line to the movie sheik's column in the newspapers. But how, newspaper men may ask you, is the press to megaphone the death of a former college president? How many newspaper readers were familiar with Doctor Eliot's name? How ballyhoo an intellect? For Valentino there were mobs, riots and a press agent. Q.E.D.

So many letters of protest flowed in on the press during the Valentino vociferation that one newspaper felt moved to offer editorial justification of the space accorded to the occasion; and its justification (precisely as in the later furore over a transatlantic flight) was that the behavior of the crowd afforded a remarkable insight into mob psychology. The picture thus conjured up, of metropolitan news editors poring over the pages of Tarde, Le Bon, Trotter, Kallen and Everett Dean Martin, in order to determine the precise significance, and therefore the number of columns to be allotted to the rioting and smashing of a plate glass window at the Valentino undertaking "parlor," is illuminating. Newspapers, be it understood, do not pander to the crowd, but afford an opportunity for study of its psychology.

Incidents such as this are reminiscent of the "compassionate superiority" noted by Matthew Arnold as characteristic of the London *Times*. What he said may be repeated here as applying to our most eminent American journals. Our metropolitan daily press is "a gigantic Sancho Panza, following by an attraction he cannot resist that poor, mad, scorned, suffering, sublime enthusiast, the modern spirit: following it, indeed, with constant grumblings, expostulation, and opposition, with airs of protection, of compassionate superiority, with an incessant by-play of nods, shrugs and winks addressed to the spectators; following it, in short, with all the incurable recalcitrancy of a lower nature, but still following it."

Following, not leading; following with winks and grimaces, in order to study its psychology, whether the path be to the bier of a movie sheik or the murder trial of a corset salesman.

IV

Charles A. Lindbergh's flight from New York to Paris, and the subsequent flight to Berlin of Clarence Chamberlin with Charles A. Levine as passenger, provoked a striking journalistic demonstration. Lindbergh was young, good-looking and modest. He went it alone, and he set a new distance record until Chamberlin surpassed it two weeks later. Neither was the first to make a transatlantic flight in a heavier-than-air machine. The palm for that had gone eight years earlier, June 15–16, 1919, to Captain John Alcock and Lieutenant Arthur W. Brown. Their flight, an historic occasion, unquestionably merited a great deal of newspaper attention; but it was not so momentous, to my notion, as Louis Bleriot's hop across the English Channel in 1909, when flying was still in its pin-feathers. To get off the ground in an airplane in that day was an adventure. Improvements in the motor and the machine, and the hazardous exploits of World War aces, took the edge off the spectacle. Aviation ceased to astound the sophisticated.

Yet even before Lindbergh accomplished his goal, when he had merely set out from Long Island, the newspapers of this country set up such a bombination as might greet a world-shaking event. For days the press had been whetting the public appetite for this thrill, whether Richard E. Byrd or Lindbergh or some other supplied it. The appetite grew by what it fed on. This much at least newspaper men knew about mass psychology. To the mere hop-off by Lindbergh the *New York Times* gave three first-page eight-column streamers, and thirty-seven columns of space, including more than a page of pictures, while it could spare but one column to a jail sentence for Harry F. Sinclair, millionaire prime mover in the Teapot Dome scandal. The successful completion of the flight moved the Cincinnati *Post* to a two-line first-page block letter headline five and one-half inches in height.

The return of the aviator to this country provoked even more surprising typographic and photographic orgies. In a single Sunday issue of one paper there were one hundred columns of text and pictures about this flier. In reporting his welcome by New York City, the *Times* used fifteen pages, the *American* ten, the *Herald Tribune* nine, the *World* eight, the *Mirror* and *News*, which are tabloids, twenty-three and sixteen pages respectively. The *Times*, which had devoted three pages of its Sunday rotogravure section to the double Armistice celebration (the celebration of the premature and of the correct report that the World War was ended), devoted that number on two different occasions to Lindbergh, and to his home-coming gave five pages!

The *Evening World* called this flight "the greatest feat of a solitary man in the records of the human race," and the *Ohio State Journal* ranked the aviator, who had followed a watery path well-blazed by other fliers, "among the great pioneers of history." "He has exalted the race of men," shrieked the Baltimore *Sun*. And the *New York Times* was moved to ask editorially: "What was the greatest story of all time? Adam eating the apple?" (Readers of the Bible may have recalled that this story was told in less than seven hundred words.) "The landing of the ark on Ararat?" (Amply reported in less than four hundred words!) "The discovery of Moses in the bulrushes?" (Fully covered in less than three hundred words!) . . . "But Lindbergh's flight," the editor concluded, "the suspense of it, the daring of it, the triumph and glory of it—these are the stuff that makes immortal news."

Suspense, daring, triumph, glory: here we have an abbreviation of the Pulitzerian formula. Lindbergh would have been the last to assert that he had done anything to compare in reckless daring with the feats of World War aviators; he had taken no new chances, and even the distance of his journey was quickly surpassed. His modest and attractive personality, however, was a Golconda for newspaper exploitation. How profitably they worked the mine may be guessed from a glance at some figures. On the day the flight was completed the Washington *Star* sold 16,000 extra copies, the Washington *Post* many thousands above its average. The Louisville *Courier-Journal* reported that it was "cleaned out early." The St. Louis *Globe-Democrat*, which had helped finance the flight and was entitled alone of them all to financial reward, gained 27,000 circulation. The St. Louis *Post-Dispatch* sold 40,000 extra copies the day the flight was completed, and the San Francisco *Call* doubled its street sales. Similar results were noted in Denver, Oklahoma City, Seattle, Chicago, Dallas, Los Angeles and Minneapolis. In New York City the *Evening World* increased its sale, its circulation manager said, by 114,000 copies in a single day, and the *Telegram* announced that its total of 380,000 papers was a clean 100,000 ahead of the sales at the time of the Gray-Snyder murder verdict. The *Times* sold from thirty-five to forty thousand extra copies a day while the excitement continued, and the *World* reported that on the Monday after the flight its sale was 68,000 above the corresponding day a year before.

A clipping bureau, reporting on the whole country, estimated that in the first four days more than 27,000 columns had been given to the flier, which makes conservative a guess that in all he was the subject of print enough to fill four volumes of the Encyclopedia Britannica. In the first four days 220,000 more stories, according to the clipping bureau, were printed about the Lindbergh flight than about the death of Woodrow Wilson, which had set a previous high record for peace times.

It may be supposed that the sale of papers bearing the tidings of the former President's death arose from genuine respect and affection. But it would be absurd to suppose that the excitement over Lindbergh was entirely spontaneous. "Newspaper talk," according to the *Times*, was "the sole cause of the vast assemblage" to welcome the flier.

The effect of the newspaper talk on a suggestible population was varied. Thousands took their pens in hand to write letters to the editor. "A great modern fairy tale," one of these volunteers called the story. Preachers took Lindbergh as their topic, and commercial commodities as well as zoölogical exhibits were named for him. A former Justice of the Supreme Court united with the Secretary of War and the Governor of New York State in dithyrambic pæans. Time and again his flight was compared in importance with the Armistice; and vastly greater space was devoted to it.

The Government of the United States took advantage of the fanfare to victimize this somewhat shrinking young carrier of commercial air mail. When newspaper men interviewed him in Paris, Ambassador Myron T. Herrick was present to signify by a nod or a shake of the head whether he should answer questions. He was brought back across the Atlantic in a naval flagship, the *Memphis*, accompanied by Vice-Admiral Burrage. Among the newspapers men aboard was the *New York Times* reporter who was writing the aviator's "signed" stories. (The stories were printed in thirty-odd newspapers, and presumably accepted as coming from Lindbergh himself.) This reporter, and the others aboard, found that their material was censored. Not even a bulletin could go out without the O.K. of Commander Bagley. Since the end of the World War American newspaper men had not submitted to censorship until the Navy manifested this acute and arrogant interest. Nor was Lindbergh consulted as to what should be deleted. The Commander of the *Memphis* took it upon himself to say what should and should not be made known to the public.

Lindbergh's father had denounced the World War, had declared that "we have been dragged into the war by the intrigue of speculators," and had written a book, "Why Is Your Country at War." The *New York times* had counted him fortunate not to be under indictment for sedition. The son refused to wear a Colonel's uniform sent out to him on the *Memphis*; but he was taken first to Washington, nevertheless, that the Government might identify itself with him, and him with the Unknown Soldier. He found his flight made the occasion for a demand for more fliers and better preparedness; he even found himself echoing these phrases! Willy-nilly, he was made a Colonel in the Air Corps Reserve of the United States Army. Addressing this modest and skillful young man at St. Louis, the Secretary of War said:

> You have almost alone reunited in spirit and soul nations whose sons shed their blood in a common cause, peoples who through mutual misunderstandings seemed to be drifting apart when the world most needed a recrudescence of the valorous spirit of comradeship which sent men of different tongues and different races into the hell of battle. With common purpose

and common courage, you flew from the night as a harbinger of international good-will.

And the daily press, which had exploited and victimized the young man to fatten its circulation figures, lent its cordial coöperation to his exploitation for the praiseworthy purposes of international relations and militarism. It uttered not a whimper about the censorship.

During all this time Lindbergh signed no commercial contracts, although vaudeville and motion picture promoters were eager to make him and themselves rich. At the crest of the newspaper-bred hysteria about him he refused to reap a harvest of millions. He had witnessed the sudden economic inflation of personalities; he had seen how the journalistic deification of "Trudy" Ederle and "Red" Grange and "Babe" Ruth and various prize-fighters had thrown tangential fortunes into their laps. If the newspapers profited, in higher milline advertising rates, how much more did these temporary idols of a gullible and suggestible populace profit! Compared to their annual earnings at the height of their pulpwood acclaim, the President of the United States drew a meagre wage. It was true that with the waning of the paroxysm earnings fell off. Ours is a restless populace, hand-cuffed to a mechanical monotony and ever atiptoe for another thrill. In a channel swimmer, a bathing beauty, a tennis player, a pugilist, a motion picture star, it may find vicarious escape from the commonplace of machinery; and the newspaper undertakes profitably to provide the escape.

V

The organized ballyhoo which I have been describing had its real beginnings in the last decade of the last century. We may trace its trends by glancing at the results of two surveys, one made in 1899, the other in 1923. In each there was set down the space allotted by sixty-three leading American newspapers to various types of news. During this twenty-four-year period, there was a decline of seventy-seven per cent in editorials, a decline of eighty-four per cent in letters to the editor, and a decline of sixty-six per cent in society items. Let us look now at the figures for certain categories of news, for advertising and illustrations.

General and political news, each increased one per cent—no ballyhoo there; business news increased four per cent; foreign, nine; sports, forty-seven; crime, fifty-eight!

Meanwhile advertising was increased forty-seven per cent, and illustrations eighty-four per cent.

Three years before the first of these surveys was made, at the time of the St. Louis tornado, the *Globe-Democrat* had never, even on an occasion so important as a Presidential election, printed a headline more than two columns wide, in type which would be considered inconspicuous in these days. The paper had become powerful and famous under the management of J. B. McCullagh; but on the day of the storm (of all days!) he was unable to reach his office. The duty of getting out the paper thus fell to a youngish assistant. The cyclone, so-called, was a big story, anywhere in the United States. In St. Louis, what with the great property loss, the death toll, the narrow escapes and heroic rescues, and the freakishness of the storm itself, it was by all odds the greatest story of a generation. The young assistant rose to the occasion. In the composing room he found some huge wooden type, intended for use in posters and handbills; and out of it he constructed a headline calculated to shock the most phlegmatic.

When McCullagh reached the office the next day the young man, so the story goes, spread the paper before him with unaffected pride. How did he like that headline? The Managing Editor gazed at it for some seconds in silence. Then, "It's a good head," he said; "it tells the story; but that type—I was saving that type for the Second Coming!"

For convenience this headline may be accepted as marking a mile-stone in American journalism. Other newspapers had used type as big and black, but no newspaper so conservative as the *Globe-Democrat*. This was in 1896; and it was not long until the press, which before had merely cried its wares, learned to shriek them. There was a riot of type and a bedlam of layouts. The Spanish-American War period witnessed the height of that fanfare. In that tempest ballyhoo was born. There came a stretch of comparative quiescence, until the World War so completely deranged all standards of news value and methods of news display that the American press has seemed unable to recover a normal and sound judgment.

These happenings cover less than the span of a generation. Let us move back something more than a century, that we may have the advantage of better perspective, and see what happened when the Battle of Waterloo was faught. The London *Times* announced Wellington's victory in less than a quarter of a column. No one will pretend that this was adequate from the modern viewpoint of enormous headlines and floods of poppycock, but the *Times* had no apologies to offer: indeed, it put the news of one of the world's decisive battles at the *bottom* of a column. Last Fall, and again last Spring, it was nothing unusual to see, in New York newspapers, as much as twenty columns devoted to a single day's proceedings in two second-rate murder trials. The first was second-rate because the victims were an obscure clergyman and a janitor's wife; the other because, even from the newspaper slant, there was never any real mystery in it, and but little suspense as to the outcome. Napoleon's defeat in 1815 was announced to a triumphant nation in about three hundred words; whereas to report the Hall-Mills case a single newspaper required twice as many words as Will Durant needed to tell "The Story of Philosophy"; and this author himself was one of the "trained seals" who helped overcrowd the press of the United States with balderdash about the Snyder-Gray trial.

On the very day of the signing of the Armistice which ended the World War, the German Empire was overthrown and the Kaiser fled from the Fatherland into Holland. I do not believe the press has ever been asked to lift into public view on any other day so great a load of news. The *New York Times* met the emergency, so far as first-page display went, by the use of four eight-column "streamer" headlines. Eight years later, when Tunney defeated Dempsey, it headlined the event with three eight-column "streamers." This was not news perspective. If the Dempsey-Tunney prize-fight were put into proper perspective with the events of Armistice Day, it would become invisible to the naked eye. Already its details have faded from the memory of all but sport fans. Not news perspective, this ballyhoo of the "cauliflower trade," but a development in the exploitation of a suggestible people.

James Melvin Lee, head of the School of Journalism at New York University, thinks news of informational value, instead of concentration on paid sports, screen stars, aviators and channel swimmers, could be made to pay. "Crowded as is the New York field," he writes (and surely what he says would prove true in less crowded fields), "it would, in my opinion, support a newspaper which adopted as its motto, 'All the news that's important.' The experiment of producing a paper living up to that motto has never been made in the United States. Some of the foreign newspapers which feature not 'what's interesting,' but 'what's important,' more than break even from their sales."

But news of genuinely instructive and informative character remains of a clearly casual nature. The inflation of matter appealing to unconscious passions and hungers continues. The news which startles, thrills and entertains is still blown up as vigorously as the toy balloon of Queen Marie's visit. Thus does the American press exemplify day by day the grandiose, the brobdingnagian art of ballyhoo.

JOHN DEWEY

Our Un-Free Press
(1935)

The question of the freedom of the press assumes a radically different aspect according as one takes for granted the permanence of the existing economic system—with minor reforms in it—or as one believes that the economic system is so chaotic and unjust in its workings as to demand radical change. If one takes the first position, one will have to be satisfied with striking a balance sheet. In this balance sheet, one will point out certain limitations upon freedom involved in the kind of irresponsible journalism engaged in by William Randolph Hearst; the limitations placed by advertisers upon what is printed; the invasions of privacy under the guise of freedom; the reckless sensationalism of many newspapers, etc., etc. But these will be regarded as abuses which are not inherent. As evidence that these things are only incidental abuses, one will point to the fact that there are "clean" journals which are at the same time successful; that there has been a great decline in merely partisan journalism; that many newspapers now print in full the speeches of politicians of the opposite parties; that there are successful newspapers that do not perceptibly color the news; that foreign news is now handled much more amply and intelligently than before the war; that there are liberal weeklies and monthlies; that a person of recognized standing can get a hearing in some publication for extreme liberal and radical views, etc., etc.

If one accepts the present economic order as inevitable and permanent, I see no reason why this sort of "on the one hand and on the other hand" argument should not go on indefinitely. There is a great deal to be said on both sides, and it is said. One may make an appalling list of suppressions, perversions and unchecked irresponsibilities. One may also point optimistically and with a good deal of justice to many encouraging symptoms of improvement in American journalism. I do not see that this line of argument is likely to get anywhere, save as specific criticism of

From *John Dewey: The Later Works, 1925–1953*, edited by Jo Ann Boydston (Carbondale, IL: Southern Illinois University Press, 1991), 269–73. First appeared in *Common Sense* 4 (November 1935): 6–7.

specific "abuses" tends to make newspaper managers more wary of committing themselves—of course a good thing.

The only really fundamental approach to the problem is to inquire concerning the necessary effect of the present economic system upon the whole system of publicity; upon the judgment of what news is, upon the selection and elimination of matter that is published, upon the treatment of news in both editorial and news columns. The question, under this mode of approach, is not how many specific abuses there are and how they may be remedied, but how far genuine intellectual freedom and social responsibility are possible on any large scale under the existing economic regime.

The question then becomes one aspect, and an exceedingly important one, of the larger problem of the existence of fundamental freedom of ideas and action under our present system. The glorification of the liberty of the press in which publishers and editors now indulge, failing to realize that they, as factors in the economic system, may be themselves its chief enemies, are based on the assumption that the government is the chief enemy to be dreaded, and are thus simply in tune with the outgivings of the self-styled Liberty League. What is glorified under the name of liberty is the power of the business entrepreneur to carry on his own business in his own way for the sake of private profit. The newspaper enterprise presents itself, according to the way one looks at the system, as the glory or the shame of rugged individualism in a *laissez-faire* system. Granted that some few publishers (and the editors who, after all, are only hired men) have an acute sense of public responsibility, what is their conception of the nature of the public to whom they are responsible? Taking these few at their best, the public and the social order to which they feel responsible is the existing economic system. It is this system which provides the standard for selection and organization of news.

There was a time after the collapse of '29, for example, when even the best newspapers (in the present sense of good) systematically suppressed the facts of growing unemployment. Many of them did it "conscientiously." Was not the depression largely "psychological" and would not publication of the facts simply increase and prolong the depression? The metropolitan papers blazoned abroad the assertion by the official head of a great private relief organization that local authorities were taking care of those who needed relief. When he appeared before a Senate Committee and was asked for evidence that might go on the records, and admitted that he had none except a few casual long-distance telephone conversation, no paper gave the fact any publicity. When the break-down of private charity became too evident to be covered up and the Federal Government began the policy of appropriations for relief, one has only to glance at the daily papers as the publicity organs of the present system, to note that they have been chiefly concerned with pointing out the effects on business of the high taxes made necessary by these appropriations.

All this, as Veblen might have said, is quite as it should be—given the economic system as a necessary concern. For the newspapers to face, even as a matter of news, unemployment and its causes, would be to engage in an assault upon the existing system. The newspaper business is a business; it is an enterprise conducted for private profit. Why then should it be expected of the managers of this business enterprise to do otherwise than as the leaders and henchmen of big business: namely, claim that business carried on for private profit is the best way of rendering social and public service, and select and treat *their* special wares from this standpoint?

In what I have said, I have put forward the best possible case for the existing press. In most of the industrial centres of the country, there are newspapers that are owned and deliberately controlled by some special industrial interest, and it is the business of the editors to select and suppress news in accord with its bearing upon the industry that owns them body and soul. When the Bethlehem Steel Company is under congressional investigation, would one expect the Bethlehem papers and those of the neighborhood under the control of this branch of the steel industry to print even the Associated Press dispatches regarding bonuses and armaments, even though the affairs in question were a matter of governmental record? It would be naive to indulge in any such expectation.

Such facts as these suggest another aspect of the problem of freedom of the press. The mangers of the press fall back upon giving the public what it "wants" and they can make out a case for the proposition that *this* is its wants, so that the responsibility goes back to the public and what it wants. Well, what *does* the public want in the present economic system? In spite of what the press does to create the wants upon which it then feeds, it is probably true by-and-large that the press is a fair reflection of the state of the public mind. The hopelessly naive and the apologist in high places (possibly a college president), will use this fact to discredit the public; its members are just too dumb, too immersed in petty affairs and in seeking their gross pleasures not to prefer news of murders and love-nests and commercialized sport to genuinely public news. The effect of the present economic system in generating intellectual indifference and apathy, in creating a demand for distraction and diversion, and almost a love for crime provided it pays, is completely ignored. A public, debauched by the ideal of getting away with whatever it can, will hardly turn away from a press that is getting away with murder.

The problem of the freedom of the press is a perfect illustration of the impasse of present society in accomplishing its own needed reconstruction. The task can hardly be accomplished in an orderly and peaceful way without knowledge of existing evils and of the causes that produce them. But the very set-up of the system that nourishes these evils is such as to prevent adequate and widespread realization of the evils and their causes; it is such as to divert the public mind into all sorts of irrelevancies. If one include the radio and the news-reel with the press, there is little exaggeration in the notion of a fourth estate, an estate which in direct and subtle ways has more power than the citizenry acting through recognized governmental channels. This power of the press is one phase of the power of the present economic system of business for private profit.

Those who believe that the end of freedom and of equality of opportunity for all are served by the freedom of concentrated capital to run production and distribution for the benefit of the owners of this capital, will be satisfied with the present freedom of the press. But the others? Does any one imagine that under a cooperative economic system, controlled in the interest of all, it would be necessary to have official censorship of, say, the Hearst press? Would not such a press under such a social system be inherently impossible? Some indication of the answer to this question may be found in the attacks in which that press and its prototypes, many of them more outwardly respectable, engage when it is a question of even a minor reform in the existing system.

MORRIS ERNST

The Vanishing Market Place of Thought
(1946)

The Big Bad Monopolists

Bigness and concentration of power in these communication fields is part of our traditional monopoly problem. For more than half a century we have seen the danger of monopolies in markets of tangible commodities for shop or home. We cherished small business, emotionally resisted the wiping out of free individual enterprise and deplored the increased prices to consumers resulting from trusts and monopolies. Our efforts have been not too well rewarded. Consistently we have starved the budget and personnel of the anti-trust division of the Department of Justice. Recently we revitalized the work. But we labored under old-fashioned economic philosophies. We refused to adopt the Brandeis approach. We have not even reduced the rate of decimation of smaller units by the giants.

When the war came we found that the army and navy gave further aid to large-scale business. It was easier to place a few orders of vast size than to employ the entire man and plant power of the nation directly by a program of Bits and Pieces such as was adopted in England. So the Big grew bigger and relieved the government of much detail by becoming the dispensers of millions of subcontracts. All of which added to the power of the big company, the primary contractor.

The essential error of our approach arose from turning our gaze more toward the evil monopolist than toward distortions of the market place. In a way we wanted a personal devil. However, as a buccaneer westward-moving people we were confused between our admiration for the man who could corner the market and our grievance against the limitation on the right of every man to engage in a profitable undertaking. Moreover, the innate business-inventive genius of our people accelerated the development of mergers, consolidations and pools of buying and selling power. It was natural for our law to develop on the theory that monopoly was in itself not an evil. We did not wish to throttle ambition until the

From *The First Freedom* (New York: The Macmillan Company, 1946), 44–55.

precise moment when success had created *unreasonable* restrictions on free enterprise.

We know that all competition is hurtful to the independent competitor. We were more concerned with the little man driven out of business than for the public inevitably hurt by monopoly. We said, "Let's look at how the monopolist got his power. Was he decent? Did he cheat? Did he wipe out competitors by *unfair* practices?"

Such queries missed the real point of the national economic inquiry. To the consumer it makes no difference whatever when he goes out to buy a radio, see a movie or purchase a paper, whether the producer or distributer was clean or dirty in the efforts which gave him control of the market. The sole test is, has he got a monopoly, not how he got it. Had we listened to Brandeis we would long ago have scrutinized the end result—the condition of the market. We would have assumed that mere exaggerated size created presumptions of anti-social power.

It's never easy to ascertain how a market place would have behaved in the absence of a monopolist. We must accept on partial faith the dogma that whenever a single buyer or seller controls the major demand or supply of any commodity, there are implicit temporary advantages to such concern by restricting the supply, eliminating competition and increasing the burdens on the consumers. The same holds true if instead of a single monopolist a group of companies act in concert. However, we seem to think group action is more anti-social than action by one alone. Again to the consumer it makes no difference.

That the monopolist or the group is malicious, or even intends to reduce or increase costs, seems to me to be irrelevant. Nor is the observation any different if a group of "little" men gets together to fight a single large giant—if their combination can control the market place. This, no matter how sympathetic we are to little merchants. A union closed at both ends—closed membership and closed shop—contains the same evil influence on the market as the practices of monopolists.

We must remove our emotions from our appraisal of this stream of economics. Our courts, until recently, endeavored to ascertain the manner in which the monopolist got his power. It seemed important, before condemning a monopoly, to find out if the company charged with the crime was fair or unfair in its treatment of competitors. All this is now beside the point. In the radio and Associated Press anti-trust decisions we have at last become adult in the law of restraint. We look at the company alleged to control an area or a commodity. Comparative, not objective, size and control is the starting point of the consideration. A million dollars in some precious rare metal may give more dominance than $100,000,000 may provide in making automobiles. Seventy per cent of movie ownership by five companies may be enough to wipe out all effective interplay of supply and demand. A single newspaper in a certain area may not spell any violation of anti-trust laws.

The most the law can do is to prevent the buying or selling end of the market place getting too far out of line. But by inaction the government distorts the market. It must act not only as a shield but also as a spear for freedom.

Communication Bottled Up

In the three major fields of communication—press, radio and movies—we now have had a series of recent decisions by our highest courts condemning in strong language the unbalancing of these market places of thought.

In the movie field, after a series of cases scolding the major elements of the industry, the court took a look at an attempt of a chain of theaters in Tennessee to wipe out all independent theaters. In that pursuit the chain was helped to no little degree by the large motion-picture producers. The product of an independent producer could not get into Tennessee except under burdensome and unfair conditions. The Supreme Court broke up the Tennessee chain. It was urged by the Tennessee exhibitor that he was powerless against the big producing companies unless he could increase his buying power by gobbling up other theaters. The court, in effect, said it might be that something should be done to destroy the overwhelming power of the movie giants, but surely we should not wait to destroy the Tennessee monopoly until such time as the producing monopoly is purged. And now at this very time the government is proceeding with great energy against the eight movie companies—that all too small group which owns the distribution system of the United States.

In the radio field the two largest networks were equally spanked. The Federal Communications Commission held protracted hearings, and issued a monopoly report. This report was not much mentioned in the press or on the air. We have not enough networks or press associations to let this kind of item find its way into the arena of public debate. The networks refused to allow a debate of the issues involved in the report. The leading officials of the major networks testified, however, that freedom of the air was finished and that networks could not function with profit if the proposed regulations were adopted. The case went up through the courts. The Federal Communications Commission was sustained. The networks prospered as never before. The calamity prophets of the mighty in radio now seem to be men without vision or schemers trying to scare the government into transferring complete ownership of the ether to the two networks involved.

The Federal Communications Commission had laid down some simple conditions. No one corporation should be allowed to own two networks. No one licensee should be allowed to own two stations in one town. No network should by contract be allowed to own the program time of affiliated stations.

There was no public debate, in democratic terms, for the proposals dealt with

media of communication and such media—at least all those which had large audiences—were intent on keeping any such debate away from public consideration.

But the Supreme Court spoke up, in the radio monopoly regulation case, sustaining the Federal Communications Commission. In the dissenting opinion we find
a statement with which the entire court agreed:

> In the dissemination of information and opinion, radio has assumed a posi-
> tion of commanding importance, rivaling the press and the pulpit . . . because
> of its vast potentialities as a medium of communication, discussion and prop-
> aganda, the character and extent of control that should be exercised over it
> by the government is a matter of deep and vital concern.

This was not censorship. There was no desire of government to censor program
content. The case involved solely greater diversity of ownership of broadcasting.
The big boys in the game naturally wanted no more competition.

Following the radio and movie cases we find the A.P. urging, under the gospel
of a free press, the right to bottleneck the news market place. The A.P. is really a
combination of an extra-governmental nature, prescribing rules for the restraint of
interstate commerce.

In the A.P. case the Supreme Court sustained the decision of the court below,
in which Judge Learned Hand wrote:

> However, neither exclusively nor even primarily are the interests of the
> newspaper industry conclusive; for that industry serves one of the most vital
> of all general interests—the dissemination of news from as many different
> sources and with as many different facets and colors as is possible.
>
> That interest is closely akin to, if indeed is not the same as, the interest
> protected by the First Amendment; it pre-supposes that right conclusions are
> more likely to be gathered out of a multitude of tongues, than through any
> kind of authoritative selection. To many this is, and always will be, folly; but
> we have staked upon it our all.
>
> For these reasons, it is impossible to treat two news services as inter-
> changeable, and to deprive a paper of the benefit of any service of the first
> rating is to deprive the reading public of means of information which it
> should have; it is only by crosslights from varying directions that full illu-
> mination can be secured.

Justice Black, in the decision of the United States Supreme Court, used the
following language in his landmark opinion:

The net effect [of the A.P. restraints] is seriously to limit the opportunity of any newspaper to enter these cities. Trade restraints of this character, aimed at the destruction of competition, tend to block the initiative which brings newcomers into a field of business and to frustrate the free enterprise system which it was the purpose of the Sherman Act to protect.

And further in relation to the need of diversity:

It would be strange indeed, however, if the grave concern for freedom of the press which prompted adoption of the First Amendment should be read as a command that the government was without power to protect that freedom. The First Amendment, far from providing an argument against application of the Sherman Act, here provides powerful reasons to the contrary. That Amendment rests on the assumption that the widest possible dissemination of information from diverse and antagonistic sources is essential to the welfare of the public, that a free press is a condition of a free society. Surely a command that the government itself shall not impede the free flow of ideas does not afford non-governmental combinations a refuge if they impose restraints upon that constitutionally guaranteed freedom. Freedom to publish means freedom for all and not for some. Freedom to publish is guaranteed by the Constitution, but freedom to combine to keep others from publishing is not. Freedom of the press from governmental interference under the First Amendment does not sanction repression of that freedom by private interests. The First Amendment affords not the slightest support for the contention that a combination to restrain trade in news and views has any constitutional immunity.

There no longer can be any doubt about the increasing concern of the Supreme Court as to the monopolists of thought. Few industries have been so thoroughly castigated by high judicial officers as have the press, movies and radio.

In these cases, and others, preceding or collateral thereto, we have made slow but great philosophical strides. Motive of aggrandizement, fairness of practices of the monopolists, economic need of domination in order to survive are all increasingly immaterial. We are concerned with the right of the consumer. And in our society the most important consumer goods are those sold by press, radio and movies.

I take some pride in the fact that, as far as I know, I first injected into documents for court perusal the theory that since the constitutional rights of the receiver are even more important than those of the utterer, diversity of opinion is essential if we want to continue to give meaning to our Bill of Rights, and no matter how we may feel about monopolies in hairpins or soap, the commodity which goes to the mind deserves and must be handled on a higher standard than that applied to all other merchandise. Material protected by our First Amendment is the preferred merchandise of our society.

It is interesting to note how long those who control media of communication have been allowed to proceed with their increasing concentration of power without governmental interference. As far back as 1915 Judge Brandeis pointed to the evil consequences of monopoly of thought, in the case of A.P. vs. I.N.S.

The movie case against the Big Five was started in 1938. It is not near the Supreme Court.

A gap of five years occurred between the start of the Federal Communications Commission inquiry into radio monopoly and the final decision of the highest court.

But at long last we are learning that failure of the government to act can be as detrimental to the rights secured by the First Amendment as an act of positive interference. Twenty years ago Justice Stone pointed out in a case in the Supreme Court—involving a law to protect apple trees from a cedar tree germ—that the failure of the state to take action in behalf of the owners of apple trees would have been tantamount to its taking action on behalf of the owners of cedar trees. The owners of press, radio and movies favor inaction on the part of the government because by inaction those in the saddle can further act to control the market place. Hence, inaction deprives the public of its right to hear, see and read. We need governmental offense as well as defense in the pursuit of liberty. The battle involves a way of life and not just named individuals.

Those men who own our minds are not evil persons. They are men of energy and vitality and ingenuity. They suffer from the sole disease of capitalism—the germ which may destroy free enterprise. While shouting free enterprise, they urge the right to destroy the enterprise of all save themselves. They are for freedom of competition for little people in all industries but their own. They chant in monotonous rhythm the dangers of governmental censorship, never realizing that the path of monopoly leads directly to government ownership. They are wise enough to see that the people will not allow uncontrolled extra-governmental groups to monopolize the market place for gas, water, electricity or even milk. They know that whenever a market gets too tight the public demands regulation. The concept of "public utility" should scare the wits out of owners of radio, press and movies. History should teach them that they are going down the monopoly road to "public utility" street. But for some odd reason the zeal for getting bigger and bigger has a self blinding effect.

I do not ask that heads of dominant businesses be brave enough to realize that mere size has dinosaurial defects. They acclaim the virtues of competition—it keeps people on their toes—and they go out and buy up the only competing newspaper of the district. Unless we wake up we will soon find that less than 100 cities have competing newspapers. Heads of the movie industry boast that their pictures are the best ever made, but play safe by buying up the main theaters of a town so that if by chance one of their pictures is not so good, it still can be shown. I don't mean exactly "can be shown." Rather that the public will have no choice but to see that picture. If they don't buy the theater they tie it up with an exclusive franchise. The air is bottlenecked through networks of dominated local stations.

The only limit to such aggrandizement is the will of the people expressed through courts and legislatures. Giants forget the qualities of humility and self-restraint. The bigger they get the less there is any chance of public criticism. So they run wild in their efforts to close the markets. Competition between three giant newsgatherers is not necessarily the acme of competition. That five movie companies struggle against each other spells—not a free market, but a limited policy of dog eat dog. Four networks may envy each other but more than four groups should have access to the public ear.

There Are No Devils

Knowing that these are not problems of individual personalities I have tried sincerely to avoid appraisals of the thirty or forty men who own the main access to America's mind. I have been urged to write this volume in terms of Sarnoff, Paley, Noble, McCosker, Reid, Sulzberger, Howard, the Cowles, Gannett, Field, Knight, the Pattersons, McCormick, Hearst, Perry, Ogden, Mayer, the Schencks, Odlum, Rubin, the Warners, Balaban, Luce, Wallace, to mention most of the important originating persons now in the saddle. Circuit theater owners like Shine, Sudekum, Griffith might be included, as well as Eastman, producer of raw film stock, and several key patent holders and apparatus manufacturers.

I am not here interested in these people as people. Nor do I care how they got their power—inheritance, ingenuity or through banker selection. By and large they are as decent, fair and wise as our present negligent democracy deserves. They differ among themselves on many issues. They are all heads of such vast empires that it is only natural they should be less adventurous than the small operator who has no great capital to lose. Moreover, some of them have so many employees under them that they are remote from the man on the park bench or the girl in the theater balcony.

Many of them I consider friends of mine. They know I agree with them in their individual, unrestricted control of their own media—right or wrong, wise or foolish. My complaint is that there are too few owners for 138,000,000 people; the proportion is unsatisfactory.

For the purpose of this volume I care not whether one of these pipeline owners is left or right, conservative or liberal, weak or strong. Let them be malicious, from my point of view, provided only there is enough opposing malice flowing into the market place.

But whenever some of these giants agree with my thesis in favor of greater diversity they nod and say, "Nothing can be done to stem the tide. This is the sweep of progress." Thus do rugged individualists revert to the gospel of fatalism and inevitability. Once in a while a movie magnate will agree that the radio bottleneck should be investigated, for certainly we have to do something about the power of the four men who own the networks. And the network men will rail against the press because of its ability to discriminate against a competing broadcasting station in favor of the station owned by a newspaper. From the great movie giants I have heard no eagerness for expansion of the democratic pattern except for one company which has stated that the United States might be better off if no producer was allowed to own a theater.

The question is: How far has the monopoly trend gone and what dangers are we facing? Let us look with pride at the record of our inventive genius and the zeal which gives us quantity production of radio programs, movies and papers. But let us not blindly worship the three gods of Quantity, Size and Mass. Variety, Selectivity, Variables are also important in a dynamic democracy.

With 2,600 dailies a few years ago are 1,700 enough today? How many will we have in 1960?

Five movie companies own 70 per cent of the movie income of the nation. Will there be only three in 1960?

Four networks have control over two-thirds of the radio stations of the nation. Will they control more in 1960? Will television and F.M. go the same way?

In what direction are we moving? Is there anything in the record to indicate that the destruction of small merchants in ideas will diminish in the next decade?

These and other queries first occurred to me about five years ago. I looked over the literature. I found very little: Huettig's book on the movies, Lee's great contribution, *The Daily Newspaper in America*, the writings on radio of Clifford Durr and James L. Fly, a few government reports and the records of many law cases. The industry associations either have no data of trends of ownership or have refused to make them available.

We have in many places and in many fields practically no market of thought left—worth calling a market in democratic terms. It's still a market infinitely richer than that of any totalitarian society. But we cannot afford to take pride in that comparison or to see it shrink farther. We cannot afford not to expand it. Our fight is for a way of life and not a battle against a few individuals.

The devil in this story is our own acceptance of fatalism plus one basic neglect. We have not only allowed these markets to get tighter and tighter but we also have failed to demand of our press and radio that the facts of their own monopolization be told to the American people. Even proceedings by the government in law suits against the monopolies of the A.P., the major movie companies and the radio networks get less play on most radio stations and in most papers than do picayune, insignificant crime stories or similar monopoly charges leveled against aluminum, steel or meat. For example, few people know that radio without "commercials" is economically possible and has been urged in Washington before the F.C.C. for months. This is also quite natural. Maybe it is asking too much for the press to report objectively on the claimed evils of the press. The heads of the radio networks emphatically refused in writing to allow even a forum discussion on the air of the famous F.C.C. radio monopoly report.

My publisher friends query, "Would you ask a cigarette manufacturer to insert in his ads a decision of the Federal Trade Commission condemning his products?"

I deny the analogy. These three media are and at times claim to be *trustees* of freedom of thought. They should act like trustees and tell their beneficiaries—the people—the story of the narrowing bottleneck to the market place of thought.

I have talked to many of the leading publishers and editors urging them to take stock of the problem. Only one network has allowed any debate of the issues. I have discussed this material and my proposed solutions with more than a score of United States Senators. All but two agreed that here is an issue of major importance. I write this book in the hope of stimulating further Congressional discussion, for we cannot be saved by judicial decree alone.

In the three following chapters I have shown statistically the evaporation of our press and the concentration into too few hands of all three media. The danger is clear to those who read these figures. There are literally hundreds of measures which will occur to any thinking person as to what to do about it all. I have listed in the final chapter in very brief form some of the answers. No one piece of legislation will do the trick. No one lawsuit will give the relief we deserve. Each industry has separate problems and requires different treatment. Nor are these three groups all there are to the tale. Books and magazines are more than tangential influences. Another book should be written to trace similar trends in the theater, music and other fields of human expression, which I do not discuss.

THE HUTCHINS COMMISSION

The Problem and the Principles
(1947)

The Problem

The Commission set out to answer the question:

Is the freedom of the press in danger? Its answer to that question is: Yes. It concludes that the freedom of the press is in danger for three reasons:

First, the importance of the press to the people has greatly increased with the development of the press as an instrument of mass communication. At the same time the development of the press as an instrument of mass communication has greatly decreased the proportion of the people who can express their opinions and ideas through the press.

Second, the few who are able to use the machinery of the press as an instrument of mass communication have not provided a service adequate to the needs of the society.

Third, those who direct the machinery of the press have engaged from time to time in practices which the society condemns and which, if continued, it will inevitably undertake to regulate or control.

When an instrument of prime importance to all the people is available to a small minority of the people only, and when it is employed by that small minority in such a way as not to supply the people with the service they require, the freedom of the minority in the employment of that instrument is in danger.

This danger, in the case of the freedom of the press, is in part the consequence of the economic structure of the press, in part the consequence of the industrial organization of modern society, and in part the result of the failure of the directors of the press to recognize the press needs of a modern nation and to estimate and accept the responsibilities which those needs impose upon them.

We do not believe that the danger to the freedom of the press is so great that

From *A Free and Responsible Press* (Chicago: University of Chicago Press, 1947), 1–19.

that freedom will be swept away overnight. In our view the present crisis is simply a stage in the long struggle for free expression. Freedom of expression, of which freedom of the press is a part, has always been in danger. Indeed, the Commission can conceive no state of society in which it will not be in danger. The desire to suppress opinion different from one's own is inveterate and probably ineradicable.

Neither do we believe that the problem is one to which a simple solution can be found. Government ownership, government control, or government action to break up the greater agencies of mass communication might cure the ills of freedom in the process. Although, as we shall see later, government has an important part to play in communications, we look principally to the press and the people to remedy the ills which have chiefly concerned us.

But though the crisis is not unprecedented and though the cures may not be dramatic, the problem is nevertheless a problem of peculiar importance to this generation. And not in the United States alone but in England and Japan and Australia and Austria and France and Germany as well; and in Russia and in the Russian pale. The reasons are obvious. The relation of the modern press to modern society is a new and unfamiliar relation.

The modern press itself is a new phenomenon. Its typical unit is the great agency of mass communication. These agencies can facilitate thought and discussion. They can stifle it. They can advance the progress of civilization or they can thwart it. They can debase and vulgarize mankind. They can endanger the peace of the world; they can do so accidentally, in a fit of absence of mind. They can play up or down the news and its significance, foster and feed emotions, create complacent fictions and blind spots, misuse the great words, and uphold empty slogans. Their scope and power are increasing every day as new instruments become available to them. These instruments can spread lies faster and farther than our forefathers dreamed when they enshrined the freedom of the press in the First Amendment to our Constitution.

With the means of self-destruction that are now at their disposal, men must live, if they are to live at all, by self-restraint, moderation, and mutual understanding. They get their picture of one another through the press. The press can be inflammatory, sensational, and irresponsible. If it is, it and its freedom will go down in the universal catastrophe. On the other hand, the press can do its duty by the new world that is struggling to be born. It can help create a world community by giving men everywhere knowledge of the world and of one another, by promoting comprehension and appreciation of the goals of a free society that shall embrace all men.

We have seen in our time a revival of the doctrine that the state is all and that the person is merely an instrument of its purposes. We cannot suppose that the military defeat of totalitarianism in its German and Italian manifestations has put an end to the influence and attractiveness of the doctrine. The necessity of finding some way through the complexities of modern life and of controlling the concentrations of power associated with modern industry will always make it look as though turning over all problems to the government would easily solve them.

This notion is a great potential danger to the freedom of the press. That freedom is the first which totalitarianism strikes down. But steps toward totalitarianism may be taken, perhaps unconsciously, because of conditions within the press itself. A technical society requires concentration of economic power. Since such concentration is a threat to democracy, democracy replies by breaking up some centers of power that are too large and too strong and by controlling, or even owning, others. Modern society requires great agencies of mass communication. They, too, are concentrations of power. But breaking up a vast network of communication is a different thing from breaking up an oil monopoly or a tobacco monopoly. If the people set out to break up a unit of communication on the theory that it is too large and strong, they may destroy a service which they require. Moreover, since action to break up an agency of communication must be taken at the instance of a department of the government, the risk is considerable that the freedom of the press will be imperiled through the application of political pressure by that department.

If modern society requires great agencies of mass communication, if these concentrations become so powerful that they are a threat to democracy, if democracy cannot solve the problem simply by breaking them up—then those agencies must control themselves or be controlled by government. If they are controlled by government, we lose our chief safeguard against totalitarianism—and at the same time take a long step toward it.*

The Principles

Freedom of the press is essential to political liberty. Where men cannot freely convey their thoughts to one another, no freedom is secure. Where freedom of expression exists, the beginnings of a free society and a means for every extension of liberty are already present. Free expression is therefore unique among liberties: it promotes and protects all the rest. It is appropriate that freedom of speech and freedom of the press are contained in the first of those constitutional enactments which are the American Bill of Rights.

Civilized society is a working system of ideas. It lives and changes by the con-

---

*A third possibility is that government itself may come into the field with an alternative system of communications. The Commission has given little consideration to this possibility, except in international communications. Yet the example of Station WNYC, controlled by New York City, suggests what government may do in domestic communications if it regards private service as inadequate.

sumption of ideas. Therefore it must make sure that as many as possible of the ideas which its members have are available for its examination. It must guarantee freedom of expression, to the end that all adventitious hindrances to the flow of ideas shall be removed. Moreover, a significant innovation in the realm of ideas is likely to arouse resistance. Valuable ideas may be put forth first in forms that are crude, indefensible, or even dangerous. They need the chance to develop through free criticism as well as the chance to survive on the basis of their ultimate worth. Hence the man who publishes ideas requires special protection.

The reason for the hostility which the critic or innovator may expect is not merely that it is easier and more natural to suppress or discourage him than to meet his arguments. Irrational elements are always present in the critic, the innovator, and their audience. The utterance of critical or new ideas is seldom an appeal to pure reason, devoid of emotion, and the response is not necessarily a debate; it is always a function of the intelligence, the prejudice, the emotional biases of the audience. Freedom of the press to appeal to reason may always be construed as freedom of the press to appeal to public passion and ignorance, vulgarity and cynicism. As freedom of the press is always in danger, so is it always dangerous. The freedom of the press illustrates the commonplace that if we are to live progressively we must live dangerously.

Across the path of the flow of ideas lie the existing centers of social power. The primary protector of freedom of expression against their obstructive influence is government. Government acts by maintaining order and by exercising on behalf of free speech and a free press the elementary sanctions against the expressions of private interest or resentment: sabotage, blackmail, and corruption.

But any power capable of protecting freedom is also capable of endangering it. Every modern government, liberal or otherwise, has a specific position in the field of ideas; its stability is vulnerable to critics in proportion to their ability and persuasiveness. A government resting on popular suffrage is no exception to this rule. It also may be tempted—just because public opinion is a factor in official livelihood—to manage the ideas and images entering public debate.

If the freedom of the press is to achieve reality, government must set limits on its capacity to interfere with, regulate, or suppress the voices of the press or to manipulate the data on which public judgment is formed.

Government must set these limits on itself, not merely because freedom of expression is a reflection of important interests of the community, but also because it is a moral right. It is a moral right because it has an aspect of duty about it.

It is true that the motives for expression are not all dutiful. They are and should be as multiform as human emotion itself, grave and gay, casual and purposeful, artful and idle. But there is a vein of expression which has the added impulsion of duty, and that is the expression of thought. If a man is burdened with an idea, he not only desires to express it; he ought to express it. He owes it to his conscience and the common good. The indispensable function of expressing ideas is one of obligation—to the community and also to something beyond the community—let us say to truth. It is the duty of the scientist to his result and of Socrates to his oracle; it is the duty of every man to his own belief. Because of this duty to what is beyond the state, freedom of speech and freedom of the press are moral rights which the state must not infringe.

The moral right of free expression achieves a legal status because the conscience of the citizen is the source of the continued vitality of the state. Wholly apart from the traditional ground for a free press—that it promotes the "victory of truth over falsehood" in the public arena—we see that public discussion is a necessary condition of a free society and that freedom of expression is a necessary condition of adequate public discussion. Public discussion elicits mental power and breadth; it is essential to the building of a mentally robust public; and, without something of the kind, a self-governing society could not operate. The original source of supply for this process is the duty of the individual thinker to his thought; here is the primary ground of his right.

This does not mean that every citizen has a moral or legal right to own a press or be an editor or have access, as of right, to the audience of any given medium of communication. But it does belong to the intention of the freedom of the press that an idea shall have its chance even if it is not shared by those who own or manage the press. The press is not free if those who operate it behave as though their position conferred on them the privilege of being deaf to ideas which the processes of free speech have brought to public attention.

But the moral right of free public expression is not unconditional. Since the claim of the right is based on the duty of a man to the common good and to his thought, the ground of the claim disappears when this duty is ignored or rejected. In the absence of accepted moral duties there are no moral rights. Hence, when the man who claims the moral rights of free expression is a liar, a prostitute whose political judgments can be bought, a dishonest inflamer of hatred and suspicion, his claim is unwarranted and groundless. From the moral point of view, at least, freedom of expression does not include the right to lie as a deliberate instrument of policy.

The right of free public expression does include the right to be in error. Liberty is experimental. Debate itself could not exist unless wrong opinions could be rightfully offered by those who suppose them to be right. But the assumption that the man in error is actually trying for truth is of the essence of his claim for freedom. What the moral right does not cover is the right to be deliberately or irresponsibly in error.

But a moral right can be forfeited and a legal right retained. Legal protection cannot vary with the fluctuations of inner moral direction in individual wills; it does not cease whenever a person has abandoned the moral ground of his right. It is not even desirable that the whole area of the responsible use of freedom should be made legally compulsory, even if it were possible; for in that case free self-control, a necessary ingredient of any free state, would be superseded by mechanism.

Many a lying, venal, and scoundrelly public expression must continue to find shelter under a "freedom of the press" built for widely different purposes, for to impair the legal right even when the moral right is gone may easily be a cure worse than the disease. Each definition of an abuse invites abuse of the definition. If the courts had to determine the inner corruptions of personal intention, honest and necessary criticisms would proceed under an added peril.

Though the presumption is against resort to legal action to curb abuses of the press, there are limits to legal toleration. The already recognized areas of legal correction of misused liberty of expression—libel, misbranding, obscenity, incitement to riot, sedition, in case of clear and present danger—have a common principle; namely, that an utterance or publication invades in a serious, overt, and demonstrable manner personal rights or vital social interests. As new categories of abuse come within this definition, the extension of legal sanctions is justified. The burden of proof will rest on those who would extend these categories, but the presumption is not intended to render society supine before possible new developments of misuse of the immense powers of the contemporary press.

The Principles in the Present Situation

The principles we have attempted to state are those general truths which are valid as goals for all civilized societies. It must be observed that freedom of the press is not a fixed and isolated value, the same in every society and in all times. It is a function within a society and must vary with the social context. It will be different in times of general security and in times of crisis; it will be different under varying states of public emotion and belief.

The freedom we have been examining has assumed a type of public mentality which may seem to us standard and universal but which is in many respects a product of our special history—a mentality accustomed to the noise and confusion of clashing opinions and reasonably stable in temper in view of the varying fortunes of ideas. But what a mind does with a fact or an opinion is widely different when it is serene and when it is anxious; when it has confidence in its environment and when it is infected with suspicion or resentment; when it is gullible and when it is well furnished with the means of criticism; when it has hope and when it is in despair.

Further, the citizen is a different man when he has to judge his press alone, and when his judgment is steadied by other social agencies. Free and diverse utterance may result in bewilderment unless he has access—through home, church, school, custom—to interpreting patterns of thought and feeling. There is no such thing as the "objectivity" of the press unless the mind of the reader can identify the objects dealt with.

Whether at any time and place the psychological conditions exist under which a free press has social significance is always a question of fact, not of theory. These mental conditions may be lost. They may also be created. The press itself is always one of the chief agents in destroying or in building the bases of its own significance.

If we now fix our problem in space and time and look at the press in the United States today, we see that the conditions of our society and of the press in our society require new applications of the principles we have stated.

The aim of those who sponsored the First Amendment was to prevent the government from interfering with expression. The authors of our political system saw that the free society they were seeking to establish could not exist without free communication. As Jefferson put it: "The basis of our governments being the opinion of the people, the very first object should be to keep that right; and were it left to me to decide whether we should have a government without newspapers or newspapers without a government, I should not hesitate a moment to prefer the latter. But I should mean that every man should receive those papers and be capable of reading them."

Our ancestors were justified in thinking that if they could prevent the government from interfering with the freedom of the press, that freedom would be effectively exercised. In their day anybody with anything to say had comparatively little difficulty in getting it published. The only serious obstacle to free expression was government censorship. If that could be stopped, the right of every man to do his duty by his thought was secure. The press of those days consisted of hand-printed sheets issuing from little printing shops, regularly as newspapers, or irregularly as broadsides, pamphlets, or books. Presses were cheap; the journeyman printer could become a publisher and editor by borrowing the few dollars he needed to set up his shop and by hiring an assistant or two. With a limited number of people who could read, and with property qualifications for the suffrage—less than 6 per cent of the adult population voted for the conventions held to ratify the Constitution— there was no great discrepancy between the number of those who could read and were active citizens and those who could command the financial resources to engage in publication.

It was not supposed that any one newspaper would represent all, or nearly all, of the conflicting viewpoints regarding public issues. Together they could be expected to do so, and, if they did not, the man whose opinions were not represented could start a publication of his own.

Nor was it supposed that many citizens would subscribe to all the local journals. It was more likely that each would take the one which would reinforce his prejudices. But in each village and town, with its relatively simple social structure and its wealth of neighborly contacts, various opinions might encounter each other in face-to-face meetings; the truth, it was hoped, would be sorted out by competition in the local market place.

Those circumstances which provided variety and interchange of opinion and easy individual access to the market place of ideas have changed so radically as to justify us in saying that this country has gone through a communications revolution.

Literacy, the electorate, and the population have increased to such a point that the political community to be served by the press includes all but a tiny fraction of the millions of the American people. The press has been transformed into an enormous and complicated piece of machinery. As a necessary accompaniment, it has become big business. There is a marked reduction in the number of units of the press relative to the total population. Although in small communities we can still see a newspaper plant and product that resemble their Colonial prototypes, these are no longer the most characteristic or the most influential agencies of communication.

The right of free public expression has therefore lost its earlier reality. Protection against government is now not enough to guarantee that a man who has something to say shall have a chance to say it. The owners and managers of the press determine which persons, which facts, which versions of the facts, and which ideas shall reach the public.

This is one side of the shield—the effect of the communications revolution on the right of the citizen to publish his beliefs. The other side is the effect of the communications revolution on the press as the agency through which the members of a free society receive, as well as exchange, the judgments, opinions, ideas, and information which they need in order to participate in the management of that society. The press has become a vital necessity in the transaction of the public business of a continental area.

In local affairs there is still a chance for face-to-face observation to get in its work. Many private groups, formal and informal, throw an extensive web of alternative communication over the country or over parts of it. But there is obviously less opportunity for direct observation and news by word of mouth in a metropolitan region, in a great nation, or in a world society than there is in a village, a small state, or a single country. For the most part the understanding of the leaders and people of China, Russia, England, and Argentina possessed by the citizens of New Hampshire, Kansas, Oregon, and Alabama will be gained from the agencies of mass communication. Hardly less is the dependence on these agencies of midwest farmers for their understanding of a strike in Detroit or a change in the discount rate by the Federal Reserve Board in Washington.

The complexity of modern industrial society, the critical world situation, and the new menaces to freedom which these imply mean that the time has come for the press to assume a new public responsibility.

Through concentration of ownership the variety of sources of news and opinion is limited. At the same time the insistence of the citizen's need has increased. He is dependent on the quality, proportion, and extent of his news supply, not only for his personal access to the world of event, thought, and feeling, but also for the materials of his duties as a citizen and judge of public affairs. The soundness of his judgment affects the working of the state and even the peace of the world, involving the survival of the state as a free community. Under these circumstances it becomes an imperative question whether the performance of the press can any longer be left to the unregulated initiative of the few who manage it.

The moral and legal right of those who manage it to utter their opinions must remain intact; this right stands for the valid kernel of individualism at the heart of all social life. But the element of duty involved in the right requires a new scrutiny; and the service of news, as distinct from the utterance of opinion, acquires a new importance. The need of the citizen for adequate and uncontaminated mental food is such that he is under a duty to get it. Thus his interest also acquires the stature of a right.

To protect the press is no longer automatically to protect the citizen or the community. The freedom of the press can remain a right of those who publish only if it incorporates into itself the right of the citizen and the public interest.

Freedom of the press means freedom from and freedom for. The press must be free from the menace of external compulsions from whatever source. To demand that it be free from pressures which might warp its utterance would be to demand that society should be empty of contending forces and beliefs. But persisting and distorting pressures—financial, popular, clerical, institutional—must be known and counterbalanced. The press must, if it is to be wholly free, know and overcome any biases incident to its own economic position, its concentration, and its pyramidal organization.

The press must be free for the development of its own conceptions of service and achievement. It must be free for making its contribution to the maintenance and development of a free society.

This implies that the press must also be accountable. It must be accountable to society for meeting the public need and for maintaining the rights of citizens and the almost forgotten rights of speakers who have no press. It must know that its faults and errors have ceased to be private vagaries and have become public dangers. The voice of the press, so far as by a drift toward monopoly it tends to become exclusive in its wisdom and observation, deprives other voices of a hearing and the public of their contribution. Freedom of the press for the coming period can only continue as an accountable freedom. Its moral right will be conditioned on its acceptance of this accountability. Its legal right will stand unaltered as its moral duty is performed.

WARREN BREED

Social Control in the Newsroom:
A Functional Analysis
(1955)

Top leaders in formal organizations are makers of policy, but they must also secure and maintain conformity to that policy at lower levels. The situation of the newspaper publisher is a case in point. As owner or representative of ownership, he has the nominal right to set the paper's policy and see that staff activities are coordinated so that the policy is enforced. In actuality the problem of control is less simple, as the literature of "human relations" and informal group studies and of the professions[1] suggests.

Ideally, there would be no problem of either "control" or "policy" on the newspaper in a full democracy. The only controls would be the nature of the event and the reporter's effective ability to describe it. In practice, we find the publisher does set news policy, and this policy is usually followed by members of his staff. Conformity is *not* automatic, however, for three reasons: (1) the existence of ethical journalistic norms; (2) the fact that staff subordinates (reporters, etc.) tend to have more "liberal" attitudes (and therefore perceptions) than the publishers and could invoke the norms to justify anti-policy writing; and (3) the ethical taboo preventing the publisher from commanding subordinates to follow policy. How policy comes to be maintained, and where it is bypassed, is the subject of this paper.

Several definitions are required at this point. As to personnel, "newsmen" can be divided into two main categories. "Executives" include the publisher and his editors. "Staffers" are reporters, rewrite men, copy readers, etc. In between there may be occasional city editors or wire editors who occupy an interstitial status. "Policy" may be defined as the more or less consistent orientation shown by a paper, not only in its editorial but in its news columns and headlines as well, concerning selected issues and events. "Slanting" almost never means prevarication. Rather, it involves omission, differential selection and preferential placement, such as "featuring" a pro-policy item, "burying" an anti-policy story in an inside page, etc. "Professional norms" are of two types: technical norms deal with the operations

From *Social Forces* 33, no. 4 (1955): 326–35.

of efficient news gathering, writing, and editing; ethical norms embrace the news-man's obligation to his readers and to his craft and include such ideals as respon-sibility, impartiality, accuracy, fair play, and objectivity.[2]

Every newspaper has a policy, admitted or not.[3] One paper's policy may be pro-Republican, cool to labor, antagonistic to the school board, etc. The principal areas of policy are politics, business, and labor; much of it stems from considerations of class. Policy is manifested in "slanting." Just what determines any publisher's policy is a large question and will not be discussed here. Certainly, however, the publisher has much say (often in veto form) in both long-term and immediate policy deci-sions (which party to support, whether to feature or bury a story of imminent labor trouble, how much free space to give "news" of advertisers' doings, etc.). Finally, policy is covert, due to the existence of ethical norms of journalism, policy often contravenes these norms. No executive is willing to risk embarrassment by being accused of open commands to slant a news story.

While policy is set by the executives, it is clear that they cannot personally gather and write the news by themselves. They must delegate these tasks to staffers, and at this point the attitudes or interests of staffers may—and often do—conflict with those of the executives.[4] Of 72 staffers interviewed, 42 showed that they held more liberal views than those contained in their publisher's policy; 27 held similar views, and only 3 were more conservative. Similarly, only 17 of 61 staffers said they were Republicans.[5] The discrepancy is more acute when age (and therefore years of newspaper experience) is held constant. Of the 46 staffers under 35 years of age, 34 showed more liberal orientations; older men had apparently "mellowed." It should be noted that data as to intensity of attitudes are lacking. Some staffers may disagree with policy so mildly that they conform and feel no strain. The present essay is pertinent only insofar as dissident newsmen are forced to make decisions from time to time about their relationship to policy.[6]

We will now examine more closely the workings of the newspaper staff. The central question will be: How is policy maintained, despite the fact that it often contravenes journalistic norms, that staffers often personally disagree with it, and that executives cannot legitimately command that it be followed? The frame of reference will be that of functional analysis, as embodied in Merton's paradigm.[7]

The present data come from the writer's newspaper experience and from inten-sive interviews with some 120 newsmen, mostly in the northeastern quarter of the country. The sample was not random and no claim is made for representativeness, but on the other hand no paper was selected or omitted purposely and in no case did a newsman refuse the request that he be interviewed. The newspapers were chosen to fit a "middle-sized" group, defined as those with 10,000 to 100,000 daily circulation. Interviews averaged well over an hour in duration.[8]

There is an "action" element inherent in the present subject—the practical democratic need for "a free and responsible press" to inform citizens about current issues. Much of the criticism of the press stems from the slanting induced by the bias of the publisher's policy.[9] This criticism is often directed at flagrant cases such as the Hearst press, the *Chicago Tribune* and New York tabloids, but also applies, in lesser degree, to the more conventional press. The description of mechanisms of policy maintenance may suggest why this criticism is often fruitless, at least in the short-run sense.

How the Staffer Learns Policy

The first mechanism promoting conformity is the "socialization" of the staffer with regard to the norms of his job. When the new reporter starts work he is not told what policy is. Nor is he ever told. This may appear strange, but interview after interview confirmed the condition. The standard remark was "Never, in my —— years on this paper, have I ever been told how to slant a story." No paper in the survey had a "training" program for its new men; some issue a "style" book, but this deals with literary style, not policy. Further, newsmen are busy and have little time for recruit training. Yet all but the newest staffers know what policy is.[10] On being asked, they say they learn it "by osmosis." Sociologically, this means they become socialized and "learn the ropes" like a neophyte in any subculture. Basically, the learning of policy is a process by which the recruit discovers and internalizes the rights and obligations of his status and its norms and values. He learns to anticipate what is expected of him so as to win rewards and avoid punishments. Policy is an important element of the newsroom norms, and he learns it in much the following way.

The staffer reads his own paper every day; some papers *require* this. It is simple to diagnose the paper's characteristics. Unless the staffer is naive or unusually independent, he tends to fashion his own stories after others he sees in the paper. This is particularly true of the newcomer. The news columns and editorials are a guide to the local norms. Thus a southern reporter notes that Republicans are treated in a "different" way in his paper's news columns than Democrats. The news about whites and Negroes is also of a distinct sort. Should he then write about one of these groups, his story will tend to reflect what he has come to define as standard procedure.

Certain editorial actions taken by editors and older staffers also serve as controlling guides. "If things are blue-pencilled consistently," one reporter said, "you learn he [the editor] has a prejudice in that regard."[11] Similarly an executive may occasionally reprimand a staffer for policy violation. From our evidence, the reprimand is frequently oblique, due to the covert nature of policy, but learning occurs nevertheless. One staffer learned much through a series of incidents:

I heard [a union] was going out on strike, so I kept on it; then the boss said
something about it, and well—I took the hint and we had less coverage of
the strike forming. It was easier that way. We lost the story, but what can
you do?

We used a yarn on a firm that was coming to town, and I got dragged out
of bed for that. The boss is interested in this industrial stuff—we have to clear
it all through him. He's an official in the Chamber. So . . . after a few times,
it's irritating, so I get fed up. I try to figure out what will work best. I learn
to try and guess what the boss will want.

In fairness it should be noted that this particular publisher was one of the most
dictatorial encountered in the study. The pattern of control through reprimand,
however, was found consistently. Another staffer wrote, on his own initiative, a
series about discrimination against Jews at hotel resorts.

It was the old "Gentlemen's Agreement" stuff, documented locally. The boss
called me in . . . didn't like the stuff . . . the series never appeared. You start
to get the idea. . . .

Note that the boss does not "command"; the direction is more subtle. Also, it
seems that most policy indications from executives are negative. They veto by a
nod of the head, as if to say, "Please don't rock the boat." Exceptions occur in the
"campaign" story, which will be discussed later. It is also to be noted that punishment is implied if policy is not followed.

Staffers also obtain guidance from their knowledge of the characteristics, interests, and affiliations of their executives. This knowledge can be gained in several
ways. One is gossip. A reporter said:

Do we gossip about the editors? Several of us used to meet—somewhere off
the beaten path—over a beer—and talk for an hour. We'd rake 'em over the
coals.

Another point of contact with executives is the news conference (which on
middle-sized papers is seldom *called* a news conference), wherein the staffer outlines his findings and executives discuss how to shape the story. The typical
conference consists of two persons, the reporter and the city editor, and can amount
to no more than a few words. (Reporter: "One hurt in auto accident uptown." City
editor: "Okay, keep it short.") If policy is at stake, the conference may involve
several executives and require hours of consideration. From such meetings, the
staffer can gain insight through what is said and what is not said by executives. It

is important to say here that policy is not stated explicitly in the news conference nor elsewhere, with few exceptions. The news conference actually deals mostly with journalistic matters, such as reliability of information, newsworthiness, possible "angles," and other news tactics.

Three other channels for learning about executives are house organs (printed for the staff by syndicates and larger papers), observing the executive as he meets various leaders and hearing him voice an opinion. One staffer could not help but gain an enduring impression of his publisher's attitudes in this incident:

> I can remember [him] saying on election night [1948], when it looked like we had a Democratic majority in both houses, "My God, this means we'll have a labor government." (Q: How did he say it?) He had a real note of alarm in his voice; you couldn't miss the point that he'd prefer the Republicans.

It will be noted that in speaking of "how" the staffer learns policy, there are indications also as to "why" he follows it.

Reasons for Conforming to Policy

There is no one factor which creates conformity-mindedness, unless we resort to a summary term such as "institutionalized statuses" or "structural roles." Particular factors must be sought in particular cases. The staffer must be seen in terms of his status and aspirations, the structure of the newsroom organization and of the larger society. He also must be viewed with reference to the operations he performs through his workday, and their consequences for him. The following six reasons appear to stay the potentially intransigent staffer from acts of deviance—often, if not always.[12]

1. INSTITUTIONAL AUTHORITY AND SANCTIONS. The publisher ordinarily owns the paper and from a purely business standpoint has the right to expect obedience of his employees. He has the power to fire or demote for transgressions. This power, however, is diminished markedly in actuality by three facts. First, the newspaper is not conceived as a purely business enterprise, due to the protection of the First Amendment and a tradition of professional public service. Secondly, firing is a rare phenomenon on newspapers. For example, one editor said he had fired two men in 12 years; another could recall four firings in his 15 years on that paper. Thirdly, there are severance pay clauses in contracts with the American Newspaper Guild (CIO). The only effective causes for firing are excessive drunkenness, sexual dalliance, etc. Most newspaper unemployment apparently comes from occasional

economy drives on large papers and from total suspensions of publication. Likewise, only one case of demotion was found in the survey. It is true, however, that staffers still fear punishment; the myth has the errant star reporter taken off murders and put on obituaries—"the Chinese torture chamber" of the newsroom. Fear of sanctions, rather than their invocation, is a reason for conformity, but not as potent a one as would seem at first glance.

Editors, for their part, can simply ignore stories which might create deviant actions, and when this is impossible, can assign the story to a "safe" staffer. In the infrequent case that an anti-policy story reaches the city desk, the story is changed; extraneous reasons, such as the pressure of time and space, are given for the change.[13] Finally, the editor may contribute to the durability of policy by insulating the publisher from policy discussions. He may reason that the publisher would be embarrassed to hear of conflict over policy and the resulting bias, and spare him the resulting uneasiness; thus the policy remains not only covert but undiscussed and therefore unchanged.[14]

2. FEELINGS OF OBLIGATION AND ESTEEM FOR SUPERIORS. The staffer may feel obliged to the paper for having hired him. Respect, admiration and gratitude may be felt for certain editors who have perhaps schooled him, "stood up for him," or supplied favors of a more paternalistic sort. Older staffers who have served as models for newcomers or who have otherwise given aid and comfort are due return courtesies. Such obligation and warm personal sentiments toward superiors play a strategic role in the pull to conformity.

3. MOBILITY ASPIRATIONS. In response to a question about ambition, all the younger staffers showed wishes for status achievement. There was agreement that bucking policy constituted a serious bar to this goal. In practice, several respondents noted that a good tactic toward advancement was to get "big" stories on Page One; this automatically means no tampering with policy. Further, some staffers see newspapering as a "stepping stone" job to more lucrative work: public relations, advertising, free-lancing, etc. The reputation for troublemaking would inhibit such climbing.

A word is in order here about chances for upward mobility. Of 51 newsmen aged 35 or more, 32 were executives. Of 50 younger men, 6 had reached executive posts and others were on their way up with such jobs as wire editors, political reporters, etc. All but five of these young men were college graduates, as against just half of their elders. Thus there is no evidence of a "break in the skill hierarchy" among newsmen.

4. ABSENCE OF CONFLICTING GROUP ALLEGIANCE. The largest formal organization of staffers is the American Newspaper Guild. The Guild, much as it might wish to, has not interfered with internal matters such as policy. It has stressed business unionism and political interests external to the newsroom. As for informal groups, there is no evidence available that a group of staffers has ever "ganged up" on policy.

5. THE PLEASANT NATURE OF THE ACTIVITY. a. *In-groupness in the newsroom.* The staffer has a low formal status vis-a-vis executives, but he is not treated as a "worker." Rather, he is a coworker with executives; the entire staff cooperates congenially on a job they all like and respect getting the news. The newsroom is a friendly, first-namish place. Staffers discuss stories with editors on a give-and-take basis. Top executives withtheir own offices sometimes come out and sit in on newsroom discussions.[15]

b. *Required operations are interesting.* Newsmen like their work. Few voiced complaints when given the opportunity to gripe during interviews. The operations required—witnessing, interviewing, briefly mulling the meanings of events, checking facts, writing—are not onerous.

c. *Non-financial perquisites.* These are numerous: the variety of experience, eyewitnessing significant and interesting events, being the first to know, getting "the inside dope" denied laymen, meeting and sometimes befriending notables and celebrities (who are well-advised to treat newsmen with deference). Newsmen are close to big decisions without having to make them; they touch power without being responsible for its use. From talking with newsmen and reading their books, one gets the impression that they are proud of being newsmen.[16] There are tendencies to exclusiveness within news ranks, and intimations that such near out-groups as radio newsmen are entertainers, not real newsmen. Finally, there is the satisfaction of being a member of a live-wire organization dealing with important matters. The newspaper is an "institution" in the community. People talk about it and quote it; its big trucks whiz through town; its columns carry the tidings from big and faraway places, with pictures.

Thus, despite his relatively low pay, the staffer feels, for all these reasons, an integral part of a going concern. His job morale is high. Many newsmen could qualify for jobs paying more money in advertising and public relations, but they remain with the newspaper.

6. NEWS BECOMES A VALUE. Newsmen define their job as producing a certain quantity of what is called "news" every 24 hours. This is to be produced *even though nothing much has happened.* News is a continuous challenge, and meeting this challenge is the newsman's job. He is rewarded for fulfilling this, his manifest function. A consequence of this focus on news as a central value is the shelving of a strong interest in objectivity at the point of policy conflict. Instead of mobilizing their efforts to establish objectivity over policy as the criterion for performance, their energies are channeled into getting more news. The demands of competition (in cities where there are two or more papers) and speed enhance this focus. Newsmen do talk about ethics, objectivity, and the relative worth of various papers, but not when there is news to get. News comes first, and there is always news to get.[17] They are not rewarded for analyzing the social structure, but for getting news. It would seem that this instrumental orientation diminishes their moral potential. A

further consequence of this pattern is that the harmony between staffers and executives is cemented by their common interest in news. Any potential conflict between the two groups, such as slowdowns occurring among informal work groups in industry, would be dissipated to the extent that news is a positive value. The newsroom solidarity is thus reinforced.

The six factors promote policy conformity. To state more exactly how policy is maintained would be difficult in view of the many variables contained in the system. The process may be somewhat better understood, however, with the introduction of one further concept—the reference group.[18] The staffer, especially the new staffer, identifies himself through the existence of these six factors with the executives and veteran staffers. Although not yet one of them, he shares their norms, and thus his performance comes to resemble theirs. He conforms to the norms of policy rather than to whatever personal beliefs he brought to the job, or to ethical ideals. All six of these factors function to encourage reference group formation. Where the allegiance is directed toward legitimate authority, that authority has only to maintain the equilibrium within limits by the prudent distribution of rewards and punishments. The reference group itself, which has as its "magnet" element the elite of executives and old staffers, is unable to change policy to a marked degree because first, it is the group charged with carrying out policy, and second, because the policy maker, the publisher, is often insulated on the delicate issue of policy.

In its own way, each of the six factors contributes to the formation of reference group behavior. There is almost no firing, hence a steady expectation of continued employment. Subordinates tend to esteem their bosses, so a convenient model group is present. Mobility aspirations (when held within limits) are an obvious promoter of inter-status bonds as is the absence of conflicting group loyalties with their potential harvest of cross pressures. The newsroom atmosphere is charged with the related factors of in-groupness and pleasing nature of the work. Finally, the agreement among newsmen that their job is to fasten upon the news, seeing it as a value in itself, forges a bond across status lines.

As to the six factors, five appear to be relatively constant, occurring on all papers studied. The varying factor is the second: obligation and esteem held by staffers for executive and older staffers. On some papers, this obligation-esteem entity was found to be larger than on others. Where it was large, the paper appeared to have two characteristics pertinent to this discussion. First, it did a good conventional job of news-getting and news-publishing, and second, it had little difficulty over policy. With staffers drawn toward both the membership and the reference groups, organization was efficient. Most papers are like this. On the few smaller papers where executives and older staffers are not respected, morale is spotty; staffers withhold enthusiasm from their stories, they cover their beats perfunctorily, they wish for a job on a better paper, and they are apathetic and sometimes hostile to policy. Thus the obligation-esteem factor seems to be the active variable in determining not only policy conformity, but morale and good news performance as well.

Situations Permitting Deviation

Thus far it would seem that the staffer enjoys little "freedom of the press." To show that this is an oversimplification, and more important, to suggest a kind of test for our hypothesis about the strength of policy, let us ask: "What happens when a staffer *does* submit an antipolicy story?" We know that this happens infrequently, but what follows in these cases?

The process of learning policy crystallizes into a process of social control, in which deviations are punished (usually gently) by reprimand, cutting one's story, the withholding of friendly comment by an executive, etc. For example, it is punishment for a staffer when the city editor waves a piece of his copy at him and says, "Joe, don't *do* that when you're writing about the mayor." In an actual case, a staffer acting as wire editor was demoted when he neglected to feature a story about a "sacred cow" politician on his paper. What can be concluded is that when an executive sees a clearly anti-policy item, he blue-pencils it, and this constitutes a lesson for the staffer. Rarely does the staffer persist in violating policy; no such case appeared in all the interviews. Indeed, the best-known cases of firing for policy reasons—Ted O. Thackrey and Leo Huberman—occurred on liberal New York City dailies, and Thackrey was an editor, not a staffer.

Now and then cases arise in which a staffer finds his anti-policy stories printed. There seems to be no consistent explanation for this, except to introduce two more specific subjects dealing first, with the staffer's career line, and second, with particular empirical conditions associated with the career line. We can distinguish three stages through which the staffer progresses. First, there is the cub stage, the first few months or years in which the new man learns techniques and policy. He writes short, non-policy stories, such as minor accidents, meeting activity, the weather, etc. The second, or "wiring-in" stage, sees the staffer continuing to assimilate the newsroom values and to cement informal relationships. Finally there is the "star" or "veteran" stage, in which the staffer typically defines himself as a full, responsible member of the group, sees its goals as his, and can be counted on to handle policy sympathetically.[19]

To further specify the conformity-deviation problem, it must be understood that newspapering is a relatively complex activity. The newsman is responsible for a range of skills and judgments which are matched only in the professional and entrepeneurial fields. Oversimplifications about policy rigidity can be avoided if we ask, "*Under what conditions* can the staffer defy or by-pass policy?" We have already seen that staffers are free to argue news decisions with executives in brief "news conferences," but the arguments generally revolve around points of "newsiness," rather than policy as such.[20] Five factors appear significant in the area of the reporter's power to by-pass policy.

1. The norms of policy are not always entirely clear, just as many norms are vague and unstructured. Policy is covert by nature and has large scope. The paper may be Republican, but standing only lukewarm for Republican Candidate A who may be too "liberal" or no friend of the publisher. Policy, if worked out explicitly, would have to include motivations, reasons, alternatives, historical developments, and other complicating material. Thus a twilight zone permitting a range of deviation appears.[21]

2. Executives may be ignorant of particular facts, and staffers who do the leg (and telephone) work to gather news can use their superior knowledge to subvert policy. On grounds of both personal belief and professional codes, the staffer has the option of selection at many points. He can decide whom to interview and whom to ignore, what questions to ask, which quotations to note, and on writing the story which items to feature (with an eye toward the headline), which to bury, and in general what tone to give the several possible elements of the story.

3. In addition to the "squeeze" tactic exploiting executives' ignorance of minute facts, the "plant" may be employed. Although a paper's policy may proscribe a certain issue from becoming featured, a staffer, on getting a good story about that issue may "plant" it in another paper or wire service through a friendly staffer and submit it to his own editor, pleading the story is now too big to ignore.

4. It is possible to classify news into four types on the basis of source of origination. These are: the policy or campaign story, the assigned story, the beat story, and the story initiated by the staffer. The staffer's autonomy is larger with the latter than the former types. With the campaign story (build new hospital, throw rascals out, etc.), the staffer is working directly under executives and has little leeway. An assigned story is handed out by the city editor and thus will rarely hit policy head on, although the staffer has some leverage of selection. When we come to the beat story, however, it is clear that the function of the reporter changes. No editor comes between him and his beat (police department, city hall, etc.), thus the reporter gains the "editor" function. It is he who, to a marked degree, can select which stories to pursue, which to ignore. Several cases developed in interviews of beat men who smothered stories they knew would provide fuel for policy—policy they personally disliked or thought injurious to the professional code. The cooperation of would-be competing reporters is essential, of course. The fourth type of story is simply one which the staffer originates, independent of assignment or beat. All respondents, executives and staffers, averred that any employee was free to initiate stories. But equally regularly, they acknowledged that the opportunity was not often assumed. Staffers were already overloaded with beats, assignments, and rou-

tine coverage, and besides, rewards for initiated stories were meager or non-existent unless the initiated story confirmed policy. Yet this area promises much, should staffers pursue their advantage. The outstanding case in the present study concerned a well-educated, enthusiastic reporter on a conventional daily just north of the Mason-Dixon line. Entirely on his own, he consistently initiated stories about Negroes and Negro-white relations, "making" policy where only void had existed. He worked overtime to document and polish the stories; his boss said he didn't agree with the idea but insisted on the reporter's right to publish them.

5. Staffers with "star" status can transgress policy more easily than cubs. This differential privilege of status was encountered on several papers. An example would be Walter Winchell during the Roosevelt administration, who regularly praised the president while the policy of his boss, Mr. Hearst, was strongly critical of the regime. A *New York Times* staffer said he doubted that any copy reader on the paper would dare change a word of the copy of Meyer Berger, the star feature writer.

These five factors indicate that given certain conditions, the controls making for policy conformity can be bypassed. These conditions exist not only within the newsroom and the news situation but within the staffer as well; they will be exploited only if the staffer's attitudes permit. There are some limitations, then, on the strength of the publisher's policy.

Before summarizing, three additional requirements of Merton's functional paradigm must be met. These are statements of the consequences of the pattern, of available alternative modes of behavior, and a validation of the analysis.

Consequences of the Pattern

To the extent that policy is maintained, the paper keeps publishing smoothly as seen both from the newsroom and from the outside, which is no mean feat if we visualize the country with no press at all. This is the most general consequence. There are several special consequences. For the society as a whole, the existing system of power relationships is maintained. Policy usually protects property and class interests, and thus the strata and groups holding these interests are better able to retain them. For the larger community, much news is printed objectively, allowing for opinions to form openly, but policy news may be slanted or buried so that some important information is denied the citizenry. (This is the dysfunction widely scored by critics.) For the individual readers, the same is true. For the executives, their favorable statuses are maintained, with perhaps occasional touches of guilt over policy. For newsmen, the consequences are the same as for executives. For more independent, critical staffers, there can be several modes of adaptation. At the extremes, the pure conformist can deny the conflict, the confirmed deviate can quit the newspaper business. Otherwise, the adaptations seem to run in this way: (1) Keep on the job but blunt the sharp corners of policy where possible ("If I wasn't here the next guy would let *all* that crap go through . . ."); (2) Attempt to repress the conflict amorally and anti-intellectually ("What the hell, it's only a job; take your pay and forget it . . ."); (3) Attempt to compensate, by "taking it out" in other contexts: drinking, writing "the truth" for liberal publications, working with action programs, the Guild and otherwise. All of these adjustments were found in the study. As has been suggested, one of the main compensations for all staffers is simply to find justification in adhering to "good news practice."

Possible Alternatives and Change

A functional analysis, designed to locate sources of persistence of a pattern, can also indicate points of strain at which a structural change may occur. For example, the popular recipe for eliminating bias at one time was to diminish advertisers' power over the news. This theory having proved unfruitful, critics more recently have fastened upon the publisher as the point at which change must be initiated. Our analysis suggests that this is a valid approach, but one requiring that leverage in turn be applied on the publisher from various sources. Perhaps the most significant of these are professional codes. Yet we have seen the weakness of these codes when policy decisions are made. Further leverage is contained in such sources as the professional direction being taken by some journalism schools, in the Guild, and in sincere criticism.

Finally, newspaper readers possess potential power over press performance. Seen as a client of the press, the reader should be entitled to not only an interesting newspaper, but one which furnishes significant news objectively presented. This is the basic problem of democracy: to what extent should the individual be treated as a member of a mass, and to what extent fashioned (through educative measures) as an active participant in public decisions? Readership studies show that readers prefer "interesting" news and "features" over penetrating analyses. It can be concluded that the citizen has not been sufficiently motivated by society (and its press) to demand and apply the information he needs, and to discriminate between worthwhile and spurious information, for the fulfillment of the citizen's role. These other forces—professional codes, journalism schools, the Guild, critics and readers—could result in changing newspaper performance. It still remains, however, for the publisher to be changed first. He can be located at the apex of a T, the crucial point of decision making. Newsroom and professional forces form the base of the T, outside forces from community and society are the arms. It is for the publisher to decide which forces to propitiate.

Suggestions for Validation

The Merton paradigm requires a statement concerning validation of the analysis. Checks could be forthcoming both from social science researchers and from newsmen. If the latter, the newsman should explicitly state the basis for his discussion, especially as regards the types of papers, executives, and staffers he knows. A crucial case for detailed description would be the situation in which staffers actively defied authority on policy matters. Another important test would be a comparative description of two papers contrasted by their situation as regards the six factors promoting conformity, with particular reference to the variable of obligation and esteem held toward superiors, and the factors permitting deviation. In any event, the present exploratory study may serve as a point of departure.

A second type of validation may be suggested. This would focus on the utility of the paradigm itself. Previous studies have been based on functional theory but before the development of the paradigm.[22] Studies of diverse social systems also lend themselves to functional analysis, and such comparative research could function not only to build systematic theory but to test and suggest modifications of the paradigm. Situations characterized by conflict and competition for scarce goals seem particularly well suited to functional analysis. Several points made in the present essay might have been overlooked without the paradigm.[23]

Summary

The problem, which was suggested by the age-old charges of bias against the press, focussed around the manner in which the publisher's policy came to be followed, despite three empirical conditions: (1) policy sometimes contravenes journalistic norms; (2) staffers often personally disagree with it; and (3) executives cannot legitimately command that policy be followed. Interview and other data were used to explain policy maintenance. It is important to recall that the discussion is based primarily on study of papers of "middle" circulation range, and does not consider either non-policy stories or the original policy decision made by the publishers.

The mechanisms for learning policy on the part of the new staffer were given, together with suggestions as to the nature of social controls. Six factors, apparently the major variables producing policy maintenance, were described. The most significant of these variables, obligation and esteem for superiors, was deemed not only the most important, but the most fluctuating variable from paper to paper. Its existence and its importance for conformity led to the sub-hypothesis that reference group behavior was playing a part in the pattern. To show, however, that policy is not ironclad, five conditions were suggested in which staffers may by-pass policy.

Thus we conclude that the publisher's policy, when established in a given subject area, is usually followed, and that a description of the dynamic socio-cultural situation of the newsroom will suggest explanations for this conformity. The newsman's source of rewards is located not among the readers, who are manifestly his clients, but among his colleagues and superiors. Instead of adhering to societal and professional ideals, he re-defines his values to the more pragmatic level of the newsroom group. He thereby gains not only status rewards, but also acceptance in a solidary group engaged in interesting, varied, and sometimes important work. Thus the cultural patterns of the newsroom produce results insufficient for wider democratic needs. Any important change toward a more "free and responsible press" must stem from various possible pressures on the publisher, who epitomizes the policy making and coordinating role.

Notes

1. See, for instance, F. J. Roethlisberger and William J. Dickson, *Management and the Worker* (Cambridge: Harvard University Press, 1947); and Logan Wilson, *The Academic Man* (New York: Oxford University Press, 1942).

2. The best-known formal code is The Canons of Journalism, of the American Society of Newspaper Editors. See Wilbur Schramm (ed.), *Mass Communications* (Urbana: University of Illinois Press, 1949), pp. 236–38.

3. It is extremely difficult to measure the extent of objectivity or bias. One recent attempt is reported in Nathan B. Blumberg, *One-Party Press?* (Lincoln: University of Nebraska Press, 1954), which gives a news count for 35 papers' performance in the 1952 election campaign. He concluded that 18 of the papers showed "no evidence of partiality," 11 showed "no conclusive evidence of partiality," and 6 showed partiality. His interpretations, however, are open to argument. A different interpretation could conclude that while about 16 showed little or no partiality, the rest did. It should be noted, too, that there are different areas of policy depending on local conditions. The chief difference occurs in the deep South, where frequently there is no "Republican" problem and no "union" problem over which the staff can be divided. Color becomes the focus of policy.

4. This condition, pointed out in a lecture by Paul F. Lazarsfeld, formed the starting point for the present study.

5. Similar findings were made about Washington correspondents in Leo C. Rosten, *The Washington Correspondents* (New York: Harcourt, Brace, 1937). Less ideological conflict was found in two other studies: Francis V. Prugger, "Social Composition and Training of the Milwaukee Journal News Staff," *Journalism Quarterly*, 18 (Sept. 1941), pp. 231–44, and Charles E. Swanson, The Mid-City Daily (Ph.D. dissertation, State University of Iowa, 1948). Possible reasons for the gap is that both papers studied were perhaps above average in objectivity; executives were included with staffers in computations; and some staffers were doubtless included who did not handle policy news.

6. It is not being argued that "liberalism" and objectivity are synonymous. A liberal paper (e.g., *PM*) can be biased too, but it is clear that few liberal papers exist

among the many conservative ones. It should also be stressed that much news is not concerned with policy and is therefore probably unbiased.

7. Robert K. Merton, *Social Theory and Social Structure* (Glencoe: Free Press, 1949), esp. pp. 49–61. Merton's elements will not be explicitly referred to but his principal requirements are discussed at various points.

8. The data are taken from Warren Breed, The Newspaperman, News and Society (Ph.D. dissertation, Columbia University, 1952). Indebtedness is expressed to William L. Kolb and Robert C. Stone, who read the present manuscript and provided valuable criticisms and suggestions.

9. For a summary description of this criticism, see Commission on the Freedom of the Press, *A Free and Responsible Press* (Chicago: University of Chicago Press, 1947), chap. 4.

10. While the concept of policy is crucial to this analysis, it is not to be assumed that newsmen discuss it fully. Some do not even use the word in discussing how their paper is run. To this extent, policy is a latent phenomenon; either the staffer has no reason to contemplate policy or he chooses to avoid so doing. It may be that one strength of policy is that it has become no more manifest to the staffers who follow it.

11. Note that such executives' actions as blue-pencilling play not only the manifest function of preparing the story for publication but also the latent one of steering the future action of the staffer.

12. Two cautions are in order here. First, it will be recalled that we are discussing not all news, but only policy news. Secondly, we are discussing only staffers who are potential non-conformers. Some agree with policy; some have no views on policy matters; others do not write policy stories. Furthermore, there are strong forces in American society which cause many individuals to choose harmonious adjustment (conformity) in any situation, regardless of the imperatives. See Erich Fromm, *Escape From Freedom* (New York: Farrar and Rinehart, 1941), and David Riesman, *The Lonely Crowd* (New Haven: Yale, 1950).

13. Excellent illustration of this tactic is given in the novel by an experienced newspaperwoman: Margaret Long, *Affair of the Heart* (New York: Random House, 1953), chap. 10. This chapter describes the framing of a Negro for murder in a middle-sized southern city, and the attempt of a reporter to tell the story objectively.

14. The insulation of one individual or group from another is a good example of social (as distinguished from psychological) mechanisms to reduce the likelihood of conflict. Most of the factors inducing conformity could likewise be viewed as social mechanisms. See Talcott Parsons and Edward A. Shils, "Values, Motives and Systems of Action," in Parsons and Shils (eds.), *Toward A General Theory of Action* (Cambridge Harvard University Press, 1951), pp. 223–30.

15. Further indication that the staffer-executive relationship is harmonious came from answers to the question, "Why do you think newspapermen are thought to be cynical?" Staffers regularly said that newsmen are cynical because they get close enough to stark reality to see the ills of their society, and the imperfections of its leaders and officials. Only two, of 40 staffers, took the occasion to criticize their executives and the enforcement of policy. This displacement, or lack of strong feelings against executives, can be interpreted to bolster the hypothesis of staff solidarity. (It further suggests that newsmen tend to analyze

their society in terms of personalities, rather than institutions comprising a social and cultural system.)

16. There is a sizeable myth among newsmen about the attractiveness of their calling. For example, the story: "Girl: 'My, you newspapermen must have a fascinating life. You meet such interesting people.' Reporter: 'Yes, and most of them are newspapermen.' " For a further discussion, see Breed, *op. cit.*, chap. 17.

17. This is a variant of the process of "displacement of goals," newsmen turning to "getting news" rather than to seeking data which will enlighten and inform their readers. The dysfunction is implied in the nation's need not for more news but for better news—quality rather than quantity. See Merton, *op. cit.*, "Bureaucratic Structure and Personality," pp. 154–5.

18. Whether group members acknowledge it or not, "if a person's attitudes are influenced by a set of norms which he assumes that he shares with other individuals, those individuals constitute for him a reference group." Theodore M. Newcomb, *Social Psychology* (New York: Dryden, 1950), p. 225. Williams states that reference group formation may segment large organizations; in the present case, the reverse is true, the loyalty of subordinates going to their "friendly" superiors and to the discharge of technical norms such as getting news. See Robin M. Williams, *American Society* (New York: Knopf, 1951), p. 476.

19. Does the new staffer, fresh from the ideals of college, really "change his attitudes"? It would seem that attitudes about socio-economic affairs need not be fixed, but are capable of shifting with the situation. There are arguments for and against any opinion; in the atmosphere of the newsroom the arguments "for" policy decisions are made to sound adequate, especially as these are evoked by the significant others in the system.

20. The fullest treatment of editor-reporter conferences appears in Swanson, *op. cit.*

21. Related to the fact that policy is vague is the more general postulate that executives seek to avoid formal issues and the possibly damaging disputes arising therefrom. See Chester I. Barnard, *Functions of the Executive* (Cambridge: Harvard University Press, 1947).

22. References are cited in Merton, *Social Theory and Social Structure, op. cit.*, and also in the works of Talcott Parsons.

23. That the paradigm might serve best as a check-list or "insurance," or as a theoretical guide to fledgling scholars, is shown by the excellence of an article published before the paradigm—and quite similar to the present article in dealing with problems of policy maintenance in a formal organization: Edward A. Shils and Morris Janowitz, "Cohesion and Disintegration in the Wehrmacht in World War II," *Public Opinion Quarterly*, 12 (Summer 1948), pp. 280–315.

COLUMBIA JOURNALISM REVIEW

Why a Review of Journalism?
(1962)

What journalism needs, it has been said time and again, is more and better criticism. There have been abundant proposals for professional study panels, for institutes with squads of researchers, for critical journals.

Columbia University's Graduate School of Journalism has decided to attempt such a journal. Two considerations brought about the decision: First, the need, magnified in a critical era like this, for some effort to assess the performance of journalism in all its forms, to call attention to its shortcomings and its strengths, and to help define—or redefine—standards of honest, responsible service. Second, the obligation that falls on a serious professional school—a graduate institution, national in character—to help stimulate continuing improvement in its profession and to speak out for what it considers right, fair, and decent.

Columbia's Faculty of Journalism cannot pretend to Olympian qualifications. It does combine the detachment needed to be reasonably impartial with the professional experience needed to sense what is possible and what is not. It can also draw upon the vast experience of its part-time teaching staff and its alumni, as well as upon the growing number of alert, inquiring minds within journalism and informed critics from outside.

All the proposals for organized criticism—whatever their intent or merit—point to one conclusion: that there exists, in and out of the profession, a widespread uneasiness about the state of journalism. The School shares this uneasiness, not over any supposed deterioration but over the probability that journalism is not yet a match for the complications of our age. It believes that the urgent arguments for a critical journal far outweigh the hazards.

In launching this experiment, the School has set for the *Review* these goals:

To deal forthrightly with what it finds to be deficient or irresponsible and to salute what it finds to be responsible, fair, and professional.

From *Columbia Journalism Review* 1, no. 1 (Spring 1962): 2.

To discuss all the means that carry news to the public, thus viewing the field whole, without the customary partitions.

To provide a meeting ground for thoughtful discussion of journalism, both by its practitioners and by observers, to encourage debate, and to provide ample space for dissent.

To attempt systematic studies of major problems in journalism, drawing not only upon published sources but upon new research and upon correspondents here and abroad, including many of the School's alumni active in the profession.

To recognize that others (like *Nieman Reports, Journalism Quarterly*, the *Saturday Review* and, in some ways, trade publications like *Editor & Publisher* and *Broadcasting*) have been doing part of the job and to acknowledge their work in the *Review*'s pages.

As a division of a large private university and as an institution that has mediated between the academic world and journalism for nearly fifty years, the School is committed to no single interest beyond its belief in good journalism and graduate education for journalism. The School has tried to prepare more than 2,500 graduates for careers in journalism. Now it believes it is time to try to assess the field they have entered.

No single issue of this publication will satisfy all the editors' standards—least of all this first pilot effort. But the *Review* will try to emulate all sincere journalism by coming as near the whole truth as possible.

THE KERNER COMMISSION

The News Media and the Disorders
(1968)

Introduction

The President's charge to the Commission asked specifically: "What effect do the mass media have on the riots?"

The question is far reaching, and a sure answer is beyond the range of presently available scientific techniques. Our conclusions and recommendations are based upon subjective as well as objective factors; interviews as well as statistics; isolated examples as well as general trends.

Freedom of the press is not the issue. A free press is indispensable to the preservation of the other freedoms this Nation cherishes. The recommendations in this chapter have thus been developed under the strong conviction that only a press unhindered by government can contribute to freedom.

To answer the President's question, the Commission:

• Directed its field survey teams to question government officials, law enforcement agents, media personnel, and ordinary citizens about their attitudes and reactions to reporting of the riots.

• Arranged for interviews of media representatives about their coverage of the riots.

• Conducted special interviews with ghetto residents about their response to coverage.

• Arranged for a quantitative analysis of the content of television programs and newspaper reporting in 15 riot cities during the period of the disorder and the days immediately before and after.

• From November 10–12, 1967, sponsored and participated in a conference of

From *Report of the National Advisory Commission on Civil Disorders* (Washington, DC: U.S. Government Printing Office, 1968), 201–13.

representatives from all levels of the newspaper, news magazine, and broadcasting industries at Poughkeepsie, N.Y.

Finally, of course, the Commissioners read newspapers, listened to the radio, watched television, and thus formed their own impressions of media coverage. All of these data, impressions, and attitudes provide the foundation for our conclusions.

The Commission also determined, very early, that the answer to the President's question did not lie solely in the performance of the press and broadcasters in reporting the riots proper. Our analysis had to consider also the overall treatment by the media of the Negro ghettos, community relations, racial attitudes, urban and rural poverty—day by day and month by month, year in and year out.

On this basis, we have reached three conclusions:

First, that despite instances of sensationalism, inaccuracies, and distortions, newspapers, radio, and television, on the whole, made a real effort to give a balanced, factual account of the 1967 disorders.

Second, that despite this effort, the portrayal of the violence that occurred last summer failed to reflect accurately its scale and character. The overall effect was, we believe, an exaggeration of both mood and event.

Third, and ultimately most important, we believe that the media have thus far failed to report adequately on the causes and consequences of civil disorders and the underlying problems of race relations.

With these comments as a perspective, we discuss first the coverage of last summer's disturbances. We will then summarize our concerns with overall coverage of race relations.

Coverage of the 1967 Disturbances

We have found a significant imbalance between what actually happened in our cities and what the newspaper, radio, and television coverage of the riots told us happened. The Commission, in studying last summer's disturbances, visited many of the cities and interviewed participants and observers. We found that the disorders, as serious as they were, were less destructive, less widespread, and less of a black-white confrontation than most people believed.

Lacking other sources of information, we formed our original impressions and beliefs from what we saw on television, heard on the radio, and read in newspapers and magazines. We are deeply concerned that millions of other Americans, who must rely on the mass media, likewise formed incorrect impressions and judgments about what went on in many American cities last summer.

As we started to probe the reasons for this imbalance between reality and impression, we first believed that the media had sensationalized the disturbances, consistently overplaying violence and giving disproportionate amounts of time to emotional events and militant leaders. To test this theory, we commissioned a systematic, quantitative analysis, covering the content of newspaper and television reporting in 15 cities where disorders occurred. The results of this analysis do not support our early belief. Of 955 television sequences of riot and racial news examined, 837 could be classified for predominant atmosphere as either "emotional," "calm," or "normal." Of these, 494 were classified as calm, 262 as emotional, and 81 as normal. Only a small proportion of all scenes analyzed showed actual mob action, people looting, sniping, setting fires, or being injured, or killed. Moderate Negro leaders were shown more frequently than militant leaders on television news broadcasts.

Of 3,779 newspaper articles analyzed, more focused on legislation which should be sought and planning which should be done to control ongoing riots and prevent future riots than on any other topic. The findings of this analysis are explained in detail later in this chapter. They make it clear that the imbalance between actual events and the portrayal of those events in the press and on the air cannot be attributed solely to sensationalism in reporting and presentation.

We have, however, identified several factors which, it seems to us, did work to create incorrect and exaggerated impressions about the scope and intensity of the disorders.

First, despite the overall statistical picture, there were instances of gross flaws in presenting news of the 1967 riots. Some newspapers printed scare headlines unsupported by the mild stories that followed. All media reported rumors that had no basis in fact. Some newsmen staged riot events for the cameras. Examples are included in the next section.

Second, the press obtained much factual information about the scale of the disorders—property damage, personal injury, and deaths—from local officials, who often were inexperienced in dealing with civil disorders and not always able to sort out fact from rumor in the confusion. At the height of the Detroit riot, some news reports of property damage put the figure in excess of $500 million.[1] Subsequent investigation shows it to be $40 to $45 million.[2] The initial estimates were not the independent judgment of reporters or editors. They came from beleaguered government officials. But the news media gave currency to these errors. Reporters uncritically accepted, and editors uncritically published, the inflated figures, leaving an indelible impression of damage up to more than 10 times greater than actually occurred.

Third, the coverage of the disorders—particularly on television—tended to define the events as black-white confrontations. In fact, almost all of the deaths, injuries, and property damage occurred in all-Negro neighborhoods, and thus the disorders were not "race riots" as that term is generally understood.

Closely linked to these problems is the phenomenon of cumulative effect. As the summer of 1967 progressed, we think Americans often began to associate more or less neutral sights and sounds (like a squad car with flashing red lights, a burning building, a suspect in police custody) with racial disorders, so that the appearance of any particular item, itself hardly inflammatory, set off a whole sequence of association with riot events. Moreover, the summer's news was not seen and heard in isolation. Events of these past few years—the Watts riot, other disorders, and the growing momentum of the civil rights movement—conditioned the responses of readers and viewers and heightened their reactions. What the public saw and read last summer thus produced emotional reactions and left vivid impressions not wholly attributable to the material itself.

Fear and apprehension of racial unrest and violence are deeply rooted in American society. They color and intensify reactions to news of racial trouble and threats of racial conflict. Those who report and disseminate news must be conscious of the background of anxieties and apprehension against which their stories are projected. This does not mean that the media should manage the news or tell less than the truth. Indeed, we believe that it would be imprudent and even dangerous to downplay coverage in the hope that censored reporting of inflammatory incidents somehow will diminish violence. Once a disturbance occurs, the word will spread independently of newspapers and television. To attempt to ignore these events or portray them as something other than what they are can only diminish confidence in the media and increase the effectiveness of those who monger rumors and the fears of those who listen.

But to be complete, the coverage must be representative. We suggest that the main failure of the media last summer was that the totality of its coverage was not as representative as it should have been to be accurate. We believe that to live up to their own professed standards, the media simply must exercise a higher degree of care and a greater level of sophistication than they have yet shown in this area— higher, perhaps, than the level ordinarily acceptable with other stories.

This is not "just another story." It should not be treated like one. Admittedly, some of what disturbs us about riot coverage last summer stems from circumstances beyond media control. But many of the inaccuracies of fact, tone, and mood were due to the failure of reporters and editors to ask tough enough questions about official reports and to apply the most rigorous standards possible in evaluating and presenting the news. Reporters and editors must be sure that descriptions and pictures of violence, and emotional or inflammatory sequences or articles, even though "true" in isolation, are really representative and do not convey an impression at odds with the overall reality of events. The media too often did not achieve this level of sophisticated, skeptical, careful news judgment during last summer's riots.

The Media and Race Relations

Our second and fundamental criticism is that the news media have failed to analyze and report adequately on racial problems in the United States and, as a related matter, to meet the Negro's legitimate expectations in journalism. By and large, news organizations have failed to communicate to both their black and white audiences a sense of the problems America faces and the sources of potential solutions. The media report and write from the standpoint of a white man's world. The ills of the ghetto, the difficulties of life there, the Negro's burning sense of grievance, are seldom conveyed. Slights and indignities are part of the Negro's daily life, and many of them come from what he now calls the "white press"—a press that repeatedly, if unconsciously, reflects the biases, the paternalism, the indifference of white America. This may be understandable, but it is not excusable in an institution that has the mission to inform and educate the whole of our society.

Our criticisms, important as they are, do not lead us to conclude that the media are a cause of riots, any more than they are the cause of other phenomena which they report. It is true that newspaper and television reporting helped shape people's attitudes toward riots. In some cities, people who watched television reports and read newspaper accounts of riots in other cities later rioted themselves. But the causal chain weakens when we recall that in other cities, people in very much the same circumstances watched the same programs and read the same newspaper stories but did not riot themselves.

The news media are not the sole source of information and certainly not the only influence on public attitudes. People obtained their information and formed their opinions about the 1967 disorders from the multiplicity of sources that condition the public's thinking on all events. Personal experience, conversations with others, the local and long-distance telephone are all important as sources of information and ideas and contribute to the totality of attitudes about riots.

No doubt, in some cases, the knowledge or the sight on a television screen of what had gone on elsewhere lowered inhibitions, kindled outrage or awakened desires for excitement or loot—or simply passed the word. Many ghetto residents we interviewed thought so themselves. By the same token, the news reports of riots must have conditioned the response of officials and police to disturbances in their own cities. The reaction of the authorities in Detroit was almost certainly affected in some part by what they saw or read of Newark a week earlier. The Commission believes that none of these private or official reactions was decisive in determining the course of the disorders. Even if they had been more significant than we think, however, we cannot envision a system of governmental restraints that could successfully eliminate these effects. And an effort to formulate and impose such restraints would be inconsistent with fundamental traditions in our society.

These failings of the media must be corrected and the improvement must come from within the media. A society that values and relies on a free press as intensely as ours is entitled to demand in return responsibility from the press and conscientious attention by the press to its own deficiencies. The Commission has seen evidence that many of those who supervise, edit, and report for the news media are becoming increasingly aware of and concerned about their performance in this field. With that concern, and with more experience, will come more sophisticated and responsible coverage. But much more must be done, and it must be done soon.

The Commission has a number of recommendations designed to stimulate and accelerate efforts toward self-improvement. And we propose a privately organized, privately funded Institute of Urban Communications as a means for drawing these recommendations together and promoting their implementation.

News Coverage of Civil Disorders—Summer 1967

The Method of Analysis

As noted, the Commission has been surveying both the reporting of disorders last summer and the broader field of race relations coverage. With respect to the reporting of disorders, we were trying to get a sense of content, accuracy, tone, and bias. We sought to find out how people reacted to it and how reporters conducted themselves while carrying out their assignments. The Commission used a number of techniques to probe these matters and to provide cross-checks on data and impressions.

To obtain an objective source of data, the Commission arranged for a systematic, quantitative analysis of the content of newspapers, local television, and network coverage in 15 cities for a period from 3 days before to 3 days after the disorder in each city.[3] The cities were chosen to provide a cross-section in terms of the location and scale of the disorders and the dates of their occurrence.

Within each city, for the period specified, the study was comprehensive. Every daily newspaper and all network and local television news films were analyzed, and scripts and logs were examined. In all, 955 network and local television sequences and 3,779 newspaper articles dealing with riot and race relations news were analyzed. Each separate analysis was coded and the cards were cross-tabulated by computer to provide results and comparisons for use by the Commission. The material was measured to determine the amount of space devoted to news of riot activity; the nature of the display given compared with other news coverage; and the types of stories, articles, and television programing presented. We sought specific statistical information on such matters as the amount of space or time devoted to different kinds of riot stories, the types and identities of persons most often depicted or interviewed, the frequency with which race relations problems were mentioned in riot stories or identified as the cause of riot activity.

The survey was designed to be objective and statistical. Within its terms of reference, the Commission was looking for broad characterizations of media tone and content.

The Commission is aware of the inherent limitations of content analysis techniques. They cannot measure the emotional impact of a particular story or television sequence. By themselves, they provide no basis for conclusions as to the accuracy of what was reported. Particular examples of good or bad journalistic conduct, which may be important in themselves, are submerged in a statistical average. The Commission therefore sought through staff interviews and personal contact with members of the press and the public to obtain direct evidence of the effects of riot coverage and the performance of the media during last summer's disturbances.

Conclusions about Content[4]

Television   1. Content analysis of television film footage shows that the tone of the coverage studied was more "calm" and "factual" than "emotional" and "rumor-laden." Researchers viewed every one of the 955 television sequences and found that twice as many "calm" sequences as "emotional" ones were shown. The amount and location of coverage were relatively limited, considering the magnitude of the events. The analysis reveals a dominant, positive emphasis on control of the riot and on activities in the aftermath of the riot (53.8 percent of all scenes broadcast), rather than on scenes of actual mob action, or people looting, sniping, setting fires, or being injured or killed (4.8 percent of scenes shown). According to participants in our Poughkeepsie conference, coverage frequently was of the post-riot or interview variety because newsmen arrived at the scene after the actual violence had subsided. Overall, both network and local television coverage was cautious and restrained.

2. Television newscasts during the periods of actual disorder in 1967 tended to emphasize law enforcement activities, thereby overshadowing underlying grievances and tensions. This conclusion is based on the relatively high frequency with which television showed and described law enforcement agents, police, National Guardsmen, and army troops performing control functions.

Television coverage tended to give the impression that the riots were confrontations between Negroes and whites rather than responses by Negroes to underlying slum problems. The control agents were predominantly white. The ratio of white male adults[5] to Negro male adults shown on television is high (1:2) considering that the riots took place in predominantly Negro neighborhoods. And some interviews with whites involved landlords or proprietors who lost property or suffered business losses because of the disturbances and thus held strongly antagonistic attitudes.

The content analysis shows that by far the most frequent "actor" appearances on television were Negro male adults, white male adults, law enforcement agents, and public officials. We cannot tell from a content analysis whether there was any preconceived editorial policy of portraying the riots as racial confrontations requiring the intervention of enforcement agents. But the content analysis does present a visual three-way alignment of Negroes, white bystanders, and public officials or enforcement agents. This alignment tended to create an impression that the riots were predominantly racial confrontations involving clashes between black and white citizens.

3. About one-third of all riot-related sequences for network and local television appeared on the first day following the outbreak of rioting, regardless of the course of development of the riot itself. After the first day there was, except in Detroit, a very sharp decline in the amount of television time devoted to the disturbance. In Detroit, where the riot started slowly and did not flare out of control until the evening of July 24, 48 hours after it started, the number of riot-related sequences shown increased until July 26 and then showed the same sharp dropoff as noted after the first day of rioting in the other cities.[6] These findings tend to controvert the impression that the riot intensifies television coverage, thus in turn intensifying the riot. The content analysis indicates that whether or not the riot was getting worse, television coverage of the riot decreased sharply after the first day.

4. The Commission made a special effort to analyze television coverage of Negro leaders. To do this, Negro leaders were divided into three categories: (a) celebrities or public figures, who did not claim any organizational following (e.g., social scientist Dr. Kenneth B. Clark, comedian Dick Gregory) ; (b) "moderate" Negro leaders, who claim a political or organizational following ; and (c) "militant" Negro leaders who claim a political or organizational following. During the riot periods surveyed, Negro leaders appeared infrequently on network news broadcasts and were about equally divided among celebrity or public figures, moderate leaders, and militant leaders. On local television, Negro leaders appeared more often. Of the three categories, "moderate" Negro leaders were shown on local stations more than twice as often as Negro leaders identified primarily as celebrities or public figures and three times more frequently than militant leaders.

Newspapers 1. Like television coverage, newspaper coverage of civil disturbances in the summer of 1967 was more calm, factual, and restrained than outwardly emotional or inflammatory. During the period of the riot there were many stories dealing exclusively with non-riot racial news. Considering the magnitude of the events, the amount of coverage was limited. Most stories were played down or put on inside pages. Researchers found that almost all the articles analyzed (3,045 of 3,770) tended to focus on one of 16 identifiable subjects. Of this group, 502 articles (16.5 percent) focused primarily on legislation which should be sought and planning which could be done to control ongoing riots and prevent future riots. The second largest category consisted of 471 articles (15.5 percent) focusing on containment or control of riot action. Newspaper coverage of the disorders reflects efforts at caution and restraint.

2. Newspapers tended to characterize and portray last summer's riots in national terms rather than as local phenomena and problems, especially when rioting was taking place in the newspaper's own city. During the actual disorders, the newspapers in each city studied tended to print many stories dealing with disorders or racial troubles in other cities. About 40 percent of the riot or racial stories in each local newspaper during the period of rioting in that city came from the wire services. Furthermore, most newspaper editors appear to have given more headline attention to riots occurring elsewhere than to those at home during the time of trouble in their own cities.

Accuracy of the Coverage

We have tested the accuracy of coverage by means of interviews with local media representatives, city and police officials, and residents of the ghettos. To provide a broad base, we used three separate sources for interview data: The Commission's field survey teams, special field teams, and the findings of a special research study.

As is to be expected, almost everyone had his own version of "the truth," but it is noteworthy that some editors and reporters themselves, in retrospect, have expressed concern about the accuracy of their own coverage. For example, one newspaper editor said at the Commission's Poughkeepsie Conference:

> We used things in our leads and headlines during the riot I wish we could have back now, because they were wrong and they were bad mistakes * * *
>
> We used the words "sniper kings" and "nests of snipers." We found out when we were able to get our people into those areas and get them out from under the cars that these sniper kings and these nests of snipers were the constituted authorities shooting at each other, most of them. There was just one confirmed sniper in the entire eight-day riot and he was * * * drunk and he had a pistol, and he was firing from a window.

Television industry representatives at the conference stressed their concern about "live" coverage of disorders and said they try, whenever possible, to view and edit taped or filmed sequences before broadcasting them. Conference participants admitted that live television coverage via helicopter of the 1965 Watts riot had been inflammatory, and network news executives expressed doubts that tele-vision would ever again present live coverage of a civil disorder.

Most errors involved mistakes of fact, exaggeration of events, overplaying of particular stories, or prominently displayed speculation about unfounded rumors of potential trouble. This is not only a local problem ; because of the wire services and networks, it is a national one. An experienced riot reporter told the Commis-sion that initial wire service reports of a disturbance tend to be inflated. The reason, he said, is that they are written by local bureau men who in most cases have not seen a civil disorder before. When out-of-town reporters with knowledge in the field or the wire services' own riot specialists arrive on the scene, the situation is put into a more accurate context.

Some examples of exaggeration and mistakes about facts are cataloged here. These examples are by no means exhaustive. They represent only a few of the incidents discovered by the Commission and, no doubt, are but a small part of the total number of such inaccuracies. But the Commission believes that they are rep-resentative of the kinds of errors likely to occur when, in addition to the confusion inherent in civil disorder situations, reporters are rushed and harried or editors are superficial and careless. We present these as examples of mistakes that we hope will be avoided in the future.

In particular, we believe newsmen should be wary of how they play rumors of impending trouble. Whether a rumor is reliable and significant enough to deserve coverage is an editorial decision. But the failure of many headlined rumors to be borne out last summer suggests that these editorial decisions often are not as care-fully made as the sensitivity of the subject requires.

- In Detroit, a radio station broadcast a rumor, based on a telephone tip, that Negroes planned to invade suburbia one night later; if plans existed, they never materialized.
- In Cincinnati, several several outlets ran a story about white youths arrested for possessing a bazooka; only a few reports mentioned that the weapon was in-operable.
- In Tampa, a newspaper repeatedly indulged in speculation about impending trouble. When the state attorney ruled the fatal shooting of a Negro youth justifi-able homicide, the paper's news columns reported: "There were fears today that the ruling would stir new race problems for Tampa tonight." The day before, the paper quoted one "top lawman" as telling reporters "he now fears that Negro res-idents in the Central Avenue Project and in the West Tampa trouble spots feel they are in competition and are trying to see which can cause the most unrest—which area can become the center of attraction."
- A West Coast newspaper put out an edition headlined: "Rioting Erupts in Washington, D.C. / Negroes Hurl Bottles, Rocks at Police Near White House." The

story did not support the headline. It reported what was actually the fact: that a number of teenage Negroes broke store windows and threw bottles and stones at police and firemen near downtown Washington, a mile or more from the White House. On the other hand, the same paper did not report unfounded local rumors of sniping when other news media did.

Television presents a different problem with respect to accuracy. In contrast to what some of its critics have charged, television sometimes may have leaned over too far backward in seeking balance and restraint. By stressing interviews, many with whites in predominantly Negro neighborhoods, and by emphasizing control scenes rather than riotous action, television news broadcasts may have given a distorted picture of what the disorders were all about.

The media—especially television—also have failed to present and analyze to a sufficient extent the basic reasons for the disorders. There have, after the disorders, been some brilliant exceptions.[7] As the content analysis findings suggest, however, coverage during the riot period itself gives far more emphasis to control of rioters and black-white confrontation than to the underlying causes of the disturbances.

Ghetto Reactions to the Media Coverage

The Commission was particularly interested in public reaction to media coverage; specifically, what people in the ghetto look at and read and how it affects them. The Commission has drawn upon reports from special teams of researchers who visited various cities where outbreaks occurred last summer. Members of these teams interviewed ghetto dwellers and middle-class Negroes on their responses to news media. In addition, we have used information from a statistical study of the mass media in the Negro ghetto in Pittsburgh.[8]

These interviews and surveys, though by no means a complete study of the subject, lead to four broad conclusions about ghetto and, to a lesser degree, middle-class Negro reactions to the media.

Most Negroes distrust what they refer to as the "white press." As one interviewer reported:

> The average black person couldn't give less of a damn about what the media say. The intelligent black person is resentful at what he considers to be a totally false portrayal of what goes on in the ghetto. Most black people see the newspapers as mouth-pieces of the "power structure."

These comments are echoed in most interview reports the Commission has read. Distrust and dislike of the media among ghetto Negroes encompass all the media, though in general, the newspapers are mistrusted more than the television. This is not because television is thought to be more sensitive or responsive to Negro needs and aspirations but because ghetto residents believe that television at least lets them see the actual events for themselves. Even so, many Negroes, particularly teenagers, told researchers that they noted a pronounced discrepancy between what they saw in the riots and what television broadcast.

Persons interviewed offered three chief reasons for their attitude. First, they believe, as suggested in the quotation above, that the media are instruments of the white power structure. They think that these white interests guide the entire white community, from the journalists' friends and neighbors to city officials, police officers, and department store owners. Publishers and editors, if not white reporters, they feel, support and defend these interests with enthusiasm and dedication.

Second, many people in the ghettos apparently believe that newsmen rely on the police for most of their information about what is happening during a disorder and tend to report much more of what the officials are doing and saying than what Negro citizens or leaders in the city are doing and saying. Editors and reporters at the Poughkeepsie conference acknowledged that the police and city officials are their main—and sometimes their only—source of information. It was also noted that most reporters who cover civil disturbances tend to arrive with the police and stay close to them—often for safety and often because they learn where the action is at the same time as the authorities—and thus buttress the ghetto impression that police and press work together and toward the same ends (an impression that may come as a surprise to many within the ranks of police and press).

Third, Negro residents in several cities surveyed cited as specific examples of media unfairness what they considered the failure of the media:

• To report the many examples of Negroes helping law enforcement officers and assisting in the treatment of the wounded during disorders.
• To report adequately about false arrests.
• To report instances of excessive force by the National Guard.
• To explore and interpret the background conditions leading to disturbances.
• To expose, except in Detroit, what they regarded as instances of police brutality.
• To report on white vigilante groups which allegedly came into some disorder areas and molested innocent Negro residents.

Some of these problems are insoluble. But more first-hand reporting in the diffuse and fragmented riot area should temper easy reliance on police information and announcements. There is a special need for news media to cover "positive" news stories in the ghetto before and after riots with concern and enthusiasm.

A multitude of news and information sources other than the established news media are relied upon in the ghetto. One of our studies found that 79 percent of a total of 567 ghetto residents interviewed in seven cities[9] first heard about the outbreak in their own city by word of mouth. Telephone and word of mouth exchanges on the streets, in churches, stores, pool halls, and bars, provide more information—and rumors—about events of direct concern to ghetto residents than the more conventional news media.

Among the established media, television and radio are far more popular in the ghetto than newspapers. Radios there, apparently, are ordinarily listened to less for news than for music and other programs. One survey showed that an overwhelmingly large number of Negro children and teenagers (like their white counterparts) listen to the radio for music alone, interspersed by disc jockey chatter. In other age groups, the response of most people about what they listen to on the radio was "anything," leading to the conclusion that radio in the ghetto is basically a background accompaniment.

But the fact that radio is such a constant background accompaniment can make it an important influence on people's attitudes, and perhaps on their actions once trouble develops. This is true for several reasons. News presented on local "rock" stations seldom constitutes much more than terse headline items which may startle or frighten but seldom inform. Radio disc jockeys and those who preside over the popular "talk shows" keep a steady patter of information going over the air. When a city is beset by civil strife, this patter can both inform transistor radio-carrying young people where the action is, and terrify their elders and much of the white community. "Burn, baby, burn," the slogan of the Watts riot, was inadvertently originated by a radio disc jockey.

Thus, radio can be an instrument of trouble and tension in a community threatened or inundated with civil disorder. It can also do much to minimize fear by putting fast-paced events into proper perspective. We have found commendable instances, for example, in Detroit, Milwaukee, and New Brunswick, of radio stations and personalities using their air time and influence to try to calm potential rioters. In the next section, we recommend procedures for meetings and consultations for advance planning among those who will cover civil disorders. It is important that radio personnel, and especially disc jockeys and talk show hosts, be included in such preplanning.

Television is the formal news source most relied upon in the ghetto. According to one report, more than 75 percent of the sample turned to television for national and international news, and a larger percentage of the sample (86 percent) regularly watched television from 5 to 7 p.m., the dinner hours when the evening news programs are broadcast.

The significance of broadcasting in news dissemination is seen in Census Bureau estimates that in June 1967, 87.7 percent of nonwhite households and 94.8 percent of white households had television sets.

When ghetto residents do turn to newspapers, most read tabloids, if available, far more frequently than standard size newspapers and rely on the tabloids primarily for light features, racing charts, comic strips, fashion news and display advertising.

Conduct of Press Representatives

Most newsmen appear to be aware and concerned that their very physical presence can exacerbate a small disturbance, but some have conducted themselves with a startling lack of common sense. News organizations, particularly television networks, have taken substantial steps to minimize the effect of the physical presence of their employees at a news event. Networks have issued internal instructions calling for use of unmarked cars and small cameras and tape recorders, and most stations instruct their cameramen to film without artificial light whenever possible. Still, some newsmen have done things "for the sake of the story" that could have contributed to tension.

Reports have come to the Commission's attention of individual newsmen staging events, coaxing youths to throw rocks and interrupt traffic, and otherwise acting irresponsibly at the incipient stages of a disturbance. Such acts are the responsibility of the news organization as well as of its individual reporter.

Two examples occurred in Newark. Television cameramen, according to officials, crowded into and in front of police headquarters, interfering with law enforcement operations and "making a general nuisance of themselves." In a separate incident, a New York newspaper photographer covering the Newark riot repeatedly urged and finally convinced a Negro boy to throw a rock for the camera. Crowding may occasionally be unavoidable; staging of events is not.

We believe every effort should be made to eliminate this sort of conduct. This requires the implementation of thoughtful, stringent staff guidelines for reporters and editors. Such guidelines, carefully formulated, widely disseminated, and strictly enforced, underlie the self-policing activities of some news organizations already, but they must be universally adopted if they are to be effective in curbing journalistic irresponsibility.

The Commission has studied the internal guidelines in use last summer at the Associated Press, United Press International, the Washington Post and the Columbia Broadcasting System. Many other news organizations, large and small, have similar guidelines. In general, the guidelines urge extreme care to ensure that reporting is thorough and balanced and that words and statistics used are appropriate and accurate. The AP guidelines call for broad investigation into the immediate and underlying causes of an incident. The CBS guidelines demand as much caution as possible to avoid the danger of camera equipment and lights exacerbating the disturbance.

Internal guidelines can, and all those studied do, go beyond problems of physical presence at a disturbance to the substantive aspects of searching out, reporting, and writing the story. But the content of the guidelines is probably less important than the fact that the subject has been thoughtfully considered and hammered out within the organization, and an approach developed that is designed to meet the organization's particular needs and solve its particular problems.

We recommend that every news organization that does not now have some form of guidelines—or suspects that those it has are not working effectively—designate top editors to (a) meet with its reporters who have covered or might be assigned to riots, (b) discuss in detail the problems and procedures which exist or are expected and (c) formulate and disseminate directives based on the discussions. Regardless of the specific provisions, the vital step is for every news-gathering organization to adopt and implement at least some minimal form of internal control.

A Recommendation to Improve Riot Coverage

A Need for Better Communication

A recurrent problem in the coverage of last summer's disorders was friction and lack of cooperation between police officers and working reporters. Many experienced and capable journalists complained that policemen and their commanding officers were at best apathetic and at worst overtly hostile toward reporters attempting to cover a disturbance. Policemen, on the other hand, charged that many reporters seemed to forget that the task of the police is to restore order.

After considering available evidence on the subject, the Commission is convinced that these conditions reflect an absence of advance communication and planning among the people involved. We do not suggest that familiarity with the other's problems will beget total amity and cooperation. The interests of the media and the police are sometimes necessarily at variance. But we do believe that communication is a vital step toward removing the obstacles produced by ignorance, confusion, and misunderstanding of what each group is actually trying to do.

Mutual Orientation

What is needed first is a series of discussions, perhaps a combination of informal gatherings and seminar-type workshops. They should encompass all ranks of the police, all levels of media employees, and a cross-section of city officials. At first these would be get-acquainted sessions—to air complaints and discuss common problems. Working reporters should get to know the police who would be likely to draw duty in a disorder. Police and city officials should use the sessions for frank and candid briefings on the problems the city might face and official plans for dealing with disturbances.

Later sessions might consider procedures to facilitate the physical movement of personnel and speed the flow of accurate and complete news. Such arrangements might involve nothing more than a procedure for designating specific locations at which police officers would be available to escort a reporter into a dangerous area. In addition, policemen and reporters working together might devise better methods of identification, communication, and training.

Such procedures are infinitely variable and depend on the initiative, needs, and desires of those involved. If there is no existing institution or procedure for convening such meetings, we urge the mayor or city manager to do so in every city where experience suggests the possibility of future trouble. To allay any apprehension that discussions with officials might lead to restraints on the freedom to seek out and report the news, participants in these meetings should stipulate beforehand that freedom of access to all areas for reporters will be preserved.

Designation of Information Officers

It is desirable to designate and prepare a number of police officers to act as media information officers. There should be enough of these so that, in the event of a disturbance, a reporter will not have to seek far to find a policeman ready and able to give him information and answer questions. Officers should be of high enough rank within the police department to have ready access to information.

Creation of an Information Center

A nerve center for reliable police and official government information should be planned and ready for activation when a disturbance reaches a predetermined point of intensity. Such a center might be located at police headquarters or city hall. It should be directed by an experienced, high-ranking information specialist with close ties to police officials. It is imperative, of course, that all officials keep a steady flow of accurate information coming into the center. Ideally, rooms would be set aside for taping and filming interviews with public officials. Local television stations might cut costs and relieve congestion by pooling some equipment at this central facility. An information center should not be thought of as replacing other news sources inside and outside the disturbance area. If anything, our studies suggest that reporters are already too closely tied to police and officials as news sources in a disorder. An information center should not be permitted to intensify this dependence. Properly conceived, however, a center can supplement on-the-spot reporting and supply news about official action.

Out-of-Town Reporters

Much of the difficulty last summer apparently revolved around relations between local law enforcement officials and out-of-town reporters. These reporters are likely to be less sensitive about preserving the "image" of the local community.

Still, local officials serve their city badly when they ignore or impede national media representatives instead of informing them about the city, and cooperating with their attempts to cover the story. City and police officials should designate liaison officers and distribute names and telephone numbers of police and other relevant officials, the place they can be found if trouble develops, and other information likely to be useful.

National and other news organizations, in turn, could help matters by selecting a responsible home office official to act as liaison in these cases and to be accessible by phone to local officials who encounter difficulty with on-the-spot representatives of an organization.

General Guidelines and Codes

In some cases, if all parties involved were willing, planning sessions might lead to the consideration of more formal undertakings. These might include: (a) agreements on specific procedures to expedite the physical movement of men and equipment around disorder areas and back and forth through police lines; (b) general guidelines on the behavior of both media and police personnel; and (c) arrangements for a brief moratorium on reporting news of an incipient disturbance. The Commission stresses once again its belief that though each of these possibilities merits consideration, none should be formulated or imposed by unilateral government action. Any procedure finally adopted should be negotiated between police and media representatives and should assure both sides the flexibility needed to do their respective jobs. Acceptance of such arrangements should be frankly based on grounds of self-interest, for negotiated methods of procedure can often yield substantial benefits to each side—and to the public which both serve.

At the request of the Commission, the Community Relations Service of the Department of Justice surveyed recent experiences with formal codes. Most of the codes studied: (a) Set forth in general terms common sense standards of good journalistic conduct, and (b) establish procedures for a brief moratorium (seldom more than 30 minutes to an hour) on reporting an incipient disturbance.

In its survey, the Community Relations Service described and analyzed experiences with codes in 11 major cities where they are currently in force. Members of the CRS staff conducted interviews with key citizens (newsmen, city officials, and community leaders) in each of the 11 cities, seeking comments on the effectiveness and practicality of the codes and guidelines used. CRS's major findings and conclusions are:

• All codes and guidelines now in operation are basically voluntary arrangements usually put forward by local authorities and accepted by the news media after consultation. Nowhere has an arrangement or agreement been effected that binds the news media without their assent.

• No one interviewed in this survey considered the code or guidelines in effect in his city as useless or harmful. CRS thought that, where they were in effect, the codes had a constructive impact on the local news media. Observers in some cities, however, thought the increased sense of responsibility manifested by press and television was due more to experience with riot coverage than to the existence of the codes.

• The more controversial and often least understood aspect of guidelines has been provision for a brief voluntary moratorium on the reporting of news. Some kind of moratorium is specified in the codes of six cities surveyed (Chicago, Omaha, Buffalo, Indianapolis, Kansas City, and Toledo), and the moratorium was invoked last summer in Chicago and Indianapolis. In each case, an effort to prevent quite minor racial incidents from escalating into more serious trouble was successful, and many thought the moratorium contributed.

• The confusion about a moratorium, and the resulting aversion to it, is unfortunate. The specific period of delay is seldom more than 30 minutes. In practice, under today's conditions of reporting and broadcasting, this often will mean little if any delay before the full story gets into the paper or on the air. The time can be used to prepare and edit the story and to verify and assess the reports of trouble. The only loss is the banner headline or the broadcast news bulletin that is released prematurely to avoid being beaten by "the competition." It is just such reflexive responses that can lead to sensationalism and inaccuracy. In cities where a moratorium is part of the code, CRS interviewers detected no discontent over its presence.

• The most frequent complaint about shortcomings in existing codes is that many of them do not reach the underpinnings of crisis situations. Ghetto spokesmen, in particular, said that the emphasis in the codes on conduct during the crisis itself tended to lead the media to neglect reporting the underlying causes of racial tension.

At the Poughkeepsie conference with media representatives, there was considerable criticism of the Chicago code on grounds that the moratorium is open-ended. Once put into effect it is supposed to be maintained until "the situation is under control." There were doubts about how effective this code had been in practice. The voluntary news blackout in Detroit for part of the first day of the riot—apparently at the request of officials and civil rights groups—was cited as evidence that suppression of news of violence does not necessarily defuse a riot situation.

On the basis of the CRS survey and other evidence, the Commission concludes that codes are seldom harmful, often useful, but no panacea. To be of any use, they must address themselves to the substance of the problems that plague relations between the press and officialdom during a disorder, but they are only one of several methods of improving those relations. Ultimately, no matter how sensitive and comprehensive a code or set of guidelines may be, efficient, accurate reporting must depend on the intelligence, judgment, and training of newsmen, police, and city officials together.

Reporting Racial Problems in the United States

A Failure to Communicate

The Commission's major concern with the news media is not in riot reporting as such, but in the failure to report adequately on race relations and ghetto problems and to bring more Negroes into journalism. Concern about this was expressed by a number of participants in our Poughkeepsie conference. Disorders are only one aspect of the dilemmas and difficulties of race relations in America. In defining, explaining, and reporting this broader, more complex and ultimately far more fundamental subject, the communications media, ironically, have failed to communicate.

They have not communicated to the majority of their audience—which is white—a sense of the degradation, misery, and hopelessness of living in the ghetto. They have not communicated to whites a feeling for the difficulties and frustrations of being a Negro in the United States. They have not shown understanding or appreciation of—and thus have not communicated—a sense of Negro culture, thought, or history.

Equally important, most newspaper articles and most television programming ignore the fact than an appreciable part of their audience is black. The world that television and newspapers offer to their black audience is almost totally white, in both appearance and attitude. As we have said, our evidence shows that the so-called "white press" is at best mistrusted and at worst held in contempt by many black Americans. Far too often, the press acts and talks about Negroes as if Negroes do not read the newspapers or watch television, give birth, marry, die, and go to PTA meetings. Some newspapers and stations are beginning to make efforts to fill this void, but they have still a long way to go.

The absence of Negro faces and activities from the media has an effect on white audiences as well as black. If what the white American reads in the newspapers or sees on television conditions his expectation of what is ordinary and normal in the larger society, he will neither understand nor accept the black American. By failing to portray the Negro as a matter of routine and in the context of the total society, the news media have, we believe, contributed to the black-white schism in this country.

When the white press does refer to Negroes and Negro problems it frequently does so as if Negroes were not a part of the audience. This is perhaps understandable in a system where whites edit and, to a large extent, write news. But such attitudes, in an area as sensitive and inflammatory as this, feed Negro alienation and intensify white prejudices.

We suggest that a top editor or news director monitor his news production for a period of several weeks, taking note of how certain stories and language will affect black readers or viewers. A Negro staff member could do this easily. Then the staff should be informed about the problems involved.

The problems of race relations coverage go beyond incidents of white bias. Many editors and news directors, plagued by shortages of staff and lack of reliable contacts and sources of information in the city, have failed to recognize the significance of the urban story and to develop resources to cover it adequately.

We believe that most news organizations do not have direct access to diversified news sources in the ghetto. Seldom do they have a total sense of what is going on there. Some of the blame rests on Negro leaders who do not trust the media and will not deal candidly with representatives of the white press. But the real failure rests with the news organizations themselves. They—like other elements of the white community—have ignored the ghettos for decades. Now they seek instant acceptance and cooperation.

The development of good contacts, reliable information, and understanding requires more effort and time than an occasional visit by a team of reporters to do a feature on a newly-discovered ghetto problem. It requires reporters permanently assigned to this beat. They must be adequately trained and supported to dig out and tell the story of a major social upheaval—among the most complicated, portentous and explosive our society has known. We believe, also, that the Negro press—manned largely by people who live and work in the ghetto—could be a particularly useful source of information and guidance about activities in the black community. Reporters and editors from Negro newspapers and radio stations should be included in any conference between media and police-city representatives, and we suggest that large news organizations would do well to establish better lines of communication to their counterparts in the Negro press.[10]

In short, the news media must find ways of exploring the problems of the Negro and the ghetto more deeply and more meaningfully. To editors who say "we have run thousands of inches on the ghetto which nobody reads" and to television executives who bemoan scores of underwatched documentaries, we say: find more ways of telling this story, for it is a story you, as journalists, must tell—honestly, realistically, and imaginatively. It is the responsibility of the news media to tell the story of race relations in America, and with notable exceptions, the media have not yet turned to the task with the wisdom, sensitivity, and expertise it demands.

Negroes in Journalism

The journalistic profession has been shockingly backward in seeking out, hiring, training, and promoting Negroes. Fewer than 5 percent of the people employed by the news business in editorial jobs in the United States today are Negroes. Fewer than 1 percent of editors and supervisors are Negroes, and most of them work for Negro-owned organizations. The lines of various news organizations to the militant blacks are, by admission of the newsmen themselves, almost nonexistent. The plaint is, "we can't find qualified Negroes." But this rings hollow from an industry where, only yesterday, jobs were scarce and promotion unthinkable for a man whose skin was black. Even today, there are virtually no Negroes in positions of editorial or executive responsibility and there is only one Negro newsman with a nationally syndicated column.

News organizations must employ enough Negroes in positions of significant responsibility to establish an effective link to Negro actions and ideas and to meet legitimate employment expectations. Tokenism—the hiring of one Negro reporter, or even two or three—is no longer enough. Negro reporters are essential, but so are Negro editors, writers and commentators. Newspaper and television policies are, generally speaking, not set by reporters. Editorial decisions about which stories to cover and which to use are made by editors. Yet, very few Negroes in this country are involved in making these decisions, because very few, if any, supervisory editorial jobs are held by Negroes. We urge the news media to do everything possible to train and promote their Negro reporters to positions where those who are qualified can contribute to and have an effect on policy decisions.

It is not enough, though, as many editors have pointed out to the Commission, to search for Negro journalists. Journalism is not very popular as a career for aspiring young Negroes. The starting pay is comparatively low and it is a business which has, until recently, discouraged and rejected them. The recruitment of Negro reporters must extend beyond established journalists, or those who have already formed ambitions along these lines. It must become a commitment to seek out young Negro men and women, inspire them to become—and then train them as— journalists. Training programs should be started at high schools and intensified at colleges. Summer vacation and part-time editorial jobs, coupled with offers of permanent employment, can awaken career plans.

We believe that the news media themselves, their audiences and the country will profit from these undertakings. For if the media are to comprehend and then to project the Negro community, they must have the help of Negroes. If the media are to report with understanding, wisdom and sympathy on the problems of the cities and the problems of the black man—for the two are increasingly intertwined—they must employ, promote and listen to Negro journalists.

The Negro in the Media

Finally, the news media must publish newspapers and produce programs that recognize the existence and activities of the Negro, both as a Negro and as part of the community. It would be a contribution of inestimable importance to race relations in the United States simply to treat ordinary news about Negroes as news of other groups is now treated.

Specifically, newspapers should integrate Negroes and Negro activities into all parts of the paper, from the news, society and club pages to the comic strips. Television should develop programing which integrates Negroes into all aspects of televised presentations. Television is such a visible medium that some constructive steps are easy and obvious. While some of these steps are being taken, they are still largely neglected. For example, Negro reporters and performers should appear more frequently—and at prime time—in news broadcasts, on weather shows, in documentaries, and in advertisements. Some effort already has been made to use Negroes in television commercials. Any initial surprise at seeing a Negro selling a sponsor's product will eventually fade into routine acceptance, an attitude that white society must ultimately develop toward all Negroes.

In addition to news-related programing, we think that Negroes should appear more frequently in dramatic and comedy series. Moreover, networks and local stations should present plays and other programs whose subjects are rooted in the ghetto and its problems.

Institute of Urban Communications

The Commission is aware that in this area, as in all other aspects of race relations, the problems are great and it is much easier to state them than to solve them. Various pressures—competitive, financial, advertising—may impede progress toward more balanced, in-depth coverage and toward the hiring and training of more Negro personnel. Most newspapers and local television and radio stations do not have the resources or the time to keep abreast of all the technical advances, academic theories, and government programs affecting the cities and the lives of their black inhabitants.

During the course of this study, the Commission members and the staff have had many conversations with publishers, editors, broadcasters, and reporters throughout the country. The consensus appears to be that most of them would like to do much more but simply do not have the resources for independent efforts in either training or coverage.

The Commission believes that some of these problems could be resolved if there were a central organization to develop, gather, and distribute talent, resources, and information and to keep the work of the press in this field under review. For this reason, the Commission proposes the establishment of an Institute of Urban Communications on a private, nonprofit basis. The Institute would have neither governmental ties nor governmental authority. Its board would consist in substantial part of professional journalists and, for the rest, of distinguished public figures. The staff would be made up of journalists and students of the profession. Funding would be sought initially from private foundations. Ultimately, it may be hoped, financial support would be forthcoming from within the profession.

The Institute would be charged, in the first instance, with general responsibility for carrying out the media recommendations of the Commission, though as it developed a momentum and life of its own it would also gain its own view of the problems and possibilities. Initial tasks would include:

1. Training and Education for Journalists in the Field of Urban Affairs. The Institute should organize and sponsor, on its own and in cooperation with universities and other institutions, a comprehensive range of courses, seminars and workshops designed to give reporters, editors, and publishers the background they need to cover the urban scene. Offerings would vary in duration and intensity from weekend conferences to grants for year-long individual study on the order of the Nieman fellowships.

All levels and all kinds of news outlets should be served. A most important activity might be to assist disc jockeys and commentators on stations that address themselves especially to the Negro community. Particularly important would be sessions of a month or more for seasoned reporters and editors, comparable to middle management seminars or midcareer training in other callings. The press must have all of the intellectual resources and background to give adequate coverage to the city and the ghetto. It should be the first duty of the Institute to see that this is provided.

2. Recruitment, Training and Placement of Negro Journalists. The scarcity of Negroes in responsible news jobs intensifies the difficulties of communicating the reality of the contemporary American city to white newspaper and television audiences. The special viewpoint of the Negro who has lived through these problems and bears their marks upon him is, as we have seen, notably absent from what is, on the whole, a white press. But full integration of Negroes into the journalistic profession is imperative in its own right. It is unacceptable that the press, itself the special beneficiary of fundamental constitutional protections, should lag so far behind other fields in giving effect to the fundamental human right to equality of opportunity.

To help correct this situation, the Institute will have to undertake far-ranging activities. Providing educational opportunities for would-be Negro journalists is not enough. There will have to be changes in career outlooks for Negro students and their counselors back to the secondary school level. And changes in these attitudes will come slowly unless there is a change in the reality of employment and advancement opportunities for Negroes in journalism. This requires an aggressive placement program, seeking out newspapers, television and radio stations that discriminate, whether consciously or unconsciously, and mobilizing the pressures, public, private, and legal, necessary to break the pattern. The Institute might also provide assistance to Negro newspapers, which now recruit and train many young journalists.

3. Police-Press Relations. The Commission has stressed the failures in this area, and has laid out a set of remedial measures for action at the local level. But if reliance is placed exclusively on local initiative we can predict that in many places—often those that need it most—our recommended steps will not be taken. Pressure from the Federal Government for action along the lines proposed would be suspect, probably, by both press and local officials. But the Institute could undertake the task of stimulating community action in line with the Commission's recommendations without arousing local hostility and suspicion. Moreover, the Institute could serve as a clearinghouse for exchange of experience in this field.

4. Review of Media Performance on Riots and Racial Issues. The Institute should review press and television coverage of riot and racial news and publicly award praise and blame. The Commission recognizes that government restraints or guidelines in this field are both unworkable and incompatible with our Constitution and traditions. Internal guidelines or voluntary advance arrangements may be useful, but they tend to be rather general and the standards they prescribe are neither self-applying nor self-enforcing. We believe it would be healthy for reporters and editors who work in this sensitive field to know that others will be viewing their work and will hold them publicly accountable for lapses from accepted standards of good journalism. The Institute should publicize its findings by means of regular and special reports. It might also set a series of awards for especially meritorious work of individuals or news organizations in race relations reporting.

5. An Urban Affairs Service. Whatever may be done to improve the quality of reporting on urban affairs, there always will be a great many outlets that are too small to support the specialized investigation, reporting and interpreting needed in this field. To fill this gap, the Institute could organize a comprehensive urban news service, available at a modest fee to any news organization that wanted it. The Institute would have its own specially trained reporters, and it would also cull the national press for news and features stories of broader interest that could be reprinted or broadcast by subscribers.

6. Continuing Research. Our own investigations have shown us that academic work on the impact of the media on race relations, its role in shaping attitudes, and the effects of the choices it makes on people's behavior, is in a rudimentary stage. The Commission's content analysis is the first study of its type of contemporary riot coverage, and it is extremely limited in scope. A whole range of questions needs intensive, scholarly exploration, and indeed the development of new modes of research and analysis. The Institute should undertake many of these important projects under its own auspices and could stimulate others in the academic community to further research.

Along with the country as a whole, the press has too long basked in a white world, looking out of it, if at all, with white men's eyes and a white perspective. That is no longer good enough. The painful process of readjustment that is required of the American news media must begin now. They must make a reality of integration—in both their product and personnel. They must insist on the highest standards of accuracy—not only reporting single events with care and skepticism, but placing each event into meaningful perspective. They must report the travail of our cities with compassion and in depth.

In all this, the Commission asks for fair and courageous journalism—commitment and coverage that are worthy of one of the crucial domestic stories in America's history.

Notes

1. As recently as Feb. 9, 1968, an Associated Press dispatch from Philadelphia said "damage exceeded $1 billion" in Detroit.

2. Michigan State Insurance Commission estimate, December 1967. See also "Meeting the Insurance Crisis of Our Cities," a report by the President's National Advisory Panel on Insurance in Riot-Affected Areas, January 1968.

3. Detroit, Mich.; Milwaukee, Wis.; Cincinnati and Dayton, Ohio ; Tampa, Fla.; Newark, Plainfield, Elizabeth, Jersey City, East Orange, Paterson, New Brunswick, and Englewood, N.J. ; New Haven, Conn.; Rochester, N.Y.

4. What follows is a summary of the major conclusions drawn from the content analysis conducted for the Commission.

5. The white male adult category in this computation does *not* include law enforcement agents or public officials.

6. Detroit news outlets substantially refrained from publicizing the riot during the early part of Sunday, the first day of rioting.

7. As examples, less than a month after the Detroit riot, the Detroit *Free Press* published the results of a landmark survey of local Negro attitudes and grievances. *Newsweek* magazine's November 20, 1967, special issue on "The Negro American— What Must Be Done" made a significant contribution to public understanding.

8. The Commission is indebted, in this regard, to M. Thomas Allen for his document on *Mass Media Use Patterns and Functions in the Negro Ghetto in Pittsburgh*.

9 Detroit, Newark, Atlanta, Tampa, New Haven, Cincinnati, Milwaukee.

10. We have not, in this report, examined the Negro press in detail. The thrust of our studies was directed at daily mass circulation, mass audience media which are aimed at the community as a whole.

GLORIA STEINEM

Night Thoughts of a Media Watcher
(1983)

Equal Rights Amendment began its long ratification process in 1972, yet to my knowledge, not one major newspaper or radio station, not one network news department or national television show, has ever done an independent investigative report on what the ERA will and will not do.

Instead, the major media have been content to present occasional interviews, debates, and contradictory reports from those who are for or against. One expert is quoted as saying that the ERA will strengthen the legal rights of women in general and homemakers in particular by causing the courts to view marriage as a partnership and the next one says the ERA will force wives to work outside the home and eliminate support payments. One political leader explains on camera that the ERA protects women and men from discriminatory federal laws; then another politician calls the ERA a federal power grab that will reduce individual rights. One activist says that the ERA is a simple guarantee of democracy that should have been part of the Bill of Rights, had the Constitution not been written by and for property-owning white males, and the next one insists it will destroy the family, eliminate heterosexuality, and integrate bathrooms.

Understandably, the audience is confused. We thought the sky was blue to begin with, but equal time and prestige given to an insistence that it's really green may finally cause us to doubt our perceptions. It's true that the majority of women and men have continued to support the ERA (by a margin that has increased since the Reagan administration demonstrated that progress could be reversed without it), but I'm not sure the media can take much credit for that fact. There is some evidence that 50–50, so-called objective reporting has actually *impeded* the building of a larger majority.

From *Outrageous Acts and Everyday Rebellions* (New York: Henry Holt and Company, 1983, 1995), 356–59.

For instance, reading or hearing the actual twenty-four words of the ERA* is the most reliable path to its support. Many people are still surprised to learn that there's no mention of *unisex* or *abortion* or *combat* in its text; such is the confusion created by anti-ERA arguments. Yet most ERA news coverage never quotes its text at all.

Among reporters and news executives, however, there is great self-righteousness. They have followed the so-called fairness doctrine. They have presented "both sides of the issue" by devoting the same number of minutes or amount of space to the "pro" and the "con." This has remained true, even though majority support for the ERA means a "con" is often tough to find. I've frequently been called by an interviewer and asked, "Would you bring an 'anti' with you?"

One result of this prizefight school of journalism is that Phyllis Schlafly, who was not a nationally famous person pre-ERA, has become the only name that most Americans can think of when asked what women oppose it. In a real sense, she is an artificial creation of the fairness doctrine. Another result is the idea that *women* voted against the ERA; not the two dozen or so aging white male state legislators, plus economic and religious interests, who are the actual culprits. A third result is the notion that black Americans don't support the ERA, though black state legislators have voted overwhelmingly for it. If black women and men had been represented in legislatures in proportion to their present numbers in the population, especially in southern states, the ERA would have passed long ago.

In the early days of the civil rights movement, most journalists followed the same "equal time" formula. When they reported on black voter registration in the South, for instance, they quoted civil rights workers saying they had been beaten up in jail. Then they quoted the sheriff saying that these young people had attacked the police or had beaten up each other. Readers were left with either their confusion or their original biases intact.

Eventually, however, most serious media assumed responsibility for doing their own investigations. They reported, to the best of their ability, what the facts really were.

Unfortunately, that has never been done for the ERA. It isn't that such independent reporting would be difficult. More than fifty years of legislative history is available to explain the impact intended by Congress. An issue of the *Yale Law Journal* and many authoritative books have been devoted to projecting its impact in scholarly detail. Finally, there are a few states that have already begun to enforce statewide ERAs with the same or similar wording as that proposed federally. Pennsylvania adopted its ERA more than a decade ago, and bathrooms have not been integrated, abortion and homosexual rights have not been affected, for better or

Equality of rights under the law shall not be denied or abridged by the United States or by any state on account of sex.

worse. On the other hand, women's economic rights have been strengthened; equality in education, employment, and insurance benefits has advanced; and sex-based discriminatory laws against men also have been struck down.

So why haven't independent, in-depth reports been done? Why don't the media of your town (and mine) take this historic issue seriously? Why do they allow legislators to vote against the majority opinion in their own districts, as reflected in independent polls, without fearing a journalistic exposé of the special interests they are responding to?

Ask them. A future with or without the ERA is at stake. And so is good or lousy journalism.

BEN BAGDIKIAN

The Growing Gap
(1983)

It appears to have five outpouchings. . . . A container of some sort?

OLIVER SACKS
The Man Who Mistook His Wife for a Hat

In 1986 when General Electric, through its acquisition of RCA, became the owner of NBC, it raised familiar questions about new ownership patterns in the American media.

General Electric activities periodically become subjects in the news. The country's tenth largest corporation and a major defense contractor, it is the biggest producer of electric lamps, a major manufacturer of power plants, nuclear reactors, jet engines, nuclear missiles, locomotives, and of almost every link in the production and distribution of electricity. Through its board of directors it interlocks with still other industries also sensitive to their treatment in the news.

To promote its business, General Electric, like most large corporations, expends formidable energies to shape its public image in positive, even heroic terms. Like other corporations, it uses whatever influence it can to sell its commercial products and win government contracts. An important part of the promotion is intensive work by public relations staffs and, on occasion, top executives, to influence the news in its favor. Now, if it desires favorable treatment it no longer has to plead with at least one major American news organization. It owns one.

Only time will tell how this will affect NBC. But the power and politics of General Electric are not very different from those of other large corporations that in the last twenty-five years have acquired control of the country's major media.

General Electric's record illustrates the problem. Throughout its history it has had public embarrassments. Each time, uncontrolled news reports damaged its advertised image as a benevolent force selling helpful household appliances. Some

From *The Media Monopoly* (Boston: Beacon Press, 6th ed., 2000 [1983]), 208–22.

news stories have periodically weakened its image as a conscientious government contractor.

In 1932, for example, one of its engineers testified that the company cut the life of light bulbs a third in order to increase sales during the Great Depression. In 1941 it was convicted of an illegal agreement with Germany's Krupp company, particularly embarrassing because World War II had started and Krupp was a major supplier for the Nazi war machine. In 1942 General Electric was convicted of fraud in supplying cable for U.S. Navy warships. In 1948 it and Westinghouse were convicted of a conspiracy to fix bids on street lighting for American cities. In 1961 it was the largest of a group of companies found guilty of having conspired for years to rig bids on electrical generating equipment; three GE executives were sentenced to jail terms.

In 1982 news stories disclosed that though GE had 1981 pretax earnings of $2.66 billion, it had paid no income tax and actually received a $90 million rebate from the Internal Revenue Service, legal under a new law but still embarrassing. In 1985, the year before its acquisition of NBC News became final, it pleaded guilty to forging 100,000 employee time cards in order to shift expenses from one of its private contracts to a Department of Defense project for intercontinental nuclear missiles.

Over the years it has taken special pains to promote its preferred politics. In the 1950s, for example, it launched Ronald Reagan as a national political spokesman by paying him to make nationwide public speeches against communism, labor unions, social security, public housing, the income tax, and to augment the corporation's support of right-wing political movements.

It is still interested in politics. Shortly after General Electric bought control of NBC, the GE executive who was appointed the new president of the National Broadcasting Company, announced that NBC should start a political action committee and contribute money to strengthen the company's influence in Washington. The new network president made it clear that failure to cooperate would raise questions about the employee's "dedication to the company." The president of NBC News had to announce that news employees would be exempted.

Question: If General Electric had owned NBC during its earlier episodes of criminal convictions and other public embarrassments, would NBC News have reported them?

Fifty years ago the answer would have been an almost certain no. Newspapers and broadcasters did not publicize bad news about their owner.

The answer in 1986, however, would probably be yes.

If General Electric in 1987 experienced a major criminal conviction, NBC News would probably report it in a straightforward way.

Another question: If NBC did report the news item of the conviction, would NBC also proceed to produce a documentary on criminality and carelessness in defense contracts, with General Electric as an obvious recent example? If it were disclosed that the company paid no income taxes during three years of multibillion profits, and General Electric owned NBC at the time, would the network produce a documentary on inequities in the national tax system?

One has to speculate, but the answer is probably no. It is unlikely that any corporate-owned medium would do so, but General Electric, recently embarrassed, might be less likely to.

These differing answers symbolize the paradoxes and problems of concentrated corporate control of the major media. The new corporate ownership has not canceled an outstanding strength of American news reporting—accurate reporting of facts—but it has increased some of the most troublesome weaknesses in the integrity and usefulness of American news.

It has been two generations since American media suffered sweeping corporate suppression of the media. The investigative and political reformist magazines of 1900–1912 included some of the most prestigious in the country—*Harper's, Scribners, Century*—and a dozen others. The "muckraker" magazines' exposure of systematic bribery of government by banks and industry, and abuses by monopolies and trusts, were an important force in the political movements that elected mayors, governors, and, finally, a reformist president, Theodore Roosevelt. That was too much, and in a series of abrupt acts J. P. Morgan and the Rockefeller interests simply bought controlling interest in the magazines—*Harper's, Scribners, Century*, and a number of others—installed their own managers, and announced that the public was tired of reading exposés of banks and business. It ended an era of American journalism and national politics.

Corporate power to influence public information has not changed, but American journalism and its audience have altered the way it is done. History seldom repeats itself precisely. In the latter half of the twentieth century, the holders of corporate media power are, like their fellow citizens, a different breed in a different time.

Compared to the years before World War II, the quality and seriousness of daily breaking news in the United States has improved significantly, thanks largely to a remarkable alteration in the perceptions and expectations of the American public.

World War II ended any remaining innocence about the horrors possible in the human race, and wiped out illusions that any society can insulate itself from the rest of the world. Nowhere was this change more significant than in the United States, where two underlying beliefs had been the inevitability of human progress and the beauties of isolation from a troublesome outside world.

Ever since, the message has been clear that, like it or not, Americans have a personal stake in unfolding history, and that awareness has created a public demand for more relevant daily news.

Shocks like the Vietnam War, the gasoline shortage of the 1970s, and hijackings of the 1980s have removed any remaining doubt that the lives of individuals are profoundly altered by remote forces. In domestic life, society changes with ever greater speed. Whole industries are born while others die, occupations alter almost overnight, sons and daughters no longer assume they will do the same work or live in the same place as their parents. Radical technologies that prolong individual life can also terminate all human life.

The demand for better public information during World War II was furthered by an almost revolutionary move in its aftermath. After World War II, the G.I. Bill promised free higher education to the 14 million men and women who had been in the armed services. That ended the perception of university education as an elite privilege, and began an alteration of the intellectual, occupational, and cultural character of the American population. Today a majority of adult Americans have had some college education and that figure is rising. With widespread travel and international communication, cosmopolitan tastes and values are growing. The American public developed wider sources of information, in textbooks, lectures, and experience with new cultures.

Journalists have been part of that transformation. Today, journalists are not only better educated, but they are more concerned with individual professional ethics than would have seemed possible fifty years ago. The conventions against lying, fictionalizing, and factual inaccuracy are strong and widespread. Collection of accurate facts is a high priority in American reporting.

The devotion to accurate facts and the rarity of suppression of dramatic public events are strengths of American reporting.

Unfortunately, that admirable professional standard in American news does not extend to other crucial kinds of news treatment.

Despite raised standards in journalism, American mainstream news is still heavily weighted in favor of corporate values, sometimes blatantly, but more often subtly in routine conventions widely accepted as "objective." One is overdependence on official sources of news. Another is a peculiar lack of social context for facts in the news, which removes much of the meaning. Third is a pattern of selective pursuit that results in some subjects regularly developed in depth and others of equal or greater importance systematically avoided.

Just Credentialed Facts

Facts supported by important figures form the bulk of contemporary news. Someone in authority makes a statement, a law is enacted, the government or a corporation releases data, an accident occurs, a natural phenomenon is reliably observed—all can be cited and proved as objective entities.

There are sound reasons for it all. Facts supported by named authorities are crucial social artifacts, whether it is a secretary of defense reporting on performance of a new weapons system or a local police chief on the subject of a crime. Citing responsible sources has reduced the worst curses in worldwide reporting—the propagation of baseless rumor, lying or lazy reporters, anonymous falsehoods planted for cynical purposes. Unless there is a body of unambiguous fact, there is no basis for reality in public discourse. And those who wield social power deserve special attention. They have a major impact on public affairs and what they say in public is part of their public accountability.

The highly credentialed fact is also commercially and professionally convenient. If a fact comes from a named source with an impressive title, it is less easy to accuse the reporter, editor, or news organization of introducing personal judgments or bias.

But overemphasis on news from titled sources of power has occurred at the expense of reporting "unofficial" facts and circumstances. In a dynamic and changing society, the voices of authority are seldom the first to acknowledge or even to know of new and disturbing developments. Officials can be wrong.

Overreliance on the official view of the world can contribute to social turbulence. Unable to attract serious media attention by conventional methods, unestablished groups have had to adopt melodramatic demonstrations that meet the other media standards of acceptable news—visible drama, conflict, and novelty. If they are sufficiently graphic, the news will report protests, demonstrations, marches, boycotts, and self-starvation in public places (though not always their underlying causes). But in the end, even that fails. Repeated melodrama ceases to be novel and goes unreported. Social malaise or injustice often are not known, or can be ignored, by officialdom. Unreported or unpursued, these realities have periodically led to turbulent surprises—such as the social explosions that came after years of officially unacknowledged structural poverty, continuation of racial oppression, or damage from failed foreign policies.

Over the years, the exaggerated demand for official credentials in the news has given the main body of American news a strong conservative cast. This is not peculiar to the United States, though many other democracies avoid it. Where there are not genuinely diverse voices in the media the result inevitably is an overemphasis on a picture of the world as seen by the authorities, or as the authorities wish it to be.

Fear of Context

Accurate facts are indispensable, but by themselves they can be misleading; a single dramatic event may be unrepresentative of the whole, or even contrary to the nature of the whole. Simple recitations of data seldom lead to public comprehension. Most naked facts are comparatively meaningless. Context is crucial.

There are good reasons to exercise care in providing context. Incompetent or propagandistic context can distort rather than clarify meaning. Simple personal opinion of the reporter should not be mistaken for informed context. Furthermore, in a news system characterized by local monopolies, there is an obligation to be attentive to the border between clarifying context and politicizing news.

But there is a difference between partisanship and placing facts in a reasonably informed context of history and social circumstance. American journalism has not made a workable distinction between them. Too often the social significance of American news is avoided for the wrong reasons.

There are powerful commercial pressures to remove social significance from standard American news. Informed social-economic context has unavoidable political implications which may disturb some in the audience whose world view differs. Those readers and viewers might grudgingly accept the briefly announced, indisputable fact but not the display of its similarly indisputable implications. In the late 1980s, for example, failures of local banks were routinely reported, but seldom the ominous growth in annual bank failures and what this could mean for the national economy. Both advertiser and owner want the audience to remain in an accepting attitude toward both the news and the advertising. The result is unnecessarily bland and unintegrated information, which too often leaves the public without a true understanding of the facts in the news.

Most serious editors agree that some interpretation is periodically needed. But the doctrine of just-the-facts is so strong that with rare exceptions the interpretations are done with self-canceling circumlocutions in order to remove any impression that political and economic judgments are being made.

The overemphasis on austere factuality makes much American news insufficiently descriptive. In the drive for rigid neutrality, American reporting style has become the journalism of nouns, at the expense of verbs of action and adjectives of states of being.

While not all journalists have the background knowledge, analytical skills, or personal insights to provide a valid context for the news, there is a large reservoir of journalists who have those qualities in their own fields.

Too often the experienced journalist is forced to imitate the patient described by Oliver Sacks (*The Man Who Mistook His Wife for a Hat*). The patient, an educated and cultivated man, suffered from a neurological disorder that kept him from perceiving the function of common objects. Shown an ordinary glove, the patient stared at it and said, "A continuous surface, infolded on itself. It appears to have five outpouchings. . . . A container of some sort?" The patient's perceptual system did not permit him to recognize its function and name the word *glove*. With too much vital news, American journalism is forbidden to call a glove a glove.

Exaggerated dependence on facts that carry the imprimatur of the authorities, combined with limitations on giving the context for facts, has left American journalism relatively defenseless when authorities lie or evade relevant facts. A generation ago, Senator Joseph McCarthy created years of chaos by lying or misusing facts. This was known by reporters covering him, but the constraints of journalism permitted the lies and distortions to prevail for years before they became plain to the public.

It is a highly cultivated art form in contemporary life for leaders to pretend to address cogent issues while evading them; almost always there are knowledgeable journalists who recognize the emptiness, but who must solemnly report the words accurately without the context that places the spoken "facts" in their real meaning, or lack of it. The limitation has contributed to the debasement of public discourse. Public and private leaders who lie with enough charm or evade compelling questions with sufficient artfulness, can usually rely on the conventions of news to tolerate it. The system penalizes truth and rewards its avoidance.

Dig Here, Not There

There is no journalistic convention for dealing with the "butcher's thumb" of owner prejudice in deciding which news events will be pursued, which will be repeated with emphasis.

The pattern is clear in American journalism: in general, items are more likely to be pursued in depth if they portray flaws in the public, tax-supported sector of American life, and less likely to be pursued if they portray flaws in the private corporate sector. Items about high costs or flaws in welfare and labor unions are likely to be emphasized and repeated. Items such as General Electric's conviction for cheating on its defense contract in 1985 are not as likely to be pursued by a series of articles in depth on flaws in defense contracting. Over long periods of time, this results in the public impression that public-sector activities are essentially flawed and should be limited while private enterprises are essentially sound and have no need for change.

The dilemma is vexing. Deciding which news to pursue in depth and which to drop quickly is legitimate, normal, and necessary. It is the most important single step in journalism. Yet, current professional standards give journalists little or no power to question systematic failures to pursue some important subjects and overemphasis on other subjects. Reporters take for granted that they have the right to resist an order to write a falsehood. There is no comparable convention for resisting the avoidance of important issues or the pursuit of self-serving ones.

When an editor makes a news decision based on corporate orders, or knowledge of ownership wishes, the editor seldom states the real reason. Thanks to raised journalistic standards, it is too embarrassing before professional subordinates. It violates the prevailing dogma of American journalism that serious news is the result of whatever is true and significant, let the chips fall where they may. It is a religious value in journalism, and like most religious values it is subject to official interpretation.

For example, it is normal and necessary for every editor to make decisions based on a variety of concerns—the inherent importance of the subject, its possible special meaning in a particular community, the strength of evidence to support a story, existence of special problems such as bad taste, unfair defamation of individuals, or whether the special interests of the owning corporation will be harmed. If the real "special problem" is the owners' private interests, the editor seldom announces the real reason. The item is dismissed for another, professionally acceptable reason, such as being insufficiently documented, or of no interest to the public.

As cited earlier in this book, 33 percent of American newspaper editors said they would not feel free to print an item damaging to their parent firm. They were not asked whether, if they decided against printing such items, they would announce the true reason to their staffs.

Overt punishment for embarrassing owners has lasting effects. In almost every news organization there has been, at some time, an editor who permitted publication of a legitimate story that unexpectedly brought retribution from the owner. A reporter or editor is fired, demoted, or otherwise reprimanded. That lesson is observed by everyone in the news organization. Future items of that nature are not aired or published. For years, no one has to speak to the editor or the news staff to know that the organization does not consider that subject "news." Eventually, the prohibition is no longer a conscious one. After a passage of time, long after the punished malefactors have disappeared, the professional staff may say, with sincerity, that owners exercise no influence on the news because they have never been told or seen a memorandum stating the prohibition. Journalists quickly learn that whatever is regularly printed in their newspaper or broadcast over their station is the definition of what is "news."

This internalized bias has special meaning in an era of ownership by a few large corporations, all with similar political and economic goals. Eighty years ago the Morgan and Rockefeller interests did not hesitate to buy politically troublesome magazines and set them in a different direction. Today, corporations whose contemporary goals are not that different from the Morgan and Rockefeller goals eighty years ago already own the most important media.

There are laudable exceptions to the prevailing pattern of news organizations avoiding pursuit of subjects that could hurt the financial interests of their owners. As cited earlier, the *Charlotte Observer* did this with tobacco. CBS in its 1971 documentary "The Selling of the Pentagon" showed waste and impropriety in the Pentagon at a time when CBS was a significant defense contractor. In 1978 CBS produced a documentary on growing concentration of ownership in newspapers (though CBS owned no newspapers it is not usual for one medium to stress problems of ownership in another). But these are rare. They are becoming more so.

The butcher's thumb that quietly tilts news in favor of corporate values has survived the rise in journalistic standards. The tilt has been so quietly and steadily integrated into the normal process of weighing news that the angle of the needle is now seen as "zero."

There is another paradox in American journalism, a seeming contradiction between heightened standards of news and a worsening deficiency. The country's newspapers and broadcast stations are rapidly, if unwittingly, abandoning a vital need of their audience. They are literally redrawing the map of American news.

The average voter in the United States is probably better equipped to consider public policy problems than the average citizen in any other major country. (The American public is too often unfairly compared with the elite of foreign countries, and it is forgotten how often those elites have blundered.) But Americans are required to know more.

Other democratic countries deal with serious issues only in national voting; practically all their primary government functions are controlled at the national level. Furthermore, most have a parliamentary system in which voters select not hundreds of individual candidates but, in effect, one of several parties, each with a distinct set of programs and policies. Consequently, the voter in other democracies makes clear choices from a relatively small number of alternatives. These choices are dealt with in the several competing national papers available to all.

Unlike voters elsewhere, Americans must know local candidates and issues as well. Each community makes its own decisions on education, land use, police, property taxes, and much else.

Presented on election day with an array of local, state, and national decisions, this is complex enough. But the task is made infinitely more complicated because political candidates in the United States, though they may run with a party label, are not committed to a party platform. For both local and national offices, the voter is supposed to know about each individual candidate, Consequently, United States citizens face a formidable task in trying to vote intelligently. They need to be informed routinely about their local schools, highways, and zoning and property taxes, something no national news medium can provide. And since every office, local and national, will be filled by a winner who is not bound by party discipline, the voter, theoretically, should know about each candidate's personal public history, including voting record, position papers, and other specific information that would permit matching the voter's wishes with each candidate.

There are strengths and weaknesses in both the parliamentary and the American system. But to be effective, the American system must be served by appropriate news about its civic governments: the map of the political system and the map of news reporting ought to have basic similarities. But the two maps are becoming more dissimilar with each passing year, a difference accelerated by the new corporate ownership.

Two gaps are widening. The first is the media's decreasing interest in news aimed at those who are not affluent or who are fifty years old or older. The second is the decreasing fit between the geographic boundaries the news media have established as their fields of operation, and the political boundaries by which people vote.

A century ago almost every city and town had its own daily paper, with systematic information about civic bodies and other politics affecting that particular community (see chapter 10). This has changed radically. The number of daily newspapers has diminished, from 2,000 in 1900 to 1,676 today. During the same period, the number of urban places increased from 1,737 to 8,765 today. Cities and towns without a paper are now the majority.

A new philosophy of American news distribution coverage has made the disparity even worse. It is a swift reversal of past patterns when newspapers, and broadcast stations, concentrated on particular municipalities. The names of American newspapers have always included colorful references to local place names—the *Oil City* (Pennsylvania) *Derrick*, or the *Bad Axe* (Michigan) *Tribune*—but colorful or not, the name of a city was an integral part of the newspaper title and the station identification.

But newspapers are rapidly eliminating their place names. For example, in California, which has more daily papers than any other state, two-thirds of all the daily papers have no city name showing on page one of their title.

The rapid disappearance of home cities in newspaper titles and in most broadcast station identifications is not an accident.

Most newspapers and broadcast stations no longer direct themselves to a particular municipality. They design themselves—and their content—to reach a particular retail market. The focus of circulation is no longer City Hall but the shopping mall.

There are 19,000 municipalities in the United States but only 210 markets. A market covers dozens and sometimes hundreds of municipalities, counties, school districts, and state and federal legislative districts. Newspapers and broadcast stations aimed at markets cannot and will not cover those hundreds of districts in any systematic way.

Candidates do not run from markets. They do not represent shopping malls. Political districts and public agencies whose actions directly affect the public do not draw their lines according to the 210 retail markets but according to the 19,000 municipal boundaries. Yet the American newspaper and local broadcast industries are in the process of a revolutionary rearrangement of their circulation and content strategies to service the market areas and to move away from focusing their primary efforts on municipalities. As a result, the country suffers from a growing gap between what the average voter in a particular city needs to know and the pattern of content and coverage by the news media.

The new corporate owners of the media did not cause the gap, but they have rapidly widened it. They have done this not out of a desire to debilitate intelligent voting, but because of the greater pressure on large corporations to maximize quick profits of their news subsidiaries. The most direct way of doing this is to rearrange their circulation to appeal to large regional advertisers, and to compete with television stations whose broad geographic reach has defined the 210 markets.

Similarly, new corporate owners of newspapers and broadcast stations have more swiftly altered their content to deal with affluent consumers instead of the whole adult population. It is an ingredient of the "better resources" and "higher managerial skills" often offered to the public as an advantage of corporate ownership.

The widening gap is the result of commercial decisions, not journalistic ones, about what each community needs to know. It is undoubtedly a contributor to the steady decline in the percentage of eligible citizens who actually vote.

Professional journalists, including their top editors, are largely powerless in determining the areas of strategic news coverage. That task has been taken over by market analysts and business consultants. The focus of journalistic effort has shifted from what the community needs to what the advertiser wants.

The average American voter is getting steadily less information about civic institutions and candidates from standard news. But neither the voter nor the professional journalist has the power to regain the lost coverage.

Defenders of the narrowing control of the media point, accurately enough, to the large numbers of media outlets available to the population: almost 1,700 daily papers, more than 8,000 weeklies, 10,000 radio and television stations, 11,000 magazines, 2,500 book publishers, more than a dozen movie studios, plus cable systems, home videotapes, and more—the usual number quoted for individual outlets is 35,000.

Unfortunately, the large numbers deepen the problem of excessively concentrated control. If the number of outlets is growing and the number of owners declining, then each owner controls ever more formidable communications power.

Furthermore, the growing numbers, ironically, accompany a growing uniformity of content. In the last generation all newspapers have become more similar in content and approach. Most magazines have become specialized in content but major magazines that deal with political, social, and economic information are increasingly similar in political and economic orientation. There is such imitativeness in radio and television that it is almost arbitrary which station is heard. Major books and movies retain more variations, though mass advertising and distribution techniques tend to favor imitative books. Cable and videotapes are almost entirely du-plications of the already uniform content of commercial television.

As the country approaches the end of this century, the major media are ex-tremely profitable and closely organized in a few powerful corporations. But un-derneath the spectacular annual profits and corporate self-satisfaction, there is a disturbing separation of most major media from the true nature of their country's population, a separation that threatens not only the future usefulness of the media, but the vitality of the American political process.

BRENT CUNNINGHAM

Re-thinking Objectivity
(2003)

In his March 6, 2003, press conference, in which he laid out his reasons for the coming war, President Bush mentioned al Qaeda or the attacks of September 11 fourteen times in fifty-two minutes. No one challenged him on it, despite the fact that the CIA had questioned the Iraq–al Qaeda connection, and that there has never been solid evidence marshaled to support the idea that Iraq was involved in the attacks of 9/11.

In a world of spin, our awkward embrace of an ideal can make us passive recipients of the news. When Bush proposed his $726 billion tax cut in January 2003, his sales pitch on the plan's centerpiece—undoing the "double-taxation" on dividend earnings—was that "It's unfair to tax money twice." In the next two months, the tax plan was picked over in hundreds of articles and broadcasts, yet a Nexis database search turned up few news stories—notably, one by Donald Barlett and James Steele in *Time* on January 27, 2003, and another by Daniel Altman in the business section of *The New York Times* on January 21—that explained in detail what was misleading about the president's pitch: that in fact there is plenty of income that is doubly, triply, or even quadruply taxed, and that those other taxes affect many more people than the sliver who would benefit from the dividend tax cut.

Before the fighting started in Iraq, in the dozens of articles and broadcasts that addressed the potential aftermath of a war, much was written and said about the maneuverings of the Iraqi exile community and the shape of a postwar government, about cost and duration and troop numbers. Important subjects all. But few of those stories, dating from late last summer, delved deeply into the numerous and plausible complications of the aftermath. That all changed on February 26, 2003, when President Bush spoke grandly of making Iraq a model for retooling the entire Middle East. After Bush's speech "aftermath" articles began to flow like the waters of the Tigris—including cover stories in *Time* and *The New York Times*

From *Columbia Journalism Review*, July/August 2003, 24–32.

Magazine—culminating in *The Wall Street Journal*'s page-one story on March 17, 2003, just days before the first cruise missiles rained down on Baghdad, that revealed how the administration planned to hand the multibillion-dollar job of rebuilding Iraq to U.S. corporations. It was as if the subject of the war's aftermath was more or less off the table until the president put it there himself.

There is no single explanation for these holes in the coverage, but I would argue that our devotion to what we call "objectivity" played a role. It's true that the Bush administration is like a clenched fist with information, one that won't hesitate to hit back when pressed. And that reporting on the possible aftermath of a war before the war occurs, in particular, was a difficult and speculative story.

Yet these three examples—which happen to involve the current White House, although every White House spins stories—provide a window into a particular failure of the press: allowing the principle of objectivity to make us passive recipients of news, rather than aggressive analyzers and explainers of it. We all learned about objectivity in school or at our first job. Along with its twin sentries "fairness" and "balance," it defined journalistic standards.

Or did it? Ask ten journalists what objectivity means and you'll get ten different answers. Some, like the *Washington Post*'s editor, Leonard Downie, define it so strictly that they refuse to vote lest they be forced to take sides. My favorite definition was from Michael Bugeja, who teaches journalism at Iowa State: "Objectivity is seeing the world as it is, not how you wish it were." In 1996 the Society of Professional Journalists acknowledged this dilemma and dropped "objectivity" from its ethics code. It also changed "the truth" to simply "truth."

Tripping Toward the Truth

As E.J. Dionne wrote in his 1996 book, *They Only Look Dead*, the press operates under a number of conflicting diktats: be neutral yet investigative; be disengaged but have an impact; be fair-minded but have an edge. Therein lies the nut of our tortured relationship with objectivity. Few would argue that complete objectivity is possible, yet we bristle when someone suggests we aren't being objective—or fair, or balanced—as if everyone agrees on what they all mean.

Over the last dozen years a cottage industry of bias police has sprung up to exploit this fissure in the journalistic psyche, with talk radio leading the way followed by Shout TV and books like Ann Coulter's *Slander* and Bernard Goldberg's *Bias*. Now the left has begun firing back, with Eric Alterman's book *What Liberal Media?* and a group of wealthy Democrats' plans for a liberal radio network. James Carey, a journalism scholar at Columbia, points out that we are entering a new age of partisanship. One result is a hypersensitivity among the press to charges of bias, and it shows up everywhere: In October 2001, with the war in Afghanistan under way, then CNN chairman Walter Isaacson sent a memo to his foreign correspondents telling them to "balance" reports of Afghan "casualties or hardship" with reminders to viewers that this was, after all, in response to the terrorist attacks of September 11. More recently, a *CJR* intern, calling newspaper letters-page editors to learn whether reader letters were running for or against the looming war in Iraq, was told by the letters editor at *The Tennessean* that letters were running 70 percent against the war, but that the editors were trying to run as many prowar letters as possible lest they be accused of bias.

Objectivity has persisted for some valid reasons, the most important being that nothing better has replaced it. And plenty of good journalists believe in it, at least as a necessary goal. Objectivity, or the pursuit of it, separates us from the unbridled partisanship found in much of the European press. It helps us make decisions quickly—we are disinterested observers after all—and it protects us from the consequences of what we write. We'd like to think it buoys our embattled credibility, though the deafening silence of many victims of Jayson Blair's fabrications would argue otherwise. And as we descend into this new age of partisanship, our readers need, more than ever, reliable reporting that tells them what is true when that is knowable, and pushes as close to truth as possible when it is not.

But our pursuit of objectivity can trip us up on the way to "truth." Objectivity excuses lazy reporting. If you're on deadline and all you have is "both sides of the story," that's often good enough. It's not that such stories laying out the parameters of a debate have no value for readers, but too often, in our obsession with, as *The Washington Post*'s Bob Woodward puts it, "the latest," we fail to push the story, incrementally, toward a deeper understanding of what is true and what is false. Steven R. Weisman, the chief diplomatic correspondent for *The New York Times* and a believer in the goal of objectivity ("even though we fall short of the ideal every day"), concedes that he felt obliged to dig more when he was an editorial writer, and did not have to be objective. "If you have to decide who is right, then you must do more reporting," he says. "I pressed the reporting further because I didn't have the luxury of saying X says this and Y says this and you, dear reader, can decide who is right."

It exacerbates our tendency to rely on official sources, which is the easiest, quickest way to get both the "he said" and the "she said," and, thus, "balance." According to numbers from the media analyst Andrew Tyndall, of the 414 stories on Iraq broadcast on NBC, ABC, and CBS from September 2002 to February 2003, all but thirty-four originated at the White House, Pentagon, and State Department. So we end up with too much of the "official" truth.

More important, objectivity makes us wary of seeming to argue with the president—or the governor, or the CEO—and risk losing our access. Jonathan Weisman, an economics reporter for *The Washington Post*, says this about the fear of losing access: "If you are perceived as having a political bias, or a slant, you're screwed."

Finally, objectivity makes reporters hesitant to inject issues into the news that aren't already out there. "News is driven by the zeitgeist," says Jonathan Weisman, "and if an issue isn't part of the current zeitgeist then it will be a tough sell to editors." But who drives the zeitgeist, in Washington at least? The administration. In short, the press's awkward embrace of an impossible ideal limits its ability to help set the agenda.

This is not a call to scrap objectivity, but rather a search for a better way of thinking about it, a way that is less restrictive and more grounded in reality. As Eric Black, a reporter at the *Minneapolis Star Tribune*, says, "We need a way to both do our job and defend it."

An Ideal's Troubled Past

American journalism's honeymoon with objectivity has been brief. The press began to embrace objectivity in the middle of the nineteenth century, as society turned away from religion and toward science and empiricism to explain the world. But in his 1998 book, *Just the Facts*, a history of the origins of objectivity in U.S. journalism, David Mindich argues that by the turn of the twentieth century, the flaws of objective journalism were beginning to show. Mindich shows how "objective" coverage of lynching in the 1890s by *The New York Times* and other papers created a false balance on the issue and failed "to recognize a truth, that African-Americans were being terrorized across the nation."

After World War I, the rise of public relations and the legacy of wartime propaganda—in which journalists such as Walter Lippmann had played key roles—began to undermine reporters' faith in facts. The war, the Depression, and Roosevelt's New Deal raised complex issues that defied journalism's attempt to distill them into simple truths. As a result, the use of bylines increased (an early nod to the fact that news is touched by human frailty), the political columnist crawled from the primordial soup, and the idea of "interpretive reporting" emerged. Still, as Michael Schudson argued in his 1978 book *Discovering the News*, journalism clung to objectivity as the faithful cling to religion, for guidance in an uncertain world. He wrote: "From the beginning, then, criticism of the 'myth' of objectivity has accompanied its enunciation. . . . Journalists came to believe in objectivity, to the extent that they did, because they wanted to, needed to, were forced by ordinary human aspiration to seek escape from their own deep convictions of doubt and drift."

By the 1960s, objectivity was again under fire, this time to more fundamental and lasting effect. Straight, "objective" coverage of McCarthyism a decade earlier had failed the public, leading Alan Barth, an editorial writer at *The Washington Post*, to tell a 1952 gathering of the Association for Education in Journalism: "There can be little doubt that the way [Senator Joseph McCarthy's charges] have been reported in most papers serves Senator McCarthy's partisan political purposes much more than it serves the purposes of the press, the interest of truth." Government lies about the U2 spy flights, the Cuban missile crisis, and the Vietnam War all cast doubt on the ability of "objective" journalism to get at anything close to the truth. The New Journalism of Tom Wolfe and Norman Mailer was in part a reaction to what many saw as the failings of mainstream reporting. In Vietnam, many of the beat reporters who arrived believing in objectivity eventually realized, if they stayed long enough, that such an approach wasn't sufficient. Says John Laurence, a former CBS News correspondent, about his years covering Vietnam: "Because the war went on for so long and so much evidence accumulated to suggest it was a losing cause, and that in the process we were destroying the Vietnamese and ourselves, I felt I had a moral obligation to report my views as much as the facts."

As a result of all these things, American journalism changed. "Vietnam and Watergate destroyed what I think was a genuine sense that our officials knew more than we did and acted in good faith," says Anthony Lewis, the former *New York Times* reporter and columnist. We became more sophisticated in our understanding of the limits of objectivity. And indeed, the parameters of modern journalistic objectivity allow reporters quite a bit of leeway to analyze, explain, and put news in context, thereby helping guide readers and viewers through the flood of information.

Still, nothing replaced objectivity as journalism's dominant professional norm. Some 75 percent of journalists and news executives in a 1999 Pew Research Center survey said it was possible to obtain a true, accurate, and widely agreed-upon account of an event. More than two-thirds thought it feasible to develop "a systematic method to cover events in a disinterested and fair way." The survey also offered another glimpse of the objectivity fissure: more than two-thirds of the print press in the Pew survey also said that "providing an interpretation of the news is a core principle," while less than half of those in television news agreed with that.

The More Things Change

If objectivity's philosophical hold on journalism has eased a bit since the 1960s, a number of other developments have bound us more tightly to the objective ideal and simultaneously exacerbated its shortcomings. Not only are journalists operating under conflicting orders, as E.J. Dionne argued, but their corporate owners don't exactly trumpet the need to rankle the status quo. It is perhaps important to note that one of the original forces behind the shift to objectivity in the nineteenth century was economic. To appeal to as broad an audience as possible, first the penny press and later the new wire services gradually stripped news of "partisan" context. Today's owners have squeezed the newshole, leaving less space for context and analysis.

If space is a problem, time is an even greater one. The nonstop news cycle leaves reporters less time to dig, and encourages reliance on official sources who can provide the information quickly and succinctly. "We are slaves to the incremental daily development," says one White House correspondent, "but you are perceived as having a bias if you don't cover it." This lack of time makes a simpleminded and lazy version of objectivity all the more tempting. In *The American Prospect* of November 6, 2000, Chris Mooney wrote about how "e-spin," a relentless diet of canned attacks and counterattacks e-mailed from the Bush and Gore campaigns to reporters, was winding up, virtually unedited, in news stories. "Lazy reporters may be seduced by the ease of readily provided research," Mooney wrote. "That's not a new problem, except that the prevalence of electronic communication has made it easier to be lazy."

Meanwhile, the Internet and cable news's Shout TV, which drive the nonstop news cycle, have also elevated the appeal of "attitude" in the news, making the balanced, measured report seem anachronistic. In the January/February 2003 issue of the *Columbia Journalism Review*, young journalists asked to create their dream newspaper wanted more point-of-view writing in news columns. They got a heavy dose of it during the second gulf war, with news "anchors" like Fox's Neil Cavuto saying of those who opposed the war, "You were sickening then; you are sickening now."

Perhaps most ominous of all, public relations, whose birth early in the twentieth century rattled the world of objective journalism, has matured into a spin monster so ubiquitous that nearly every word a reporter hears from an official source has been shaped and polished to proper effect. Consider the memo from the Republican strategist Frank Luntz, as described in a March 2, 2003, *New York Times* story, that urged the party—and President Bush—to soften their language on the environment to appeal to suburban voters. "Climate change" instead of "global warming," "conservationist" rather than "environmentalist." To the extent that the threat of being accused of bias inhibits reporters from cutting through this kind of manipulation, challenging it, and telling readers about it, then journalism's dominant professional norm needs a new set of instructions.

Joan Didion got at this problem while taking Bob Woodward to task in a 1996 piece in *The New York Review of Books* for writing books that she argued were too credulous, that failed to counter the possibility that his sources were spinning him. She wrote:

> The genuflection toward "fairness" is a familiar newsroom piety, in practice the excuse for a good deal of autopilot reporting and lazy thinking but in

theory a benign ideal. In Washington, however, a community in which the management of news has become the single overriding preoccupation of the core industry, what "fairness" has often come to mean is a scrupulous passivity, an agreement to cover the story not as it is occurring but as it is presented, which is to say as it is manufactured.

Asked about such criticism, Woodward says that for his books he has the time and the space and the sources to actually uncover what really happened, not some manufactured version of it. "The best testimony to that," he says, "is that the critics never suggest how any of it is manufactured, that any of it is wrong." Then, objectivity rears its head. "What they seem to be saying," Woodward says of his critics, "is that I refuse to use the information I have to make a political argument, and they are right, I won't." Yet some of Woodward's critics do suggest how his material is manufactured. Christopher Hitchens, reviewing Woodward's latest book, *Bush at War*, in the June 2003 issue of *The Atlantic Monthly*, argues that, while reporting on a significant foreign-policy debate, Woodward fully presents the point of view of his cooperative sources, but fails to report deeply on the other sides of the argument. Thus he presents an incomplete picture. "Pseudo-objectivity in the nation's capital," Hitchens writes, "is now overripe for regime change."

To Fill the Void

Jason Riley is a young reporter at the *Louisville Courier-Journal*. Along with a fellow reporter, R.G. Dunlop, he won a Polk award this year for a series on dysfunction in the county courts, in which hundreds of felony cases dating back to 1983 were lost and never resolved. Riley and Dunlop's series was a classic example of enterprise reporting: poking around the courthouse, Riley came across one felony case that had been open for several years. That led to more cases, then to a drawer full of open cases. No one was complaining, at least publicly, about this problem. In a first draft, Riley wrote that the system was flawed because it let cases fall off the docket and just disappear for years. "I didn't think it needed attribution because it was the conclusion I had drawn after six months of investigation," he writes in an e-mail. But his editor sent it back with a note: "Says who?"

In a follow-up profile of the county's lead prosecutor, a man Riley has covered for three years, many sources would not criticize the prosecutor on the record. He "knew what people thought of him, knew what his strengths and weaknesses were," Riley says. "Since no one was openly discussing issues surrounding him, I raised many in my profile without attribution." Again his editors hesitated. There were discussions about the need to remain objective. "Some of my conclusions and questions were left out because no one else brought them up on the record," he says.

Riley discovered a problem on his own, reported the hell out of it, developed an understanding of the situation, and reached some conclusions based on that. No official sources were speaking out about it, so he felt obliged to fill that void. Is that bias? Good reporters do it, or attempt to do it, all the time. The strictures of objectivity can make it difficult. "I think most journalists will admit to feeding sources the information we want to hear, for quotes or attribution, just so we can make the crucial point we are not allowed to make ourselves," Riley says. "But why not? As society's watchdogs, I think we should be asking questions, we should be bringing up problems, possible solutions . . . writing what we know to be true."

Last fall, when America and the world were debating whether to go to war in Iraq, no one in the Washington establishment wanted to talk much about the aftermath of such a war. For the Bush administration, attempting to rally support for a preemptive war, messy discussions about all that could go wrong in the aftermath were unhelpful. Anything is better than Saddam, the argument went. The Democrats, already wary of being labeled unpatriotic, spoke their piece in October 2002 when they voted to authorize the use of force in Iraq, essentially putting the country on a war footing. Without the force of a "she said" on the aftermath story, it was largely driven by the administration, which is to say stories were typically framed by what the administration said it planned to do: work with other nations to build democracy. Strike a blow to terrorists. Stay as long as we need to and not a minute longer. Pay for it all with Iraqi oil revenue. There were some notable exceptions—a piece by Anthony Shadid in the October 20, 2002, *Boston Globe*, for instance, and another on September 22, 2002, by James Dao in *The New York Times*, pushed beyond the administration's broad assumptions about what would happen when Saddam was gone—but most of the coverage included only boilerplate reminders that Iraq is a fractious country and bloody reprisals are likely, that tension between the Kurds and Turks might be a problem, and that Iran has designs on the Shiite region of southern Iraq.

David House, the reader advocate for the *Fort Worth Star-Telegram*, wrote a piece on March 23, 2003, that got at the press's limitations in setting the agenda. "Curiously, for all the technology the news media have, for all the gifted minds that make it all work . . . it's a simple thing to stop the media cold. Say nothing, hide documents."

In November 2002, James Fallows wrote a cover story for *The Atlantic Monthly* entitled "The Fifty-First State? The Inevitable Aftermath of Victory in Iraq." In it, with the help of regional experts, historians, and retired military officers, he gamed out just how difficult the aftermath could be. Among the scenarios he explored: the financial and logistical complications caused by the destruction of Baghdad's infrastructure; the possibility that Saddam Hussein would escape and join Osama bin Laden on the Most Wanted list; how the dearth of Arabic speakers in the U.S. government would hinder peacekeeping and other aftermath operations; how the need for the U.S., as the occupying power, to secure Iraq's borders would bring it face to face with Iran, another spoke in the "axis of evil"; the complications of working with the United Nations after it refused to support the war; what to do about the Iraqi debt from, among other things, UN-imposed reparations after the first gulf war, which some estimates put as high as $400 billion.

Much of this speculation has since come to pass and is bedeviling the U.S.'s attempt to stabilize—let alone democratize—Iraq. So are some other postwar realities that were either too speculative or too hypothetical to be given much air in the prewar debate. Looting, for instance, and general lawlessness. The fruitless (thus far) search for weapons of mass destruction. The inability to quickly restore power and clean water. A decimated health-care system. The difficulty of establishing an interim Iraqi government, and the confusion over who exactly should run things in the meantime. The understandably shallow reservoir of patience among the long-suffering Iraqis. The hidden clause in Halliburton's contract to repair Iraq's oil wells that also, by the way, granted it control of production and distribution, despite the administration's assurances that the Iraqis would run their own oil industry.

In the rush to war, how many Americans even heard about some of these possibilities? Of the 574 stories about Iraq that aired on NBC, ABC, and CBS evening news broadcasts between September 12, 2002 (when Bush addressed the UN), and March 7, 2003 (a week and a half before the war began), only twelve dealt primarily with the potential aftermath, according to Andrew Tyndall's numbers.

The Republicans were saying only what was convenient, thus the "he said." The Democratic leadership was saying little, so there was no "she said." "Journalists are never going to fill the vacuum left by a weak political opposition," says *The New York Times*'s Steven R. Weisman. But why not? If something important is being ignored, doesn't the press have an obligation to force our elected officials to address it? We have the ability, even on considerably less important matters than war and nation-building. Think of the dozens of articles *The New York Times* published between July 10, 2002, and March 31, 2003, about the Augusta National Country Club's exclusion of women members, including the one from November 25, 2002, that carried the headline CBS STAYING SILENT IN DEBATE ON WOMEN JOINING AUGUSTA. Why couldn't there have been headlines last fall that read: BUSH STILL MUM ON AFTERMATH, or BEYOND SADDAM: WHAT COULD GO RIGHT, AND WHAT COULD GO WRONG? And while you're at it, consider the criticism the *Times*'s mini-crusade on Augusta engendered in the media world, as though an editor's passion for an issue never drives coverage.

This is not inconsequential nitpicking. *The New Yorker*'s editor, David Remnick, who has written in support of going to war with Iraq, wrote of the aftermath in the March 31, 2003, issue: "An American presence in Baghdad will carry with it risks and responsibilities that will shape the future of the United States in the world." The press not only could have prepared the nation and its leadership for the aftermath we are now witnessing, but should have.

The Real Bias

In the early 1990s, I was a statehouse reporter for the *Charleston Daily Mail* in West Virginia. Every time a bill was introduced in the House to restrict access to abortion, the speaker, who was solidly pro-choice, sent the bill to the health committee, which was chaired by a woman who was also pro-choice. Of course, the bills never emerged from that committee. I was green and, yes, pro-choice, so it took a couple of years of witnessing this before it sunk in that—as the antiabortion activists had been telling me from day one—the committee was stacked with pro-choice votes and that this was how "liberal" leadership killed the abortion bills every year while appearing to let the legislative process run its course. Once I understood, I eagerly wrote that story, not only because I knew it would get me on page one, but also because such political maneuverings offended my reporter's sense of fairness. The bias, ultimately, was toward the story.

Reporters are biased, but not in the oversimplified, left-right way that Ann Coulter and the rest of the bias cops would have everyone believe. As Nicholas Confessore argued in *The American Prospect*, most of the loudest bias-spotters were not reared in a newsroom. They come from politics, where everything is driven by ideology. Voting Democratic and not going to church—two bits of demography often trotted out to show how liberal the press is—certainly have some bearing on one's interpretation of events. But to leap to the conclusion that reporters use their precious column inches to push a left-wing agenda is specious reasoning at its worst. We all have our biases, and they can be particularly pernicious when they are unconscious. Arguably the most damaging bias is rarely discussed—the bias born of class. A number of people interviewed for this story said that the lack of socioeconomic diversity in the newsroom is one of American journalism's biggest blind spots. Most newsroom diversity efforts, though, focus on ethnic, racial, and gender minorities, which can often mean people with different skin color but largely the same middle-class background and aspirations. At a March 13, 2003, panel on media bias at Columbia's journalism school, John Leo, a columnist for *U.S. News & World Report*, said, "It used to be that anybody could be a reporter by walking in the door. It's a little harder to do that now, and you don't get the working-class Irish poor like Hamill or Breslin or me. What you get is people from Ivy League colleges with upper-class credentials, what you get is people who more and more tend to be and act alike." That, he says, makes it hard for a newsroom to spot its own biases.

Still, most reporters' real biases are not what political ideologues tend to think.

"Politically I'm a reporter," says Eric Nalder, an investigative reporter at the *San Jose Mercury News*. Reporters are biased toward conflict because it is more interesting than stories without conflict; we are biased toward sticking with the pack because it is safe; we are biased toward event-driven coverage because it is easier; we are biased toward existing narratives because they are safe and easy. Consider the story—written by reporters around the country—of how Kenneth L. Lay, the former CEO of Enron, encouraged employees to buy company stock as he was secretly dumping his. It was a conveniently damning narrative, and easy to believe. Only it turned out, some two years later, to be untrue, leading *The New York Times*'s Kurt Eichenwald to write a story correcting the record on February 9, 2003.

Mostly, though, we are biased in favor of getting the story, regardless of whose ox is being gored. Listen to Daniel Bice, an investigative columnist at the *Milwaukee Journal-Sentinel*, summarize his reporting philosophy: "Try not to be boring, be a reliable source of information, cut through the political, corporate, and bureaucratic bullshit, avoid partisanship, and hold politicians' feet to the fire." It would be tough to find a reporter who disagrees with any of that.

In his 1979 book *Deciding What's News*, the Columbia sociologist Herbert Gans defined what he called the journalist's "paraideology," which, he says, unconsciously forms and strengthens much of what we think of as news judgment. This consists largely of a number of "enduring values"—such as "altruistic democracy" and "responsible capitalism"—that are reformist, not partisan. "In reality," Gans writes, "the news is not so much conservative or liberal as it is reformist; indeed, the enduring values are very much like the values of the *Progressive* movement of the early twentieth century." My abortion story, then, came from my sense that what was happening violated my understanding of "altruistic democracy." John Laurence distills Gans's paraideology into simpler terms: "We are for honesty, fairness, courage, humility. We are against corruption, exploitation, cruelty, criminal behavior, violence, discrimination, torture, abuse of power, and many other things." Clifford Levy, a reporter for *The New York Times* whose series on abuse in New York's homes for the mentally ill won a Pulitzer this year, says, "Of all the praise I got for the series, the most meaningful was from other reporters at the paper who said it made them proud to work there because it was a classic case of looking out for those who can't look out for themselves."

This "paraideology," James Carey explains, can lead to charges of liberal bias. "There is a bit of the reformer in anyone who enters journalism," he says. "And reformers are always going to make conservatives uncomfortable to an extent because conservatives, by and large, want to preserve the status quo."

Gans, though, notes a key flaw in the journalist's paraideology. "Journalists cannot exercise news judgment," he writes, "without a composite of nation, society, and national and social institutions in their collective heads, and this picture is an aggregate of reality judgments . . . In doing so, they cannot leave room for the reality judgments that, for example, poor people have about America; nor do they ask, or even think of asking, the kinds of questions about the country that radicals, ultraconservatives, the religiously orthodox, or social scientists ask as a result of their reality judgments."

This understanding of "the other" has always been—and will always be—a central challenge of journalism. No individual embodies all the perspectives of a society. But we are not served in this effort by a paralyzing fear of being accused of bias. In their recent book *The Press Effect*, Kathleen Hall Jamieson and Paul Waldman make a strong case that this fear was a major factor in the coverage of the Florida recount of the 2000 presidential election, and its influence on journalists was borne out in my reporting for this piece. "Our paper is under constant criticism by people alleging various forms of bias," says the *Star-Tribune*'s Eric Black. "And there is a daily effort to perform in ways that will make it harder to criticize. Some are reasonable, but there is a line you can cross after which you are avoiding your duties to truth-telling." In a March 10, 2003, piece critical of the press's performance at Bush's prewar press conference, *USA Today*'s Peter Johnson quoted Sam Donaldson as saying that it is difficult for the media—especially during war—"to press very hard when they know that a large segment of the population doesn't want to see a president whom they have anointed having to squirm." If we're about to go to war—especially one that is controversial—shouldn't the president squirm?

It is important, always, for reporters to understand their biases, to understand what the accepted narratives are, and to work against them as much as possible. This might be less of a problem if our newsrooms were more diverse—intellectually and socioeconomically as well as in gender, race, and ethnicity—but it would still be a struggle. There is too much easy opinion passing for journalism these days, and this is in no way an attempt to justify that. Quite the opposite. We need deep reporting and real understanding, but we also need reporters to acknowledge all that they don't know, and not try to mask that shortcoming behind a gloss of attitude, or drown it in a roar of oversimplified assertions.

Toward a Better Definition of Objectivity

In the last two years, Archbishop Desmond Tutu has been mentioned in more than 3,000 articles on the Nexis database, and at least 388 (11 percent) included in the same breath the fact that he was a Nobel Peace Prize winner. The same search criteria found that Yasser Arafat turned up in almost 96,000 articles, but only 177 (less than .2 percent) mentioned that he won the Nobel prize. When we move beyond stenography, reporters make a million choices, each one subjective. When, for example, is it relevant to point out, in a story about Iraq's weapons of mass destruction, that the U.S. may have helped Saddam Hussein build those weapons in the 1980s? Every time? Never?

The rules of objectivity don't help us answer such questions. But there are some steps we can take to clarify what we do and help us move forward with confidence. A couple of modest proposals:

Journalists (and journalism) must acknowledge, humbly and publicly, that what we do is far more subjective and far less detached than the aura of objectivity implies—and the public wants to believe. If we stop claiming to be mere objective observers, it will not end the charges of bias but will allow us to defend what we do from a more realistic, less hypocritical position.

Secondly, we need to free (and encourage) reporters to develop expertise and to use it to sort through competing claims, identify and explain the underlying assumptions of those claims, and make judgments about what readers and viewers need to know to understand what is happening. In short, we need them to be more willing to "adjudicate factual disputes," as Kathleen Hall Jamieson and Paul Waldman argue in *The Press Effect*. Bill Marimow, the editor of the *Baltimore Sun*, talks of reporters "mastering" their beats. "We want our reporters to be analysts," he told a class at Columbia in March 2003. "Becoming an expert, and mastering the whole range of truth about issues will give you the ability to make independent judgments."

Timothy Noah, writing in *The Washington Monthly* for a 1999 symposium on objectivity, put it this way: "A good reporter who is well-steeped in his subject matter and who isn't out to prove his cleverness, but rather is sweating out a detailed understanding of a topic worth exploring, will probably develop intelligent opinions that will inform and perhaps be expressed in his journalism." This happens every day in ways large and small, but it still happens too rarely. In a March 18, 2003, piece headlined BUSH CLINGS TO DUBIOUS ALLEGATIONS ABOUT IRAQ, *The Washington Post*'s Walter Pincus and Dana Milbank laid out all of Bush's "allegations" about Saddam Hussein "that have been challenged—and in some cases disproved—by the United Nations, European governments, and even U.S. intelligence." It was noteworthy for its bluntness, and for its lack of an "analysis" tag. In commenting on that story, Steven Weisman of *The New York Times* illustrates how conflicted journalism is over whether such a piece belongs in the news columns: "It's a very good piece, but it is very tendentious," he says. "It's interesting that the editors didn't put it on page one, because it would look like they are calling Bush a liar. Maybe we should do more pieces like it, but you must be careful not to be argumentative."

Some reporters work hard to get these same "argumentative" ideas into their stories in more subtle ways. Think of Jason Riley's comment about "feeding information" to sources. Steven Weisman calls it making it part of the "tissue" of the story. For example, in a March 17, 2003, report on the diplomatic failures of the Bush administration, Weisman worked in the idea that the CIA was questioning the Iraq–al Qaeda connection by attributing it to European officials as one explanation for why the U.S. casus belli never took hold in the UN.

The test, though, should not be whether it is tendentious, but whether it is true.

There are those who will argue that if you start fooling around with the standard of objectivity you open the door to partisanship. But mainstream reporters by and large are not ideological warriors. They are imperfect people performing a difficult job that is crucial to society. Letting them write what they know and encouraging them to dig toward some deeper understanding of things is not biased, it is essential. Reporters should feel free, as Daniel Bice says, to "call it as we see it, but not be committed to one side or the other." Their professional values make them, Herbert Gans argues, akin to reformers, and they should embrace that aspect of what they do, not hide it for fear of being slapped with a bias charge. And when actual bias seeps in—as it surely will—the self-policing in the newsroom must be vigorous. Witness the memo John Carroll, editor of the *Los Angeles Times*, wrote last month to his staff after a front-page piece on a new Texas abortion law veered left of center: "I want everyone to understand how serious I am about purging all political bias from our coverage."

Journalists have more tools today than ever to help them "adjudicate factual disputes." In 1993, before the computer-age version of "precision journalism" had taken root in the newsroom, Steve Doig helped *The Miami Herald* win a Pulitzer with his computer-assisted stories that traced damage done by Hurricane Andrew to shoddy home construction and failed governmental oversight of builders. "Precision journalism is arguably activist, but it helps us approach the unobtainable goal of objectivity more than traditional reporting strategies," says Doig, who now teaches computer-assisted reporting at Arizona State University. "It allows you to measure a problem, gives you facts that are less controvertible. Without the computer power, our Hurricane Andrew stories would have essentially been finger-pointing stories, balanced with builders saying there is no way any structure could have withstood such winds."

On April 1, 2003, Ron Martz, a reporter from the *Atlanta Journal-Constitution* embedded with the Army in Iraq, delivered a "war diary" entry on National Public Radio in which he defended his battlefield decision to drop his reporter's detachment and take a soldier's place holding an intravenous drip bag and comforting a wounded Iraqi civilian. The "ethicists," Martz said on NPR, tell us this is murky territory. That Martz, an accomplished reporter, should worry at all that his reputation could suffer from something like this says much about journalism's relationship with objectivity. Martz concluded that he is a human being first and a reporter second, and was comfortable with that. Despite all our important and necessary attempts to minimize our humanity, it can't be any other way.

Free Press and Democracy

AMERICAN NEWSPAPER GUILD

Code of Ethics
(1934)

1. That the newspaper man's first duty is to give the public accurate and unbiased news reports, and that he be guided in his contacts with the public by a decent respect for the rights of individuals and groups.

2. That the equality of all men before the law should be observed by the men of the press; that they should not be swayed in news reporting by political, economic, social, racial or religious prejudices, but should be guided only by facts and fairness.

3. That newspaper men should presume persons accused of crime of being innocent until they are convicted, as is the case under the law, and that news accounts dealing with accused persons should be in such form as not to mislead or prejudice the reading public.

4. That the Guild should work through efforts of its members or by agreement with editors and publishers to curb the suppression of legitimate news concerning "privileged" persons or groups, including advertisers, commercial powers and friends of newspapers.

5. That newspaper men shall refuse to reveal confidences or disclose sources of confidential information in court or before other judicial or investigating bodies, and that the newspaperman's duty to keep confidences shall include those he shared with one employer even after he has changed his employment.

6. That the news be edited exclusively in the editorial rooms instead of in the business office of the daily newspapers.

7. That newspaper men shall behave in a manner indicating independence and decent self-respect in the city room as well as outside, and shall avoid any demeanor that might be interpreted as a desire to curry favor with any person.

From the Founding Statements of the American Newspaper Guild (1934), reprinted as an appendix in George Seldes, *Freedom of the Press* (Garden City, NY: Garden City Publishing Company, 1935), 370–71.

Integrity of the Press

Resolution Adopted by the Newspaper Guild, in Convention, St. Paul, June, 1934

WHEREAS, freedom of the press is a right of the readers of news and a responsibility upon the producers of news; and is not a privilege for owners of news channels to exploit; and

WHEREAS, reporting is a high calling which has fallen into disrepute because news writers have been too often degraded as hirelings compelled by their employers to serve the purposes of politicians, monopolists, speculators in the necessaries of life, exploiters of labor, and fomenters of war; therefore be it

RESOLVED, that the American Newspaper Guild strive tirelessly for integrity of news columns and opportunity for its members to discharge their social responsibility; not stopping until the men and women who write, graphically portray, or edit news have achieved freedom of conscience to report faithfully, when they occur, and refuse by distortion and suppression, to create political, economic, industrial and military wars.

LEO C. ROSTEN

The Corps, the Press, and Democracy
(1937)

There is ample evidence to support the belief that some newspapers are more interested in furthering the interests of their publishers than in enlightening the public. Other newspapers possess great journalistic integrity, permit their reporters freedom to operate as honest newspapermen, and draw a meticulous line between the editorial and the news columns. This point of view was expressed several years ago by Paul Y. Anderson:

> It required no particular courage to write the truth for the *Baltimore Sun*, the *St. Louis Post-Dispatch* or the Scripps-Howard papers. Such newspapers as these expect it. But what would happen to the correspondent who tried to write the truth about "Coolidge economy" for the *Boston Transcript*, or about the Mellon tax refunds for the *Philadelphia Public Ledger*, or about the social lobby for the *Washington Star?* What would happen to any man who insisted on dishing up the bald truth about any Republican administration for such papers as the *New York Herald Tribune*, the *Detroit Free Press*, the *St. Louis Globe-Democrat*, the *Chicago Tribune*, or the *Los Angeles Times?* The Washington corps of correspondents has its inevitable percentage of sycophants, climbers, politicians and lads with an eye on the main chance, and it has, sad to relate, a solemn bevy of "gallery statesmen" who have been duped into a bogus sense of being "part" of the government, and hence bound to conceal its blunders and knaveries. But on the whole they are ten times better men than the owners of their papers.[1]

How much journalistic integrity is to be expected from the reporter who testified, in an interview with Professor H. Gilpatrick of Columbia University:

From *The Washington Correspondents* (New York: Harcourt, Brace and Company, 1937), 271–306.

Hearst decided he wanted the McLeod Bill to go through. We were instructed that we were in favor of the bill and were to go out and make everyone else in favor of it. We were instructed to get one hundred telegrams from various people sent to Congress saying they favored the bill. I don't think I found a single person who knew what the bill was or cared, but we got the telegrams because of the obligations they felt to the paper.[2]

Or from the reporter who said:

We do just what the Old Man orders. One week he orders a campaign against rats. The next week he orders a campaign against dope peddlers. Pretty soon he is going to campaign against college professors. It's all the bunk, but orders are orders.[3]

Newspaper "policy" is sharpened during political controversies in which the interests of publishers are involved, or during the heat of national elections. In the Presidential campaign of 1936 the newspapers of the nation were characterized by singularly undisguised preferences; the issue was not merely that of a choice between Roosevelt and Landon but between a program and philosophy of government which directly threatened the estates of the wealthy—including newspaper proprietors—and one which proposed to free them from the legislative and economic attacks of the four years in which the New Deal had operated. A swift examination of the emphases of the press during this campaign will place the meaning of newspaper policy in bolder relief.

The Baltimore *Sun*, the St. Louis *Post-Dispatch*, and the Kansas City *Star* conducted energetic criticisms of Mr. Roosevelt and the New Deal in their editorial columns. (Roy Roberts of the Kansas City *Star* acted as Governor Landon's campaign manager.) But these papers did not carry their political disposition into the news columns. News about Roosevelt and Landon was treated with a regard for the equities of both space and emphasis. Similarly, although the New York *Times* supported Mr. Roosevelt in its editorials, Mr. Landon received scrupulously fair treatment in its news columns. This is one type of journalism.

A less laudable record was left by other newspapers. The honest reporting of their Washington correspondents was negated by misleading headlines, inconspicuous placing, and the sundry devices of what is most euphemistically called "unethical journalism." Correspondents found that the impartiality of their dispatches from the capital was lost in the total effect of their papers' make-up. In some cases members of the press corps were subjected to such psychological pressure that they took the safe path of least resistance. One Washington correspondent told this writer: "I'm sick of fighting my home office. I'm sick of being criticized, accused of being 'sold' on the New Deal simply because I don't attack Roosevelt and because

I honestly think he will make a better President than Landon. From now on I'm giving my paper what it wants. That's what I'm being paid to do, I suppose. If I don't swing into line they can fire me in a second and get some trained seal who will write to please the Boss."

The Chicago *Tribune*, for example, was transformed into what was virtually a personal organ, disseminating the biases of its publisher in its news columns. For over a week, during the height of the Presidential campaign, the President of the United States, a candidate for re-election, was mentioned on the front page of "The World's Greatest Newspaper" only once. On one day he was left out of the paper entirely. On another he was given a few perfunctory lines on page 13.[4] It is difficult to cite a more unabashed manipulation of news in the service of policy. When an investigation divulged immoral practices in two Wisconsin cities, the Chicago *Tribune* captioned its dispatch:

Roosevelt Area in Wisconsin is Hotbed of Vice.[5]

In reporting the meeting of the American Labor Party, which endorsed President Roosevelt, the *Tribune* dispatch of October 29, 1936, used this language: "More than 90 per cent of the audience . . . were persons of foreign birth. . . . The leaders of the new party who addressed the meeting one after another spoke with a foreign accent."

On September 1, 1937, the *Tribune*, in an editorial, spoke of a forthcoming La Follette senatorial investigation on labor spies and the violation of civil liberties as "a form of self-advertisement," "another New Deal importation of European methods employed by dictatorships both communist and fascist." The *Tribune* placed this editorial on its front page. There is historic irony in the spectacle of a newspaper in a democratic society labeling an investigation of civil liberties as a "Fascist-Communist" tactic.

The practices of the Hearst newspapers in 1936 are still vivid enough to make extended analysis unnecessary. During the last weeks of the campaign, reporters for the Hearst papers were estopped from writing anything that suggested the *possibility* of Mr. Roosevelt's re-election. References to the President's future plans were not welcomed. The phrase "if re-elected" disappeared from the news columns. Only near the end of October, 1936, did Mr. Hearst, in a confidential "rush" cable to all his editors, order his newspapers to give news of Roosevelt equal space and prominence with news of Landon. This policy was to go into effect on October 26, 1936—exactly eight days before the country went to the polls.[6]

The Hearst policy may be indicated more sharply by comparing the form in which the syndicated column of Robert S. Allen and Drew Pearson, "The Daily Washington Merry-Go-Round," was printed in the Hearst and other papers on several occasions. In November, 1935, Allen and Pearson conducted a poll on the question: "Should President Roosevelt Be Re-elected?" This was an effort to check upon the validity of the *Literary Digest* poll, which had asked the question: "Do you now approve of the acts and policies of the New Deal to date?" The *Literary Digest* had found 55.6 per cent of the voters against "the acts and policies of the New Deal." The Allen-Pearson poll showed that 69.7 percent of their radio listeners favored President Roosevelt's re-election—a more pertinent issue. The comparison was striking and significant. In "The Daily Washington Merry-Go-Round" for December 9, 1935, these facts were analyzed. The Washington *Herald*, a Hearst property, simply deleted this part of the column: the rest was intact, exactly similar to the column as printed that day in the Philadelphia *Record*, for example. The space which had been occupied by the paragraphs discussing the 69.7 per cent majority for Roosevelt was filled in, instead, by "filler" material which Messrs. Allen and Pearson supply to their clients: comments on processing taxes, farm contracts, "The Mail Bag," etc.

At the end of 1935, Messrs. Allen and Pearson reviewed what they called "The End of the Pedestal Era," pointing out that President Roosevelt's popularity had declined in the early part of 1935 but had risen strongly since the adjournment of Congress. A comparison of the column as printed in the Philadelphia *Record* and the Washington *Herald* on December 31, 1935, shows that the Hearst paper printed that part of the column which analyzed the *decline* in Mr. Roosevelt's popularity, but cut out the part which discussed his rise back to public favor. This time the space was filled in with miscellaneous tid-bits about the Department of Agriculture's ice-cream reports.

Random items from the news columns of several other newspapers are illuminating examples of policy-governed "news." For several months before the election, the New York *Herald Tribune* printed the daily Jeremiads of Mrs. Preston Davie, famous for the slogan, "Twelve days left before election. Twelve days left to save the American way of life." Mrs. Davie, an amateur journalist, ended her daily attack on the President with these words:

Will you join us?
Call, write or telephone,
Forty-one East Forty-second Street,
Twelfth floor, Vanderbilt 3-5600.

This can hardly be called news. It was not marked advertising. It was propaganda—on the news pages. Mrs. Davie urged voters "to save our country, our homes, and our children from Communism, from the Dubinskys, the Hillmans, the Zaritskys."[7] That this type of tub-thumping was permitted in the columns of the *Herald Tribune* is no tribute to its record.

Colonel Frank Knox's Chicago *Daily News* is part-owner of Westbrook Pegler's daily column, "Fair Enough." In several instances, when Pegler's speculations were pointedly unfavorable to the Republican cause, the column was omitted from the Chicago *Daily News*.[8]

The coloring, slanting, or suppression of political news in the 1936 campaign was not confined to Republican or anti-Roosevelt papers.* Many papers in the South did not welcome news favorable to the cause of Governor Landon. The Washington correspondent for one of the most powerful Southern newspapers told this writer that he "wouldn't dream" of sending a story which did not support President Roosevelt and the Democratic party, or which did not seem to injure the chances of Mr. Landon and "the other party." The New York *Post* (and the Philadelphia *Record*) set about an uncompromising pro-Roosevelt campaign which resulted in such misrepresentation as this:

Pro-Hitler Staff at Headquarters of Republicans.[9]

Robert S. Lynd has shown that in Middletown both daily newspapers are committed to the same political party; the assumption of the founding fathers that each community will develop an "opposition" newspaper has thus been negated.

> The fact that the heavy majority of American newspapers sided with big business interests in actively backing the campaign of Governor Landon in 1936 suggests that this clash between symbol and reality, between the newspaper as a public agency for the dissemination of necessary information and the newspaper as a privately owned business venture is in no sense peculiar to Middletown.[10]

Underlying the behavior of publishers there is a structure of interests which makes their journalistic strategies intelligible.

1. Newspapers are properties. As properties they are dedicated to the making of profit. And as men of property, publishers find their interests coinciding with the interests of other property-holding groups. Their sincere editorial policies may, *without* deliberate intent, mirror the preferences of the economic stratum with which they are identified. Hence the precision with which newspapers reflected the anti-Roosevelt line which characterized those whose property and estate were threatened by the New Deal.

Newspapers are not necessarily guardians of the public welfare or organs of political enlightenment. Given the private ownership and freedom from social responsibility of the American press, it is gratuitous to expect publishers, with

---

*Professor Barlow of the University of Illinois analyzed the news columns of several dozen papers and concluded that of twenty-nine large dailies examined, nineteen consistently printed more pro-Landon than pro-Roosevelt news.[11]

acknowledged exceptions, to adhere to a different ethic or a more detached consideration of the public good than bankers, business magnates, or manufacturers of patent medicines. The *Wall Street Journal*, in an editorial on January 20, 1925, printed a refreshingly candid statement of this point:

> A newspaper is a private enterprise, owing nothing whatever to the public, which grants it no franchise. It is therefore "affected" with no public interest. It is emphatically the property of its owner who is selling a manufactured product at his own risk. . . . Editors, except where they own their own newspapers, take their policy from their employers. . . . But for ridiculously obvious reasons, there are many newspaper owners willing enough to encourage the public in the delusion that it is the editor of a newspaper who dictates the selection of news and expression of opinion. He only does so subject to correction and suggestion of the proprietor of the paper who, most properly, considers his newspaper as a plain business proposition. It is just that, no more and certainly no less.

R. G. Bauer of the University of Wisconsin investigated the editorial policies of leading American newspapers from 1895 to 1923, using outstanding decisions of the Supreme Court as points of analysis. Wherever clear-cut issues were involved (states rights versus federal centralization, for example, or individualism versus collectivism) newspapers which had traditionally championed one side promptly deserted it when their own economic interests were involved. The study concluded that editorial policies tend to reflect not a philosophical point of view or a set of political principles but "sympathy for an economic class."[12]

2. Publishers are employers. The publisher's relation to his employees is precisely that of any other employer to his employees: he can hire, fire, promote, penalize. He faces the same industrial problems that other employing groups do: the challenge of unionization, the problem of wages, the threat of strikes.

Many newspaper publishers make no pretense at maintaining "objectivity" during industrial crises. During the San Francisco General Strike of 1934, the publishers of that city and Oakland formed a council which, according to *Editor and Publisher*, was responsible for breaking the strike. Despite the protestations of Secretary of Labor Perkins ("You have no right to say there is radicalism or communism in this situation.") newspaper owners adopted a red-baiting, red-herring strategy. They treated the suggestions of General Hugh S. Johnson in such a manner that, upon leaving San Francisco, he remarked: "This is the first time I have ever been up against a newspaper oligarchy."[13]

In the field of social legislation the attitude of newspaper proprietors springs, once again, from their employer status. The Committee on Social Security of the American Newspaper Publishers' Association urged publishers to join with "other employer groups . . . (to) watch closely every rule, instruction or interpretation issued by your respective state administration" with reference to the social security laws. The committee urged "co-operation wherever possible with representatives of other industries" and said rather flatly:

> Newspaper publishers as employers have interests that are identical and in common with all other employers in their respective areas. . . . It has been the belief of your Committee that newspaper publishers, as employers, are charged with an especial responsibility to co-operate with other employer groups in studying this whole problem and its effects upon industry, developing, as a result, a constructive attitude in presenting the employers' side of the problem. It is our feeling that newspaper publishers as employers fail to . . . appreciate the extent to which business generally looks to them for guidance and leadership, especially with respect to problems that are as broad in their effect and definite in their form as the ones contained in this social security program. Wherever possible, in an informal manner, the members of your Committee have endeavored to meet this situation and render constructive service.[14]

The Wagner Bill, before it was upheld by the Supreme Court, was attacked by newspapers on every ground from "un-Americanism" to "bureaucracy." Most publishers fought the Child Labor clause of the NRA code proposals bitterly. They protested on every ground from the sacrosanct "Freedom of the Press" to the claim that the government was trying to "regiment" American youth.*

In a confidential bulletin issued November 20, 1935, the A.N.P.A. warned its members against the progress of the Child Labor Amendment, referred to as the "federal control of youth [sic] amendment."[15] In the news columns of the New York *Herald Tribune*, the Child Labor Amendment was referred to as "youth control," a term which scarcely suggests objective news treatment.

The fight of most publishers against the American Newspaper Guild is another illustration of primary business behavior. Unionization will unquestionably result in higher salaries, shorter hours, greater security of tenure, and improved working conditions. It will also raise publishing costs and cut into publishing profits. Publishers contend that membership in a union will rob the reporter of his detachment and will result in his "slanting" the news with a pro-union or pro-labor bias. They insist that

---

*The Louisville *Courier-Journal* had its carriers deliver letters to all subscribers asking them to write General Hugh S. Johnson "in my behalf" because "reformers are attempting to prohibit . . . boys under eighteen years from being gainfully employed." The newsboys provided the writing paper and picked up the letters the next day; they were mailed from the *Courier-Journal* office at that newspaper's expense.[16]

reporters should avoid extra-journalistic ties. Such logic is a two-edged weapon, for reporters may legitimately reply that, to safeguard the objectivity of the press, the American Newspaper Publishers' Association should promptly disband, publishers should give up their business connections and club memberships, publishers should withdraw their investments in stocks, bonds, and factories, etc. In England, Sweden and Australia, reporters' unions have bettered working conditions and raised the quality and the dignity of journalism without interfering with editorial policy.[17]

When the directors of the Associated Press were considering a more expensive wire-photo service, Roy Howard of the Scripps-Howard papers said tartly: "We shortly will be met with the task of meeting the arguments of the newspaper guilds, and they can't be laughed off. When they say we have money for everything but editorial brains, they've got to be answered."[18]

Mr. William Randolph Hearst's argument against a guild is worthy of preservation for future historians. Mr. Hearst said: "Frankly, I do not believe in a newspaper guild. . . . I like to feel that a newspaperman is like a soldier in war. . . . The guild would tend to deprive the reporter of the character which makes the newspaperman a romantic figure."[19]

4. Publishers have vested interests in non-journalistic enterprises. A newspaper owner may also be a mine owner, a real estate operator, a large investor in utilities, a stock-holder in a manufacturing plant, a director of a bank. Elizabeth Maier studied the biographies of 162 living editors and publishers and discovered that 30 per cent of them were directors of business corporations.[20] Elmer O. Fehlhaber examined the "Purely Personal" columns of *Editor and Publisher* and concluded that editors and publishers were identified, personally or financially, "with practically every non-journalistic enterprise in their respective communities." Editors and publishers were on committees pushing the sale of refunding bonds; one was president of the local telephone company; one was president of the Chamber of Commerce; one was district governor of Rotary International; one was head of the American Legion; one was running for State Senator.[21]

A publisher's temptation to use his newspaper to buttress his extra-journalistic stakes is difficult to resist. Newspaper proprietors do not publish newspapers in one insulated compartment of their identity, and own stocks, direct banks, or vote on corporation policies in another.

Mr. Moses (New York Commissioner of Parks) came out with the statement that he didn't like the approach to the Tri-Borough Bridge. The next morning we all got instructions that we were to kill that idea—stir up people, get telegrams, etc., to the effect that people didn't want the approach changed. Well, we all knew *Hearst has been buying up property around there.*[*22]

*The italics are the writer's.

5. Publishers possess human preferences and inhibitions which are projected, often unconsciously, into the organization which they control. According to *Time* magazine, the publisher of the Kansas City *Star* has "snake phobia." The *Star* avoids snake stories, and where that is impossible refers to snakes as "moving objects." When a Moon Mullins cartoon strip had a picture of a circus character charming snakes, the sequence was cut out and a strip from 1927 was substituted.[23] Now the injection of a publisher's snake phobia into news-treatment is of trivial consequence. But what if a publisher has a political "red," "yellow," or "pink" phobia and incorporates this into his newspaper policy? The consequences to the community are too serious to be ignored.

6. As men of property, wealth, and power, publishers rotate in certain sets. They marry into certain families; they move in rarefied social circles; their children study, play, and travel together. Publishers cannot help absorbing the psychology of their associates and approximating a social philosophy which is common to their circle. William Allen White has said:

I know of no editor so high that his mind is not affected by his industrial environment. The fact that he lives in daily contact with the rich people of his community, whether the community be large or small, that he gangs with them at the country clubs, eats with them at leading hotels, and, indeed, prays with what might be called a plutocratic congregation, colors his mind and he sees things as his friends and associates see them.[24]

The testimony of the late Arthur Brisbane, intellectual doyen of the Hearst properties, is equally pertinent:

Newspaper success today means great wealth, and the rich man . . . 99 times out of 100, lets his money think for him. There are men owning newspapers in this country who could not be bribed by any amount of money outside of their own pockets. But the money in their pockets edits their editorial columns every day. . . . A man's newspaper, like his God, is likely to reflect his own peculiarities.[25]

7. Newspapers derive the largest part of their income from advertising, not circulation.* (Increased circulation is valued primarily because it raises advertising

*A survey of a dozen representative newspapers in 1935 concluded that the average revenue from circulation was 20.6 per cent of the total income. Evening and Sunday papers got only 13.3 per cent of their receipts from circulation. Six morning metropolitan newspapers reached the highest circulation percentage, which was only 28.9 per cent.[26] Advertising superseded sales-to-readers as a major source of revenue in the period from 1830 to 1840.[27]

rates.) But direct advertising control over the news columns is far less common than is generally assumed, and thrives, for the most part, in smaller towns and with less successful newspapers.[28] The well-known feud which exists between the city room and the business office of a newspaper generally revolves around the desire of a large advertiser to get free publicity in the news columns for a sales campaign, the annual employees' dance, or some anniversary. Such items may be marked "B.O.M." ("Business Office Must") but they are about as harmful as the free publicity given to church picnics or club outings. Department stores generally succeed in keeping the names of their institutions out of stories of accidents, and often a prominent advertiser's wayward son is spared publicity on some unfortunate *amour* or arrest for speeding. Paul Bellamy of the Cleveland *Plain Dealer* told the 1928 convention of the American Society of Newspaper Editors:

> Better be frank and admit that we have one rule for the strong and another for the weak. . . . Who of us will deny that the paper he serves (excepting only the *Christian Science Monitor*) has published scores, if not hundreds of . . . misadventures . . . when the actors were humble persons? Why, such stories are the warp and woof of the newspaper. . . . But here, forsooth, stands the great John Goodman, pillar in society and an advertiser to boot. At once that kind of editorial sixth sense, the trouble detector, flashes red, and we hesitate. . . . [29]

In larger matters the power of the advertiser has again and again been checked by metropolitan newspapers.* For advertisers need newspapers no less than newspapers need them. Rising rates have driven business concerns to try many substitutes for newspaper advertising: "Shopper's dailies," leaflets, neighborhood papers, "fliers" delivered to homes, etc. In no case have these been satisfactory. Advertisers generally find it difficult to suppress news of significance for several reasons. Such suppression cannot be kept secret: too many men participate in the mechanism of publishing. Furthermore, *all* newspapers cannot be bribed; an item suppressed in one sheet may be given prominence in another precisely because of the pressure brought to bear.

The solicitude of newspapers for the interests of their advertisers takes a less overt but a more important form. The Tugwell Bill, a significant move in government service and an effort to check the false advertising of commodities which affect the health and even the lives of consumers, threatened some $350,000,000

---

*John B. Sheridan, publicity man for certain Missouri utilities, offered the bait of million-dollar advertising contracts for favorable utilities stories, but he could get nowhere with such journals as the St. Louis *Post-Dispatch* and the Kansas City *Star*.[30] The examples can be multiplied at length.

worth of publishers' revenue. The bill was fought tooth-and-nail by newspapers and advertisers. So aroused were newspaper publishers by this threat to their income that many of them would not print such unmistakable news as Mrs. Franklin D. Roosevelt's endorsement of the bill.[31]

Where consumers' problems are concerned, the affinity which exists between newspaper owners and their advertisers has resulted in offenses against the public welfare. Perhaps the most consistent violations of accepted journalistic ethics occur with reference to rulings of the Federal Trade Commission, the Food and Drug Administration, or the reports of the Departments of Labor and Agriculture. When a nationally advertised cosmetic is found to contain dangerous ingredients that fact is ignored by the press. When a standard brand of peaches or soap or gasoline is condemned by an official government bureau the public is given no wide recognition of it. Washington correspondents have learned that it is pointless to "waste telegraph tolls" on such stories. Within one week in 1935 the Federal Trade Commission called the following organizations to account for misleading advertising claims: the Jergen-Woodbury Sales Corporation, the Musterole Company, Pine Brothers, and the distributors of Feen-a-mint, and Pro Ker (a treatment for baldness). Few, if any, newspapers opened an inch of their news-space for any account of these events.[32] Apologists may retort that the "news" element was missing in these items; but it is clear that *had* the newspapers printed the stories they would have been news. If news is that which interests or affects a great number of readers then events which affect the consumers' health or purse* are news of unquestionable legitimacy.

In the larger view, the press is most vitally affected not by advertisers but by *advertising*. Because the welfare of newspapers rests upon the profitability of their advertising, publishers tend to emphasize a psychological setting which fosters buying—and therefore more advertising. One of the most marked characteristics of the American press is its continuous, self-conscious, and spurious optimism. Newspapers are singularly sensitive, in both their editorial and news columns, to the general business conditions from which their major source of income flows. Thus, a paper as intelligent as the Baltimore *Sun* used "idle" instead of "unemployed" during the early part of the depression, and preferred "the business situation" to "the depression." Similarly, several newspapers in the Middle West cut out the gloomy notes of their Washington correspondents in describing the Supreme Court's decision on the AAA and suggested a preference for "optimistic angles."

It may be argued that in a time of economic uncertainty enormous damage may result if newspapers act the dour Cassandra: banks may be wrecked by depositors' runs, purchasing habits upset, the vicious spiral of depression set into motion. But it is proper to examine the harm done by the efforts of the press to disseminate a

---

*Taxation stories are always considered good news.

misleading optimism in a day when reality contradicts it. Newspapers may deepen the severity of cyclical unemployment, for instance, by accentuating the general outlines of the business cycle. The American press played a significant role from 1926 to 1929 in building up a speculative psychology and a boom—with a correspondingly sharp deflation as its aftermath. The false hopes for business recovery aroused by optimistic treatments of the depression led to "unhealthy speculative situations and greater maladjustment."[33] Marlan Pew, then editor of *Editor and Publisher*, said that in the years preceding 1929 financial pages were loaded with " 'inspired' news, press-agent written" and that this "constituted as wicked an exploitation of the reading public as our press has ever been guilty of."[34] In *Mobilizing for Chaos*, Professor O. W. Riegel has commented upon the tendency of the American press to defend the *status quo*, and to indulge in "only those forms of sensationalism that will not shake the political and economic set-up of the country and thus endanger the financial security of the big newspaper properties or the great business interests which support them."[35]

8. Newspapers are Big Businesses. The character of American journalism has been radically transformed from what the founding fathers visualized. In the eighteenth and early nineteenth century, publishing was a profession. Newspapers were published by men to whom journalism was a career. It took relatively little capital for a journalistically minded man to become a publisher. Today the press is an industry and a business, subject to the laws, the problems, and the aspirations of economic enterprise. Newspaper publishing involves enormous investments and expenditures. The Chicago *Daily News* was placed on the market at a price of $13,000,000. The value of the Kansas City *Star* was set at $11,000,000. The Dallas *News*, in a city which had a population of less than 160,000 at the time, was appraised at over $2,000,000.[36]

Publishing has become an enterprise *which is no longer accessible* except to the wealthy. This means that, as in other realms of our economy, power has gravitated to few hands, power has tended to multiply itself, economic power has been translated into political power of a magnitude incongruous with the assumptions of a democratic society. Competition, from which the general good of a free competitive society is assumed to grow, has been limited, restrained, and strangulated. Competition has given way to imperfect competition or to near-monopoly. The consequences are far-reaching—perhaps more so in the realm of public opinion, where men have become lords over facts, than in the sphere of finance. For control over the dissemination of the information upon which a democratic society acts and according to which democratic citizens make political choices, is exercised by men who often recognize no social responsibility, and who may manipulate what is almost a public agency for the sake of private ends.

This does not ignore the fact that the radio has entered the scene and may publicize facts, or interpretations of fact, which newspapers suppress, mutilate, or de-emphasize. For the radio does not possess the curious authority of print; nor does the spoken word contain the *permanence* of the printed word. More important, the radio listener is conscious of the human agent, whereas the newspaper reader tends to accept printed dispatches as impersonal events. The newspaper is still "the bible of democracy, the only serious book most people read. It is the only book they read every day."[37] Nor can one dismiss the influence of the press with the blithe statement that people *know* that newspapers are not to be trusted. Charles E. Merriam has made the seminal suggestion that even where readers are skeptical of the reliability of newspapers the repetition of news has a somewhat hypnotic effect. "Journalistic repetition is in some ways reminiscent of the beat, beat, beat, of the drum in the primitive tribe."[38]

Ten years ago the Lynds said that it was safe to predict that in any given controversy the two leading papers in Middletown could be expected "to support . . . the business class rather than the working class, the Republican party against any other, but especially against any 'radical' party."[39] Today, "Middletown's press, like its pulpit, has largely surrendered its traditional role of leader; both have bartered their peculiar rights to proclaim sharply dissident truths for the right to be well supported by the reigning economy."[40] If these conditions exist in a town which at least has formally competing newspapers, how much more dire is the situation in cities in which the inhabitants have access to only one morning or evening newspaper? Even in such important centers as the following, there is only one morning newspaper: Pittsburgh, Buffalo, Cleveland, Cincinnati, Detroit, Milwaukee, Baltimore, Indianapolis, Kansas City, St. Louis, Des Moines, Louisville, Memphis, Seattle, Denver, Atlanta, Minneapolis, Syracuse, Portland (Ore.), Houston, Dallas.[41] The historical movement of journalism, reflecting the movement of the larger economy of which it is a part, is suggested by the fact that in 1890, when Chicago was one-half its present size, it had no less than eleven newspapers; today it has but five.*

Book publishing does not demand the investments or the advertising foundation

---

*The semi-monopolistic character of journalism is strikingly indicated by the following: one newspaper (or publishing company) has an exclusive monopoly in 93 per cent of the cities in the United States with populations under 10,000; in 87 per cent of the cities between 10,000 and 25,000; in 78 per cent of the cities between 25,000 and 50,000; in 66 per cent of the cities between 60,000 and 75,000; in 46 per cent of the cities between 75,000 and 100,000. Of all the dailies in the United States 82 per cent had a complete monopoly in their communities in 1934. And of the 1,305 cities in the United States with populations under 100,000 only 163 have more than one newspaper, or one newspaper publishing company. The extraordinary growth of "chain ownership" has accentuated this movement towards monopolization. In 1933, sixty-four chains owned over 315 daily newspapers in the United States.[42]

of newspaper publishing. And the American reader of books has access to political concepts and interpretations of fact which range from the most reactionary to the most radical; he has a similar choice in weekly or monthly magazines. But what choice does the vast majority of American readers have in the political emphases of the editorial columns of daily newspapers, or the political color of their news columns? Of Middletown, the Lynds have written:

> Here, then, is a community of nearly 40,000 individuals, founded upon the two principles that one adult's judgment is as good as another's and that ignorance is no excuse for incompetency, and increasingly dependent upon information furnished by its daily press. But despite the assumption of the adequacy of the information of each citizen, it is left to the whim and economic status of the individual whether he shall see a paper at all, obstructions, political, economic and personal, are thrown at many points in the way of our newspapers . . . (publishing) . . . the facts needed by the citizens to carry on a democratic form of government.[43]

In a democratic society one cannot challenge the right of Mr. William Randolph Hearst to utter the most arrant nonsense in his editorial columns, nor the privilege of Colonel Robert R. McCormick to project his personal phobias into the Chicago *Tribune's* editorials, nor the license of the respective publishers and editors of the Los Angeles *Times*, the Philadelphia *Record*, or the *Daily Worker* to stride through their editorial columns breathing hell-fire of their own particular type. Editorials are the soap-boxes of journalism. They are approached by readers as recognizable efforts to influence opinion. Their influence may be discounted accordingly. But when editorial opinions are stamped into the news columns, when facts are colored, twisted, suppressed, or mutilated, then a crime is being committed against the society which sanctions journalistic freedom. For the news columns are common carriers. As Walter Lippmann pointed out some twenty years ago:

> When those who control them (the news columns) arrogate to themselves the right to determine by their own consciences what shall be reported and for what purpose, democracy is unworkable. Public opinion is blockaded. For when a people can no longer confidently repair "to the best fountains" for their information, then anyone's guess and anyone's rumor, each man's hope and each man's whim becomes the basis of government. All that the sharpest critics of democracy have alleged is true, if there is no steady supply of trustworthy and relevant news.[44]

In the larger view, the ills with which contemporary journalism is afflicted are an integral aspect of our society rather than a disease with an etiology of its own.

One may question whether newspapers are any more derelict in their duty to democratic society than the schools, the church, or the bar. The character of American journalism is, in a sense, an indictment of our educational system, for insofar as readers have not learned to be critical of evidence, or to effect better journalism by protesting against that which is offered to them, our schools have neglected an important task. "We must advance, if we are to advance at all, along the entire front at once. Our journalism can never be truly free until our society is free."[45] But long-range perspectives may tend to obscure immediate problems. Mature political orientation consists partly in subordinating utopian preferences to the recognition of available alternatives. This is not the place to suggest panaceas for our society, but we may properly devote some attention to the newspapers which are so influential an aspect of it.

A free press can exist only in a free society. It would appear, therefore, that publishers would defend the greater, inclusive freedom of the order in which they thrive. They would recognize and seek to help in the solution of the contradictions into which the growth of our economy has plunged our polity: the disparity between political and economic freedom; the precipitation of federal centralization, unionization, collective bargaining, etc., partly *as a consequence* of monopolies, the corporate structure, and imperfect competition; the violations of basic civil liberties by men more determined to defend their power than the political rights upon which the system from which they derived their power is founded; the new role of the United States in the international scene. The Washington correspondents probably recognize these manifestations of historical change more sharply than do their employers. In the scramble for immediate profit, and in the fight to keep immediate gains, men of property lose sight of the consequences of their behavior. The steel baron who defies his union is more concerned over the threat of collective bargaining than the implications of his defiance of what is now national law. The publisher who corrupts his news-columns or ignores his duties under the Wagner Labor Relations Act is, in no less measure, blind to the attack on orderly democratic government which his intransigence entails. One of the leading economists in the country has written:

> In an individualistic-utilitarian view of life, freedom means freedom to use power, and economic freedom means freedom to use economic power, without political interference or restraint. Such freedom may in effect become slavery for the person who has little power at his disposal, since life itself requires practically continuous control of a certain minimum of economic power.[46]

The historical line along which the United States seems to be traveling cannot leave the proprietary foundations of the press unaffected. The movement towards

centralization of political authority is commensurate with the scale and the problems of the American economy and—perhaps more critical—with the position of
the United States in the world "balancing of power" process. The rise to political
self-consciousness of workers, and their identification in terms other than "Republican" or "Democrat," is a revolution which, for better or for worse, has begun.
This, too, the Washington correspondents seem to recognize with more precision
than do their employers. Insofar as publishers are indifferent to, or overly apolo-
getic for, the excesses of contemporary society, and insofar as they fail to expose
its weakness and its problems simply by the untrammeled publication of facts, they
function to undermine the very political structure with which their own welfare is
inextricably identified. It is not gratuitous to remind newspaper proprietors that
the result of the 1936 Presidential campaign was a severe blow to their methods
and philosophy. The press was discredited, in effect, by the size of the vote for the
candidate they had so vehemently opposed.

There is a disturbing side to the publishers' conduct in the 1936 campaign which
has not been commented upon. By the manner in which they presented the issues
and the candidates, the newspapers increased the importance of an area of political
combat which it would be better for democratic citizens to treat with skepticism:
the competition of personalities and of oratory. In proportion as the newspapers
did not grant a just hearing to Mr. Roosevelt they increased the public's receptivity
to his voice, his phrases, and his oratorical virtuosity. They forced the public, as it
were, to turn to the radio. They forced the public to give greater credence to the
very things which they warned against: dramatic phrases. Those who rejoice over
Mr. Roosevelt's victory may well ask themselves whether they would have welcomed a vote influenced by vocal brilliance had Mr. Landon been the better speaker
and showman. Suppose, for example, that in the 1940's the Presidency becomes a
contest between an honest democratic leader and a demagogue with dictatorial
aspirations. Suppose the press once again enters the campaign with such undisguised animus that citizens discount even its legitimate points and turn, in disgust,
to the radio as a guide? Suppose this time it is the democratic candidate, the "American" candidate, who is no master of the golden voice, but, rather, the demagogue.
. . . By branding Mr. Roosevelt as a "dictator," a "radical," or a "Communist," the
newspapers have robbed the words of their meaning and have built an indifference
to them as negative concepts in political controversy.* The thoughtless reiteration
of "red scare" phrases calculated to stampede the public had the paradoxical effect
of accustoming people to the words and, by identifying a man as popular as Mr.
Roosevelt with them, tended to *legitimize* their sound. Similarly, by using "freedom
of the press" as a moral smoke-screen behind which to defend child labor and low

---

*In an article entitled "AWAKE, AMERICAN PATRIOTS!" published in the Los An-
geles *Examiner*, November 24, 1935, Robert H. Hemphill, "financial authority" of

salaries, publishers dissipate the moral authority of the slogan; in doing so they negate its potency for some day when freedom of the press may actually be endangered. One might without flippancy recommend a reading of the "Wolf! Wolf!" fable to the next convention of the A.N.P.A.

The norms of contemporary journalism are anachronistic. The individualism of an earlier and more healthy competitive system still dominates the substance of newspaper dispatches. Personal ingenuity, personal success, and personal responsibility are over-emphasized and extolled at a time when widespread recognition is being given to the social foundations of individual success and the social responsibilities of individual power. The dislocations of industrial conflict are interpreted in terms of over-simplified personal equations. The wider and more important aspects of social change and political growth are lost sight of in the emphasis upon romantic personalities. "Reds" or "agitators" are blamed for protest formations which transcend the influence of persons. "John L. Lewis" becomes a too-simple rhetorical substitute for "the labor movement." Newspaper dispatches operate to concentrate attention on the individual at the expense of the societal.

> The focus of attention is thus absorbed by personal problems . . . The particular incident is not written about as representative of a context of relationships. Not desperation through unemployment, not insecurity through crop failure, not diminished administrative efficiency because of greater burdens of prohibitory regulation, but personal motives and struggles are the subject matter of the secondary means of communication in the bourgeois world.
>
> When such an ideology impregnates life from start to finish, the thesis of collective responsibility runs against a wall of non-comprehension.[47]

---

the Hearst press, declared: "I do not know what catastrophe will be required to shock this nation into a realization of the enormous consequences which are planned and ARE BEING EXECUTED by the Federal Administration and its little band of fanatic adventurers. . . .

"This band of revolutionary radicals PROPOSE TO OVERTHROW THIS GOVERNMENT.

"AND THEY ARE DOING IT!"[48]

In the New York *American* Mr. Hearst addressed the President and his associates as "you and your fellow Communists." On October 8, 1936, the *American* printed a poem, under an inflammatory cartoon, of which the first stanza read:

> A Red New Deal with a Soviet seal
> Endorsed by a Moscow hand,
> The strange result of an alien cult
> In a liberty-loving land.[49]

The premium which journalism places upon an attack, and the spurious daily "crises" which clutter the pages of the newspapers, tend to (1) over-emphasize the errors and inefficiencies of representative government at a time when democratic agencies should concern themselves with buttressing its prestige; (2) deaden the perception of the public in advance to genuine crises which may arise; (3) heighten tensions and foster an impatience with democratic government which demagogues may use to their advantage. The campaign of the newspapers against "professors," "theories," and "theorists" has exalted the pragmatic at the expense of the analytic; it has, in effect, disparaged the value of the expert and discouraged the contribution to government of knowledge derived from systematic study. It is ironic that in a country which values education so highly that it has made it compulsory (a democracy must deny the freedom to be ignorant), the men who help make opinion have discouraged the application of knowledge to social problems.

It is worth noticing that American journalism does not possess any agency, public, private, or professional, to guard its standards and supervise its practitioners. We have an American Medical Association, bar associations, societies of engineers, architects, etc.; but we have no comparable organization of journalists. The American Newspaper Publishers' Association is primarily interested in publishers' problems and is dominated by a business ethic. The American Society of Newspaper Editors does not reach into the ranks of journalism and lacks both scope and authority. The American Newspaper Guild has devoted its brief life to the problems of unionization and recognition and has so far indicated no program along personnel lines.

In England two organizations guard the professional standards of their craft: the Institute of Journalism, founded in 1880 and composed of newspaper proprietors as well as workers, and the National Union of Journalists, which publishes the monthly organ *The Journalist*.[50] Efforts to license journalists in our country, to set up standards by which newspapermen are to be judged, or by which their integrity and competence may be tested, have invariably failed.* Since newspapermen are skeptical of the suggestions of laymen or scholars it is valuable, at this point, to quote the admonition of one of the most distinguished editors in the country, William Allen White:

> Until the people of this country get it well into their heads that journalism
> is a profession that must be licensed and controlled, as the medical and legal
> profession are licensed and controlled, there can be no freedom of the press
> that is not liable to abuses. . . . The most important thing in a democracy is

---

*In many cases there was an understandable fear that such measures might be an encroachment on the freedom of the press.

the dissemination of intelligent information upon important matters. Until a man is equipped to know what are important matters and until he is trained to discuss important matters and disseminate facts intelligently, democracy is in danger. . . . Until journalism is recognized as a profession for trained men who have certain defined qualifications the newspaper business will vacillate.[51]

For over 150 years the right of American publishers to print what they please has not been challenged. They have enjoyed freedom of expression and freedom of reporting. But they have not been held responsible for the *uses* to which they put their constitutional prerogative. If a doctor falsely or incompetently prescribes strychnine and his patient dies, the doctor is subject to prosecution. If a maniac puts poison into a public-drinking system, he is incarcerated in a stronghold where his possibilities of injuring society are minimized. But a newspaper publisher can give criminal advice, lie to the public, poison its intelligence, and conduct campaigns against civil liberties, decent morals, and the democratic system itself without being held accountable for his conduct, or without having to accept responsibility for the consequences of his action. He is granted legal sanction for behavior which may range from the incendiary to the psychopathic.

The journalist with a power comprehending all things requires no sanction. He derives his authority from no election, he receives support from no one. . . . It is hard to imagine a despotism more irresponsible than the despotism of printed words. Is it not strange and irrational that those who struggle most for the preservation of this despotism are the most impassioned champions of freedom, the ferocious enemies of legal restrictions and of all interference by established authority? . . . For conduct such as this a monarch would lose his throne, a minister would be disgraced, impeached and punished; but the journalist stands dry above the waters he has disturbed; from the ruin he has caused he rises triumphant and briskly continues his destructive work.[52]

Professor Merriam has said that in one sense newspaper proprietors have become an informal and irresponsible House of Lords.[53] This position assumes enormous significance if we remember that the newspaper becomes to the layman what the school is to the child: a dispensary of facts; a crucible in which political ideas are resolved; an opinion-making institution which disseminates the symbols of political life and, however unintentionally, assigns moral values to them.

The American press is free in the sense that there are no legal or political interferences with its editorial and news-columns. But the freedom of the press does not mean the freedom of the *news*. It is the contention of this writer that in abusing the freedom which they possess newspaper publishers are strengthening the possibility of political interference with that freedom. The danger of distorted news-columns and of colored dispatches lies not merely in the fact that the public is misled—(the radio has removed some of the dangers in this direction)—but that aspiring demagogues and potential dictators are provided with impressive arguments for controlling the press. A public which has learned to be skeptical of the sources of its news, and which has been given evidence of the falsifications practiced by its newspapers, may be receptive to the oratory of those who ask for the power to "cleanse" the press and "remove" those who pollute the news. This is a danger which few publishers seem to recognize, but it cannot be ignored in a day in which democratic society is being threatened. The best guarantee of freedom is the intelligent use of it. In no society has license long gone uncorrected: when liberty is used to violate the privileges which liberty confers, men of force and eloquence may win public support to suppress those violations—and freedom with it. It is not academic to suggest to the proprietors of the American newspapers that one of the gravest threats to their freedom lies in the very use which they are making of it. They would do well to ponder the words of Franz Höllering, formerly editor of the Berlin *Zeitung am Mittag*, who speaks from direct experience when he says:

> But I must say that Hitler had a fatal attraction for the big publishers as he did for the rest of big business. He promised to free them from labor unions and from government regulations. In economic matters he promised them absolute freedom. May things which today are said in America against the New Deal, Hitler said against the Weimar Republic.[54]

From whatever point of departure one chooses to analyze the function and the influence of the Washington representatives of the American press, the following generalizations, suggested in earlier chapters, seem defensible: newspapers get the type of reporting which they encourage; publishers get the kind of Washington correspondents that they deserve; and the public receives Washington correspondents of a character which newspaper publishers, and ultimately they alone, make possible.

Notes

1. Quoted in George Seldes, *Freedom of the Press* (Indianapolis and New York: Bobbs-Merrill, 1935), p. 338.

2. Ernest Sutherland Bates and Oliver Carolson, *Hearst: Lord of San Simeon* (New York: Viking, 1936), pp. 254–55.

3. Frederick L. Schuman, "Hearst's Campaign Against Professors," a letter to the editors of the *New Republic*, April 17, 1935, pp. 287–88.

4. "The Press and the Public," *New Republic*, Special Section, Prepared by the Editors, March 17, 1937, Part Two, pp. 180–81.

5. In Virginius Dabney, "The Press and the Election," *Public Opinion Quarterly*, April, 1937, p. 123. For a detailed analysis of the Chicago *Tribune's* methods in the 1936 campaign see "The Press and the Public," *New Republic*, *op. cit.*, pp. 180–82.

6. Paul W. Ward, "Washington Weekly: Farley Captures Labor," *Nation*, October 31, 1936, p. 512. Also *Time*, November 2, 1936, p. 14.

7. New York *Herald Tribune*, October 22, 1936, p. 15.

8. Heywood Broun, "Roosevelt Shows up the Press," *Nation*, October 31, 1936, p. 522.

9. *Ibid.*

10. Robert S. and Helen Merrell Lynd, *Middletown in Transition*, pp. 377–78.

11. In Virginius Dabney, *op. cit.*, p. 123.

12. In Chilton R. Bush, *Editorial Thinking and Writing* (New York and London: Appleton, 1932), p. 307, footnote.

13. Earl Burke, "Dailies Helped Break General Strike," *Editor and Publisher*, July 28, 1934, p. 5. Also see "The Press As Strike-Breakers," *New Republic*, August 8, 1934, p. 333.

14. "Report of the Committee on Social Security of the ANPA," *Editor and Publisher*, April 25, 1936, p. 14.

15. *Editor and Publisher*, November 30, 1935, p. 43.

16. *Time*, June 25, 1934, p. 64.

17. "Conditions of Work and Life of Journalists," *International Labor Office, Series and Reports*, Series L, No. 2 (London: E. S. King, 1928). See also Dexter Merriam Keezer, "Press," *Encyclopedia of the Social Sciences*, XII, pp. 325–43; and Allan Nevins, "Journalism," *ibid.*, VIII, pp. 420–24.

18. *Time*, May 7, 1934, p. 48.

19. *Ibid.*

20. C. R. Bush, *op. cit.*, p. 312, footnote.

21. "Whose Hands Need Washing?" *Guild Reporter*, June, 1934, p. 11.

22. In Bates and Carlson, *op. cit.*, p. 255.

23. *Time*, October 28, 1935, p. 48.

24. Quoted by C. R. Bush, *op. cit.*, p. 311.

25. John K. Winkler, *William Randolph Hearst: An American Phenomenon* (New York: Simon and Schuster, 1928), p. 120.

26. *Editor and Publisher*, March 14, 1936, p. 28.

27. "Conditions of Work and Life of Journalists," *op. cit.*, p. 2. See also Julius Ochs Adler, "Do Advertisers Control Newspaper Policy?" *American Press*, April, 1937, p. 1.

28. See "The Press and the Public," *New Republic*, *op. cit.*, pp. 188–89.

29. *Problems of Journalism: 1928*, Proceedings of the American Society of Newspaper Editors (Washington, D.C.: Published by the Society, 1928), pp. 139–40.

30. *Editor and Publisher*, June 30, 1928, p. 5.

31. James Rorty, "Call for Mr. Throttlebottom," *Nation*, January 10, 1934, p. 37. The National Editorial Association printed an appeal entitled: "Fight the Tugwell Bill," *National Printer Journalist*, January, 1934, p. 40. Also see Seldes, *op. cit.*, p. 56.

32. See the Consumers' columns of Ruth Brindze, *Nation*, December 18, 1935, p. 716, and November 20, 1935, pp. 592–94.

33. Burrus S. Dickinson, "The Influence of the Press in Labor Affairs," *Journalism Quarterly*, September, 1932, p. 280.

34. Quoted by Seldes, *op. cit.*, p. 155.

35. *Mobilizing for Chaos: the Story of the New Propaganda*. (New Haven: Yale University Press, 1934), pp. 138–39.

36. Silas Bent, *Ballyhoo: the Voice of the Press* (New York: Boni and Liveright, 1927), p. 252.

37. *Liberty and the News* (New York: Harcourt, Brace and Howe, 1920), p. 47.

38. *The Making of Citizens: A Comparative Study of Methods of Civic Training* (Chicago: University of Chicago Press, 1931), p. 267.

39. Robert S. and Helen Merrell Lynd, *Middletown* (New York: Harcourt, Brace & Co., 1929), p. 476.

40. *Middletown in Transition*, p. 381.

41. Willard Grosvenor Bleyer, "Freedom of the Press and the New Deal," *Journalism Quarterly*, March, 1934, p. 29.

42. *Ibid.*

43. *Middletown*, p. 477.

44. *Liberty and the News*, pp. 10–11.

45. Bruce Bliven, "Bliven Sees Losing Fight Against Press Repressions," *Editor and Publisher*, March 23, 1935, p. 14.

46. Frank H. Knight, *The Ethics of Competition* (New York and London: Harpers, 1935), p. 292.

47. Lasswell, *Politics: Who Gets What, When, How* (New York and London: McGraw-Hill, 1936), p. 33.

48. Bates and Carlson, *op. cit.*, p. 269.

49. "The Press and the Public," *New Republic, op. cit.*, p. 182.

50. Allan Nevins, *op. cit.*, p. 423.

51. Quoted by John E. Drewry, "The Journalist's Inferiority Complex," *Journalism Quarterly*, March, 1931, p. 69.

52. Count Constantine K. Pobyedenostseff, Minister of Education for Czar Nicholas II, *Recollections of a Russian Statesman*, quoted in A. J. Beveridge, *The Russian Advance* (New York: Harpers, 1903), p. 456.

53. *The Making of Citizens*, p. 213.

54. In "Newspapers, Dare To Be Free!" *Nation*, February 5, 1936, p. 145.

ALFRED McCLUNG LEE

Violations of Press Freedom in America
(1938)

Every Thinking Citizen of the United States places beyond dispute the fundamental utility of Freedom of the Press in this Free Land. This Cardinal Principle of Democracy is essential to the preservation of all our other Liberties. It is, in short, a fine thing. Any who doubt it are immediately referred to some satisfactory statement by that Dangerous Red of the eighteenth century, that Saint of twentieth century Conservatives, Thomas Jefferson. A favorite quotation is the one setting forth that "our liberty . . . cannot be guarded but by freedom of the press, nor that be limited without danger of losing it."[1]

Col. R. R. McCormick,[2] editor and publisher of the Chicago *Tribune*, believes that newspapers blessed with Freedom of the Press are able "to present the news of the day, to foster commerce and industry, to inform and lead public opinion, and to furnish that check upon government which no constitution has ever been able to provide." These objectives, the Colonel implies, are all quite laudable. So that no one will think that he has in mind only his *Tribune* and the other dailies owned by members of the American Newspaper Publishers' Association and the Associated Press, this redoubtable Soldier for and of the Right has carefully placed himself on record as opposed to any such delusion. Freedom of the Press, he[3] insists, "is not a special privilege to the owners of newspapers or the owners of presses, but is a privilege of every American citizen which Congress may not pass any law to abridge."

The foregoing statements fill with satisfaction both those who think legalistically and those who believe that the intentions as well as the words of Jefferson and McCormick are similar. The former would do well to study the writings of such jurists as Justice Oliver Wendell Holmes on the evolution of law. The latter would clarify their perspective by learning what the words Freedom of the Press mean in the writings of Jefferson and McCormick. Let us assume that all of us have not overcome these obstacles as yet and examine very briefly what may be gained from

From *Journalism Quarterly* 15, no. 1 (1938): 19–27.

these suggestions. Unfortunately, within the space available, only an outline may be made of the facts upon which are based the views here given. This lack is at least partially met through references to more adequate treatments of specific points. For convenience, too, only the daily newspaper aspect of the situation is treated.

Various writers on law, among them Holmes,[4] have concluded that the "provisions of the Constitution are not mathematical formulas having their essence in their form; they are organic living institutions transplanted from English soil." By the latter statement, Holmes evidently meant that the interpretation of such provisions ought to take account of changes in life conditions and culture. On another occasion, in a decision dealing with the constitutionality of a tax statute, he[5] observed: "Upon this point a page of history is worth a volume of logic." Such judges as Holmes focus their attention on facts; they take "no stock in grand principles, 'natural law,' or other figments, and would never assert, in the style of Moses, that: 'This is The Law.' "[6] Law books rarely take this attitude. Incurious of the nature of their subject, intent merely upon the technical job of winning cases, authorities on law usually assume in a tacit way and occasionally even state explicitly that Law is a gradually perfecting instrument. In this, they reflect professional and popular mores more accurately than do the statements of Holmes.[7]

By his conclusion that constitutional provisions "are not mathematical formulas having their essence in their form," Holmes meant that the things for which the symbols in the formulas stand are not fixed once and for all. The things that the words label in such a phrase as Freedom of the Press, like all things societal, persist in changing. The assertions of special pleaders for an industry that has a vested interest in the maintenance of a fiction of permanence in a principle, and the judicial sanctioning of outworn legal precedents aid in perpetuating the delusion of changelessness. This delusion has temporary utility to those with vested interests in any given principle, but it merely delays change and makes the ultimate adjustment more drastic and costly when it finally comes. Regardless of the plausibility of the assertions of the special pleaders and of the judicial sanctionings of outworn legal precedents, the maintenance of a delusion of changelessness does not alter the trend of basic life conditions.

But the authors of the federal constitution, like the people they represented, wanted fixed formulas. In absolute phrases they sought insurance against the selfish expedients adopted by untrammeled rulers. They did not want to leave their words open to distortion. The "true key for the construction of everything doubtful in a law," wrote Jefferson,[8] "is the intention of the law-givers." Let us see what Jefferson, as one of the leading exponents of press freedom, intended by his often-quoted statements regarding Freedom of the Press.[9]

———

During the years in which Jefferson was agitating for what he regarded as inalien-
able human rights, the great oppressive power that he saw standing between the
people and their rights was a political one. While he was well aware of the oppressive power that economic monopolists might exert, he wishfully thought that
America would remain for a long time an agricultural nation in which no one man
or small group could obtain a dangerously disproportionate share in the state's
control through economic means. In his autobiography,[10] he warned that an "ar-
istocracy of wealth" is "of more harm and danger, than benefit, to society." By the
time that this was written, in 1821, he could see the beginnings of great American
fortunes and of the undemocratic uses to which they would more and more be
placed. This statement recalls a note he[11] made in 1787 while traveling in southern
France: "What a cruel reflection, that a rich country cannot long be a free one."
When he[12] claimed, therefore, that "our liberty . . . cannot be guarded but by freedom of the press, nor can that be limited without danger of losing it," he was not
advocating giving a privilege to all the people that could only be exercised by an
economically limited minority. It is explicit many places in his writings that he did
not wish to help construct democratic checks against political tyranny that would
in turn be used as legalistic guarantees of economically monopolistic privileges. In
many cases, however, that is precisely the fate currently observable for legal devices
that he advocated.

Colonel McCormick and his fellow editors and publishers of the twentieth century accept the dicta of Jefferson and his fellow patriots on Freedom of the Press
without admitting that they modify drastically the intent of such statements. Their
contemporary rationalization of the doctrine runs like this:

Freedom of the Press "would be abridged by any law passed by Congress
which, by the exercise of a code or otherwise, would do any of the following
things: First, unreasonably raise the cost of production . . . second, unreasonably
decrease the return from publishing . . . third, interfere with the transmission of
news by telegraph or otherwise . . . And, finally, anything that would unreasonably
interfere with the freedom of the press in any way which may ever be invented."[13]
*In short, the federal government and, for that matter, the state governments may not do any
of the things limiting press freedom that the industry itself has already put into effective
operation.*[14]

Freedom of the Press, to continue the rationalization in the words of Colonel
McCormick,[15] "is a privilege of every American citizen" and "not a special privilege
to the owners of newspapers or the owners of presses." Since Everyman cannot,
however, afford to issue his own personal organ, at the very outset this privilege
was economically restricted to those with funds who made a convincing effort to
represent their fellows, in other words to specialists. The further restriction of this
group of those who controlled our presses eventually led some to conclude that

"only a rich man can own a paper, so obviously press policy is based on protection of the big fellow." This statement did not embarrass the rationalists for the industry, however. To it, they were sometimes so naïve as to reply as does Casper S. Yost,[16] editor of the editorial page of the St. Louis *Globe-Democrat*, in this statement:

> The modern newspaper, in America and Great Britain at least, is a capitalistic institution and it is that which makes it free. I would not have it otherwise. The assumption that capital and labor are necessarily antagonistic grows out of the Marxian teachings that are burdening the world with class strife.

This is an amusing effort to label a typically Jeffersonian position Marxian. Even William Randolph Hearts,[17] a man whom few would presume to call a Marxian, has picturesquely disagreed with Yost's position. He was asked in 1924, "Is the political influence of the American press, in general, declining or increasing, and why?" To this, he replied as follows:

> I rather think that the influence of the American press is on the whole declining. This, I believe, is because so many newspapers are owned or influenced by reactionary interests and predatory corporations, and are used selfishly, to promote the welfare of these reactionary interests, rather than the welfare of the public. This tends to weaken the confidence of the public in all newspapers more or less.

Testimony from a man who has been so successfully branded a reactionary himself[18] as to the reactionary control of the American press is testimony indeed.

A less moralistic and hence less naïve—but no more convincing—rationalization of the monopolistic nature of press control runs along these lines: The subscriber to a daily newspaper casts a vote each day in favor of his paper's editorial policies by his act of purchasing it. If he does not think that the daily he buys serves his interests satisfactorily, he can tell his newsboy to stop delivering it. As the inimitable Mr. Hearst[19] put it, "Newspapers do not form the opinion of the public; but if they are to be successful, they must express the opinion of the public." The circulation record of his own dailies tends to substantiate this theory, but be it observed that *it does so only in cities in which his papers had local competition.*

The two chief difficulties with this subscriber-vote theory are these: Newspapers are frequently bought *in spite of* their editorial page and their general editorial policies on politico-economic matters and *because of* their comics, sports, and other features and their non-controversial announcements and advertisements. The number of cities, too, in which competing dailies furnish a choice for subscribers, is rapidly diminishing. The number of one-daily-newspaper cities has risen from 353 in 1899, 504 in 1909, 686 in 1919, and 913 in 1929 to 1,083 in 1937.[20] The speed of this process is emphasized by comparing figures for 1936 and 1937 on the number of cities with allegedly competing dailies. In this one year, the number fell from 251 to 230. In 1,206 of the 1,457 cities of the United States (48 states and D.C.) in which dailies were published in 1936, the one or more local dailies available were owned or controlled by one man or a single organization. In the other 251 cities, only 222 morning and 416 evening papers were published. In 1,230 of the 1,460 daily newspaper cities of 1937, local monopolies existed. In the other 230 cities, 212 morning and 371 evening papers were published.[21] Only in such large cities as New York, Chicago, and Philadelphia, and in a few smaller ones, however, can one find dailies that compete for subscribers on the politico-economic front. Only in such cities can one find the real choice represented by the Chicago *Times* and *Daily News*, by the New York *Daily News* and *Herald Tribune*, and by the Philadelphia *Record* and *Inquirer*. The issue elsewhere is most frequently one between the sensational and the conservative treatment of news or between one set of comics and another. In less than 100 American cities does the much vaunted Freedom of the Press bear some resemblance to what we mean by press freedom.

With this brief résumé of the status of that catch phrase, Freedom of the Press, and of press freedom, it is now possible to approach the subject of violations of press freedom. What are some of the most outstanding instances of violation? Who were the chief culprits? What steps can be taken to protect press freedom in the future? Let us take up these three questions one at a time.

What, then, are some of the most striking instances of violation? If one were to ask this question of J. G. Stahlman, president of the ANPA, and of Heywood Broun, president of the American Newspaper Guild, they would probably furnish quite different lists. Passing over the many current irritations bothering each of these worthies, both would—oddly enough—find many of their instances in the list to be given here.

To record the most striking incidents that gradually restricted press freedom would be to outline the history of the American daily newspaper industry. In fact, such incidents as one can list are merely symbols of a long-time societal process. Our daily newspapers as they are today, like our universities, our trade associations, and our trade unions, have grown as integral parts of the evolving American scene. During this evolution, the long-time tendency has been in the direction of an economic restriction of press freedom. This cannot be assigned to a series of simple causes; the causes are as numerous and as complex as American society. The events to be mentioned will merely illustrate these points. Since news-gathering combines and agencies have promoted local monopolies and the integration and standardization of the industry nationally, the list can well start with the formation of the Associated Presses of New York State in 1846 and of New York City in 1848. Since the demands of unionized mechanical workers and the introduction of mass-

production machinery and raw materials have helped decisively to make daily publication a "rich man's game," at least these developments are outstanding enough
to be relevant: the introduction of the type-revolving press in 1847; the formation
of the National Typographical Union in 1852; the adaptation of stereotyping to
newspaper printing needs in the late 1850's and the 1860's; the importation of a
knowledge of the methods for manufacturing newsprint from mechanical wood-
pulp, resulting in its use from 1867; the production of a workable Linotype machine
in 1886; the appointment of a Special Standing Committee on labor relations by
the ANPA in 1900; and the establishment of the ANPA's Open Shop Department
in 1922. The organization of the ANPA itself in 1887 signalized the passing of the
old-time rugged individualism of small operators. The enactment of the National
Industrial Recovery Act in 1933, vastly over-rated by publishers as a direct threat
to Freedom of the Press, powerfully stimulated the integrative process. It finally
permitted the crystallization of a national union of newswriters in 1933 and finally
of other white-collar employees, the fruition of efforts in this direction over a period
of more than forty years.[22] That act plus the other problems of depression and
recovery in 1931–37 made both the American Newspaper Publishers' Association
and such other coöperative efforts as the Associated Press far more effective means
for bolstering up the current control of the press.[23]

From a legislative standpoint, strictly speaking, the most striking violation cannot be symbolized even as well as the foregoing by one or a group of incidents.
This violation was the inevitable differentiation between the "proper" exercise of
Freedom of the Press and "license," between "decent" and "indecent" utterances in
print. With the progressive tendency toward a standardization of viewpoint in daily
newspapers, and the gradual broadening of the politico-economic powers of dailies
of wide circulation, restrictive legislation came to weigh more and more heavily on
minority publications.[24] In 1911, Congress widened the definition of what the postmaster general might exclude from the mails by amending postal legislation to
include "matter of a character tending to incite arson, murder or assassination"
within the meaning of "indecent."[25] During the World War, under the Espionage
Acts of 1917 and 1918, authorities "often shut their eyes to slips or deliberate
violations on the part of powerful newspapers with orthodox political opinions and
exerted their powers over the unorthodox."[26]

After the War, "while still under the influence of 'war psychology,' a large number of states sought to curb the activities of radical political groups such as the I.
W. W. and communists by enacting the so-called peace-time criminal syndicalism
or sedition acts." These penalized "publications which tend to incite insurrection or
sedition or which advocate the subversion and destruction by force of the government of the state or of the United States or which 'encourage, incite, abet or promote' hostility to either government." One had to stick to the dispassionate
advocacy of change by what are called "lawful means."[27] These laws render illegal,

of course, certain passages in the Declaration of Independence and such statements as the following by Abraham Lincoln[28] in his first inaugural address:

> This country, with its institutions, belongs to the people who inhabit it. Whenever they shall grow weary of the existing Government, they can exercise their constitutional right of amending it or their revolutionary right to dismember or overthrow it.

Against such repressive legislation an exponent of liberalism[29] cried, little heeded:

> There should be no legislation against sedition and anarchy. We must legislate and enforce the laws against the use of force, but protect ourselves against bad thinking and speaking by the strength of argument and a confidence in American common sense and American institutions, including that most characteristic of all, which stands at the head of the Bill of Rights, freedom of thought.

These laws, the constitutionality of which has been upheld,[30] do not, after all, affect the members of the American Newspaper Publishers' Association or those of the state and sectional publishers' bodies. The time of violent clashes over fundamental politico-economic issues between papers of general circulation has, at least temporarily, passed. Prof. Zechariah Chafee, Jr.,[31] of the Harvard Law School, however, makes this highly cogent comment on this tendency:

> It is one of the unfortunate results of governmental action against freedom of speech that the persons who retain sufficient courage to come into conflict with the law are often of a heedless and aggressive character, which makes them unattractive and devoid of a personal appeal. Too often we assume that such persistent trouble-makers are the only persons injured by a censorship or a sedition law, and conclude from the indiscreet and unreasonable qualities of their speech and writing that after all the loss to the world of thought has been very slight. Too often we forget the multitude of cautious and sensitive men, men with wives and children dependent upon them, men who abhor publicity, who prefer to keep silent in the hope of better days. We cannot know what is lost through the effect upon them of repression, for it is simply left unsaid.

All who are convinced of the societal utility of freedom of thought and speech owe Professor Chafee a debt of gratitude for that clear statement of the crux of the matter as well as for the rest of his great book entitled *Freedom of Speech*.

The instances of violation of press freedom, then, are a vast series of events, a vast number of largely unplanned actions, expedient to the individuals involved within the limits of their foresight. In selecting between alternatives, neither publishers nor their employees apply tests beyond the immediate factors—the so-called "selfish" factors—involved. To ask a publisher whether or not he realizes that a contemplated merger is probably a step toward precipitating the limitation of press freedom through stabilizing his policies would be to invite ridicule. The publisher would talk about his vested interests, his property rights, the fact that he has to "meet payrolls," and academic idealism. The publisher *knows* that he will make more money if he makes his venture less subject to competition. He *knows* that he represents and will continue to Fight for the Best Interests of The People. He can trust The People, he believes, to listen to Reason. The People appreciate the Rights they assured to themselves in The Constitution of the United States. He would not care to mention in this connection, of course, the Declaration of Independence, an incendiary document at best. To ask a trade union member whether or not he realizes that he is aiding and abetting the same tendency toward greater rigidity when he raises the costs of production in a marginal shop, a shop that depends upon "operating efficiencies" to exist, is also to invite derision. A worker, he would reply, has to look after "Number One." The vagaries of long-time industrial and societal trends are beyond his as well as his publisher's mental horizon.

This brings our discussion to the second question asked above: Who have the chief culprits been in the limitation of press freedom? To this, the social scientists and social historians can make but one answer: No one in particular and yet everyone. The blind forces of society and not appreciably the creative urge of a few great editors and publishers have molded the course of the daily newspaper industry. It is scientifically naïve, therefore, to hold up individuals either to praise or to scorn on this count. The greatest newspaper leaders—Bennett, Sr., Greeley, Dana, Pulitzer, Scripps, Brearley, Broun, McCormick and the rest—have served as implements of society and particularly of the societal groups and classes they represented both in the extension of and in the limitation of Freedom of the press and press freedom.

In view of these considerations, what steps can be taken to protect press freedom in the future? To this question, as all objective students of the press well know, no cure-all answer can be offered. To combat economic restrictions with legalistic restrictions would merely multiply our ills. On this point, it is easy to agree with Colonel McCormick[32] when he says,

Men who are given dictatorial powers invariably become tyrants, with the tyrannical conviction that they are heaven-sent, that what they do is divinely inspired, and that dissent is treason.

This statement, intended for politicians, applies in the economic realm as well as in the political.

Two definite steps may be taken, I believe, to protect in the future what press freedom we have and to aid in developing more. In both of these, journalism teachers can be particularly serviceable. These are in the fields first of research and second of instruction. Journalism teachers can boldly and objectively test the premises and theories of journalism in the light of verified observations, carefully and impartially gathered. From their fairly detached positions on university campuses, they can analyze the practices of working newspaper men for the purpose of advocating useful methods and advising the rejection of outworn ones. Journalism teachers have made many excellent studies of this sort, but many more are needed. On the basis of these candid analyses of the industry's practices, then, journalism teachers can do an ever more efficient job of producing level-headed, curious-minded apprentices for the industry, young men who have a far greater respect for facts than for theories, for societal necessities than for short-range personal expedients. It has been asserted that journalism teachers cannot produce William Allen Whites, Joseph Medill Pattersons, and J. David Sterns. Possibly not. That job depends to a large extent upon parents. But journalism teachers can certainly help to grow them.

Notes

1. *The Writings of Thomas Jefferson*, ed. by P. L. Ford, IV (New York: G. P. Putnam's Sons, 1894), 186, quoting a letter to John Jay, dated at Paris, January 25, 1786.

2. Quoted in *Editor & Publisher*, Vol. 70, No. 50 (December 11, 1937), Sec. 1, p. 9. The quotation given is part of a formula that he has repeated many, many times. It is his definition of the rôle of the newspaper, *Cf.* his *What Is a Newspaper* (Chicago: The Tribune Company, 1924), p. 32, and his *The Newspaper* (Chicago: The Tribune Company, 1932), p. 15.

3. R. R. McCormick, *How Stands the Constitution!* (Chicago: The Tribune Company, 1934), p. 10.

4. "Gompers v. United States," *United States Reports*, Vol. 233 (1914), p. 610.

5. "New York Trust Company *et. al.*, as Executors of Purdy, v. Eisner," *United States Reports*, Vol. 256 (1921), p. 349.

6. A. G. Keller, *Societal Evolution* (2nd ed.; New York: The Macmillan Company, 1931), pp. 168–9.

7. See A. M. Lee, "Freedom of the Press: Services of a Catch Phrase," in *Studies in the Science of Society*, ed. by G. P. Murdock (New Haven: Yale University Press, 1937), pp. 355–75.

8. *The Writings of Thomas Jefferson*, ed. by H. A. Washington, V. (Washington: Taylor & Maury, 1853), 291, quoting a letter to A. Gallatin, dated at Monticello, May 20, 1808.

9. Throughout this paper, a differentiation is made between the shifting doctrine labeled by the catch phrase, Freedom of the Press, and the phenomenon described by the expression, "press freedom." The latter refers to the comparative ability of special interest groups—of the spokesmen for societal classes and for the less extensive societal groupings—to present their views in print.

10. *The Writings of Thomas Jefferson*, ed. by Ford, I (1892), 49: written in 1821.

11. *The Writing of Thomas Jefferson*, ed. by Washington, IX (1854), 319.

12. *The Writings of Thomas Jefferson*, ed. by Ford, IV (1894), 186, quoting a letter to John Jay, dated at Paris, January 25, 1786.

13. R. R. McCormick, *The Freedom of the Press Still Furnishes That Check Upon Government Which No Constitution Has Ever Been Able to Provide* (Chicago: The Tribune Company, 1934), pp. 33–4.

14. For a description of the manner in which publication conditions "unreasonably raise the cost of production," see A. M. Lee, *The Daily Newspaper in America* (New York: The Macmillan Company, 1937), Chaps. V and VII in particular; for a reply to McCormick's second point, see *ibid.*, esp. Chaps. IX and X; and for a reply to his third point, see *ibid.*, esp. Chaps. XIII and XIV, also those two excellent recent books: R. W. Desmond, *The Press and World Affairs* (New York: D. Appleton-Century Company, 1937), and L. C. Rosten, *The Washington Correspondents* (New York: Harcourt, Brace and Company, 1937).

15. *How Stands the Constitution!*, p. 10.

16. Quoted in "Maybe Press Needs 'Publicity Agent,' " *The Bulletin of the American Society of Newspaper Editors*, No. 132 (October 15, 1936), p. 1.

17. Quoted in *Editor & Publisher*, Vol. 57, No. 3 (June 14, 1924), p. 3.

18. See esp. Oliver Carlson and E. S. Bates, *Hearst: Lord of San Simeon* (New York: Viking Press, 1936), and Ferdinand Lundberg, *Imperial Hearst* (New York: Equinox Cooperative Press, 1936).

19. Quoted in *Editor & Publisher*, Vol. 57, No. 3 (June 14, 1924), p. 3.

20. The 1937 figure was tabulated from the list in *Editor & Publisher*, Vol. 71. No. 5 (January 29, 1938). Sec. 2, pp. 16–115. Earlier figures from M. M. Willey and S. A. Rice, *Communication Agencies and Social Life* (New York, McGraw-Hill Book Company, 1933), p. 164; compiled by W. C. Masche from N. W. Ayer and Son's directories dated 1900, 1910, 1920, and 1930 but more comparable with other data for each year preceding.

21. Tabulated from lists in *Editor & Publisher*, Vol. 70, No. 5 (January 30, 1937), Sec. 2, pp. 16–114, and Vol. 71, No. 5 (January 29, 1938), Sec. 2, pp. 16–115. These lists, said to include only English-language dailies of general circulation, nevertheless contain some business and a few other special-interest dailies.

22. See Lee, *The Daily Newspaper*, pp. 666–99.

23. *Ibid.*, pp. 240–50, Chap. XIV, etc.

24. *Ibid.*, Chaps. IX, XII, XVII.

25. *United States Compiled Statutes* (St. Paul: West Publishing Co., 1918), Sec. 10381: Criminal Code, Sec. 211, as amended March 4, 1911. This provision has been used to sanction the withdrawal of postal privileges from a half-dozen publications, including the New York *Call*, a Socialist daily, especially during the World War.

26. Will Irwin, *Propaganda and the News* (New York: McGraw-Hill Book Company, 1936), p. 184.

27. F. S. Siebert, *The Rights and Privileges of the Press* (New York: D. Appleton-Century Company, 1934), pp. 270–1. On p. 271, this author cites thirty-four such state and territorial laws, mostly enacted in 1919.

28. *A Compilation of the Messages and Papers of the Presidents*, VI (Washington: James D. Richardson, 1897), 10.

29. Zechariah Chafee, Jr., *Freedom of Speech* (New York: Harcourt, Brace and Howe, 1920), p. 228.

30. Siebert, *op. cit.*, p. 271.

31. *Op. cit.*, p. 294.

32. *The Freedom of the Press Still Furnishes That Check Upon Government Which No Constitution Has Ever Been Able to Provide*, p. 31.

W.E.B. DU BOIS

On the Collection of Honest News
(1953)

Our first line of duty today is simple. It is to know and evaluate the facts about the present situation in the world. Or, in other words, to collect and distribute the news and to keep open a free platform for discussion. There was a time when such a program was axiomatic. But we should realize that this is not true today. In the collection of the news of the world, of our own city and nation and of foreign lands, facts are often omitted, distorted or actually invented. Opinions are regularly suppressed or misrepresented. And this, we must remember, is not simply by mistake. It is often done deliberately and scientifically.

We all know this to a certain extent, and yet few of us fully realize the sinister possibilities of this method of newspaper publishing and periodical making. If we do not realize what is taking place, if we supinely or negligently submit to this kind of literature and information, we are not simply deceived but are courting disaster. We may easily be led unprotesting into misunderstanding, hate and war. We may ruin civilization because we did not know the truth and were willing slaves.

If the wrong in this case is clear and easily understood, the remedy also is simple. But it is so simple as to seem relatively unimportant. We could change the face of the world today without disaster or upheaval, if we simply insisted on the accuracy of the news collected for us, upon its wide distribution or easy availability to the mass of men; and if we realized that in order to accomplish this we have simply to be willing to pay for the collection of facts, on receiving no news service as a gift, on trusting no newspaper or periodicals whose bills are paid by persons not interested in the dissemination of the truth but interested in having readers believe something that owners want believed and the truth of which is unimportant to the very persons who pretend to collect and distribute the news.

To overturn this system what the individual has to do is a simple thing. He must

From *Newspaper Columns by W.E.B. Du Bois*, compiled and edited by Herbert Aptheker, vol. 2, *1945–1961* (White Plains, NY: Kraus-Thomson Organization Limited, 1986), 907–8. Originally published in the *National Guardian*, January 29, 1953.

buy and adequately pay for honest collection of facts and their interpretation by experts and scholars. This is not nearly as costly as it sounds. Huge sums are certainly spent on news collection now because men are not trying to collect facts, and lies are costly. It would be possible—it is possible—to have a newspaper like the *NATIONAL GUARDIAN* which collects facts and interprets them through the medium of honest men and women.

But this service has got to be paid for. Its workers have got to have social security, and therefore the paper must have a broad circulation, a subscription list which covers the nation, to compete with their competitors whose expenses are paid by department stores and drug companies. The securing of such a circulation is not a matter of pastime, and a little spare change. It is a matter of the same deliberate care and budgeting on the part of the citizen that he applies to his grocery bill, to the repairs on his house, and the clothing and education of his children.

The time of those persons who are conducting the *GUARDIAN* should not be wasted in seeing that their bills are paid and their salaries kept up-to-date or even to preparing delightful occasions like this Fourth Anniversary get-together. But they should put their whole time and thought into the arduous duty of collecting the facts of human thought and action the world over, and of using science and knowledge for its proper and complete interpretation.

This attitude of determination; this stern refusal to be misled by pictures, false reputations and cunning phrases, can do more than a thousand peace rallies to make peace possible. It will do more than millions of chance bits of literature to restore sanity to our thought and to make this world again a place where human beings can act and think and live without being covered by a pall of fear and continually distracted by shrieks of hysterics.

The *NATIONAL GUARDIAN* consists of eight closely-packed, ingeniously selected and thoughtfully-written pages. In contrast, the average New York Sunday paper is a vast bundle of pounds of advertisements enmeshed in a mass of propaganda, and wrapped in a rag bag of entertainment, distraction and escapism, written by every kind of person from scientist to well-known liar—all calculated to make upon the reader the impression which the owners of this vast economic organization want made on the people of the U.S. and the world. What we ask is not the suppression of such monstrosities as our Sunday papers, not to mention our evening tabloids and morning prophets; but we do plead for a few pages of real facts and honestly interpreted truth, to give at least to the intelligent part of the U.S. that correct picture of the world which the *GUARDIAN* can do. And to spread this over 12 pages each week instead of only eight.

This is not much to ask for a great purpose.

On the Right to Express and Hear
Unpopular Opinion
(1953)

Quite honestly, I would like to know the inner working of the minds of what we call the "average American." Let us assume that he is neither a Communist nor a member of the U.S. Chamber of Commerce; that he is just an ordinary citizen who wants to earn enough to live decently, educate his children and provide something for his old age. He is confronted today by a number of serious questions which as citizen, taxpayer and voter he must help decide. There is first and foremost the question of war, then the question of civil rights, the right to vote and the right to work.

Now in order to decide these questions he must know facts; and for the facts he depends on the newspapers, the radio, public meetings, and general gossip. The last, of course, he does not rate highly, but it may have more influence than he realizes.

His chief dependence is upon the newspaper; and lately he is quite aware that in collecting facts, omitting information and slanting interpretation, most of the newspapers he reads are not giving him the full and fair picture of the world. Their reports need not necessarily be altogether wrong, but they certainly are not complete.

The Other Side

Now I have been brought up with the idea that in any controversy or question I should, as a matter of duty, read the other side; that is, read the newspaper with whose general attitude I do not agree, and listen to the speaker whose position on

From *Newspaper Columns by W.E.B. Du Bois*, compiled and edited by Herbert Aptheker, vol. 2, *1945–1961* (White Plains, NY: Kraus-Thomson Organization Limited, 1986), 918–19. Originally published in the *National Guardian*, May 25, 1953.

the whole I believe is wrong. That I must do this is because otherwise I may possibly, and even probably, get a one-sided view of the facts—or at any rate not know and not give due weight to certain facts which I do not know or have not considered.

I have been taught to believe and have convinced myself therefore that any system of spreading information, in any country which denies the intelligent citizen and voter certain facts or groups of facts, is fundamentally and dangerously wrong. Yet it is just this situation that I see developing in the U.S. today.

The facts which the ruling powers of this country want known can easily be learned. There is no way of escaping their revelation and repeated statement by most of the newspapers. On the other hand, certain groups of facts, particularly concerning socialism and communism, concerning Eastern Europe, the Middle East, Asia and Africa, are not easily obtained nor fully reported. For additional facts and dissident opinions the intelligent reader must depend upon newspapers like the *Guardian*, the *Daily Worker*, the *People's World*, the defunct *PM* and *Compass*.

Slavery of the Mind

It is not a question as to whether these facts and opinions are right or wrong, true or false. It is the more basic question as to who is going to be the judge of this, and as to how far honest people can remain intelligent if they refuse to listen to unpopular opinions or to facts which they do not want to believe.

There is a determined effort today to put papers like these out of existence, to harass and harry them, to make readers afraid to subscribe to them or to buy them on news stands; to keep newspaper distributors from handling them; and in these and other ways to make their continued existence impossible. Quite outside of all questions as to what is true or false, as to what our aims or ideals should be, this program seems to me the most vicious and indefensible attack upon the fundamentals of American democracy that can be imagined. It makes impartial judgment impossible. It is precisely the kind of procedure that made reasonable opposition to Negro slavery find voice only in civil war.

Fight or Be Shamed

It should be the duty of every honest citizen, whether he be reactionary or radical, rich or poor, capitalist or laborer, to fight this attack on the freedom of the press in every way possible; because unless this is done we are headed toward an intellectual dark age of which all of our descendants, physical and spiritual, will be thoroughly ashamed and will ask what on earth we who live today were thinking of when we permitted this program to triumph!

I would like, then, quite honestly to know what the average American citizen really thinks of the present inquisition into men's thoughts and into their right to seek information where they will.

C. WRIGHT MILLS

The Mass Society
(1956)

In the standard image of power and decision, no force is held to be as important as The Great American Public. More than merely another check and balance, this public is thought to be the seat of all legitimate power. In official life as in popular folklore, it is held to be the very balance wheel of democratic power. In the end, all liberal theorists rest their notions of the power system upon the political role of this public; all official decisions, as well as private decisions of consequence, are justified as in the public's welfare; all formal proclamations are in its name.

1

Let us therefore consider the classic public of democratic theory in the generous spirit in which Rousseau once cried, 'Opinion, Queen of the World, is not subject to the power of kings; they are themselves its first slaves.'

The most important feature of the public of opinion, which the rise of the democratic middle class initiates, is the free ebb and flow of discussion. The possibilities of answering back, of organizing autonomous organs of public opinion, of realizing opinion in action, are held to be established by democratic institutions. The opinion that results from public discussion is understood to be a resolution that is then carried out by public action; it is, in one version, the 'general will' of the people, which the legislative organ enacts into law, thus lending to it legal force. Congress, or Parliament, as an institution, crowns all the scattered publics; it is the archetype for each of the little circles of face-to-face citizens discussing their public business.

This eighteenth-century idea of the public of public opinion parallels the economic idea of the market of the free economy. Here is the market composed of freely competing entrepreneurs; there is the public composed of discussion circles of opinion peers. As price is the result of anonymous, equally weighted, bargaining

From *The Power Elite* (New York: Oxford University Press, 1956), 298–324.

individuals, so public opinion is the result of each man's having thought things out for himself and contributing his voice to the great chorus. To be sure, some might have more influence on the state of opinion than others, but no one group monopolizes the discussion, or by itself determines the opinions that prevail.

Innumerable discussion circles are knit together by mobile people who carry opinions from one to another, and struggle for the power of larger command. The public is thus organized into associations and parties, each representing a set of viewpoints, each trying to acquire a place in the Congress, where the discussion continues. Out of the little circles of people talking with one another, the larger forces of social movements and political parties develop; and the discussion of opinion is the important phase in a total act by which public affairs are conducted.

The autonomy of these discussions is an important element in the idea of public opinion as a democratic legitimation. The opinions formed are actively realized within the prevailing institutions of power; all authoritative agents are made or broken by the prevailing opinions of these publics. And, in so far as the public is frustrated in realizing its demands, its members may go beyond criticism of specific policies; they may question the very legitimations of legal authority. That is one meaning of Jefferson's comment on the need for an occasional 'revolution.'

The public, so conceived, is the loom of classic, eighteenth-century democracy; discussion is at once the threads and the shuttle tying the discussion circles together. It lies at the root of the conception of authority by discussion, and it is based upon the hope that truth and justice will somehow come out of society as a great apparatus of free discussion. The people are presented with problems. They discuss them. They decide on them. They formulate viewpoints. These viewpoints are organized, and they compete. One viewpoint 'wins out.' Then the people act out this view, or their representatives are instructed to act it out, and this they promptly do.

Such are the images of the public of classic democracy which are still used as the working justifications of power in American society. But now we must recognize this description as a set of images out of a fairy tale: they are not adequate even as an approximate model of how the American system of power works. The issues that now shape man's fate are neither raised nor decided by the public at large. The idea of the community of publics is not a description of fact, but an assertion of an ideal, an assertion of a legitimation masquerading—as legitimations are now apt to do—as fact. For now the public of public opinion is recognized by all those who have considered it carefully as something less than it once was.

These doubts are asserted positively in the statement that the classic community of publics is being transformed into a society of masses. This transformation, in fact, is one of the keys to the social and psychological meaning of modern life in America.

I. In the democratic society of publics it was assumed, with John Locke, that the individual conscience was the ultimate seat of judgment and hence the final court of appeal. But this principle was challenged—as E. H. Carr has put it—when Rousseau 'for the first time thought in terms of the sovereignty of the whole people, and faced the issue of mass democracy.'[1]

II. In the democratic society of publics it was assumed that among the individuals who composed it there was a natural and peaceful harmony of interests. But this essentially conservative doctrine gave way to the Utilitarian doctrine that such a harmony of interests had first to be created by reform before it could work, and later to the Marxian doctrine of class struggle, which surely was then, and certainly is now, closer to reality than any assumed harmony of interests.

III. In the democratic society of publics it was assumed that before public action would be taken, there would be rational discussion between individuals which would determine the action, and that, accordingly, the public opinion that resulted would be the infallible voice of reason. But this has been challenged not only (1) by the assumed need for experts to decide delicate and intricate issues, but (2) by the discovery—as by Freud—of the irrationality of the man in the street, and (3) by the discovery—as by Marx—of the socially conditioned nature of what was once assumed to be autonomous reason.

IV. In the democratic society of publics it was assumed that after determining what is true and right and just, the public would act accordingly or see that its representatives did so. In the long run, public opinion will not only be right, but public opinion will prevail. This assumption has been upset by the great gap now existing between the underlying population and those who make decisions in its name, decisions of enormous consequence which the public often does not even know are being made until well after the fact.

Given these assumptions, it is not difficult to understand the articulate optimism of many nineteenth-century thinkers, for the theory of the public is, in many ways, a projection upon the community at large of the intellectual's ideal of the supremacy of intellect. The 'evolution of the intellect,' Comte asserted, 'determines the main course of social evolution.' If looking about them, nineteenth-century thinkers still saw irrationality and ignorance and apathy, all that was merely an intellectual lag, to which the spread of education would soon put an end.

How much the cogency of the classic view of the public rested upon a restriction of this public to the carefully educated is revealed by the fact that by 1859 even John Stuart Mill was writing of 'the tyranny of the majority,' and both Tocqueville and Burckhardt anticipated the view popularized in the recent past by such political moralists as Ortega y Gasset. In a word, the transformation of public into mass—and all that this implies—has been at once one of the major trends of modern societies and one of the major factors in the collapse of that liberal optimism which determined so much of the intellectual mood of the nineteenth century.

By the middle of that century: individualism had begun to be replaced by collective forms of economic and political life; harmony of interests by inharmonious struggle of classes and organized pressures; rational discussions undermined by expert decisions on complicated issues, by recognition of the interested bias of argument by vested position; and by the discovery of the effectiveness of irrational appeal to the citizen. Moreover, certain structural changes of modern society, which we shall presently consider, had begun to cut off the public from the power of active decision.

2

The transformation of public into mass is of particular concern to us, for it provides an important clue to the meaning of the power elite. If that elite is truly responsible to, or even exists in connection with, a community of publics, it carries a very different meaning than if such a public is being transformed into a society of masses.

The United States today is not altogether a mass society, and it has never been altogether a community of publics. These phrases are names for extreme types; they point to certain features of reality, but they are themselves constructions; social reality is always some sort of mixture of the two. Yet we cannot readily understand just how much of which is mixed into our situation if we do not first understand, in terms of explicit dimensions, the clear-cut and extreme types:

At least four dimensions must be attended to if we are to grasp the differences between public and mass.

I. There is first, the ratio of the givers of opinion to the receivers, which is the simplest way to state the social meaning of the formal media of mass communication. More than anything else, it is the shift in this ratio which is central to the problems of the public and of public opinion in latter-day phases of democracy. At one extreme on the scale of communication, two people talk personally with each other; at the opposite extreme, one spokesman talks impersonally through a network of communications to millions of listeners and viewers. In between these extremes there are assemblages and political rallies, parliamentary sessions, law-court debates, small discussion circles dominated by one man, open discussion circles with talk moving freely back and forth among fifty people, and so on.

II. The second dimension to which we must pay attention is the possibility of answering back an opinion without internal or external reprisals being taken. Technical conditions of the means of communication, in imposing a lower ratio of speakers to listeners, may obviate the possibility of freely answering back. Informal rules, resting upon conventional sanction and upon the informal structure of opinion leadership, may govern who can speak, when, and for how long. Such rules may or may not be in congruence with formal rules and with institutional sanctions which govern the process of communication. In the extreme case, we may conceive of an absolute monopoly of communication to pacified media groups whose members cannot answer back even 'in private.' At the opposite extreme, the conditions may allow and the rules may uphold the wide and symmetrical formation of opinion.

iii. We must also consider the relation of the formation of opinion to its realization in social action, the ease with which opinion is effective in the shaping of decisions of powerful consequence. This opportunity for people to act out their opinions collectively is of course limited by their position in the structure of power. This structure may be such as to limit decisively this capacity, or it may allow or even invite such action. It may confine social action to local areas or it may enlarge the area of opportunity; it may make action intermittent or more or less continuous.

iv. There is, finally, the degree to which institutional authority, with its sanctions and controls, penetrates the public. Here the problem is the degree to which the public has genuine autonomy from instituted authority. At one extreme, no agent of formal authority moves among the autonomous public. At the opposite extreme, the public is terrorized into uniformity by the infiltration of informers and the universalization of suspicion. One thinks of the late Nazi street-and-block-system, the eighteenth-century Japanese kumi, the Soviet cell structure. In the extreme, the formal structure of power coincides, as it were, with the informal ebb and flow of influence by discussion, which is thus killed off.

By combining these several points, we can construct little models or diagrams of several types of societies. Since 'the problem of public opinion' as we know it is set by the eclipse of the classic bourgeois public, we are here concerned with only two types: public and mass.

In a *public*, as we may understand the term, (1) virtually as many people express opinions as receive them. (2) Public communications are so organized that there is a chance immediately and effectively to answer back any opinion expressed in public. Opinion formed by such discussion (3) readily finds an outlet in effective action, even against—if necessary—the prevailing system of authority. And (4) authoritative institutions do not penetrate the public, which is thus more or less autonomous in its operations. When these conditions prevail, we have the working model of a community of publics, and this model fits closely the several assumptions of classic democratic theory.

At the opposite extreme, in a *mass*, (1) far fewer people express opinions than receive them; for the community of publics becomes an abstract collection of individuals who receive impressions from the mass media. (2) The communications that prevail are so organized that it is difficult or impossible for the individual to answer back immediately or with any effect. (3) The realization of opinion in action is controlled by authorities who organize and control the channels of such action. (4) The mass has no autonomy from institutions; on the contrary, agents of authorized institutions penetrate this mass, reducing any autonomy it may have in the formation of opinion by discussion.

The public and the mass may be most readily distinguished by their dominant modes of communication: in a community of publics, discussion is the ascendant means of communication, and the mass media, if they exist, simply enlarge and animate discussion, linking one *primary public* with the discussions of another. In a mass society, the dominant type of communication is the formal media, and the publics become mere *media markets*: all those exposed to the contents of given mass media.

3

From almost any angle of vision that we might assume, when we look upon the public, we realize that we have moved a considerable distance along the road to the mass society. At the end of that road there is totalitarianism, as in Nazi Germany or in Communist Russia. We are not yet at that end. In the United States today, media markets are not entirely ascendant over primary publics. But surely we can see that many aspects of the public life of our times are more the features of a mass society than of a community of publics.

What is happening might again be stated in terms of the historical parallel between the economic market and the public of public opinion. In brief, there is a movement from widely scattered little powers to concentrated powers and the attempt at monopoly control from powerful centers, which, being partially hidden, are centers of manipulation as well as of authority. The small shop serving the neighborhood is replaced by the anonymity of the national corporation: mass advertisement replaces the personal influence of opinion between merchant and customer. The political leader hooks up his speech to a national network and speaks, with appropriate personal touches, to a million people he never saw and never will see. Entire brackets of professions and industries are in the 'opinion business,' impersonally manipulating the public for hire.

In the primary public the competition of opinions goes on between people holding views in the service of their interests and their reasoning. But in the mass society of media markets, competition, if any, goes on between the manipulators with their mass media on the one hand, and the people receiving their propaganda on the other.

Under such conditions, it is not surprising that there should arise a conception of public opinion as a mere reaction—we cannot say 'response'—to the content of the mass media. In this view, the public is merely the collectivity of individuals each rather passively exposed to the mass media and rather helplessly opened up to the suggestions and manipulations that flow from these media. The fact of manipulation from centralized points of control constitutes, as it were, an expropriation of the old multitude of little opinion producers and consumers operating in a free and balanced market.

In official circles, the very term itself, 'the public'—as Walter Lippmann noted thirty years ago—has come to have a phantom meaning, which dramatically reveals its eclipse. From the standpoint of the deciding elite, some of those who clamor publicly can be identified as 'Labor,' others as 'Business,' still others as 'Farmer.' Those who can *not* readily be so identified make up 'The Public.' In this usage, the public is composed of the unidentified and the non-partisan in a world of defined and partisan interests. It is socially composed of well-educated salaried professionals, especially college professors; of non-unionized employees, especially white-collar people, along with self-employed professionals and small businessmen.

In this faint echo of the classic notion, the public consists of those remnants of the middle classes, old and new, whose interests are not explicitly defined, organized, or clamorous. In a curious adaptation, 'the public' often becomes, in fact, 'the unattached expert,' who, although well informed, has never taken a clear-cut, public stand on controversial issues which are brought to a focus by organized interests. These are the 'public' members of the board, the commission, the committee. What the public stands for, accordingly, is often a vagueness of policy (called open-mindedness), a lack of involvement in public affairs (known as reasonable-ness), and a professional disinterest (known as tolerance).

Some such official members of the public, as in the field of labor-management mediation, start out very young and make a career out of being careful to be informed but never taking a strong position; and there are many others, quite unofficial, who take such professionals as a sort of model. The only trouble is that they are acting as if they were disinterested judges but they do not have the power of judges; hence their reasonableness, their tolerance, and their open-mindedness do not often count for much in the shaping of human affairs.

4

All those trends that make for the decline of the politician and of his balancing society bear decisively upon the transformation of public into mass.* One of the most important of the structural transformations involved is the decline of the voluntary association as a genuine instrument of the public. As we have already seen, the executive ascendancy in economic, military, and political institutions has lowered the effective use of all those voluntary associations which operate between the state and the economy on the one hand, and the family and the individual in the primary group on the other. It is not only that institutions of power have become large-scale and inaccessibly centralized; they have at the same time become

*See, especially, the analysis of the decline of the independent middle classes, ELEVEN: The Theory of Balance.

less political and more administrative, and it is within this great change of frame-work that the organized public has waned.

In terms of *scale*, the transformation of public into mass has been underpinned by the shift from a political public decisively restricted in size (by property and education, as well as by sex and age) to a greatly enlarged mass having only the qualifications of citizenship and age.

In terms of *organization*, the transformation has been underpinned by the shift from the individual and his primary community to the voluntary association and the mass party as the major units of organized power.

Voluntary associations have become larger to the extent that they have become effective; and to just that extend they have become inaccessible to the individual who would shape by discussion the policies of the organization to which he be-longs. Accordingly, along with older institutions, these voluntary associations have lost their grip on the individual. As more people are drawn into the political arena, these associations become mass in scale; and as the power of the individual becomes more dependent upon such mass associations, they are less accessible to the indi-vidual's influence.*

Mass democracy means the struggle of powerful and large-scale interest groups and associations, which stand between the big decisions that are made by state, corporation, army, and the will of the individual citizen as a member of the public. Since these middle-level associations are the citizen's major link with decision, his relation to them is of decisive importance. For it is only through them that he exercises such power as he may have.

The gap between the members and the leaders of the mass association is becom-ing increasingly wider. As soon as a man gets to be a leader of an association large enough to count he readily becomes lost as an instrument of that association. He does so (1) in the interest of maintaining his leading position in, or rather over, his mass association, and he does so (2) because he comes to see himself not as a mere delegate, instructed or not, of the mass association he represents, but as a member of 'an elite' composed of such men as himself. These facts, in turn, lead to (3) the big gap between the terms in which issues are debated and resolved among members of this elite, and the terms in which they are presented to the members of the various mass associations. For the decisions that are made must *take into account* those who are important—other elites—but they must be *sold* to the mass memberships.

The gap between speaker and listener, between power and public, leads less to any iron law of oligarchy than to the law of spokesmanship: as the pressure group

---

*At the same time—and also because of the metropolitan segregation and distrac-tion, which I shall discuss in a moment—the individual becomes more dependent upon the means of mass communication for his view of the structure as a whole.

expands, its leaders come to organize the opinions they 'represent.' So elections, as we have seen, become contests between two giant and unwieldy parties, neither of which the individual can truly feel that he influences, and neither of which is capable of winning psychologically impressive or politically decisive majorities. And, in all this, the parties are of the same general form as other mass associations.[2]

When we say that man in the mass is without any sense of political belonging, we have in mind a political fact rather than merely a style of feeling. We have in mind (I.) a certain way of belonging (II.) to a certain kind of organization.

I. The way of belonging here implied rests upon a belief in the purposes and in the leaders of an organization, and thus enables men and women freely to be at home within it. To belong in this way is to make the human association a psychological center of one's self, to take into our conscience, deliberately and freely, its rules of conduct and its purposes, which we thus shape and which in turn shape us. We do not have this kind of belonging to any political organization.

II. The kind of organization we have in mind is a voluntary association which has three decisive characteristics: first, it is a context in which reasonable opinions may be formulated; second, it is an agency by which reasonable activities may be undertaken; and third, it is a powerful enough unit, in comparison with other organizations of power, to make a difference.

It is because they do not find available associations at once psychologically meaningful and historically effective that men often feel uneasy in their political and economic loyalties. The effective units of power are now the huge corporation, the inaccessible government, the grim military establishment. Between these, on the one hand, and the family and the small community on the other, we find no intermediate associations in which men feel secure and with which they feel powerful. There is little live political struggle. Instead, there is administration from above, and the political vacuum below. The primary publics are now either so small as to be swamped, and hence give up; or so large as to be merely another feature of the generally distant structure of power, and hence inaccessible.

Public opinion exists when people who are not in the government of a country claim the right to express political opinions freely and publicly, and the right that these opinions should influence or determine the policies, personnel, and actions of their government.[3] In this formal sense there has been and there is a definite public opinion in the United States. And yet, with modern developments this formal right—when it does still exist as a right—does not mean what it once did. The older world of voluntary organization was as different from the world of the mass organization, as was Tom Paine's world of pamphleteering from the world of the mass media.

Since the French Revolution, conservative thinkers have Viewed With Alarm the rise of the public, which they called the masses, or something to that effect. 'The populace is sovereign, and the tide of barbarism mounts,' wrote Gustave Le Bon. 'The divine right of the masses is about to replace the divine right of kings,' and already 'the destinies of nations are elaborated at present in the heart of the masses, and no longer in the councils of princes.'[4] During the twentieth century, liberal and even socialist thinkers have followed suit, with more explicit reference to what we have called the society of masses. From Le Bon to Emil Lederer and Ortega y Gasset, they have held that the influence of the mass in unfortunately increasing.

But surely those who have supposed the masses to be all powerful, or at least well on their way to triumph, are wrong. In our time, as Chakhotin knew, the influence of autonomous collectivities within political life is in fact diminishing.[5] Furthermore, such influence as they do have is guided; they must now be seen not as publics acting autonomously, but as masses manipulated at focal points into crowds of demonstrators. For as publics become masses, masses sometimes become crowds; and, in crowds, the psychical rape by the mass media is supplemented up-close by the harsh and sudden harangue. Then the people in the crowd disperse again—as atomized and submissive masses.

In all modern societies, the autonomous associations standing between the various classes and the state tend to lose their effectiveness as vehicles of reasoned opinion and instruments for the rational exertion of political will. Such associations can be deliberately broken up and thus turned into passive instruments of rule, or they can more slowly wither away from lack of use in the face of centralized means of power. But whether they are destroyed in a week, or wither in a generation, such associations are replaced in virtually every sphere of life by centralized organizations, and it is such organizations with all their new means of power that take charge of the terrorized or—as the case may be—merely intimidated, society of masses.

5

The institutional trends that make for a society of masses are to a considerable extent a matter of impersonal drift, but the remnants of the public are also exposed to more 'personal' and intentional forces. With the broadening of the base of politics within the context of a folk-lore of democratic decision-making, and with the increased means of mass persuasion that are available, the public to public opinion has become the object of intensive efforts to control, manage, manipulate, and increasingly intimidate.

In political, military, economic realms, power becomes, in varying degrees, uneasy before the suspected opinions of masses, and, accordingly, opinion-making becomes an accepted technique of power-holding and power-getting. The minority electorate of the propertied and the educated is replaced by the total suffrage—and intensive campaigns for the vote. The small eighteenth-century professional army is replaced by the mass army of conscripts—and by the problems of nationalist morale. The small shop is replaced by the mass-production industry—and the national advertisement.

As the scale of institutions has become larger and more centralized, so has the range and intensity of the opinion-makers' efforts. The means of opinion-making, in fact, have paralleled in range and efficiency the other institutions of greater scale that cradle the modern society of masses. Accordingly, in addition to their enlarged and centralized means of administration, exploitation, and violence, the modern elite have had placed within their grasp historically unique instrument of psychic management and manipulation, which include universal compulsory education as well as the media of mass communication.

Early observers believed that the increase in the range and volume of the formal means of communication would enlarge and animate the primary public. In such optimistic views—written before radio and television and movies—the formal media are understood as simply multiplying the scope and pace of personal discussion. Modern conditions, Charles Cooley wrote, 'enlarge indefinitely the competition of ideas, and whatever has owed its persistence merely to lack of comparison is likely to go, for that which is really congenial to the choosing mind will be all the more cherished and increased.'[6] Still excited by the break-up of the conventional consensus of the local community, he saw the new means of communication as furthering the conversational dynamic of classic democracy, and with it the growth of rational and free individuality.

No one really knows all the functions of the mass media, for in their entirety these functions are probably so pervasive and so subtle that they cannot be caught by the means of social research now available. But we do now have reason to believe that these media have helped less to enlarge and animate the discussions of primary publics than to transform them into a set of media markets in mass-like society. I do not refer merely to the higher ratio of deliverers of opinion to receivers and to the decreased chance to answer back; nor do I refer merely to the violent banalization and stereotyping of our very sense organs in terms of which these media now compete for 'attention.' I have in mind a sort of psychological illiteracy that is facilitated by the media, and that is expressed in several ways:

I. Very little of what we think we know of the social realities of the world have we found out first-hand. Most of 'the pictures in our heads' we have gained from these media—even to the point where we often do not really believe what we see before us until we read about it in the paper or hear about it on the radio.[7] The media not only give us information; they guide our very experiences. Our standards of credulity, our standards of reality, tend to be set by these media rather than by our own fragmentary experience.

Accordingly, even if the individual has direct, personal experience of events, it is not really direct and primary: it is organized in stereotypes. It takes long and skillful training to so uproot such stereotypes that an individual sees things freshly, in an unstereotyped manner. One might suppose, for example, that if all the people went through a depression they would all 'experience it,' and in terms of this experience, that they would all debunk or reject or at least refract what the media say about it. But experience of such a *structural* shift has to be organized and interpreted if it is to count in the making of opinion.

The kind of experience, in short, that might serve as a basis for resistance to mass media is not an experience of raw events, but the experience of meanings. The fleck of interpretation must be there in the experience if we are to use the word experience seriously. And the capacity for such experience is socially implanted. The individual does not trust his own experience, as I have said, until it is confirmed by others or by the media. Usually such direct exposure is not accepted if it disturbs loyalties and beliefs that the individual already holds. To be accepted, it must relieve or justify the feelings that often lie in the back of his mind as key features of his ideological loyalties.

Stereotypes of loyalty underlie beliefs and feelings about given symbols and emblems; they are the very ways in which men see the social world and in terms of which men make up their specific opinions and views of events. They are the results of previous experience, which affect present and future experience. It goes without saying that men are often unaware of these loyalties, that often they could not formulate them explicitly. Yet such general stereotypes make for the acceptance or the rejection of specific opinions not so much by the force of logical consistency as by their emotional affinity and by the way in which they relieve anxieties. To accept opinions in their terms is to gain the good solid feeling of being correct without having to think. When ideological stereotypes and specific opinions are linked in this way, there is a lowering of the kind of anxiety which arises when loyalty and belief are not in accord. Such ideologies lead to a willingness to accept a given line of belief; then there is no need, emotionally or rationally, to overcome resistance to given items in that line; cumulative selections of specific opinions and feelings become the pre-organized attitudes and emotions that shape the opinion-life of the person.

These deeper beliefs and feelings are a sort of lens through which men experience their worlds, they strongly condition acceptance or rejection of specific opinions, and they set men's orientation toward prevailing authorities. Three decades ago, Walter Lippmann saw such prior convictions as biases: they kept men from defining reality in an adequate way. They are still biases. But today they can often be seen as 'good biases'; inadequate and misleading as they often are, they are less so than the crackpot realism of the higher authorities and opinion-makers. They are the lower common sense and as such a factor of resistance. But we must recognize, especially when the pace of change is so deep and fast, that common sense is more often common than sense. And, above all, we must recognize that 'the common sense' of our children is going to be less the result of any firm social tradition than of the stereotypes carried by the mass media to which they are now so fully exposed. They are the first generation to be so exposed.

II. So long as the media are not entirely monopolized, the individual can play one medium off against another; he can compare them, and hence resist what any one of them puts out. The more genuine competition there is among the media, the more resistance the individual might be able to command. But how much is this now the case? *Do* people compare reports on public events or policies, playing one medium's content off against another's?

The answer is: generally no, very few do: (I) We know that people tend strongly to select those media which carry contents with which they already agree. There is a kind of selection of new opinions on the basis of prior opinions. No one seems to search out such counter-statements as may be found in alternative media offerings. Given radio programs and magazines and newspapers often get a rather consistent public, and thus reinforce their messages in the minds of that public. (2) This idea of playing one medium off against another assumes that the media really have varying contents. It assumes genuine competition, which is not widely true. The media display an apparent variety and competition, but on closer view they seem to compete more in terms of variations on a few standardized themes than of clashing issues. The freedom to raise issues effectively seems more and more to be confined to those few interests that have ready and continual access to these media.

III. The media have not only filtered into our experience of external realities, they have also entered into our very experience of our own selves. They have provided us with new identities and new aspirations of what we should like to be, and what we should like to appear to be. They have provided in the models of conduct they hold out to us a new and larger and more flexible set of appraisals of our very selves. In terms of the modern theory of the self,[8] we may say that the media bring the reader, listener, viewer into the sight of larger, higher reference groups—groups, real or imagined, up-close or vicarious, personally known or distractedly glimpsed—which are looking glasses for his self-image. They have multiplied the groups to which we look for confirmation of our self-image.

More than that: (1) the media tell the man in the mass who he is—they give him identity; (2) they tell him what he wants to be—they give him aspirations; (3) they tell him how to get that way—they give him technique; and (4) they tell him how to feel that he is that way even when he is not—they give him escape. The gaps between the identity and aspiration lead to technique and/or to escape. That is probably the basic psychological formula of the mass media today. But, as a formula, it is not attuned to the development of the human being. It is the formula of a pseudo-world which the media invent and sustain.

IV. As they now generally prevail, the mass media, especially television, often encroach upon the small-scale discussion, and destroy the chance for the reasonable and leisurely and human interchange of opinion. They are an important cause of the destruction of privacy in its full human meaning. That is an important reason why they not only fail as an educational force, but are a malign force: they do not articulate for the viewer or listener the broader sources of his private tensions and anxieties, his inarticulate resentments and half-formed hopes. They neither enable the individual to transcend his narrow milieu nor clarify its private meaning.

The media provide much information and news about what is happening in the world, but they do not often enable the listener or the viewer truly to connect his daily life with these larger realities. They do not connect the information they provide on public issues with the troubles felt by the individual. They do not increase rational insight into tensions, either those in the individual or those of the society which are reflected in the individual. On the contrary, they distract him and obscure his chance to understand himself or his world, by fastening his attention upon artificial frenzies that are resolved within the program framework, usually by violent action or by what is called humor. In short, for the viewer they are not really resolved at all. The chief distracting tension of the media is between the wanting and the not having of commodities or of women held to be good looking. There is almost always the general tone of animated distraction, of suspended agitation, but it is going nowhere and it has nowhere to go.

But the media, as now organized and operated, are even more than a major cause of the transformation of America into a mass society. They are also among the most important of those increased means of power now at the disposal of elites of wealth and power; moreover, some of the higher agents of these media are themselves either among the elites or very important among their servants.

Alongside or just below the elite, there is the propagandist, the publicity expert, the public-relations man, who would control the very formation of public opinion in order to be able to include it as one more pacified item in calculations of effective power, increased prestige, more secure wealth. Over the last quarter of a century, the attitudes of these manipulators toward their task have gone through a sort of dialectic:

In the beginning, there is great faith in what the mass media can do. Words win wars or sell soap; they move people, they restrain people. 'Only cost,' the advertising man of the 'twenties proclaims, 'limits the delivery of public opinion in any direction on any topic.'[9] The opinion-maker's belief in the media as mass persuaders almost amounts to magic—but he can believe mass communications omnipotent only so long as the public is trustful. It does not remain trustful. The mass media say so very many and such competitively exaggerated things; they banalize their message and they cancel one another out. The 'propaganda phobia,' in reaction to wartime lies and postwar disenchantment, does not help matters, even though memory is both short and subject to official distortion. This distrust of the magic of media is translated into a slogan among the opinion managers. Across their banners they write: 'Mass Persuasion Is Not Enough.'

Frustrated, they reason; and reasoning, they come to accept the principle of social context. To change opinion and activity, they say to one another, we must pay close attention to the full context and lives of the people to be managed. Along with mass persuasion, we must somehow use personal influence; we must reach people in their life context and *through* other people, their daily associates, those whom they trust: we must get at them by some kind of 'personal' persuasion. We must not show our hand directly; rather than merely advise or command, we must manipulate.

Now this live and immediate social context in which people live and which exerts a steady expectation upon them is of course what we have called the primary public. Anyone who has seen the inside of an advertising agency or public-relations office knows that the primary public is still the great unsolved problem of the opinion-makers. Negatively, their recognition of the influence of social context upon opinion and public activity implies that the articulate public resists and re-fracts the communications of the mass media. Positively, this recognition implies that the public is not composed of isolated individuals, but rather of persons who not only have prior opinions that must be reckoned with, but who continually influence each other in complex and intimate, in direct and continual ways.

In their attempts to neutralize or to turn to their own use the articulate public, the opinion-makers try to make it a relay network for their views. If the opinion-makers have so much power that they can act directly and openly upon the primary publics, they may become authoritative; but, if they do not have such power and hence have to operate indirectly and without visibility, they will assume the stance of manipulators.

Authority is power that is explicit and more or less 'voluntarily' obeyed; ma-nipulation is the 'secret' exercise of power, unknown to those who are influenced. In the model of the classic democratic society, manipulation is not a problem, be-cause formal authority resides in the public itself and in its representatives who are made or broken by the public. In the completely authoritarian society, manipula-tion is not a problem, because authority is openly identified with the ruling insti-tutions and their agents, who may use authority explicitly and nakedly. They do not, in the extreme case, have to gain or retain power by hiding its exercise.

Manipulation becomes a problem wherever men have power that is concen-trated and willful but do not have authority, or when, for any reason, they do not wish to use their power openly. Then the powerful seek to rule without showing their powerfulness. They want to rule, as it were, secretly, without publicized le-gitimation. It is in this mixed case—as in the intermediate reality of the American today—that manipulation is a prime way of exercising power. Small circles of men are making decisions which they need to have at least authorized by indifferent or recalcitrant people over whom they do not exercise explicit authority. So the small circle tries to manipulate these people into willing acceptance or cheerful support of their decisions or opinions—or at least to the rejection of possible counter-opinions.

Authority *formally* resides 'in the people,' but the power of initiation is in fact held by small circles of men. That is why the standard strategy of manipulation is to make it appear that the people, or at least a large group of them, 'really made the decision.' That is why even when the authority is available, men with access to it may still prefer the secret, quieter ways of manipulation.

But are not the people now more educated? Why not emphasize the spread of education rather than the increased effects of the mass media? The answer, in brief, is that mass education, in many respects, has become—another mass medium.

The prime task of public education, as it came widely to be understood in this country, was political: to make the citizen more knowledgeable and thus better able to think and to judge of public affairs. In time, the function of education shifted from the political to the economic: to train people for better-paying jobs and thus to get ahead. This is especially true of the high-school movement, which has met the business demands for white-collar skills at the public's expense. In large part education has become merely vocational; in so far as its political task is concerned, in many schools, that has been reduced to a routine training of nationalist loyalties.

The training of skills that are of more or less direct use in the vocational life is an important task to perform, but ought not to be mistaken for liberal education: job advancement, no matter on what levels, is not the same as self-development, although the two are now systematically confused.[10] Among 'skills,' some are more and some are less relevant to the aims of liberal—that is to say, liberating—education. Skills and values cannot be so easily separated as the academic search for supposedly neutral skills causes us to assume. And especially not when we speak seriously of liberal education. Of course, there is a scale, with skills at one end and values at the other, but it is the middle range of this scale, which one might call sensibilities, that are of most relevance to the classic public.

To train someone to operate a lathe or to read and write is pretty much education of skill; to evoke from people an understanding of what they really want out of their lives or to debate with them stoic, Christian and humanist ways of living, is pretty much a clear-cut education of values. But to assist in the birth among a group of people of those cultural and political and technical sensibilities which would make them genuine members of a genuinely liberal public, this is at once a training in skills and an education of values. It includes a sort of therapy in the ancient sense of clarifying one's knowledge of one's self; it includes the imparting of all those skills of controversy with one's self, which we call thinking;

and with others, which we call debate. And the end product of such liberal education of sensibilities is simply the self-educating, self-cultivating man or woman.

The knowledgeable man in the genuine public is able to turn his personal troubles into social issues, to see their relevance for his community and his community's relevance for them. He understands that what he thinks and feels as personal troubles are very often not only that but problems shared by others and indeed not subject to solution by any one individual but only by modifications of the structure of the groups in which he lives and sometimes the structure of the entire society.

Men in masses are gripped by personal troubles, but they are not aware of their true meaning and source. Men in public confront issues, and they are aware of their terms. It is the task of the liberal institution, as of the liberally educated man, continually to translate troubles into issues and issues into the terms of their human meaning for the individual. In the absence of deep and wide political debate, schools for adults and adolescents could perhaps become hospitable frameworks for just such debate. In a community of publics the task of liberal education would be: to keep the public from being overwhelmed; to help produce the disciplined and informed mind that cannot be overwhelmed; to help develop the bold and sensible individual that cannot be sunk by the burdens of mass life. But educational practice has not made knowledge directly relevant to the human need of the troubled person of the twentieth century or to the social practices of the citizen. This citizen cannot now see the roots of his own biases and frustrations, nor think clearly about himself, nor for that matter about anything else. He does not see the frustration of idea, of intellect, by the present organization of society, and he is not able to meet the tasks now confronting 'the intelligent citizen.'

Educational institutions have not done these things and, except in rare instances, they are not doing them. They have become mere elevators of occupational and social ascent, and, on all levels, they have become politically timid. Moreover, in the hands of 'professional educators,' many schools have come to operate on an ideology of 'life adjustment' that encourages happy acceptance of mass ways of life rather than the struggle for individual and public transcendence.*

There is not much doubt that modern regressive educators have adapted their notions of educational content and practice to the idea of the mass. They do not effectively proclaim standards of cultural level and intellectual rigor; rather they often deal in the trivia of vocational tricks and 'adjustment to life'—meaning the

---

*'If the schools are doing their job,' A. E. Bestor has written, 'we should expect educators to point to the significant and indisputable achievement in raising the intellectual level of the nation—measured perhaps by larger per capita circulation of books and serious magazines, by definitely improved taste in movies and radio programs, by higher standards of political debate, by increased respect for freedom of speech and of thought, by marked decline in such evidences of mental retardation as the incessant reading of comic books by adults.'[11]

slack life of masses. 'Democratic schools' often mean the furtherance of intellectual mediocrity, vocational training, nationalistic loyalties, and little else.

6

The structural trends of modern society and the manipulative character of its communication technique come to a point of coincidence in the mass society, which is largely a metropolitan society. The growth of the metropolis, segregating men and women into narrowed routines and environments, causes them to lose any firm sense of their integrity as a public. The members of publics in smaller communities know each other more or less fully, because they meet in the several aspects of the total life routine. The members of masses in a metropolitan society know one another only as fractions in specialized milieux: the man who fixes the car, the girl who serves your lunch, the saleslady, the women who take care of your child at school during the day. Prejudgment and stereotype flourish when people meet in such ways. The human reality of others does not, cannot, come through.

People, we know, tend to select those formal media which confirm what they already believe and enjoy. In a parallel way, they tend in the metropolitan segregation to come into live touch with those whose opinions are similar to theirs. Others they tend to treat unseriously. In the metropolitan society they develop, in their defense, a blasé manner that reaches deeper than a manner. They do not, accordingly, experience genuine clashes of viewpoint, genuine issues. And when they do, they tend to consider it mere rudeness.

Sunk in their routines, they do not transcend, even by discussion, much less by action, their more or less narrow lives. They do not gain a view of the structure of their society and of their role as a public within it. The city is a structure composed of such little environments, and the people in them tend to be detached from one another. The 'stimulating variety' of the city does not stimulate the men and women of 'the bedroom belt,' the one-class suburbs, who can go through life knowing only their own kind. If they do reach for one another, they do so only through stereotypes and prejudiced images of the creatures of other milieux. Each is trapped by his confining circle; each is cut off from easily identifiable groups. It is for people in such narrow milieux that the mass media can create a pseudo-world beyond, and a pseudo-world within themselves as well.

Publics live in milieux but they can transcend them—individually by intellectual effort; socially by public action. By reflection and debate and by organized action, a community of publics comes to feel itself and comes in fact to be active at points of structural relevance.

But members of a mass exist in milieux and cannot get out of them, either by mind or by activity, except—in the extreme case—under 'the organized spontaneity' of the bureaucrat on a motorcycle. We have not yet reached the extreme case, but observing metropolitan man in the American mass we can surely see the psychological preparations for it.

We may think of it in this way: When a handful of men do not have jobs, and do not seek work, we look for the causes in their immediate situation and character. But when twelve million men are unemployed, then we cannot believe that all of them suddenly 'got lazy' and turned out to be 'no good.' Economists call this 'structural unemployment'—meaning, for one thing, that the men involved cannot themselves control their job chances. Structural unemployment does not originate in one factory or in one town, nor is it due to anything that one factory or one town does or fails to do. Moreover, there is little or nothing that one ordinary man in one factory in one town can do about it when it sweeps over his personal milieu.

Now, this distinction, between social structure and personal milieu, is one of the most important available in the sociological studies. It offers us a ready understanding of the position of 'the public' in America today. In every major area of life, the loss of a sense of structure and the submergence into powerless milieux is the cardinal fact. In the military it is most obvious, for here the roles men play are strictly confining; only the command posts at the top afford a view of the structure of the whole, and moreover, this view is a closely guarded official secret. In the division of labor too, the jobs men enact in the economic hierarchies are also more or less narrow milieux and the positions from which a view of the production process as a whole can be had are centralized, as men are alienated not only from the product and the tools of their labor, but from any understanding of the structure and the processes of production. In the political order, in the fragmentation of the lower and in the distracting proliferation of the middle-level organization, men cannot see the whole, cannot see the top, and cannot state the issues that will in fact determine the whole structure in which they live and their place within it.

This loss of any structural view or position is the decisive meaning of the lament over the loss of community. In the great city, the division of milieux and of segregating routines reaches the point of closest contact with the individual and the family, for, although the city is not the unit of prime decision, even the city cannot be seen as a total structure by most of its citizens.

On the one hand, there is the increased scale and centralization of the structure of decision; and, on the other, the increasingly narrow sorting out of men into milieux. From both sides, there is the increased dependence upon the formal media of communication, including those of education itself. But the man in the mass does not gain a transcending view from these media; instead he gets his experience stereotyped, and then he gets sunk further by that experience. He cannot detach himself in order to observe, much less to evaluate, what he is experiencing, much less what he is not experiencing. Rather than that internal discussion we call reflection, he is accompanied through his life-experience with a sort of unconscious, echoing monologue. He has no projects of his own: he fulfills the routines that exist. He does not transcend whatever he is at any moment, because he does not, he cannot, transcend his daily milieux. He is not truly aware of his own daily experience and of its actual standards: he drifts, he fulfills habits, his behavior a result of a planless mixture of the confused standards and the uncriticized expectations that he has taken over from others whom he no longer really knows or trusts, if indeed he ever really did.

He takes things for granted, he makes the best of them, he tries to look ahead—a year or two perhaps, or even longer if he has children or a mortgage—but he does not seriously ask, What do I want? How can I get it? A vague optimism suffuses and sustains him, broken occasionally by little miseries and disappointments that are soon buried. He is smug, from the standpoint of those who think something might be the matter with the mass style of life in the metropolitan frenzy where self-making is an externally busy branch of industry. By what standards does he judge himself and his efforts? What is really important to him? Where are the models of excellence for this man?

He loses his independence, and more importantly, he loses the desire to be independent: in fact, he does not have hold of the idea of being an independent individual with his own mind and his own worked-out way of life. It is not that he likes or does not like this life; it is that the question does not come up sharp and clear so he is not bitter and he is not sweet about conditions and events. He thinks he wants merely to get his share of what is around with as little trouble as he can and with as much fun as possible.

Such order and movement as his life possesses is in conformity with external routines; otherwise his day-to-day experience is a vague chaos—although he often does not know it because, strictly speaking, he does not truly possess or observe his own experience. He does not formulate his desires; they are insinuated into him. And, in the mass, he loses the self-confidence of the human being—if indeed he has ever had it. For life in a society of masses implants insecurity and furthers impotence; it makes men uneasy and vaguely anxious; it isolates the individual from the solid group; it destroys firm group standards. Acting without goals, the man in the mass just feels pointless.

The idea of a mass society suggests the idea of an elite of power. The idea of the public, in contrast, suggests the liberal tradition of a society without any power elite, or at any rate with shifting elites of no sovereign consequence. For, if a genuine public is sovereign, it needs no master; but the masses, in their full development, are sovereign only in some plebiscitarian moment of adulation to an elite as authoritative celebrity. The political structure of a democratic state requires the public; and, the democratic man, in his rhetoric, must assert that this public is the very seat of sovereignty.

But now, given all those forces that have enlarged and centralized the political order and made modern societies less political and more administrative; given the transformation of the old middle classes into something which perhaps should not even be called middle class; given all the mass communications that do not truly communicate; given all the metropolitan segregation that is not community; given the absence of voluntary associations that really connect the public at large with the centers of power—what is happening is the decline of a set of publics that is sovereign only in the most formal and rhetorical sense. Moreover, in many countries the remnants of such publics as remain are now being frightened out of existence. They lose their will for rationally considered decision and action because they do not possess the instruments for such decision and action; they lose their sense of political belonging because they do not belong; they lose their political will because they see no way to realize it.

The top of modern American society is increasingly unified, and often seems willfully co-ordinated: at the top there has emerged an elite of power. The middle levels are a drifting set of stalemated, balancing forces: the middle does not link the bottom with the top. The bottom of this society is politically fragmented, and even as a passive fact, increasingly powerless: at the bottom there is emerging a mass society.

Notes

1. See E. H. Carr, *The New Society* (London: Macmillan, 1951), pp. 63–6, on whom I lean heavily in this and the following paragraphs.

2. On elections in modern formal democracies, E. H. Carr has concluded: "To speak today of the defence of democracy as if we were defending something which we knew and had possessed for many decades or many centuries is self-deception and sham—mass democracy is a new phenomenon—a creation of the last half-century—which it is inappropriate and misleading to consider in terms of the philosophy of Locke or of the liberal democracy of the nineteenth century. We should be nearer the mark, and should have a far more convincing slogan, if we spoke of the need, not to defend democracy, but to create it.' (ibid. pp. 75–6).

3. Cf. Hans Speier, *Social Order and The Risks of War* (New York: George Stewart, 1952), pp. 323–39.

4. Gustave Le Bon, *The Crowd* (London: Ernest Benn Ltd., 1952—first English edition, 1896), pp. 207. Cf. also pp. 6, 23, 30, 187.

5. Sergei Chakhotin, *The Rape of the Masses* (New York: Alliance, 1940), pp. 289–91.

6. Charles Horton Cooley, *Social Organization* (New York: Scribner's, 1909), p. 93. Cf. also Chapter IX.

7. See Walter Lippmann, *Public Opinion* (New York: Macmillan, 1922), which is still the best account of this aspect of the media. Cf. especially pp. 1–25 and 59–121.

8. Cf. Gerth and Mills, *Character and Social Structure* (New York: Harcourt, Brace, 1953), pp. 84 ff.

9. J. Truslow Adams, *The Epic of America* (Boston: Little, Brown, 1931) p. 360.

10. Cf. Mills, 'Work Milieu and Social Structure,' a speech to 'The Asilomar Conference' of the Mental Health Society of Northern California, March 1954, reprinted in their bulletin, *People At Work: A Symposium*, pp. 20 ff.

11. A. E. Bestor, *Educational Wastelands* (Urbana, Ill.: University of Illinois, 1953), p. 7. Cf. also p. 80.

JEROME A. BARRON

Access to the Press—A New First Amendment Right (1967)

The press, long enshrined among our most highly cherished institutions, was thought a cornerstone of democracy when its name was boldly inscribed in the Bill of Rights. Freed from governmental restraint, initially by the first amendment and later by the fourteenth, the press was to stand majestically as the champion of new ideas and the watchdog against governmental abuse. Professor Barron finds this conception of the first amendment, perhaps realistic in the eighteenth century heyday of political pamphleteering, essentially romantic in an era marked by extraordinary technological developments in the communications industry. To make viable the time-honored "marketplace" theory, he argues for a twentieth century interpretation of the first amendment which will impose an affirmative responsibility on the monopoly newspaper to act as sounding board for new ideas and old grievances.

There is an anomaly in our constitutional law. While we protect expression once it has come to the fore, our law is indifferent to creating opportunities for expression. Our constitutional theory is in the grip of a romantic conception of free expression, a belief that the "market place of ideas" is freely accessible. But if ever there were a self-operating marketplace of ideas, it has long ceased to exist. The mass media's development of an antipathy to ideas requires legal intervention if novel and unpopular ideas are to be assured a forum—unorthodox points of view which have no claim on broadcast time and newspaper space as a matter of right are in poor position to compete with those aired as a matter of grace.

The free expression questions which now come before the courts involve individuals who have managed to speak or write in a manner that captures public attention and provokes legal reprisal. The conventional constitutional issue is whether expression already uttered should be given first amendment shelter or whether it may be subjected to sanction as speech beyond the constitutionally protected pale. To those

From *Harvard Law Review* 80, no. 8 (June 1967): 1641–78.

who can obtain access to the media of mass communications first amendment case
law furnishes considerable help. But what of those whose ideas are too unacceptable
to secure access to the media? To them the mass communications industry replies:
The first amendment guarantees our freedom to do as we choose with our media.
Thus the constitutional imperative of free expression becomes a rationale for repress-
ing competing ideas. First amendment theory must be reexamined, for only by responding to the present reality of the mass media's repression of ideas can the
constitutional guarantee of free speech best serve its original purposes.

I. The Romantic View of the First Amendment:
A Rationale for Repression

The problem of access to the press is not a new one. When the Newspaper Guild
was organizing in the late 1930's, a statement opposing that organization was prepared by the American Newspaper Publishers Association. Not surprisingly that
statement was given publicity in almost all the newspapers in the United States.
Mr. Heywood Broun, a celebrated American journalist, prepared a two hundred
word reply for the Guild organizers and asked the hostile newspapers to print it:[1]
"A very large number of newspaper owners who had beaten their breasts as evidence of their devotion to a 'free press' promptly threw the Guild statement into
the waste basket and printed not a line of it."

Mr. Broun's experience illustrates the danger posed by the ability of mass communications media to suppress information, but an essentially romantic view of
the first amendment has perpetuated the lack of legal interest in the availability to
various interest groups of access to means of communication. Symptomatic of this
view is Mr. Justice Douglas's eloquent dissent in *Dennis v. United States:*[2]

> When ideas compete in the market for acceptance, full and free discussion
> exposes the false and they gain few adherents. Full and free discussion even
> of ideas we hate encourages the testing of our own prejudices and precon-
> ceptions. Full and free discussion keeps a society from becoming stagnant and
> unprepared for the stresses and strains that work to tear all civilizations apart.
> *Full and free discussion has indeed been the first article of our faith.*

The assumption apparent in this excerpt is that, without government intervention,
there is a free market mechanism for ideas. Justice Douglas's position expresses the
faith that, if government can be kept away from "ideas," the self-operating and
self-correcting force of "full and free discussion" will go about its eternal task of
keeping us from "embracing what is cheap and false" to the end that victory will
go to the doctrine which is "true to our genius."[3]

This romantic view of the first amendment had its origin in Mr. Justice Holmes's free speech opinions; a typical statement of his "marketplace of ideas" theory is found in his dissent in *Abrams v. United States*:[4]

> But when men have realized that time has upset many fighting faiths, they may come to believe even more than they believe the very foundations of their own conduct that the ultimate good desired is better reached by free trade in ideas—that the best test of truth is the power of thought to get itself accepted in the competition of the market, and that truth is the only ground upon which their wishes safely can be carried out. That at any rate is the theory of our Constitution.

It is interesting, perhaps anomalous, that the same Justice who reminded his brethren in *Lochner v. New York*[5] that the Constitution was not "intended to embody a particular economic theory, whether of paternalism and the organic relation of the citizen to the state or of *laissez faire*," nevertheless rather uncritically accepted the view that constitutional status should be given to a free market theory in the realm of ideas.

The possibility of governmental repression is present so long as government endures, and the first amendment has served as an effective device to protect the flow of ideas from governmental censorship: "Happily government censorship has put down few roots in this country. . . . We have in the United States no counterpart of the Lord Chamberlain who is censor over England's stage."[6] But this is to place laurels before a phantom—our constitutional law has been singularly indifferent to the reality and implications of nongovernmental obstructions to the spread of political truth. This indifference becomes critical when a comparatively few private hands are in a position to determine not only the content of information but its very availability, when the soap box yields to radio and the political pamphlet to the monopoly newspaper.

II. Obstacles to Access: The Changing Technology of the Communications Process

The British M.P. and publicist, R.H.S Crossman, has observed that the modern world is witnessing at present a Political Revolution as searing and as consequential as the Industrial Revolution, a revolution which "has concentrated coercive power and thought control in a few hands."[7] Power, he contends, has shifted from those who control the "means of production" to "those who control the media of mass communication and the means to destruction (propaganda and the armed forces)."[8] Mr. Crossman, to be sure, writes from the vantage point of the British Labor Party, but his observations have the ring of urgency and contemporaneity. Difficulties in securing access, unknown both to the draftsmen of the first amendment and to the early proponents of its "marketplace" interpretation, have been wrought by the changing technology of mass media.

Mr. Broun's experience as representative of the Newspaper Guild in the 1930's led him to write an article in which he expressed concern about the implications of the newspapers' refusal to print his reply at a time when "[e]very day brings the news that one or two or three more papers have collapsed or combined with their rivals."[9] He has proved a good prophet, for where fourteen English language dailies were published in New York City in 1900, only two morning papers and two afternoon dailies survive. Many American cities have become one newspaper towns. This is a "disquieting" development for American journalist J. Russell Wiggins since "[t]his noncompetitive situation puts it within the power of the monopoly newspaper to suppress facts at its discretion . . ."[10]

Mr. Wiggins suggests that the economics of newspaper publication—rising costs of everything from newsprint to labor—may be a more significant cause of the withholding of news than conspiratorial efforts of publishers. Less sympathetic to the mass media in evaluating the practical obstacles which confront the group seeking an adequate forum for its opinion is Marshall McLuhan's view that the very nature of modern media is at war with a point of view orientation.[11] McLuhan observes that each medium engenders quite different degrees of participation. The new modes of communication engage us by their form rather than by their content; what captivates us is the television screen itself. In his view the electronic media which have eclipsed the typographical age entail a high degree of nonintellectual and emotional participation and involvement.[12] We have become mesmerized by the new forms of communication to the point of indifference to their content and to the content of the older media. The electronic media which dominate modern communications are, in McLuhan's analysis, ill suited to the problem of making public issues meaningful.

Another commentator on communications, Dan Lacy, has explained this indifference to content somewhat differently. More critical than popular obsession with the forms of technological advance is the dull emphasis on majoritarian values which characterizes all our media, old and new:[13]

> We have seen that the very technology of films and especially of broadcasting is such that their efficiency can be realized only when they are reaching very large audiences. This is a constant factor that is just as present in the BBC as in the advertising-supported networks of the United States. This technological fact predisposes all the mass media to conform to an already widely accepted taste. It also makes it very difficult for a novel point of view or a just emerging problem to gain access to network broadcasts or other mass components of

the mass communications system. Let me make it clear once more that I am not talking about the ability of each of two conflicting points of views to get on the air so long as each is a well-recognized point of view about a controversy that already commands attention. It is rather the subject or point of view in which people are not yet interested, but ought to be, that finds understandable difficulty in gaining access to the mass media.

The aversion of the media for the novel and heretical has escaped attention for an odd reason. The controllers of the media have no ideology. Since in the main they espouse no particular ideas, their antipathy to all ideas has passed unnoticed.[14] What has happened is not that the controllers of opinion, Machiavellian fashion, are subtly feeding us information to the end that we shall acquiesce in their political view of the universe. On the contrary, the communications industry is operated on the whole with an intellectual neutrality consistent with V.O. Key's theory that the commercial nature of mass communications makes it "bad business" to espouse the heterodox or the controversial.[15]

But retreat from ideology is not bereft of ideological and practical consequences. In a commentary about television, but which applies equally well to all mass media, Gilbert Seldes has complained that, in a time demanding more active intelligence than has ever before been necessary if we are to survive, the most powerful of all our media are inducing inertia.[16] The contemporary structure of the mass media direct the media away from rather than toward opinion-making. In other words, it is not that the mass communication industry is pushing certain ideas and rejecting others but rather that it is using the free speech and free press guarantees to avoid opinions instead of acting as a sounding board for their expression. What happens of course is that the opinion vacuum is filled with the least controversial and bland ideas. Whatever is stale and accepted in the status quo is readily discussed and thereby reinforced and revitalized.

The failures of existing media are revealed by the development of new media to convey unorthodox, unpopular, and new ideas. Sit-ins and demonstrations testify to the inadequacy of old media as instruments to afford full and effective hearing for all points of view. Demonstrations, it has been well said, are "the free press of the movement to win justice for Negroes. . . ."[17] But, like an inadequate underground press, it is a communications medium by default, a statement of the inability to secure access to the conventional means of reaching and changing public opinion. By the bizarre and unsettling nature of his technique the demonstrator hopes to arrest and divert attention long enough to compel the public to ponder his message. But attention-getting devices so abound in the modern world that new ones soon become tiresome. The dissenter must look for ever more unsettling assaults on the mass mind if he is to have continuing impact. Thus, as critics of protest are eager and in a sense correct to say, the prayer-singing student demonstration is the prelude to Watts. But the difficulty with this criticism is that it wishes to throttle protest rather than to recognize that protest has taken these forms because it has had nowhere else to go.

III. Making the First Amendment Work

The Justices of the United States Supreme Court are not innocently unaware of these contemporary social realities, but they have nevertheless failed to give the "marketplace of ideas" theory of the first amendment the burial it merits. Perhaps the interment of this theory has been denied for the understandable reason that the Court is at a loss to know with what to supplant it. But to put off inquiry under today's circumstances will only aggravate the need for it under tomorrow's.

A. Beyond Romanticism

There is inequality in the power to communicate ideas just as there is inequality in economic bargaining power; to recognize the latter and deny the former is quixotic. The "marketplace of ideas" view has rested on the assumption that protecting the right of expression is equivalent to providing for it.[18] But changes in the communications industry have destroyed the equilibrium in that marketplace. While it may have been still possible in 1925 to believe with Justice Holmes that every idea is "acted on unless some other belief outweighs it or some failure of energy stifles the movement at its birth,"[19] it is impossible to believe that now. Yet the Holmesian theory is not abandoned, even though the advent of radio and television has made even more evident that philosophy's unreality. A realistic view of the first amendment requires recognition that a right of expression is somewhat thin if it can be exercised only at the sufferance of the managers of mass communications.

Too little attention has been given to defining the purposes which the first amendment protection is designed to achieve and to identifying the addressees of that protection. An eloquent exception is the statement of Justice Brandeis in *Whitney v. California*[20] that underlying the first amendment guarantee is the assumption that free expression is indispensable to the "discovery and spread of political truth" and that the "greatest menace to freedom is an inert people." In *Thornhill v. Alabama*[21] Justice Murphy described his view of the first amendment:

> The exigencies of the colonial period and the efforts to secure freedom from oppressive administration developed a broadened conception of these liberties as adequate to supply *the public need for information and education with respect to the significant issues of the times.* . . . Freedom of discussion, if it would fulfill its historic function in this nation, must embrace all issues about which

information is needed or appropriate to enable the members of society to cope with the exigencies of their period.

That public information is vital to the creation of an informed citizenry is, I suppose, unexceptionable. Both Justices recognize the importance of confronting citizens, as individual decision makers, with the widest variety of competing ideas. But accuracy does demand one to remember that Justice Brandeis was speaking in *Whitney*, as was Justice Murphy in *Thornhill*, of the constitutional recognition that is given to the necessity of inhibiting "the occasional tyrannies of governing majorities" from throttling opportunities for discussion. But is it such a large constitutional step to take the same approach to nongoverning minorities who control the machinery of communication? Is it too bold to suggest that it is necessary to ensure access to the mass media for unorthodox ideas in order to make effective the guarantee against repression?

Another conventionally stated goal of first amendment protection—the "public order function"—also cries out for recognition of a right of access to the mass media. The relationship between constitutional assurance of an opportunity to communicate ideas and the integrity of the public order was appreciated by both Justice Cardozo and Justice Brandeis. In *Palko v. Connecticut*[22] Justice Cardozo clearly indicated that while many rights could be eliminated and yet "justice" not undone, "neither liberty nor justice would exist . . . [without] freedom of thought and speech" since free expression is "the matrix, the indispensable condition, of nearly every other form of freedom." If freedom of expression cannot be secured because entry into the communication media is not free but is confined as a matter of discretion by a few private hands, the sense of the justice of existing institutions, which freedom of expression is designed to assure, vanishes from some section of our population as surely as if access to the media were restricted by the government.

Justice Brandeis, in his seminal opinion in *Whitney*—one of the few efforts of a Supreme Court Justice to go beyond the banality of the "marketplace of ideas"— also stressed the intimacy of the relationship between the goals of a respect for public order and the assurance of free expression. For Brandeis one of the assumptions implicit in the guarantee of free expression is that "it is hazardous to discourage thought, hope and imagination; that fear breeds repression; that repression breeds hate; that hate menaces stable government; that the path of safety lies in the opportunity to discuss freely supposed grievances and proposed remedies. . . ."[23] I would suggest that the contemporary challenge to this "path of safety" has roots in the lack of opportunity for the disadvantaged and the dissatisfied of our society to discuss supposed grievances effectively.

The "sit-in" demonstrates that the safety valve value of free expression in preserving public order is lost when access to the communication media is foreclosed to dissident groups. It is a measure of the jaded and warped standards of the media that ideas which normally would never be granted a forum are given serious network coverage if they become sufficiently enmeshed in mass demonstration or riot and violence. Ideas are denied admission into media until they are first disseminated in a way that challenges and disrupts the social order. They then may be discussed and given notice. But is it not the assumption of a constitutional guarantee of freedom of expression that the process ought to work just the other way— that the idea be given currency first so that its proponents will not conclude that unrest and violence alone will suffice to capture public attention? Contemporary constitutional theory has been indifferent to this task of channeling the novel and the heretical into the mass communications media, perhaps because the problem is indeed a recent one.

B. The Need for a Contextual Approach

A corollary of the romantic view of the first amendment is the Court's unquestioned assumption that the amendment affords "equal" protection to the various media. According to this view new media of communication are assimilated into first amendment analysis without regard to the enormous differences in impact these media have in comparison with the traditional printed word. Radio and television are to be as free as newspapers and magazines, sound trucks as free as radio and television.

This extension of a simplistic egalitarianism to media whose comparative impacts are gravely disproportionate is wholly unrealistic. It results from confusing freedom of media content with freedom of the media to restrict access. The assumption in romantic first amendment analysis that the same postulates apply to different classes of people, situations, and means of communication obscures the fact, noted explicitly by Justice Jackson in *Kovacs v. Cooper*,[24] that problems of access and impact vary significantly from medium to medium: "The moving picture screen, the radio, the newspaper, the handbill, the sound truck and the street corner orator have differing natures, values, abuses and dangers. Each, in my view, is a law unto itself, and all we are dealing with now is the sound truck."

However, this enlightened view, suggesting the creation of legal principles which fit the dimensions of the particular medium, was probably not accepted by the majority in *Kovacs* and appeared to be rejected by the dissenters. For the Court Justice Reed declared that the right of free speech is guaranteed each citizen that he may reach the minds of willing listeners, and to do so there must be opportunity to win their attention. This statement would have had tremendous impact had Justice Reed meant that the free speech guarantee applied with particular force to those media where the greatest public attention was focused. But what he probably meant was that because some media, albeit the most important ones, are closed, it is important that other means of communication remain more or less unregulated.

The dissenters, in an opinion by Justice Black, are explicit in rejecting any attempt to shape legal principles to the particular medium, reasoning that government cannot restrain a given mode of communication because that would disadvantage the others—"favoritism" would result because "[l]aws which hamper the free use of some instruments of communication thereby favor competing channels."[25] Justice Black's theory appears to be that if all instrumentalities of communication are "free" in the sense of immunization from governmental regulations, problems of access will work themselves out. But what happens in fact is that the dominant media become even more influential and the media which are freely available, such as sound trucks and pamphlets, become even less significant. Thus, we are presented with the anomaly that the protagonist of the "absolute" view of free speech has helped to fashion a protective doctrine of greatest utility to the owners and operators of the mass communications industry. By refusing to treat media according to their peculiar natures Justice Black has done that very thing he so heartily condemns—he has favored some channels of communication.

Justice Black is not unaware of the inequality in the existing operation of the mass media, but he blurs distinctions among the media and acquiesces in their differing impacts:[26]

> Yet everybody knows the vast reaches of these powerful channels of communication which from the very nature of our economic system must be under the control and guidance of comparatively few people . . .
>
> . . . For the press, the radio, and the moving picture owners have their favorites, and it assumes the impossible to suppose that these agencies will at all times be equally fair as between the candidates and officials they favor and those whom they vigorously oppose.

For all the intensity of his belief that "it is of particular importance" in a system of representative government that the "fullest opportunity be afforded candidates" to express their views to the voters,[27] Justice Black is nevertheless of the opinion that courts must remain constitutionally insensitive to the problem of getting ideas before a forum. That his approach affords greatest protection to mass media does not come about because of a belief that such protection is particularly desirable. Rather it results from a constitutional approach which looks only to protecting the communications which are presently being made without inquiry as to whether freedom of speech and press, in defense of which so much judicial rhetoric is expended, is a realistically available right. While we have taken measures to ensure the sanctity of that which is said, we have not inquired whether, as a practical matter, the difficulty of access to the media of communication has made the right of expression somewhat mythical.

Once again Justice Jackson was the author of one of the few judicial statements which recognizes that first amendment interpretation is uselessly conceptual unless it attempts to be responsive to the diverse natures of differing modes of communication. Dissenting in *Kunz v. New York*[28] he thought absolutist interpretations of the first amendment too simplistic and suggested that the susceptibility to public control of a given medium of communication should be in direct proportion to its public impact: "Few are the riots caused by publication alone, few are the mobs that have not had their immediate origin in harangue. *The vulnerability of various forms of communication to community control must be proportioned to their impact upon other community interests.*" Although originally made in a context of the greater likelihood that a riot would be initiated by an harangue than by a newspaper publication, the principle applies equally well to the impact which the new technology has on the informational and public-order goals of the first amendment.

An analysis of the first amendment must be tailored to the context in which ideas are or seek to be aired. This contextual approach requires an examination of the purposes served by and the impact of each particular medium. If a group seeking to present a particular side of a public issue is unable to get space in the only newspaper in town, is this inability compensated by the availability of the public park or the sound truck? Competitive media only constitute alternative means of access in a crude manner. If ideas are criticized in one forum the most adequate response is in the same forum since it is most likely to reach the same audience. Further, the various media serve different functions and create different reactions and expectations—criticism of an individual or a governmental policy over television may reach more people but criticism in print is more durable.

The test of a community's opportunities for free expression rests not so much in an abundance of alternative media but rather in an abundance of opportunities to secure expression in media with the largest impact. Such a test embodies Justice Jackson's observation that community control must be in proportion to the impact which a particular medium has on the community.

C. A New Perspective

The late Professor Meiklejohn, who has articulated a view of the first amendment which assumes its justification to be political self-government, has wisely pointed out that "what is essential is not that everyone shall speak, but that everything worth saying shall be said"—that the point of ultimate interest is not the words of the speakers but the minds of the hearers.[29] Can everything worth saying be effectively said? Constitutional opinions that are particularly solicitous of the interests of mass media—radio, television, and mass circulation newspaper—devote little thought to the difficulties of securing access to those media. If those media are unavailable, can the minds of "hearers" be reached effectively? Creating opportunities for expression is as important as ensuring the right to express ideas without fear of governmental reprisal.

The problem of private restrictions on freedom of expression might, in special circumstances, be attacked under the federal antitrust laws.[30] In *Associated Press v. United States*,[31] involving an attempt to exclude from membership competitors of existing members of the Associated Press in order to deprive them of the use of the AP's wire service, Justice Black wrote for the Court that nongovernmental combinations are not immune from governmental sanction if they impede rather than expedite free expression:

> *[The First] Amendment rests on the assumption that the widest possible dissemination of information from diverse and antagonistic sources is essential to the welfare of the public, that a free press is a condition of a free society.* Surely a command that the government itself shall not impede the free flow of ideas does not afford nongovernmental combinations a refuge if they impose restraints upon that constitutionally guaranteed freedom ... *Freedom to publish is guaranteed by the Constitution, but freedom to combine to keep others from publishing is not. Freedom of the press from governmental interference under the First Amendment does not sanction repression of that freedom by private interests.*

Despite these unusual remarks this opinion reflects a romantic view of the first amendment, for Justice Black assumes the "free flow of ideas" and the "freedom to publish" absent a combination of publishers. Moreover, this was an unusual case; antitrust law operates too indirectly in assuring access to be an effective device.

But the case is important in its acknowledgment that the public interest, here embodied in the antitrust statutes, can override the first amendment claims of the mass media; it would seem that the public interest in expression of divergent viewpoints should be weighted as heavily when the mass media invoke the first amendment to shield restrictions on access. In the opinion for the trial court, Judge Learned Hand at least suggests first amendment protection for the interest which the individual members of the body politic have in the communications process itself. Identification of first amendment beneficiaries is not complete if only the interest of the "publisher" are protected:[32]

> However, neither exclusively, nor even primarily, are the interests of the newspaper industry conclusive; for that industry serves one of the most vital of all general interests: the dissemination of news from as many different sources, and with as many different facets and colors as is possible. That interest is closely akin to, if indeed it is not the same as, the interest protected

by the First Amendment; it presupposes that right conclusions are more likely to be gathered out of a multitude of tongues, than through any kind of authoritative selection.

Our constitutional theory, particularly in the free speech area, has historically been inoperative unless government restraint can be shown. If the courts or the legislature were to guarantee some minimal right to access for ideas which could not otherwise be effectively aired before the public, there would be "state action"[33] sufficient to support a claim by the medium involved that this violated its first amendment rights. However, the right of free expression is not an absolute right, as is illustrated by *Associated Press*, and to guarantee access to divergent, otherwise unexpressed ideas would so promote the societal interests underlying the first amendment as perhaps to outweigh the medium's claim. Nor is the notion of assuring access or opportunity for discussion a novel theory. In *Near v. Minnesota ex rel. Olson*[34] Chief Justice Hughes turned to Blackstone to corroborate the view that freedom from prior restraint rather than freedom from subsequent punishment was central to the eighteenth century notion of liberty of the press. This concern with suppression before dissemination was doubtless to assure that ideas would reach the public:[35] "Every freeman has an undoubted right to lay what sentiments he pleases before the public; to forbid this, is to destroy the freedom of the press; but if he publishes what is improper, mischievous or illegal, he must take the consequence of his own temerity.' "

The avowed emphasis of free speech is still on a freeman's right to "lay what sentiments he pleases before the public." But Blackstone wrote in another age. Today ideas reach the millions largely to the extent they are permitted entry into the great metropolitan dailies, news magazines, and broadcasting networks. The soap box is no longer an adequate forum for public discussion. Only the new media of communication can lay sentiments before the public, and it is they rather than government who can most effectively abridge expression by nullifying the opportunity for an idea to win acceptance. As a constitutional theory for the communication of ideas, laissez faire is manifestly irrelevant.

The constitutional admonition against abridgment of speech and press is at present not applied to the very interests which have real power to effect such abridgement. Indeed, nongoverning minorities in control of the means of communication should perhaps be inhibited from restraining free speech (by the denial of access to their media) even more than governing majorities are restrained by the first amendment—minorities do not have the mandate which a legislative majority enjoys in a polity operating under a theory of representative government. What is required is an interpretation of the first amendment which focuses on the idea that restraining the hand of government is quite useless in assuring free speech if a restraint on access is effectively secured by private groups. A constitutional prohibition against governmental restrictions on expression is effective only if the Constitution ensures an adequate opportunity for discussion. Since this opportunity exists only in the mass media, the interests of those who control the means of communication must be accommodated with the interests of those who seek a forum in which to express their point of view.

IV. New Winds of Constitutional Doctrine: The Implications for a Right to Be Heard

A. *New York Times Co. v. Sullivan: A Lost Opportunity*

The potential of existing law to support recognition of a right of access has gone largely unnoticed by the Supreme Court. Judicial blindness to the problem of securing access to the press is dramatically illustrated by *New York Times Co. v. Sullivan*,[36] one of the latest chapters in the romantic and rigid interpretation of the first amendment. There the Court reversed a five hundred thousand dollar judgment of civil libel which Montgomery Commissioner Sullivan had won against the *Times* in the Alabama state courts. The Court created the "*Times* privilege" whereby a defamed "public official" is constitutionally proscribed from recovering damages from a newspaper unless he can show that the offending false publication was made with "actual malice."

The constitutional armor which *Times* now offers newspapers is predicted on the "principle that debate on public issues should be uninhibited, robust, and wide-open, and that it may well include vehement, caustic, and sometimes unpleasantly sharp attacks on government and public officials."[37] But it is paradoxical that although the libel laws have been emasculated for the benefit of defendant newspapers where the plaintiff is a "public official,"[38] the Court shows no corresponding concern as to whether debate will in fact be assured. The irony of *Times* and its progeny lies in the unexamined assumption that reducing newspaper exposure to libel litigation will remove restraints on expression and lead to an "informed society." But in fact the decision creates a new imbalance in the communications process. Purporting to deepen the constitutional guarantee of full expression, the actual effect of the decision is to perpetuate the freedom of a few in a manner adverse to the public interest in uninhibited debate. Unless the *Times* doctrine is deepened to require opportunities for the public figure to reply to a defamatory attack, the *Times* decision will merely serve to equip the press with some new and rather heavy artillery which can crush as well as stimulate debate.[39]

Justice Black's concurring opinion in *Times*, joined in by Justice Douglas, is perhaps even more disappointing than the opinion of the Court in its failure to recognize the balancing problems created by the changing nature of the communications process. Once again Justice Black insisted that newspapers be entirely immune from libel actions where public officials are being attacked, and once again his absolutist rhetoric obscured fundamental problems. He seems to identify the "press" with the "people" and to think that immunity from suit for newspapers is equivalent to enhancing the right of free expression for all members of the community:[40]

> . . . I doubt that a country can live in freedom where its people can be made to suffer physically or financially for criticizing their government, its actions, or its officials. . . . An unconditional right to say what one pleases about public affairs is what I consider to be the minimum guarantee of the First Amendment.

The law of libel is not the only threat to first amendment values; problems of equal moment are raised by judicial inattention to the fact that the newspaper publisher is not the only addressee of first amendment protection. Supreme Court efforts to remove the press from judicial as well as legislative control do not necessarily stimulate and preserve that "multitude of tongues" on which "we have staked . . . our all."[41] What the Court has done is to magnify the power of one of the participants in the communications process with apparently no thought of imposing on newspapers concomitant responsibilities to assure that the new protection will actually enlarge and protect opportunities for expression.

If financial immunization by the Supreme Court is necessary to ensure a courageous press, the public officials who fall prey to such judicially reinforced lions should at least have the right to respond or to demand retraction in the pages of the newspapers which have published charges against them. The opportunity for counterattack ought to be at the very heart of a constitutional theory which supposedly is concerned with providing an outlet for individuals "who wish to exercise their freedom of speech even though they are not members of the press."[42] If no such right is afforded or even considered, it seemes meaningless to talk about vigorous public debate.

By severely undercutting a public official's ability to recover damages when he has been defamed, the *Times* decision would seem to reduce the likelihood of retractions since the normal mitigation incentive to retract will be absent. For example, the *Times* failed to print a retraction as requested by Sullivan even though an Alabama statute provided that a retraction eliminates the jury's ability to award punitive damages. On the other hand, *Times* was a special case and the Court explicitly left open the question of a public official's ability to recover damages if there were a refusal to retract:[43]

> Whether or not a failure to retract may ever constitute such evidence [of "actual malice"], there are two reasons why it does not here. *First*, the letter

written by the Times reflected a reasonable doubt on its part as to whether the advertisement could reasonably be taken to refer to respondent at all. *Second*, it was not a final refusal, since it asked for an explanation on this point—a request that respondent chose to ignore.

Although the Court did not foreclose the possibility of allowing public officials to recover damages for a newspaper's refusal to retract, its failure to impose such a responsibility represents a lost opportunity to work out a more relevant theory of the first amendment. Similarly, the Court's failure to require newspapers to print a public official's reply ignored a device which could further first amendment objectives by making debate meaningful and responsive.[44] Abandonment of the romantic view of the first amendment would highlight the importance of giving constitutional status to these responsibilities of the press.

However, even these devices are no substitute for the development of a general right of access to the press. A group that is not being attacked but merely ignored will find them of little use. Indifference rather than hostility is the bane of new ideas and for that malaise only some device of more general application will suffice. It is true that Justice Brennan, writing for the Court in *Times*, did suggest that a rigorous test for libel in the public criticism area is particularly necessary where the offending publication is an "editorial advertisement," since this is an "important outlet for the promulgation of information and ideas by *persons who do not themselves have access to publishing facilities*—who wish to exercise their freedom of speech *even though they are not members of the press*."[45] This statement leaves us at the threshold of the question of whether these individuals—the "nonpress"—should have a right of access secured by the first amendment: should the newspaper have an obligation to take the editorial advertisement? As Justice Brennan appropriately noted, newspapers are an important outlet for ideas. But currently they are outlets entry to which is granted at the pleasure of their managers. The press having been given the *Times* immunity to promote public debate, there seems little justification for not enforcing coordinate responsibility to allocate space equitably among ideas competing for public attention. And, some quite recent shifts in constitutional doctrine may at last make feasible the articulation of a constitutionally based right of access to the media.

B. Ginzburg v. United States: The Implications of the "Commercial Exploitation" Doctrine

The *Times* decision operates on the assumption that newspapers are fortresses of vigorous public criticism, that assuring the press freedom over its content is the only prerequisite to open and robust debate. But if the *raison d'être* of the mass media is not to maximize discussion but to maximize profits, inquiry should be directed to the possible effect of such a fact on constitutional theory. The late Professor V. O. Key stressed the consequences which flow from the fact that communications is big business:[46]

> [A]ttention to the economic aspects of the communications industries serves to emphasize the fact that they consist of commercial enterprises, not public service institutions. . . . They sell advertising in one form or another, and they bait it principally with entertainment. Only incidentally do they collect and disseminate political intelligence.
>
>   . . . .
>
>   . . . The networks are in an unenviable economic position. They are not completely free to sell their product—air time. If they make their facilities available to those who advocate causes slightly off color politically, they may antagonize their major customers.

The press suffers from the same pressures—"newspaper publishers are essentially people who sell white space on newsprint to advertisers"; [47] in large part they are only processors of raw materials purchased from others.[48]

Professor Key's conclusion—indifference to content follows from the structure of contemporary mass communications—compares well with Marshall McLuhan's view that the nature of the communications process compels a "strategy of neutrality." For McLuhan it is the technology or form of television itself, rather than the message, which attracts public attention. Hence the media owners are anxious that media content not get enmeshed with unpopular views which will undermine the attraction which the media enjoy by virtue of their form alone:[49]

> Thus the commercial interests who think to render media universally acceptable, invariably settle for "entertainment" as a strategy of neutrality. A more spectacular mode of the ostrich-head-in-sand could not be devised, for it ensures maximum pervasiveness for any medium whatever.

Whether the mass media suffer from an institutional distaste for controversy because of technological or of economic factors, this antipathy to novel ideas must be viewed against a background of industry insistence on constitutional immunity from legally imposed responsibilities. A quiet truth emerges from such a study: industry opposition to legally imposed responsibilities does not represent a flight from censorship but rather a flight from points of view. Points of view suggest disagreement and angry customers are not good customers.

However, there is emerging in our constitutional philosophy of the first amendment a strain of realism which contrasts markedly with the prevailing romanticism.

The much publicized case of *Ginzburg v. United States*[50] contains the seeds of a new pragmatic approach to the first amendment guarantee of free expression. In *Ginzburg* the dissemination of books was held to violate the federal obscenity statute not because the printed material was in itself obscene but because the publications were viewed by the Court "against a background of commercial exploitation of erotica solely for the sake of their prurient appeal."[51] The books were purchased by the reader "for titillation, not for saving intellectual content."

The mass communications industry should be viewed in constitutional litigation with the same candor with which it has been analyzed by industry members and scholars in communication. If dissemination of books can be prohibited and punished when the dissemination is not for any "saving intellectual content" but for "commercial exploitation," it would seem that the mass communications industry, no less animated by motives of "commercial exploitation," could be legally obliged to host competing opinions and points of view.[52] If the mass media are essentially business enterprises and their commercial nature makes it difficult to give a full and effective hearing to a wide spectrum of opinion, a theory of the first amendment is unrealistic if it prevents courts or legislatures from requiring the media to do that which, for commercial reasons, they would be otherwise unlikely to do. Such proposals only require that the opportunity for publication be broadened and do not involve restraint on publication or punishment after publication, as did *Ginzburg* where the distributor of books was jailed under an obscenity statute even though the books themselves were not constitutionally obscene.[53] In a companion case to *Ginzburg*, Justice Douglas remarked that the vice of censorship lies in the substitution it makes of "majority rule where minority tastes or viewpoints were to be tolerated."[54] But what is suggested here is merely that legal steps be taken to provide for the airing and publication of "minority tastes or viewpoints," not that the mass media be prevented from publishing their views.

In *Ginzburg* Justice Brennan observed:[55]

[T]he circumstances of presentation and dissemination of material are equally relevant to determining whether social importance claimed for material in the courtroom was, in the circumstances, pretense or reality—whether it was the basis upon which it was traded in the marketplace or a spurious claim for litigation purposes.

The same approach should be taken in evaluating the protests of mass media against the prospect of a right to access. Is their argument—that the development of legally assured rights of access to mass communications would hinder media freedom of expression—"pretense or reality"? The usefulness of *Ginzburg* lies in its recognition of the doctrine that when commercial purposes dominate the matrix of expression seeking first amendment protection, first amendment directives must be restructured. When commercial considerations dominate, often leading the media to repress ideas, these media should not be allowed to resist controls designed to promote vigorous debate and expression by cynical reliance on the first amendment.

C. Office of Communication of the United Church of Christ v. FCC: A Support for the Future?

There are other signs of change in legal doctrine, among the more significant the recent decision in *Office of Communication of the United Church of Christ v. FCC*.[56] In *Church of Christ*, individuals and organizations claiming to represent the Negro community of Jackson, Mississippi—forty-five percent of the city's total population—requested the FCC to grant an evidentiary hearing to challenge the renewal application of a television broadcast licensee in Jackson. The petitioners contended that the station discriminated against Negroes, both by failure to give meaningful expression to integrationist views contrary to the segregationist position taken by it and by the relatively tiny segment of religious programming assigned to Negro churches. The Commission held that the petitioners were merely members of the public and had no standing to claim a hearing since there was no showing of competitive economic injury or electrical interference. However, in an opinion which may be the harbinger of a new approach for the whole field of communications, the court of appeals reversed the Commission, radically expanding the grounds for standing by holding the interests of community groups in broadcast programming sufficient to obtain an evidentiary hearing on license renewal applications.

The court of appeals rested its decision on the FFC's "fairness" doctrine, an administrative creation[57] first adopted in 1949 and later codified in a 1959 amendment to section 315 of the Federal Communications Act.[58] The statute requires licensees "to afford reasonable opportunity for the discussion of conflicting views on issues of public importance," which in operation means that where a licensee has taken a position he must permit spokesmen for the other side or sides to reply. Of course, the defect of the statute is that, as interpreted, the obligation to provide access for ideas of "public importance" arises only after the licensee has taken a position on an issue. By avoiding controversy the licensee can evade the fairness rule—there is no duty to report the other side of silence. Beyond this, if the licensee chooses to violate the requirements of the doctrine by only reporting one side of a controversy, little can be done about it until license renewal. Formerly not much was done even at the time of renewal since a refusal to renew is an extremely harsh penalty. However, groups and individuals representing the public now have been authorized to challenge license renewal in their own right.

Church of Christ, holding the listener's reaction to programming sufficient to fur-nish standing to contest license renewal, is one of the most significant cases in public law in recent years. It is unfortunate that the constitutional basis of the case, though readily discernible, was not made more explicit. The court's opinion relied on the FCC's *Report on Editorializing by Broadcast Licensees*, the document which gave life to the Commission's "fairness" doctrine. The court emphasized principally the primary status of "the 'right of the public to be informed, rather than any right on the part of the Government, any broadcast licensee or any individual member of the public to broadcast his own particular views on any matter. . . .' "[59] This state-ment was accompanied in the *Report* by citation to two formative first amendment cases.[60]

It is noteworthy that prior to the promulgation of the *Report* the alleged uncon-stitutionality of the fairness doctrine was vigorously asserted by industry witnesses in the hearings before the Commission.[61] To the challenge that programming stan-dards such as the "fairness" doctrine were violations of the first amendment, the Commission made remarks which are quite pertinent to the achievement of a healthy symbiosis between the first amendment and modern mass communications media:[62]

> The freedom of speech protected against governmental abridgment by the first amendment does not extend any privilege to government licensees of means of public communications to exclude the expression of opinions and ideas with which they are in disagreement. We believe, on the contrary, that a requirement that broadcast licensees utilize their franchises in a manner in which the listening public may be assured of hearing varying opinions on the paramount issues facing the American people is within both the spirit and letter of the first amendment.

Church of Christ marks the beginning of a judicial awareness that our legal system must protect not only the broadcaster's right to speak but also, in some measure, public rights in the communications process. Perhaps this new awareness will stim-ulate inquiry into the stake a newspaper's readership has in the content of the press. Understanding that *Church of Christ* has a constitutional as well as statutory basis helps to expose the distinction typically made between newspapers and broad-cast stations. An orthodox dictum in Judge Burger's otherwise pioneering opinion in *Church of Christ* illustrates the traditional approach:[63]

> A broadcaster seeks and is granted the free and exclusive use of a limited and valuable part of the public domain; when he accepts that franchise it is bur-dened by enforceable public obligations. A newspaper can be operated at the whim or caprice of its owners; a broadcast station cannot.

But can a valid distinction be drawn between newspapers and broadcasting stations, with only the latter subject to regulation? It is commonly said that because the number of possible radio and television licenses is limited, regulation is the natural regimen for broadcasting.[64] Yet the number of daily newspapers is certainly not infinite[65] and, in light of the fact that there are now three times as many radio stations as there are newspapers, the relevance of this distinction is dubious. Consolidation is the established pattern of the American press today, and the need to develop means of access to the press is not diminished because the limitation on the number of newspapers is caused by economic rather than technological factors. Nor is the argument that other newspapers can always spring into existence persuasive—the ability of individuals to publish pamphlets should not preclude regulation of mass circulation, monopoly newspapers any more than the availability of sound trucks precludes regulation of broadcasting stations.

If a contextual approach is taken and a purposive view of the first amendment adopted, at some point the newspaper must be viewed as impressed with a public service stamp and hence under an obligation to provide space on a nondiscriminatory basis to representative groups in the community.[66] It is to be hoped that an awareness of the listener's interest in broadcasting will lead to an equivalent concern for the reader's stake in the press, and that first amendment recognition will be given to a right of access for the protection of the reader, the listener, and the viewer.

V. Implementing a Right of Access to the Press

The foregoing analysis has suggested the necessity of rethinking first amendment theory so that it will not only be effective in preventing governmental abridgment but will also produce meaningful expression despite the present or potential repressive effects of the mass media. If the first amendment can be so invoked, it is necessary to examine what machinery is available to enforce a right of access and what bounds limit that right.

A. Judicial Enforcement

One alternative is a judicial remedy affording individuals and groups desiring to voice views on public issues a right of nondiscriminatory access to the community newspaper. This right could be rooted most naturally in the letter-to-the-editor column[67] and the advertising section. That pressure to establish such a right exists in our law is suggested by a number of cases in which plaintiffs have contended, albeit unsuccessfully, that in certain circumstances newspaper publishers have a common law duty to publish advertisements. In these cases the advertiser sought nondiscriminatory access, subject to even-handed limitations imposed by rates and space.

Although in none of these cases did the newspaper publisher assert lack of space, the right of access has simply been denied.[68] The drift of the cases is that a newspaper is not a public utility and thus has freedom of action regardless of the objectives of the claimant seeking access. One case has the distinction of being the only American case which has recognized a right of access. In *Uhlman v. Sherman*[69] an Ohio lower court held that the dependence and interest of the public in the community newspaper, particularly when it is the only one, imposes the reasonable demand that the purchase of advertising should be open to members of the public on the same basis.

But none of these cases mentions first amendment considerations. What is encouraging for the future of an emergent right of access is that it has been resisted by relentless invocation of the freedom of contract notion that a newspaper publisher is as free as any merchant to deal with whom he chooses.[70] But the broad holding of these commercial advertising cases need not be authoritative for political advertisement. Indeed, it has long been held that commercial advertising is not the type of speech protected by the first amendment,[71] and hence even an abandonment of the romantic view of the first amendment and adoption of a purposive approach would not entitle an individual to require publication of commercial material. However, at the heart of the first amendment is political speech. In this area of speech, a revised, realistic view of the first amendment would permit the encouragement of expression by providing not only for its protection after publication but also for its emergence by publication. The constitutional interest in "uninhibited," "robust" debate, expressed anew in *Times*, supplies new impetus for recognition of a right of access for political and public issue advertising generally.

Nevertheless, courts in two fairly recent cases have refused to require the publication of political advertisements. In *Mid-West Electric Cooperative, Inc. v. West Texas Chamber of Commerce*[72] an electrical cooperative, a member of the chamber, had tendered an advertisement to be placed in the chamber's magazine. The chamber refused to publish the advertisement because it was "contrary to the policies of the organization," but it offered to publish it if "any presentation of political or economic philosophy" contrary to the chamber's policies were omitted. The court refused to require publication, rejecting the cooperative's contention that, although the chamber had the right to choose what to print, the right was to be enforced by a rule of reasonableness. The candor of the censorship requirement in *Mid-West* highlights an area where groups and individuals are at the mercy of censors, unchecked because of a romantic view of the first amendment. On the other hand, even if a realistic view of the first amendment had been adopted by the court, application of a contextual approach might not have dictated an enforcement of a right of access since the medium was not a newspaper, but a magazine, and the scope of its impact on the community was apparently not great.

The second case, *Lord v. Winchester Star, Inc.*,[73] presented an even more compelling situation for recognition of a first amendment right of access. A Boston attorney, residing in Winchester, Massachusetts, took a position on a local matter adverse to that taken by the newspaper in town. Although the newspaper gave space to its side of the controversy, it refused to publish Mr. Lord's letter to the editor—hence debate in the only available local forum was effectively cut off. Lord petitioned the Superior Court for a writ of mandamus requiring the editor to publish his letter. The writ was denied and the Supreme Judicial Court of Massachusetts affirmed. Lord appealed to the United States Supreme Court which dismissed for want of jurisdiction and, treating the appeal as a petition for certiorari, denied certiorari. Plaintiff was unable to provoke a single court to write an opinion, illustrating the lack of recognition given to the reader's interest in "freedom of the press." Although these cases would augur ill for judicial creation of a constitutionally recognized right of access, it must be noted that the interdependence of free access and a free press was neither argued to the courts nor considered by them.

The courts could provide for a right of access other than by reinterpreting the first amendment to provide for the emergence as well as the protection of expression. A right of access to the pages of a monopoly newspaper might be predicated on Justice Douglas's open-ended "public function" theory which carried a majority of the Court in *Evans v. Newton*.[74] Such a theory would demand a rather rabid conception of "state action," but if parks in private hands cannot escape the stigma of abiding "public character," it would seem that a newspaper, which is the common journal of printed communication in a community, could not escape the constitutional restrictions which quasi-public status invites. If monopoly newspapers are indeed quasi-public, their refusal of space to particular viewpoints is state action abridging expression in violation of even the romantic view of the first amendment.[75]

B. A Statutory Solution

Another, and perhaps more appropriate, approach would be to secure the right of access by legislation. A statute might impose the modest requirement, for example, that denial of access not be arbitrary but rather be based on rational grounds. Although some cases have involved a statutory duty to publish,[76] a constitutional basis for a right of access has never been considered. In *Chronicle & Gazette Publishing Co. v. Attorney General*[77] legislation limiting the rates for political advertising to the rates charged for commercial advertising was held constitutional by the Supreme Court of New Hampshire. In upholding the statute Justice Kenison stated:[78] "It is not necessary to consider the extent to which such regulation may go but so long as it does not involve suppression or censorship, the regulation of newspapers is as broad as that over . . . private business." This decision is consistent with a view of the first amendment which permits legislation to effectuate freedom of expression, although the court did not uphold the statute on a theory of constitutional power to equalize opportunities for expression. However, in a dissenting opinion Chief Justice Marble pointed out that the "real purpose" of the statute was to provide for an "economical means of [political] advertising" rather than to counteract the dangers of bribery. Although clearly not put forth for this purpose,[79] Chief Justice Marble's intriguing analysis of the legislative intent is consistent with an access-oriented view of the first amendment—limiting the amount that can be charged for political advertising provides equal opportunities of access for political candidates and views not buttressed by heavy financial support.

Justice Kenison, writing for the court in *Chronicle*, thought that the legislature's failure to compel some measure of access to the press made it an easy case:[80] "The present statute does not compel the plaintiff or any other newspaper to accept political advertising." This remark at least leaves open the validity of a statute requiring access for political advertising. However, such a statute was given explicit judicial consideration in *Commonwealth v. Boston Transcript Co.*,[81] where the elegant and now vanished *Boston Evening Transcript* was charged with violation of a statute requiring newspapers to publish the findings of the state minimum wage commission. The court struck the statute down on a freedom of contract theory, the opinion bare of any mention of free expression problems. Although it was not until 1925 that Justice Sanford observed for the United States Supreme Court that freedom of press was hidden in the underbrush of the fourteenth amendment,[82] failure to discuss freedom of the press in 1924 is probably not pardonable since the Supreme Judicial Court ignored a provision in the Massachusetts constitution prohibiting abridgment of freedom of the press.

But the Massachusetts court in *Boston Transcript* stopped short of suggesting that any statutory compulsion to publish was an invasion of freedom to contract. Rather, the case clearly implies that some regulation in this area is permissible. But it did find one of the constitutional defects of the statute to be the fact that no legitimate state interest was served by the restriction on the publisher. The court was convinced that even without the statute the minimum wage board would "have ample opportunity to print its notice in other newspapers than that published by the defendant at the statutory price."[83] This less pressing need for publication contrasts with the more compelling state interest in equalizing opportunities to reach the electorate presented in *Chronicle* and the interest in access presented by the contemporary character of the mass media, illustrating the importance of a contextual approach.

Another thread common to the *Chronicle* and *Boston Transcript* cases was the concern of both courts with the increased risk of libel litigation if a duty to publish were compelled by statute. In *Chronicle* the majority did not find the objection fatal, but Chief Justice Marble relied specifically on it in his dissent; in *Boston Transcript* at least one reason for invalidation of the statute was the fear that the publisher might be exposed to libel suits. However, the treatment of editorial advertisements by the *Times* Court substantially reduces the risk of the publisher's liability for defamation. Furthermore, the statute granting the right of access could provide that the publisher would not be held for libel for publishing a statement under the statutory mandate.[84]

A recent United States Supreme Court case, *Mills v. Alabama*,[85] places new significance on opportunity for reply in the press and thus provides by implication new support for a statutory right of access to the press. In *Mills*, as in *Chronicle*, the state legislature had regulated newspapers under a state corrupt practices act. The Alabama statute[86] made it a criminal offense to electioneer or solicit votes "on the day on which the election affecting such candidates or propositions is being held." The *Birmingham Post Herald*, a daily newspaper, carried a very strong editorial urging the electorate to adopt a mayor-council form of government in place of the existing commission form. The editor of the newspaper, who had written the editorial, was arrested on a charge of violating the statute. The trail court sustained a demurrer to the complaint, but the Supreme Court of Alabama reversed on the ground that reasonable restriction of the press by the legislature was permissible.

In reversing this decision, Justice Black's opinion for the Supreme Court was based on the familiar concept that the press is a kind of constitutionally anointed *defensor fidei* for democracy:[87]

> The Constitution specifically selected the press, which includes not only newspapers, books, and magazines, but also humble leaflets and circulars . . . to play an important role in the discussion of public affairs. Thus the press serves and was designed to serve as a powerful antidote to any abuses of power by governmental officials and as a constitutionally chosen means for keeping officials elected by the people responsible to all the people whom they were selected to serve.

Mr. Justice Black observes that insofar as the Alabama statute is construed to prohibit the press from praising or criticizing the government, it frustrates the informing function of the press. But all this is familiar theory. What makes the *Mills* case something of a departure, and in its own way quietly original, is an interesting commentary by Justice Black. In rebutting Alabama's claim that the legislature's aim was a constitutionally permissible one—to purge the air of propaganda and induce momentary reflection in a brief period of tranquillity before election day—Justice Black suggested that this argument failed on its own terms since "last-minute" charges could be made on the day before election and no statutory provision had been made for effective answers:[88] "Because the law prevents any adequate reply to these charges, it is wholly ineffective in protecting the electorate 'from confusive last-minute charges and counter-charges.' "

This statement suggests a substitution of the sensitive query "Does the statute prohibit or provide for expression?" for the more wooden and formal question "Does the statute restrain the press?" It is of course clear that *Mills* did not grant a constitutionally endorsed status to legislative or judicial provisions conferring a right of access to assure debate. Quite the contrary, Justice Black prefaced his discussion of the significance of lack of opportunity to reply to "last-minute" charges with the remark that the state's argument about the reflective intent of the statute is illogical *"even if it were relevant* to the constitutionality of the law." But it is the writer's contention that the existence of adequate opportunity for debate, for charge and countercharge, is an extremely relevant consideration in any determination of the constitutionality of legislation in this area. Justice Black's inquiry into the pragmatics of debate is an encouraging step in this direction.

Evidence of an awakening to a more realistic view of the first amendment can be found in another recent case, *Time, Inc. v. Hill.*[89] Directly presented with the issue of whether the first amendment is always to be interpreted as a grant of press immunity and never as a mandate for press responsibility, a divided Court extended the *Times* doctrine by immunizing newspapers from liability under the New York right of privacy statute unless there is a finding that the publication was made in knowing or reckless disregard of the truth. But in a sensitive and thoughtful opinion, concurring in part and dissenting in part, Justice Harlan protested this "sweeping extension of the principles" of *Times*, largely because he thought an attack on private individuals was unlikely to create the "competition among ideas" which an attack on a public figure might create; the *Hill* situation was thought to be an area where the "marketplace of ideas' does not function."[90] I would argue that the marketplace theory will not function even in the *Times* situation without legal imposition of affirmative responsibilities. Nonetheless, Justice Harlan's words may augur well for the future, as may the attitude expressed in Justice Fortas's dissent, joined in by the Chief Justice and Justice Clark:[91]

> The courts may not and must not permit either public or private action that censors the press. But part of this responsibility is to preserve values and procedures which assure the ordinary citizen that the press is not above the reach of the law—that its special prerogatives, granted because of its special and vital functions, are reasonably equated with its needs in the performance of these functions.

The disenchantment of Justices Harlan and Fortas with the mindless expansion of *Times* discloses a new awareness of the range of interests protected by the first amendment.

Constitutional power exists for both federal and state legislation in this area. Turning first to the constitutional basis for federal legislation, it has long been held that freedom of expression is protected by the due process clause of the fourteenth amendment.[92] The now celebrated section five of the fourteenth amendment, authorizing Congress to "enforce, by appropriate legislation" the provisions of the fourteenth amendment, appears to be as resilient and serviceable a tool for effectuating the freedom of expression guarantee of the fourteenth amendment as for implementing the equal protection guarantee. Professor Cox has noted that our recent experience in constitutional adjudication has revealed an untapped reservoir of federal legislative power to define and promote the constitutional rights of individuals in relation to state government.[93] When the consequence of private conduct is to deny to individuals the enjoyment of a right owed by the state, legislation which assures public capacity to perform that duty should be legitimate.[94] Alternatively, legislation implementing responsibility to provide access to the mass media may be justified on a theory that the nature of the communications process imposes quasi-public functions on these quasi-public instrumentalities.[95]

It is interesting to note that the late Professor Meiklejohn did not anticipate the new uses that the long dormant section five of the fourteenth amendment could be put in order to implement in a positive manner the great negatives of section one of the fourteenth amendment. Consequently, he believed that the only solution to what I have styled the romantic approach to the first amendment was by way of constitutional amendment. Mr. W. H. Ferry of the Center for Democratic Institutions has made public Professor Meiklejohn's despair at the unintended result which had been wrought by the first amendment—freedom of the press had become an excuse for the controllers of mass communication to duck responsibility and to exercise by default the same censorship role which had been denied the government.[96] Mr. Ferry says that shortly before his death Professor Meiklejohn proposed, in an unpublished paper for the Center, that the first amendment be revised by adding the following:[97]

> In view of the intellectual and cultural responsibilities laid upon the citizens of a free society by the political institutions of self-government, the Congress, acting in cooperation with the several states and with nongovernmental organizations serving the same general purpose, shall have power to provide for the intellectual and cultural education of all of the citizens of the United States.

What is especially interesting about Professor Meiklejohn's suggested addition is the depth of its criticism of contemporary first amendment theory. However, it is not necessary to amend the first amendment to attain the goal of greater access to the mass media. I do not think it adventurous to suggest that, if Congress were to pass a federal right of access statute, a sympathetic court would not lack the constitutional text necessary to validate the statute. If the first amendment is read to state affirmative goals, Congress is empowered to realize them. My basic premise in these suggestions is that a provision preventing government from silencing or dominating opinion should not be confused with an absence of governmental power to require that opinion be voiced.

If public order and an informed citizenry are, as the Supreme Court has repeatedly said, the goals of the first amendment, these goals would appear to comport well with state attempts to implement a right of access under the rubric of its traditional police power. If a right of access is not constitutionally proscribed, it would seem well within the powers reserved to the states by the tenth amendment of the Constitution to enact such legislation, the federal legislation would control. Yet, the whole concept of a right of access is so embryonic that it can scarcely be argued that congressional silence preempts the field.

The right of access might be an appropriate area for experimental, innovative legislation. The right to access problems of a small state dominated by a single city with a monopoly press will vary, for example, from those of a populous state with many cities nourished by many competing media. These differences may be more accurately reflected by state autonomy in this area, resulting in a cultural federalism such as that envisaged by Justice Harlan in the obscenity cases.[98]

C. Administrative Feasibility of Protecting a Right of Access

If a right of access is to be recognized, considerations of administrative feasibility require that limitations of the right be carefully defined. The recent case of *Office of Communication of the United Church of Christ v. FCC*[99] suggests, by analogy, the means by which such a right of nondiscriminatory access can be rendered judicially manageable. In *Church of Christ* the court, while expanding the concept of standing, did not hold that every listener's taste provides standing to challenge the applicant in broadcast license renewal proceedings. Similarly, the daily press cannot be placed at the mercy of the collective vanity of the public. *Church of Christ* suggests an approach to give bounds to a right of access which could be utilized cautiously, but nevertheless meaningfully.

The organizations and individuals requesting standing in *Church of Christ* represented the Negro community in Jackson, Mississippi, almost half of the city's population. Therefore, the court of appeal's grant of standing did not hold that all those who sought standing to challenge the application for license renewal were entitled to it. The court held, instead, that certain of the petitioners could serve as "responsible representatives" of the Negro community in order to assert claims of inadequate and distorted coverage.

A right of access, whether created by court or legislature, necessarily would have to develop a similar approach. One relevant factor, using *Church of Christ* as an analogue, would be the degree to which the petitioner seeking access represents a significant sector of the community. But this is perhaps not a desirable test—"divergent" views, by definition, may not command the support of a "significant sector" of the community, and these may be the very views which, by hypothesis, it is desirable to encourage. Perhaps the more relevant consideration is whether the material for which access is sought is indeed suppressed and underrepresented by the newspaper. Thus, if there are a number of petitioners seeking access for a particular matter or issue, it may be necessary to give access to only one. The unimpressed response of Judge Burger in *Church of Christ* to the FCC's lamentations about that enduring tidal phenomenon of the law, the "floodgates," strikes an appropriate note of calm:[100] "The fears of regulatory agencies that their processes will be inundated by expansion of standing criteria are rarely borne out."

Utilization of a contextual approach highlights the importance of the degree to which an idea is suppressed in determining whether the right to access should be enforced in a particular case. If all media in a community are held by the same ownership, the access claim has greater attractiveness. This is true although the various media, even when they do reach the same audience, serve different functions and create different reactions and expectations. The existence of competition within the same medium, on the other hand, probably weakens the access claim, though competition within a medium is no assurance that significant opinions will have no difficulty in securing access to newspaper space or broadcast time. It is significant that the right of access cases that have been litigated almost invariably involve a monopoly newspaper in a community.[101]

VI. Conclusion

The changing nature of the communications process has made it imperative that the law show concern for the public interest in effective utilization of media for the expression of diverse points of view. Confrontation of ideas, a topic of eloquent affection in contemporary decisions, demands some recognition of a right to be heard as a constitutional principle. It is the writer's position that it is open to the courts to fashion a remedy for a right of access, at least in the most arbitrary cases, independently of legislation. If such an innovation is judically resisted, I suggest that our constitutional law authorizes a carefully framed right of access statute which would forbid an arbitrary denial of space, hence securing an effective forum for the expression of divergent opinions.

With the development of private restraints on free expression, the idea of a free marketplace where ideas can compete on their merits has become just as unrealistic in the twentieth century as the economic theory of perfect competition. The world in which an essentially rationalist philosophy of the first amendment was born has vanished and what was rationalism is now romance.

Notes

1. Broun, *Those Charming People*, in ONE HUNDRED YEARS OF THE NATION 197, 199 (H. Christman ed. 1965).
2. 341 U.S. 494, 584 (1951) (emphasis added).
3. *Id.* at 584–85.
4. 250 U.S. 616, 630 (1919).
5. 198 U.S. 45, 75 (1905) (dissenting opinion).
6. Kingsley Int'l Pictures Corp. v. Regents of the Univ. of the State of N.Y., 360 U.S. 684, 699 (1959) (Douglas, J., concurring).
7. R.H.S. CROSSMAN, THE POLITICS OF SOCIALISM 44 (1965).
8. *Id.*
9. Bround, *supra* note I, at 197.
10. J.R. WIGGINS, FREEDOM OR SECRECY 178 (rev. ed. 1964). Wiggins offers these statistics on the diminishing competitive character of the American press:

> The number of daily newspapers in the United States declined from 2202 in 1909–10 to 1760 in 1953–4. The number of cities with competing daily newspaper declined from 689 to only 87. The number of cities with non-competing dailies increased from 518 to 1361. Eighteen states are now without any locally competing daily newspapers. *Id.* at 177.

But Mr. Wiggins cautions that the danger of suppressing varied viewpoints as a result of the rise of the monopoly newspaper can be exaggerated since newspapers compete not only with each other but with other media.

11. H.M. MCLUHAN, UNDERSTANDING MEDIA (1964).
12. *Id.* at 173. The first amendment implications of this phenomenon are very great indeed. In the Supreme Court decisions we find a theory of knowledge which revolves around an outmoded conception of decision making: Information is distributed by advocates of various points of view and, after assimilation and reflection, the citizen makes his judgment. But, according to McLuhan, the media defeat this step-ladder approach to decision making: "As the speed of information increases, the tendency is for politics to move away from representation and delegation of constituents toward immediate involvement of the entire community in the central acts of decision. Slower speeds of information make delegation and representation mandatory." *Id.* at 204.
13. D. LACY, FREEDOM AND COMMUNICATIONS 69 (1961).
14. That the media have had a cutting edge in the past, however, should not be forgotten. On the phenomenon of the political radio "voices" of the thirties it has been remarked:

> There were many opportunities in the early years for commentators to convert listeners to a point of view. None succeeded until the beginning of the second decade of radio, when the Depression made home entertainment

mandatory for most families . . . Men like Father Charles E. Coughlin and Huey Long could start a movement to bring to America a Fascist brand of social justice or to make it possible for Americans to share the wealth. Long was stopped in 1935 by a bullet in Baton Rouge, Louisiana; Father Coughlin was silenced in 1940 by his bishop. Both had long demonstrated how magnetic a radio voice could be.

B. ULANOV, THE TWO WORLDS OF AMERICAN ART 404 (1965).

15. *See* p. 1661 *infra*.

16. Seldes, *Public Entertainment and the Subversion of Ethical Standards*, 363 ANNALS 87 (1966).

17. Ferry, *Masscomm as Educator*, 35 AM. SCHOLAR 293, 300 (1966).

18. *See, e.g.,* Weiman v. Updegraff, 344 U.S. 183, 194 (1952) (Black, J., concurring):

> With full knowledge of this danger the Framers rested our First Amendment on the premise that the slightest suppression of thought, speech, press, or public assembly is still more dangerous. This means that individuals are guaranteed an undiluted and unequivocal right to express themselves on questions of current public interest.

19. Gitlow v. New York, 268 U.S. 652, 673 (1925) (dissenting opinion).

20. 274 U.S. 357, 375 (1927) (concurring opinion).

21. 310 U.S. 88, 102 (1940) (emphasis added).

22. 302 U.S. 319, 325–27 (1937).

23. 274 U.S. 357, 375 (1927). Chief Justice Hughes made a similar reference to the connection between free speech and public order in De Jonge v. Oregon, 299 U.S. 353, 365 (1937):

> The greater the importance of safeguarding the community from incitements to the overthrow of our institutions by force and violence, the more imperative is the need to preserve inviolate the constitutional rights of free speech, free press and free assembly in order to maintain the opportunity for free political discussion, to the end that government may be responsive to the will of the people and that changes, if desired, may be obtained by peaceful means.

However, although all Justices would probably agree that there is a public order function underlying the free expression guarantee, others have pointed out that the guarantee contemplates a measure of disorder as well. Thus Justice Douglas declared for the Court in Terminiello v. Chicago, 337 U.S. 1, 4 (1949):

> Accordingly a function of free speech under our system of government is to invite dispute. In may indeed best serve its high purpose when it induces a condition of unrest, creates dissatisfaction with conditions as they are, or even stirs people to anger.

24. 336 U.S. 77, 97 (1949) (concurring opinion).

25. *Id*. at 102.

26. *Id*. at 102–03.

27. *Id*. at 103.

28. 340 U.S. 290, 307–08 (1951) (emphasis added).

29. A MEIKLEJOHN, POLITICAL FREEDOM: THE CONSTITUTIONAL POWERS OF THE PEOPLE 25–28 (1960).

30. *See* Lorain Journal Co. v. United States, 342 U.S. 143 (1951).

31. 326 U.S. I, 20 (1945) (emphasis added).

32. United States v. Associated Press, 52 F. Supp. 362, 372 (S.D.N.Y. 1943).

33. *Cf.* Shelly v. Kraemer, 334 U.S. 1 (1948).

34. 283 U.S. 697 (1931).

35. *Id.* at 713–14.

36. 376 U.S. 254 (1964).

37. *Id.* at 270.

38. This protection bestowed on the press may extend far beyond that suggested by the "public official" language of *Times*. Expansion has already been made by the Supreme Court. Garrison v. Louisiana, 379 U.S. 64 (1964) (criticism of "private" behavior which reflects on judge's fitness for office is protected by *Times*); Rosenblatt v. Baer, 383 U.S. 75 (1966) (local nonelected official may be a "public official"). Lower court cases have begun further extensions. The *Times* privilege may come to bar recovery by a private individual who is "incidentally" defamed by a criticism directed at a public official. *See* Gilberg v. Goffi, 21 App. Div. 2d 517, 251 N.Y.S.2d 823 (Sup. Ct. 1964), *aff'd*, 15 N.Y.2d 1023, 207 N.E.2d 620, 260 N.Y.S.2d 29 (1965); Note, *Defamation à Deux: Incidental Defamation and the Sullivan Doctrine*, 114 U. PA. L. REV. 241 (1965). The privilege may also be extended to protect defamatory statements about "public men." Walker v. Courier-Journal & Louisville Times Co., 246 F. Supp. 231 (W.D. Ky. 1965) ("public man"); Pauling v. National Review Inc., 49 Misc. 2d 975, 269 N.Y.S.2d II (Sup. Ct. 1966) ("public figure").

39. The decision may have a direct impact on discouraging debate if extended, as Judge Friendly suggests, to protect a defamatory statement about "the participant in public debate on an issue of grave public concern." Pauling v. News Syndicate Co., 335 F.2d 659, 671 (2d Cir.) (dictum), *cert. denied*, 379 U.S. 968 (1964). Individuals will be less willing to engage in public debate if that participation will allow newspapers to defame with relative impunity. Despite this undesirable consequence, the Supreme Court might abandon its "public official" standard in favor of protecting the publication of statements about "public issues." *See* Note, *The Scope of First Amendment Protection for Good-Faith Defamatory Error*, 75 YALE L.J. 642, 648 (1966); *cf.* Time, Inc. v. Hill, 385 U.S. 374 (1967) (right of privacy case).

40. 376 U.S. at 297.

41. United States v. Associated Press, 52 F. Supp. 362, 372 (S.D.N.Y. 1943) (L. Hand, J.), quoted with approval in New York Times Co. v. Sullivan, 376 U.S. 254, 270 (1964).

42. 376 U.S. at 266.

43. *Id.* at 286. Retraction statutes have some bearing on enforcing responsive dialogue. These statutes, common in this country, require the publisher to "take back" what has already been said if damages in a defamation suit are to be mitigated. If false statements have been made, and the complainant can convince the publisher to retract on the basis of correct information, such a procedure certainly serves a cleansing function for the information process. For a discussion of the status of retractions after the *Times* decision, see Note, *Vindication of the Reputation of a Public Official*, 80 HARV. L. REV. 1730, 1740–43 (1967).

44. The right of reply is commonly used in Europe and South America, constituting more than a remedy for defamation since it is available to anyone named or designated in a publication. There are essentially two approaches to the right of reply, one modelled on French law, which allows the reply to contain a statement of the individual's point of view, and one on German law, which limits the reply to corrections of factual misstatements. For a thorough study of these devices, see Donnelly, *The Right of Reply: An Alternative to an Action for Libel*, 34 VA. L. REV. 867 (1948). If either approach were to be adopted here, the French method would appear appropriate since assurance of debate is the stated purpose of *Times*, suggesting the exchange of opinion. For a discussion of right of reply after *Times*, see 80 HARV. L. REV., *supra* note 43, at 1745–47. *Cf.* Mills v. Alabama, 384 U.S. 214 (1966), discussed pp. 1672–73 *infra. See also* Pedrick, *Freedom of the Press and the Law of Libel: The Modern Revised Translation*, 49 CORNELL L.Q. 581 (1964).

45. 376 U.S. at 266 (emphasis added).

46. V. O. KEY, PUBLIC OPINION AND AMERICAN DEMOCRACY 378–79, 387 (1961).

47. *Id.* at 379.

48. *Id.* at 380.

49. H.M. McLUHAN, UNDERSTANDING MEDIA 305 (1964).

50. 383 U.S. 463 (1966).

51. *Id.* at 466.

52. The *Ginzburg* theory that an overriding commercial purpose may alter first amendment imperatives vis-à-vis legislative power to regulate a particular area is not new doctrine. For example, the *Ginzburg* Court cites Valentine v. Chrestensen, 316 U.S. 52 (1942), which upheld an ordinance forbidding the distribution of commercial matter in the streets when applied to an individual who had attempted to avoid the statute by printing noncommercial information on the opposite side of a commercial handbill.

53. "The Court today appears to concede that the materials Ginzburg mailed were themselves protected by the First Amendment." 383 U.S. at 500 (Stewart, J., dissenting).

54. A Book Named "John Cleland's Memoirs of a Woman of Pleasure" v. Attorney General of Massachusetts, 383 U.S. 413, 427 (1966) (concurring opinion).

55. 383 U.S. at 470.

56. F.2d 994 (D.C. Cir. 1966), *noted in* 80 HARV. L. REV. 670 (1967).

57. The doctrine was promulgated by the FCC in its *Report on Editorializing by Broadcast Licensees*, 13 F.C.C. 1246 (1949).

58. 47 U.S.C. § 315 (a) (1964).

59. 13 F.C.C. at 1249, cited in 359 F.2d at 999 n.5.

60. Associated Press v. United States, 326 U.S. I (1945), discussed pp. 1654–55 *supra*; Thornhill v. Alabama, 310 U.S. 88 (1940), discussed pp. 1648–49 *supra*.

61. Some feeling for the intensity of the debate may be gleaned from Commissioner Jones's separate opinion on the *Report*. 13 F.C.C. at 1259.

62. *Id.* at 1256.

63. 359 F.2d at 1003.

64. *See Report on Editorializing by Broadcasting Licensees*, 13 F.C.C. 1246, 1257 (1940).

65. *See* p. 1644 & note 10 *supra*.

66. This is reminiscent of Professor Chafee's query as to whether the monopoly newspaper ought to be treated like a public utility. Contrary to my position, however, he concluded that a legally enforceable right of access would not be feasible. 2 Z. CHAFEE, GOVERNMENT AND MASS COMMUNICATIONS 624–50 (1947).

67. In Wall v. World Publishing Co., 263 P.2d 1010 (Okla. 1953), a reader of the *Tulsa World* contended that the newspaper's invitation to its readers to submit letters on matters of public importance was a contract offer from the newspaper which was accepted by submission of the letter. The plaintiff argued that, by refusal to publish, the newspaper had breached its contract. Despite the ingenuity of the argument, the court held for defendant. Note, however, that a first amendment argument was not made to the court.

68. Shuck v. Carroll Daily Herald, 215 Iowa 1276, 247 N.W. 813 (1933); J. J. Gordon, Inc. v. Worcester Telegram Publishing Co., 343 Mass. 142, 177 N.E.2d 586 (1961); Mack v. Costello, 32 S.D. 511, 143 N.W. 950 (1913). These cases do not consider legislative power to compel access to the press. Other cases have denied a common law right but have suggested that the area is a permissible one for legislation. Approved Personnel, Inc. v. Tribune Co., 177 So. 2d 704 (Fla. 1965); Friedenberg v. Times Publishing Co., 170 La. 3, 127 So. 345 (1930); *In re* Louis Wohl, Inc., 50 F.2d 254 (E.D. Mich. 1931); Poughkeepsie Buying Service, Inc. v. Poughkeepsie Newspapers, Inc., 205 Misc. 982, 131 N.Y.S.2d 515 (Sup. Ct. 1954).

69. 22 Ohio N.P. (n.s.) 225, 31 Ohio Dec. 54 (C.P. 1919).

70. *See, e.g.*, Shuck v. Carroll Daily Herald, 215 Iowa 1276, 247 N.W. 813 (1933).

71. *See Developments in the Law—Deceptive Advertising*, 80 HARV. L. REV. 1005, 1027–38 (1967).

72. 369 S.W.2d 842 (Tex. Ct. Civ. App. 1963).

73. 346 Mass. 764, 190 N.E.2d 875 (1963), *appeal dismissed and cert. denied*, 376 U.S. 221 (1964).

74. 382 U.S. 296 (1966).

75. *Cf.* Marsh v. Alabama, 326 U.S. 501 (1946).

76. Belleville Advocate Printing Co. v. St. Clair County, 336 Ill. 359, 168 N.E. 312 (1929); Lake County v. Lake County Publishing & Printing Co., 280 Ill. 243, 117 N.E. 452 (1917) (dictum) (statute setting rates chargeable for official notices imposed no duty to publish); Wooster v. Mahaska County, 122 Iowa 300, 98 N.W. 103 (1904) (dictum) (newspaper had no duty to publish and legislature could not impose one).

77. 94 N.H. 148, 48 A.2d 478 (1946), *appeal dismissed*, 329 U.S. 690 (1947).

78. *Id.* at 153, 48 A.2d at 482.

79. I surmise that Chief Justice Marble offers this view of the statute because he believes the legislative interest in equalizing opportunities for political advertising is outweighed by the publisher's freedom of contract. Whether he would think the statute unconstitutional if it were defended on a theory that states have power to provide for "freedom of the press," so long as they do not expressly inhibit it, is arguable.

80. 94 N.H. 148, 152–53, 48 A.2d 478, 481 (1946). Another important aspect of the case was the court's answer to the argument that regulation of political advertising rates in the press, without corresponding regulation of other advertising facilities such as job printing and billboard advertising, was unconstitutionally dis-

criminatory: "It is sufficient answer to this argument that the 'state is not bound to cover the whole field of possible abuses.' " *Id.* at 152, 48 A.2d at 481.

81. 249 Mass. 477, 144 N.E. 400 (1924).

82. Gitlow v. New York, 268 U.S. 652 (1925).

83. 249 Mass. 477, 484, 144 N.E. 400, 402 (1924).

84. In Farmer's Educ. & Cooperative Union v. WDAY, Inc., 360 U.S. 525 (1959), a station was held not liable for the defamatory utterance of a candidate exercising his right to speak under the Federal Communications Act of 1934, 47 U.S.C. § 315 (Supp. V, 1964).

85. 384 U.S. 214 (1966).

86. ALA. CODE tit. 17 § 285 (1958).

87. 384 U.S. at 219.

88. *Id.* at 220.

89. 385 U.S. 374 (1967).

90. *Id.* at 407–08.

91. *Id.* at 420.

92. Gitlow v. New York, 268 U.S. 652 (1925).

93. Cox, *Foreword: Constitutional Adjudication and the Promotion of Human Rights,* 80 HARV. L. REV. 91 (1966). *See,* e.g., Katzenbach v. Morgan, 384 U.S. 641 (1966); South Carolina v. Katzenbach, 383 U.S. 301 (1966).

94. United States v. Price, 383 U.S. 787 (1966); United States v. Guest, 383 U.S. 745 (1966); Bullock v. United States, 265 F.2d 683 (6th Cir.) (by implication), *cert. denied,* 360 U.S. 909 (1959); Brewer v. Hoxie School District No. 46, 238 F.2d 91 (8th Cir. 1956) (by implication). *See generally* Cox, *supra* note 93, at 110–14.

95. Evans v. Newton, 382 U.S. 296 (1966); Marsh v. Alabama, 326 U.S. 501 (1946). Both decisions find that private property may become quasi-public without a statute in extreme cases. The Court should surely defer to a congressional determination in an arguable case.

96. Ferry, *supra* note 17.

97. *Id.* at 301.

98. Ginzburg v. United States, 383 U.S. 463, 493 (1966) (dissenting opinion); Roth v. United States, 354 U.S. 476, 503–07 (1957) (dissenting opinion).

99. F.2d 994 (D.C. Cir. 1966); *see* pp. 1663–66 *supra.*

100. F.2d at 1006.

101. *Cf.,* e.g., *In re* Louis Wohl, Inc., 50 F.2d 254 (E.D. Mich. 1931).

GAYE TUCHMAN

News as the Reproduction of the Status Quo:
A Summary
(1978)

Let me review once more the constituent features of the news frame, stressing that frames both produce and limit meaning. To return to the analogy of news as a window frame, characteristics of the window, its size and composition, limit what may be seen. So does its placement, that is, what aspect of the unfolding scene it makes accessible. Furthermore, simultaneously, news draws on social and cultural resources to present accounts, and is itself a social and cultural resource for social actors.

Definitions of news are historically derived and embedded. At any one moment, defining what is newsworthy entails drawing on contemporary understandings of the significance of events as rules for human behavior, institutional behavior, and motives. Members of society and participants in its institutions, newsworkers have rules available to them as social resources. Among those rules as resources are some that newsworkers use to define the relationship between news and other forms of knowledge, between newsworkers and other workers, and between news organizations and other social institutions. For instance, in the 1920s, when newsworkers defined themselves as professionals and news as a veridical representation of events, they drew on two cultural resources. One was popular notions of science current in the 1920s. The second was the professionals' distrust of the "reasonableness" of public opinion, because public opinion was no longer identified as the articulation of reason. The claims to both professionalism and veridical representation served, with other factors, as resources for an additional assertion. News articulated itself as he embodiment of provisions of the First Amendment (a historical resource) and as the protector of the people (a class interest).

Needless to say, all social actors did not have to accept this definition of the role of news. But although news professionalism conflicted with the rights of owners and managers to freedom of speech as an attribute of private property ("Freedom

From *Making News: A Study in the Construction of Reality* (New York: The Free Press, 1978), 209–16.

of the press is guaranteed only to those who own one"), news professionalism also served the owner's articulation of other interests. For professionalism ignored the impact of the socioeconomic processes of concentration, centralization, and conglomeration on the applicability of existing ideas to economic and political life. News organizations simultaneously participated in these processes—inventing wire services, newspaper chains, news syndicates, and radio and television networks—and sought to define conglomerates and corporations as private enterprise. By invoking eighteenth-century concepts (such as its model of free speech) and applying nineteenth-century distinctions (such as public and private rights) to twentieth-century phenomena, news limits knowledge. News obfuscates social reality instead of revealing it. It confirms the legitimacy of the state by hiding the state's intimate involvement with, and support of, corporate capitalism.

Additionally, news both draws upon and reproduces institutional structures. Through its arrangement of time and space as intertwined social phenomena, the news organization disperses a news net. By identifying centralized sources of information as legitimated social institutions, news organizations and newsworkers wed themselves to specific beats and bureaus. Those sites are then objectified as the appropriate sites at which information should be gathered. Additionally, those sites of news gathering are objectified as the legitimate and legitimating sources of both information and governance. Through naive empiricism, that information is transformed into objective facts—facts as a normal, natural, taken-for-granted description and constitution of a state of affairs. And through the sources identified with facts, newsworkers create and control controversy; they contain dissent.

The dispersion of reporters to glean facts generates its own organizational structure replete with assigned responsibilities and priorities. These are the territorial, institutional, and topical chains of command. Distinctions between and among these three spheres, which necessarily overlap one another, require ongoing negotiations of responsibility and newsworthiness. At least in part, newsworthiness is a product of these negotiations intended to sort out strips of everyday occurrences as news. These negotiations also legitimate the status quo. Each day the editors reproduce their living compromise—the hierarchy among the editors. They also reestablish the supremacy of the territorial chain of command, which incorporates political beats and bureaus but excludes topical specialties such as women's news and sports. These sorts of news are thus rendered institutionally uninteresting. In contrast, the topics of the territorial chain of command—stories about legitimated institutions—receive attention and so substantiate the power of those institutions.

Social actors also produce the rhythm of daily life, which they base in societal institutions. In newswork that rhythm is embedded in the intersection of news organizations and legitimated institutions. Faced with a glut of information by the dispersion of the news net, newsworkers and news organizations battle to impose a uniform rhythm of processing upon occurrences. They impose deadlines on defined stages of processing, and so objectify a news rhythm. They draw on the way occurrences are thought to happen, in order to reproduce a state of affairs conducive to news processing. Using past experiences as guides for the present, they typify occurrences as news events. The application of a typification to an event is subject to revision, redefinition, and reformulation, as are the typifications themselves. For typifications are based in present understandings of past situations, and such understandings of the past are continually revised. For instance, the events associated with Watergate were successively cast as a break-in (spot news), a conspiracy uncovered by news investigation (soft news), a scandal prompting comment by officials (spot news), legislative and judicial investigations (continuing news), and a presidential resignation contravening historical precedent (what-a-story). Associated with taken-for-granted assumptions about institutional processes and practices, typification may generate newsworthiness.

When an occurrence does not unfold as professionals had predicted it would, the newsworkers revise the typifications applied to it. President Johnson's speech announcing that he would not run for another term of office is one example of typification and retypification, replete with a call to historical precedent—Calvin Coolidge's statement, "I will not run." That example is interesting theoretically because newsworkers had previously invoked their objectified (taken-for-granted) knowledge to predict that Johnson would turn back Senator Eugene McCarthy's campaign for the Democratic presidential nomination. They then interpreted the error as an affirmation that Johnson's announcement was particularly newsworthy. In this case, too, the invocation of professional knowledge generates newsworthiness. Furthermore, the appeal to history and the immediate redispersion of the news net to gather reaction stories about politicians' responses to the announcement also reaffirm the status quo.

News processing is itself routinized according to the way occurrences at legitimated institutions are thought to unfold; predicting the course of continuing stories at legitimated institutions enables editors to plan which reporters will be available for spot-news coverage on any one day. The news net is based in legitimated institutions. So, too, the redispersion of the news net to gather reaction stories invokes legitimate authority by seeking out governors, mayors, presidential aspirants, senators, other legislators, and quasi-legitimated leaders. It evenhandedly gathers comments from Republicans and Democrats as the embodiment of political processes and so affirms the legitimacy of those processes. The symbolic "man [or woman] on the street" contributes his or her opinion as a representation of others, not as a representative of others. Representativeness is thought to rest in either legitimated institutions or amassed quantities of supporters.

Although typifications limit the idiosyncrasy of occurrences as the raw material of news, they still enable great flexibility. Newsworkers' activities are relatively unsupervised, and the lack of direct supervision provides room for newsworkers to claim professionalism and to both modify and ignore organizational rules. Sharing and hoarding, working together at the scene of stories, reading one another's work, socializing together, newsworkers produce professional understandings of how work is to be done. These understandings are subject to negotiation and reformulation: Editors and bureau chiefs negotiate who will cover a story and how it will be covered. Reporters negotiate their intricate relationships with one another and with sources, including the kind and amount of sharing appropriate to situations. Through this ongoing interaction, they identify the sorts of people who will serve as good sources of information about occurrences at legitimated institutions. Again invoking past experience, they extend those ideas and practices to social movements as well, creating quasi-legitimated leaders as they do so. They also blur distinctions between public and private, for they objectify political representatives and bureaucrats as "the city," "the state," or "the country." They identify the population as "the public." Simultaneously, then, politicians and bureaucrats are said to be representatives and are divorced from the population they are said to represent. Newsworkers and the news itself are left to adjudicate between "the city" (or country) and "the public." The newsworkers legitimate the role they have claimed for themselves and they legitimate politicians and bureaucrats as embodiments of political units.

Additionally, through their interaction with sources and with one another, newsworkers develop ways of identifying facts. Facts and the need for facts, sources and methods of reporting are mutually self-constituting phenomena. I do not mean to imply either that one person's fact is another's bias or that facticity is relative and unobjective. Rather, I mean that methods of identifying facts, including methods of identifying appropriate sources, objectify social life and, at times, *reify* social phenomena.

Berger and Luckmann explain:

> Reification can be described as an extreme step in the process of objectification, whereby the objectivated world loses its comprehensibility as a human enterprise and becomes fixated as a non-human, non-humanizable inert facticity. . . . Man [sic], the producer of the world, is apprehended as its product, and human activity as an epiphenomenon of non-human processes [1967: 89].

As we have seen, news sometimes uses symbols as the representation of reality and presents them as the product of forces outside human control. That is the typical presentation of economic activity and civil disorders, such as riots. These facets of social life are presented as alien, reified forces, akin to fluctuations in the weather, a natural phenomenon. Indeed, television's visual representation of the web of facticity frames riots and tornadoes in a similar manner and insistently distinguishes them from interviews with talking heads.

The reification of economic activity and civil disorders also reaffirms the status quo. First, reification affirms that the individual is powerless to battle either the forces of nature or the forces of the economy. The individual as symbol is presented as a representation of a common plight. The news consumer is encouraged to sympathize or to rejoice, but not to organize politically. Writing of radio, Lazarsfeld and Merton describe the news consumer's reaction as a narcotizing dysfunction:

> The individual takes his secondary [media] contact with the world of political reality . . . as a vicarious performance. He comes to mistake *knowing* about problems of the day for *doing* something about them. His social conscience remains spotlessly clean. He is concerned. He is informed. . . . But, after he has gotten through his dinner and listened to his favorite radio programs and after he has read his second newspaper of the day, it is time for bed [1948, reprinted 1964: 464].

That dysfunction is partially based on the news consumers' relationship to the media: Walter Cronkite of CBS or James Reston of the *New York Times* may enter their homes, but neither Cronkite nor Reston interacts directly with the consumer. They do not mutually negotiate definitions of reality.

Second, news presentations soothe the news consumers even as they reify social forces. To present the facts, newsworkers go to centralized sources responsible for handling the problems created by reified forces. Accordingly, a governor and a high-ranking officer in the National Guard may be quoted to describe a riot or a flood area. They may also be quoted about what they are doing to solve the crisis. Similarly, the president's economic advisors may describe a problem and the solution they propose. If they fail, it is because they contend with reified "natural forces." If they succeed, success symbolizes the legitimacy of their activities. If experts look into a "freak accident," it is to ensure that a similar disaster could never happen again. By implication, news consumers have decided correctly by watching television, reading the newspaper, and going to bed. They are ill equipped to deal with reified forces, and legitimated experts and authorities are doing everything they can.

In addition to reifying some phenomena, the mutual constitution of facts and sources imposes sequences of questions and answers on news events. By their very availability as resources, these professionally validated sequences encourage a trained incapacity to grasp the significance of new ideas. Instead, new ideas and emerging social issues—innovations—are framed by past experience and are typified as soft news. Lacking the appropriate questions and answers, blind to the possibility that there are questions and answers they do not know, reporters may not "be able to get a handle" on innovation. To make it a suitable topic of news, they may dismiss it, mock it, or otherwise transform it. The news professionals have many justifications they can invoke to explain their inability to deal with innovation. All are their own organizational and professional objectifications of experiences as constraints or resources. Among the constraints are the press of work, the omnipresence of deadlines, and the struggle to present factual accounts of events. Collectively derived typifications serve as constraint and resource: They are intended to facilitate news processing. But if an occurrence does not readily present itself as news easily packaged in a known narrative form, that occurrence is either soft news (requiring more reportorial time and editorial attention) or nonnews. It is dismissed by the limits inherent in the news frame.

To do otherwise, news professionals would have to question the very premises of the news net and their own routine practices. They would have to see the ways their affirmation of professionalism serves to legitimate both news as an account and social institutions as the source of news. They would have to recognize the inherent limitations of the narrative forms associated with the web of facticity. And they would have to come to terms with news as an indexical and reflexive phenomenon—a resource for social action in their own lives, in the lives of news consumers, and in the lives of the socially, politically, and economically powerful.

It seems trite to observe that knowledge is power. Yet that rationalist dictum is both a tenet of our society and a ruling premise of newswork. For power may be realized through the dissemination of some knowledge and the suppression of other ideas. And it may be reinforced by the way knowledge is framed as a resource for social action. News, I have argued, is a social resource whose construction limits an analytic understanding of contemporary life. Through its dispersion of the news net, its typifications, the claimed professionalism of newsworkers, the mutual constitution of fact and source, the representational forms of the news narrative, the claim to First Amendment rights of both private property and professionalism—through all these phenomena, objectified as constraints or as resources—news legitimates the status quo.

I do not mean to accuse newsworkers of bias. The news professionals rightfully insist that those who shout "bias" be able to define objective truth in a definitive manner. I do not claim that ability. But I do claim that it is valuable to identify news as an artful accomplishment attuned to specific understandings of social reality. Those understandings, constituted in specific work processes and practices, legitimate the status quo. Furthermore, I claim that the theories developed here might fruitfully be applied to the social construction of other sorts of knowledge and other ideologies.

EDWARD S. HERMAN and NOAM CHOMSKY

Propaganda Mill
(1988)

It is a primary function of the mass media in the United States to mobilize public support for the special interests that dominate the Government and the private sector.

This is our conclusion after years of studying the media. Perhaps it is an obvious point—but the common assumption seems to be that the media are independent and committed to discovering and reporting the truth. Leaders of the media claim that their news judgments rest on unbiased, objective criteria. We contend, on the other hand, that the powerful are able to fix the premises of discourse, decide what the general populace will be allowed to see, hear, and think about, and "manage" public opinion by mounting regular propaganda campaigns.

We do not claim this is all the mass media do, but we believe the propaganda function to be a very important aspect of their overall service.

In countries where the levers of power are in the hands of a state bureaucracy, monopolistic control of the media, often supplemented by official censorship, makes it clear that media serve the ends of the dominant elite. It is much more difficult to see a propaganda system at work where the media are private and formal censorship is absent.

This is especially true where the media actively compete, periodically attack and expose corporate and governmental malfeasance, and aggressively portray themselves as spokesmen for free speech and the general community interest. What is not evident (and remains undiscussed in the media) is the severely limited access to the private media system and the effect of money and power on the system's performance.

Critiques of this kind are often dismissed by Establishment commentators as "conspiracy theories," but this is merely an evasion. We don't rely on any kind of conspiracy hypothesis to explain the performance of the media; in fact, our treatment is much closer to a "free-market" analysis.

From *The Progressive*, June 1988, 14–17.

Most of the bias in the media arises from the selection of right-thinking people, the internalization of preconceptions until they are taken as self-evident truths, and the practical adaptation of employees to the constraints of ownership, organization, market, and political power.

The censorship practiced within the media is largely self-censorship, by reporters and commentators who adjust to the "realities" as they perceive them. But there are important actors who do take positive initiatives to define and shape the news and to keep the media in line. This kind of guidance is provided by the Government, the leaders of the corporate community, the top media owners and executives, and assorted individuals and groups who are allowed to take the initiative.

The media are not a solid monolith on all issues. Where the powerful are in disagreement, the media will reflect a certain diversity of tactical judgments on how to attain generally shared aims. But views that challenge fundamental premises or suggest that systemic factors govern the exercise of State power will be excluded.

The pattern is pervasive. Consider the coverage from and about Nicaragua. The mass media rarely allow their news columns—or, for that matter, their opinion pages—to present materials suggesting that Nicaragua is more democratic than El Salvador and Guatemala; that its government does not murder ordinary citizens, as the governments of El Salvador and Guatemala do on a routine basis; that it has carried out socioeconomic reforms important to the majority that the other two governments somehow cannot attempt; that Nicaragua poses no military threat to its neighbors but has, in fact, been subjected to continuous attack by the United States and its clients and surrogates, and that the U.S. fear of the Nicaraguan government is based more on its virtues than on its alleged defects.

The mass media also steer clear of discussing the background and results of the closely analogous attempt of the United States to bring "democracy" to Guatemala in 1954 by means of a CIA-supported invasion, which terminated Guatemalan democracy for an indefinite period. Although the United States supported elite rule and organized terror in Guatemala (among many other countries) for decades, actually subverted or approved the subversion of democracy in Brazil, Chile, and the Philippines (again, among others), is now "constructively engaged" with terror regimes around the world, and had no concern about democracy in Nicaragua so long as the brutal Somoza regime was firmly in power, the media take U.S. Government claims of a concern for "democracy" in Nicaragua at face value.

In contrast, El Salvador and Guatemala, with far worse records, are presented as struggling toward democracy under "moderate" leaders, thus meriting sympathetic approval.

In criticizing media biases, we often draw on the media themselves for at least some of the "facts." That the media provide some information about an issue, however, proves absolutely nothing about the adequacy or accuracy of media coverage. The media do, in fact, suppress a great deal of information, but even more important is the way they present a particular fact—its placement, tone, and frequency of repetition—and the framework of analysis in which it is placed. That a careful reader looking for a fact can sometimes find it, with diligence and a skeptical eye, tells us nothing about whether that fact received the attention and context it deserved, whether it was intelligible to most readers, or whether it was effectively distorted or suppressed.

The standard media pattern of indignant campaigns and suppressions, of shading and emphasis, of carefully selected context, premises, and general agenda, is highly useful to those who wield power. If, for example, they are able to channel public concern and outrage to the abuses of enemy states, they can mobilize the population for an ideological crusade.

Thus, a constant focus on the victims of communism helps persuade the public that the enemy is evil, while setting the stage for intervention, subversion, support for terrorist regimes, an endless arms race, and constant military conflict—all in a noble cause. At the same time, the devotion of our leaders—and our media—to this narrow set of victims raises public patriotism and self-esteem, demonstrating the essential humanity of our nation and our people.

The public does not notice media silence about victims of America's client states, which is as important as the media's concentration on victims of America's enemies. It would have been difficult for the Guatemalan government to murder tens of thousands over the past decade if the U.S. press had provided the kind of coverage it gave to the difficulties of Andrei Sakharov in the Soviet Union or the murder of Jerzy Popieluszko in Poland. It would have been impossible to wage a brutal war against South Vietnam and the rest of Indochina, leaving a legacy of misery and destruction that may never be overcome, if the media had not rallied to the cause, portraying murderous aggression as a defense of freedom.

Propaganda campaigns may be instituted either by the Government or by one or more of the top media firms. The campaigns to discredit the government of Nicaragua, to support the Salvadoran elections as an exercise in legitimizing democracy, and to use the Soviet shooting down of the Korean airliner KAL 007 as a means of mobilizing support for the arms buildup were instituted and propelled by the Government. The campaigns to publicize the crimes of Pol Pot in Cambodia and the allegations of a KGB plot to assassinate the Pope were initiated by the *Reader's Digest*, with strong follow-up support from NBC television, *The New York Times*, and other major media companies.

Some propaganda campaigns are jointly initiated by the Government and the media; all of them require the media's cooperation.

The mass media are drawn into a symbiotic relationship with powerful sources of information by economic necessity and reciprocity of interest. The media need a steady, reliable flow of the raw material of news. They have daily news demands and imperative news schedules. They cannot afford to have reporters and cameras at all places where important stories may break, so they must concentrate their resources where significant news often occurs, where important rumors and leaks abound, and where regular press conferences are held.

The White House, the Pentagon, and the State Department are central nodes of such news activity at the national level. On a local basis, city hall and the police department are regular news beats for reporters. Corporations and trade groups are also regular and credible purveyors of stories deemed newsworthy. These bureaucracies turn out a large volume of material that meets the demands of news organizations for reliable, scheduled flows. They also have the great merit of being recognizable and credible because of their status and prestige.

Another reason for the heavy weight given to official sources is that the mass media claim to be "objective" dispensers of the news. Partly to maintain the image of objectivity, but also to protect themselves from criticism of bias and the threat of libel suits, they need material that can be portrayed as presumptively accurate. This also reduces cost: Taking information from sources that may be presumed credible reduces investigative expense, whereas material from sources that are not *prima facie* credible, or that will draw criticism and threats, requires careful checking and costly research.

The Government and corporate bureaucracies that constitute primary news sources maintain vast public-relations operations that ensure special access to the media. The Pentagon, for example, has a public-information service that involves many thousands of employees, spending hundreds of millions of dollars every year and dwarfing not only the public-information resources of any dissenting individual or group but the aggregate of *all* dissenters.

During a brief interlude of relative openness in 1979 and 1980, the U.S. Air Force revealed that its public-information outreach included 140 newspapers with a weekly total circulation of 690,000; *Airman* magazine with a monthly circulation of 125,000; thirty-four radio and seventeen television stations, primarily overseas; 45,000 headquarters and unit news releases; 615,000 hometown news releases; 6,600 news media interviews; 3,200 news conferences; 500 news media orientation flights; fifty meetings with editorial boards, and 11,000 speeches. Note that this is just the Air Force. In 1982, *Air Force Journal International* indicated that the Pentagon was publishing 1,203 periodicals.

To put this into perspective, consider the scope of public-information activities of the American Friends Service Committee and the National Council of the Churches of Christ, two of the largest nonprofit organizations that consistently challenge the views of the Pentagon. The Friends' main office had an information services budget of less than $500,000 and a staff of eleven in 1984–1985. It issued about 200 press releases a year, held thirty press conferences, and produced one film and two or three slide shows. The Council of Churches office of information has an annual budget of about $350,000, issues about 100 news releases, and holds four press conferences a year.

Only the corporate sector has the resources to produce public information and propaganda on the scale of the Pentagon and other Government bodies. These large actors provide the media with facilities and with advance copies of speeches and reports. They schedule news conferences at hours geared to news deadlines. They write press releases in usable language. They carefully organize "photo-opportunity" sessions.

In effect, the large bureaucracies of the powerful subsidize the mass media, and thereby gain special access. They become "routine" news sources, while non-routine sources must struggle for access and may be ignored.

Because of the services they provide, the continuous contact they sustain, and the mutual dependency they foster, the powerful can use personal relationships, threats, and rewards to extend their influence over the news media. The media may feel obligated to carry extremely dubious stories, or to mute criticism, to avoid offending sources and disturbing a close relationship. When one depends on authorities for daily news, it is difficult to call them liars even if they tell whoppers.

Powerful sources may also use their prestige and importance as a lever to deny critics access to the media. The Defense Department, for example, refused to participate in discussions of military issues on National Public Radio if experts from the Center for Defense Information were invited to appear on the same program. Assistant Secretary of State Elliott Abrams would not appear on a Harvard University program dealing with human rights in Central America unless former Ambassador Robert White were excluded. Claire Sterling, a principal propagandist for the "Bulgarian connection" to the plot to assassinate the Pope, refused to take part in television programs on which her critics would appear.

The relation between power and sourcing extends beyond official and corporate provision of news to shaping the supply of "experts." The dominance of official sources is undermined when highly respectable unofficial sources give dissident views. This problem is alleviated by "coopting the experts"—that is, putting them on the payroll as consultants, funding their research, and organizing think tanks that will hire them directly and help disseminate their messages.

The process of creating a body of experts who will confirm and distribute the opinions favored by the Government and "the market" has been carried out on a deliberate basis and a massive scale. In 1972, Judge Lewis Powell, later elevated to the Supreme Court, wrote a memo to the U.S. Chamber of Commerce in which he urged business "to buy the top academic reputations in the country to add credibility to corporate studies and give business a stronger voice on the campuses."

During the 1970s and early 1980s, new institutions were established and old ones reactivated to help propagandize the corporate viewpoint. Hundreds of intellectuals were brought to these institutions, their work funded, and their output disseminated to the media by a sophisticated propaganda effort.

The media themselves also provide "experts" who regularly echo the official view. John Barron and Claire Sterling are household names as authorities on the KGB and terrorism because the *Reader's Digest* has funded, published, and publicized their work. The Soviet defector Arkady Shevchenko became an expert on Soviet arms and intelligence because *Time*, ABC television, and *The New York Times* chose to feature him, despite his badly tarnished credentials. By giving these vehicles of the preferred view much exposure, the media confer status and make them the obvious candidates for opinion and analysis.

Another class of experts whose prominence is largely a function of their serviceability to power consists of former radicals who have "come to see the light." The motives that induce these individuals to switch gods, from Stalin (or Mao) and communism to Reagan and free enterprise, may vary, but so far as the media are concerned, the ex-radicals have simply seen the error of their ways. The former sinners, whose previous work was ignored or ridiculed by the mass media, are suddenly elevated to prominence and anointed as experts.

Media propaganda campaigns have generally been useful to elite interests. The Red Scare of 1919–1920 helped abort the postwar union-organizing drive in steel and other major industries. The Truman-McCarthy Red Scare of the early 1950s helped inaugurate the Cold War and the permanent war economy, and also weakened the progressive coalition that had taken shape during the New Deal years.

The chronic focus on the plight of Soviet dissidents, on enemy killings in Cambodia, and on the Bulgarian Connection helped weaken the Vietnam Syndrome, justify a huge arms buildup and a more aggressive foreign policy, and divert attention from the upward distribution of income that was the heart of the Reagan Administration's domestic economic program. The recent propaganda attacks on Nicaragua have averted eyes from the savageries of the war in El Salvador and helped justify the escalating U.S. investment in counterrevolution in Central America.

Conversely, propaganda campaigns are *not* mobilized where coverage of victimization, though it may be massive, sustained, and dramatic, fails to serve the interests of the elite.

The focus on Cambodia in the Pol Pot era was serviceable, for example, because Cambodia had fallen to the communists and useful lessons could be drawn from the experience of their victims. But the many Cambodian victims of U.S. bombing *before* the communists came to power were scrupulously ignored by the U.S. press. After Pol Pot was ousted by the Vietnamese, the United States quietly shifted its support to this "worse than Hitler" villain, with little or no notice in the press, which once again adjusted to the official political agenda.

Attention to the Indonesian massacres of 1965–1966, or to the victims of the Indonesian invasion of East Timor since 1975, would also be distinctly unhelpful as bases of media campaigns, because Indonesia is a U.S. ally and client that maintains an open door to Western investment. The same is true of the victims of state terror in Chile and Guatemala—U.S. clients whose basic institutional structures, including the state terror system, were put in place by, or with crucial assistance from, the United States.

No propaganda campaigns are mounted in the mass media on behalf of such victims. To publicize their plight would, after all, conflict with the interests of the wealthy and powerful.

MARK HERTSGAARD

A Palace Court Press
(1988)

"If there is anything deficient about press coverage of the Reagan administration, and there of course is, it has to do simply with our own deficiencies and laziness, and no especial cleverness, or blandishments, or seductions, or threats on their part," asserted Meg Greenfield, the editorial-page editor of *The Washington Post*. "I think we in this newspaper are situated in an absolutely blessed position," she added. "We have a very supportive, journalistically minded management. We have a lot of dough. We have a lot of resources. We have a lot of really smart people. And we have the commanding newspaper position in the [nation's] capital. We can do any damn thing that is important that we have the wit to see and pursue. . . . I really think that anyone who works for this newspaper has every chance imaginable in journalism to go out and get the Story."

"The odds against us [in the press] are not overwhelming," declared *Washington Post* executive editor Ben Bradlee. "Their weapons are enormous, but we're not unarmed in this struggle, we're not unarmed." Beyond the extraordinary array of resources and the journalistic license mentioned by Ms. Greenfield, there was above all the simple fact that, collectively, the press exercised perhaps the greatest power there was in politics: the power to define reality, to say what was—and what was not—important at any given time. The three major television networks in particular could cause big trouble for the White House virtually anytime they wanted simply by focusing sustained attention on any of the scandals, inequities, dangerous or bankrupt policies or other shortcomings common to every Washington administration. True, they usually didn't, but the threat was always there.

All this made the news media a force to be reckoned with for any administration. Yet at the same time, the press's freedom to operate as an independent force within the American political system was constrained by the environment in which mainstream journalists lived and worked. Adversarial behavior was discouraged by certain basic facts of journalistic life. For instance, as employees of some of the largest

From *On Bended Knee* (New York: Farrar, Straus, Giroux, 1988), 54–76.

and most profitable corporations in the land, journalists and news executives ultimately answered to superiors whose individual and collective self-interest mitigated against strong or consistent criticism of a government as pro-corporate as Ronald Reagan's. There was also the age-old challenge of maintaining good and reliable sources without becoming a captive of them.

According to the old journalistic truism, a reporter was only as good as his sources. For White House reporters, this raised a troubling dilemma. Most news organizations' definition of proper White House coverage stressed reporting the views and actions of the President and his aides above all else. Thus the officials with whom reporters were, in theory, supposed to have an adversarial relationship were the very people upon whom they were most dependent for the information needed to produce their stories. As Lee Lescaze, who covered the White House for *The Washington Post* in 1981, explained, "There are only six or seven real sources in the White House who know anything. So you can't write a tough story if you're one of the 90 percent of the press corps who can be frozen out. . . . [Jim] Baker has three hundred phone message slips waiting for him, and he's going to call back the ones he likes or needs."

For obvious reasons, the White House propaganda apparatus concentrated its efforts on the big-circulation outlets: the major networks, the wire services and the big papers. "Anybody else," noted CBS White House correspondent Bill Plante, "can whistle 'Dixie.' "

White House officials recognized that television's commercial imperatives gave them a strategic edge. "I think by temperament, by inclination, by desire, [White House reporters] are highly adversarial," said one senior Reagan aide. "They are very smart. They are hardworking, by and large, the good ones. They simply have an extraordinarily difficult problem, because their subject, the President, is what the network wants to run."

The great demand for White House news stories meant that the Reagan media apparatus could sharply restrict reporters' access, and thereby gain greater control over coverage, without inhibiting its own access to the nation's airwaves and newspapers. It meant that top White House officials could mount the stage in the West Wing pressroom and brief the entire press corps on a "background" basis—that is, their names would not be attached to any quoted statements—without eliciting a peep of protest from the journalists gathered below. It meant that President Reagan could be made available to cameras only under the most carefully controlled conditions but with utter confidence that his remarks would nonetheless be widely printed and broadcast.

"What the Reagan White House does is say you can't have access to the President and his principal aides; you'll write what we want you to," said Juan Williams of *The Washington Post*. "And instead of the press saying this is bullshit and pushing for more press conferences, more access of all kinds, they compete with one another to get that one interview or that one scoop."

"The reason this can go on is that the reporters on the White House beat have been deadened," said Vicki Barker, a United Press International Radio general assignment reporter who covered the White House during the summer of 1985. "It's like that scene in *A Clockwork Orange* where the droog is strapped into a chair with Beethoven blasting away at him and he's being reprogrammed. That's the White House beat. [The administration] keeps up a steady drip-drop of [what is] barely news, and you have to scramble to keep up with it, because otherwise your editors ask why the competition has it."

"A lot of reporters recognized that they were dealing not with real news but pseudo-news," said Rich Jaroslovsky, a White House reporter for *The Wall Street Journal*. "[In private] network correspondents complain that a lot of it is bilge, but they still want that story to go on. They don't sit around on Air Force One asking why they're writing these stories. They know how the system works, and they accept it." As George Watson, Washington bureau chief of ABC News, commented, "We aren't consciously sitting around saying, 'How can we be more adversarial?' "

White House reporters were occupied with a much more immediate and pressing concern: getting the story, getting it first, and getting on the air or in the paper with it. As they had to be, one might add, if they were to keep their high-profile jobs. Why should their bosses keep them on the beat and pay them strong five-figure salaries—in the case of TV reporters, strong *six*-figure salaries—if they did not produce plenty of stories, or if they consistently got "beaten" by their competitors? There was also the goad of ego, which in the case of most White House correspondents was a powerful goad indeed. One did not rise as high within the journalistic profession as these reporters had if one did not really want to be—indeed, *have* to be—number one. Appearances on the evening news and the morning front page were a large part of keeping score in that contest.

Perhaps because he tended to be in the direct path of the stampeding herd, White House spokesman Larry Speakes complained that this collective urge on the reporters' part led to "distortion of the news. The correspondents never go back to their desk and say, 'There's no story here today.' . . . If Chris [Wallace of NBC] gets a piece for the evening news, then Andrea [Mitchell] has to find another angle on it to get it on the air [the next morning on the *Today* show]. And in some cases, the story gets distorted looking for that other angle. The next afternoon, Chris is looking to Sam [Donaldson] and Lesley [Stahl], so he's trying to figure out how he can hype it more and more and make sure he's got something a little bit more than they have."

Michael Deaver, on the other hand, believed that the pack mentality of the White House press corps played into his hands—it meant they tended to come to him and take what stories he offered. "You know, they'd be much better off if they were in offices scattered all over town," said Deaver. "But they beat on each other, and if they don't have a story, sure, they're going to take [ours]. Whereas if they were out on their own, they'd be hustling and digging and getting their own stories."

To be sure, the White House needed the major outlets as much as vice versa, but that did not necessarily embolden reporters at such news organizations. There was enough competitiveness on the White House beat so that even reporters with audience clout had to worry about being discriminated against. Coverage too sharply or consistently critical could well provoke. White House officials into favoring one's rival with the next inside tip.

Lou Cannon, the White House correspondent for *The Washington Post*, was the journalist widely regarded as enjoying the closest contacts with high Reagan officials. Appropriately enough, his stock-in-trade was stories revealing the inner workings of the Reagan White House. As Cannon's former editor William Greider explained, "What Lou lives for is that exclusive story that he gets not just twenty-four hours before anybody else but weeks before anybody else." Maintaining the kind of access that yielded such leaked stories, however, exacted a cost. Cannon's regular Monday column on the Reagan White House often contained wonderful inside stuff and useful insights available nowhere else. Unfortunately, it just as often was marred by an "on the one hand, on the other hand" point of view that greatly diluted the power of Cannon's information. Comments critical of the President were invariably balanced by an equal dose of approving remarks, resulting in essays that sounded eminently fair-minded to most of the reading public even as they preserved the author's special relationship with the Reagan White House.

According to Lee Lescaze, who said he "got on extremely well" with Cannon when they covered the White House together for the *Post* in 1981, Cannon was "very sympathetic" toward Reagan. "If [a reporter assigned to work with Cannon] began by saying to Lou, 'Look, you like Reagan, I don't. So you can write all the puff you want, but I'll still be tearing the lid off of it,' Lou would think he was dealing with a wild man. He'd want to keep control over the major pieces and make sure they were written with what he'd call the right sensitivity."

"As all my former and present editors know," responded Cannon, "I've got two imperatives in covering the White House: to be critical and to be fair." Noting that he spent most of 1981 on a leave of absence to complete his biography of Reagan, Cannon defended his toughness by recalling that his first story upon returning to the White House beat in January 1982 "ended by saying that the question about Ronald Reagan was the same that it was when he became President a year earlier: is he up to the job?" Cannon went on to complain that he had a hard time covering the Reagan administration precisely because he was so critical. And it was true: his coverage was relatively critical. But the emphasis belongs on the word "relatively." Lou Cannon ranked a notch above his peers because he occasionally engaged in what should have been standard practice: stating (albeit in carefully qualified language) the obvious about Ronald Reagan.

"It's hard to avoid the analogy of the White House press corps as a bunch of caged hamsters thoroughly dependent on their masters for their daily feeding," remarked *The Boston Globe*'s Walter Robinson, who was assigned to the beat in 1985. "There is so little real information there that people really do end up competing for crumbs. And they consider it a badge of honor to get one of the crumbs, even though most of them turn out to be not as nourishing as advertised."

In reaction to the intense competition, said Robinson, "people lower their standards [and] take single-source things that you'd never take in another kind of environment. . . . It's a generally held view within the press corps that the *New York Times* coverage of the White House is shameless. It's so important for the *Times* to be first that they throw their standards out the window. There's general resentment among other print reporters of the *Times* and the *Post* because of their access. It's so much easier for [second-term White House chief of staff] Donald Regan to drop something in there as a trial balloon, and then everybody else will pick it up." Beyond the front-page scoops, added Robinson, "the *Times* is also shameless with the fawning profiles of White House officials who will later be leaking stories [to the authors of said profiles]."

Tom Oliphant, Robinson's predecessor as the *Globe*'s White House reporter, agreed that reporters at "second tier" news corporations were afforded less access to officials, but asked, "So what if you can't get Don Regan on the phone twice a week? I prefer this in some ways to being a *New York Times* reporter with official sources which produce official stories that are beside the point."

Fame and fortune, whether in the form of being read by the Washington power elite or perhaps being invited to join the Sunday talk-show panels, were powerful temptations to which White House reporters were especially susceptible. After all, they were members, in former NBC White House correspondent Emery King's words, of "the most pampered press corps in the world." And their position of privilege inevitably, if subtly, shaped their reporting. "There are no whores in the [White House] press corps," declared Tom Oliphant. "They're all independent journalists. They work hard. None of them want to report just what the White House says is true. But there is subtle entrapment. . . . The perks, the trips, the *life*, as they say, are more than any human being should be expected to withstand. There are too many tender traps to report strongly there for long."

To be sure, some White House reporters resisted these traps more vigorously than others. Sam Donaldson of ABC, for example, was not one to pull punches for reasons of decorum. When White House press aides prevented reporters from getting close enough to the President to ask questions, Donaldson was not shy about shouting loud enough so that even the hard-of-hearing Mr. Reagan couldn't ignore the question. Donaldson was the man right-wing press bashers loved to hate, yet he was just as willing to hound Democrats as Republicans.

Yet not even Donaldson, probably the best television reporter covering the White House during the Reagan years, was genuinely as adversarial as commonly supposed. True, he was not afraid of challenging the official line, but he hardly made a habit of it. As befit a television journalist, his image as a mad dog was more a function of form than substance; the bark was much worse than the bite. Often, what was interpreted as hard-nosed reporting on his part had more to do with Donaldson's aggressive manner and nettlesome appearance than with the actual content of his reports, which usually were only marginally more adversarial than those of his colleagues.

Stan Opotowsky, director of political operations at ABC News and a man who worked closely with Donaldson years before he became a star, told me that to understand Sam Donaldson one had to bear in mind that he was really two persons: the loudmouth maverick of his public persona and the shrewd professional who is very much part of the establishment. *Hold On, Mr. President!*, Donaldson's 1987 autobiography, confirmed that analysis. For all his apparently outrageous behavior and growling aggressiveness, Sam Donaldson held to rather conventional opinions about news, politics and the connection between them. Which perhaps helps explain an apparent paradox: of the network correspondents on the White House beat, Donaldson was unanimously considered by the top Reagan press aides interviewed for this book to be the fairest of them all.

The sources dilemma was not quite as acute for reporters on beats other than the White House, if only because they tended to have a larger pool of potential sources on which to draw. Still, if they were to provide the kind of daily stories most desired by their editorial and executive superiors, maintaining cordial relations with top government officials was an occupational necessity. As a foreign policy reporter, "you need to be on speaking terms with the Secretary of State and the Assistant Secretary of State for Latin American Affairs, or Soviet Affairs," said ABC national security correspondent John McWethy. But how likely was a reporter to stay on speaking terms with such officials if he was consistently engaged in full-bore adversarial journalism? President Reagan's Assistant Secretary for Inter-American Affairs, Elliott Abrams, actually refused to take questions from or appear on talk shows or in public debates with certain journalists and policy analysts because he considered them politically biased. "It is time we begin to define what constitutes the borders of responsible criticism," Abrams told the *Columbia Journalism Review* in defending his refusal to grant an interview to CBS's Jane Wallace, who contributed some of the most aggressive reporting on Central America to appear on network television during the Reagan years. Because she was not restricted to the Central America beat, Ms. Wallace was not greatly

harmed by Abrams's ban. But for journalists who did do the bulk of their reporting on that beat, such a blacklisting would have amounted to a significant competitive handicap.

"How do you develop sources on a beat without becoming captive to them? I
don't know. It's one of the real dilemmas for any reporter," said Stephen Engelberg
of *The New York Times*. Commenting on press coverage of the Iran-contra affair,
Engelberg added, "That's why the people who have done the best on this story are
those who came out of left field. [*Miami Herald* reporter Alfonso] Chardy didn't
have to make the White House like him. Neither did [*Los Angeles Times* reporter
Michael] Wines. . . . Ollie North was a Pulitzer waiting to happen for anybody on
the White House or national security beat, but reporters are human beings. The
fewer sources there are, the more you think about how they'll react to your story.
You'll gore somebody's ox if you have to, but you'll think about it carefully beforehand."

During the late 1960s Jeff Gralnick was one of Walter Cronkite's favorite young
producers at CBS News. When Cronkite made his famous fact-finding journey to
Vietnam following the Tet offensive of 1968, Gralnick had already been "in-
country" seven or eight weeks, trying to figure out, as he later recalled, "whether
I should be in front of the camera or behind it." It was in the latter capacity that
he assisted in preparing what would be one of Cronkite's most important broadcasts
ever: a special primetime report in which Cronkite, who, like most other dominant
news media voices in the United States, had thus far been quite supportive of the
war, contradicted the Johnson administration's claims that the war was being won
and suggested that the United States think about withdrawing. It was a half hour
of television regarded by war supporters and critics alike, and indeed by Johnson
himself, as a clear sign that mass American opinion was turning irreversibly against
the war. And it was remarkable for another reason as well: Walter Cronkite, the
man thought to embody objective journalism, had expressed a clear opinion in the
broadcast; he had taken a stand *against* the government.

Fifteen years later, a mature Jeff Gralnick held one of the most powerful jobs
in American television news: executive producer of ABC's *World News Tonight*. Naturally he answered to executive superiors in that job, but on a day-to-day basis it
was he who exercised ultimate control over what stories appeared on *World News
Tonight* and which correspondents and producers were assigned to report them,
and over the length, emphasis and general tone of those stories. As the man who
controlled the broadcast from September 1979 until July 1983, Gralnick decided
what approximately twelve million Americans learned about their government and
the world five nights a week during the first two and a half years of Ronald Reagan's presidency.

The journalistic philosophy he brought to the job differed considerably from that which had informed Cronkite's Vietnam broadcast years before. For example, when asked how he as executive producer responded to Reagan administration efforts to restrict journalists' access to Reagan, he replied, "It's not my job to respond to it. . . . It is not my position to say, 'For shame, Public Agency.' It's my job to take the news as they choose to give it to us and then, in the amount of time that's available, put it into the context of the day or that particular story." Later in the same interview, Gralnick declared, "The evening newscast is not supposed to be the watchdog on the government. It never was, never will be. We are a national front page, five days a week."

When asked about Lou Cannon's belief that President Reagan had gotten "a fairer press than he deserves," Gralnick shot back, "I wouldn't consider talking about what the President does or does not deserve. It's a political, subjective judgment."

"Aren't those kinds of judgments made in anyone's journalism?"

"Better not be. *The Village Voice* may make those kinds of judgments, but I sure as hell don't."

Asked finally whether he was saying that *The Village Voice* had a point of view while such mainstream news organizations as *The New York Times* and ABC News did not, the network vice president seemed suddenly impatient. Grabbing that morning's *Times* from under a pile of papers on his desk, he held it up with both hands, nodded toward the fully extended front page and in a schoolteacher tone explained, "On its front page the only point of view exhibited by *The New York Times* is the view of what stories are on the right-hand lead, the left-hand lead, above and below the fold." He then ripped through the paper's front section, flung it open to the opinions and editorials page, smacked the page with the back of his hand and announced, "*That* is where *The New York Times*'s point of view is."

"He is either very naïve or a real liar," responded television critic Tom Shales of *The Washington Post*. "For Jeff Gralnick to say no political judgments go into those broadcasts is just silly."

"*The New York Times* is a very good newspaper with lots of good reporters, but to say it's value-free I think is wrong," offered Bill Wheatley, then senior (and later promoted to executive) producer of the *NBC Nightly News*. "There are values expressed just by what stories are placed on the front page, by what facts lead the story and what facts are in the middle of the story."

" 'Objectivity' contradict[s] the essentially subjective nature of journalism," wrote former *Post* editor Ben Bagdikian in his landmark 1983 study, *The Media Monopoly*. "Every basic step in the journalistic process involves a value-laden decision: Which of the infinite number of events in the environment will be assigned for coverage and which ignored? Which of the infinite observations confronting the reporter will be noted? . . . Which story will be prominently displayed on page 1 and which buried inside or discarded? . . . 'Objectivity' place[s] overwhelming emphasis on established, official voices and tend[s] to leave unreported large areas of genuine relevance that authorities choose not to talk about."

Objectivity also prohibited reporters from exercising much intelligence and judgment on behalf of their readers, according to author and former *New York Times* reporter David Halberstam. Reflecting on news coverage of the 1972 presidential campaign, Halberstam once wrote: "Despite all the fine talk of objectivity, the only thing that mildly approached objectivity was the form in which the reporter wrote the news, a technical style which required the journalist to appear to be much dumber and more innocent than in fact he was. So he wrote in a bland, uncritical way which gave greater credence to the utterances of public officials, no matter how mindless these utterances. . . . Thus the press voluntarily surrendered a vast amount of its real independence; it treated the words and actions of the government of the United States with a credence that those words and actions of the government of the United States with a credence that those words and actions did not necessarily merit."

Notwithstanding such criticisms, objectivity remained the dominant journalistic philosophy in the United States throughout the Reagan years. True, few articulated so extreme a version of that philosophy as did Jeff Gralnick. In the aftermath of Vietnam and Watergate, objectivity had come under sufficient criticism from within the profession so that now most journalists, if pushed, would concede that perfect objectivity was impossible; explicitly or implicitly, every news story unavoidably expressed a point of view. As NBC News Washington bureau chief Robert McFarland pointed out: "Do you lead your newscast with the story of how inflation is falling, or how unemployment is still 14 percent in Detroit? That's a value judgment."

The value judgments American journalists made in reporting the news were inevitably influenced by their own backgrounds. "Even as an objective journalist, you're an American first and a journalist second," observed *CBS Evening News* Washington producer Susan Zirinsky. "You come from a framework to every story, and I'm an American, that's where I come from." Former ABC Pentagon correspondent Dean Reynolds made a similar point when I asked why the press had generally refrained from highlighting the obvious potential of President Reagan's Strategic Defense Initiative space weapons system to function as a first-strike nuclear weapon. Reynolds said that he and other reporters had asked Defense Secretary Caspar Weinberger about this possibility. "And he ultimately falls back on 'Well, you have to look at the two systems [the United States versus the Soviet Union]. Which one do you believe?' That's a pretty fundamental question. And I believe this administration and this Defense Secretary [when they] say we are not attempting to build a first-strike weapon."

Even journalists who rejected simplistic notions of value-free news nevertheless usually embraced more refined versions of the doctrine of objectivity. If it was impossible to avoid a point of view entirely, they would do their best to minimize it. As much as possible, they would leave explanations and interpretations to others. They would strive for "fairness" and "balance" (the two buzzwords that had arisen to replace "objectivity" in the journalistic lexicon). They would, above all, remain politically neutral.

In accordance with their avoidance of partisanship, many journalists seemed to regard strenuous challenging of the government as an improper violation of the rules of objectivity. Honest adversarial journalism they equated with, and often dismissed as, "advocacy" journalism. NBC's Tom Brokaw was but one of those who argued that it was not the press's job to protect the public from White House efforts to manipulate opinion; rather, the press was to share with the public "the biggest, most thorough picture of what [the White House] is up to in the policy and the manipulation, and let the public respond to that."

As much as any other constraint, it was this allegiance to objectivity that put the press at such a strategic disadvantage vis-à-vis the Reagan White House. Whatever it promised in theory, in practice objective journalism was far from politically neutral, largely because of its overwhelming reliance on official sources of information. In fact, in its own way, it was no less slanted than the advocacy journalism that mainstream reporters and editors so self-righteously shunned. It was just that its slant was in deference, rather than opposition, to the reigning conventions and authorities of the day.

"Objectivity is fine if it's real," said independent journalist I. F. Stone. "Every society has its dogmas, and a genuinely objective approach can break through them. But most of the time objectivity is just the rationale for regurgitating the conventional wisdom of the day. If what you're saying challenges the stereo-types of the day, it's hard to get it printed."

It was an article of faith within the American press that everyone was free to say whatever they liked; there were no limits on opinion, and all serious views were given fair representation. In fact, however, subtle but definite limits were imposed on the nation's political debate by the press's definition of who constituted responsible, and thus quotable, news sources. As a practical matter, the definition of who was worth listening to was limited to official Washington: administration officials (past and present), members of Congress, the occasional well-connected academic specialist. "What you see are the people who are the movers and shakers, who have the power to change things in the short term," explained Sanford Socolow, former executive producer of the *CBS Evening News*. "They're the ones you see on the news."

Emphasizing the statements and actions of officials above all else often resulted in woefully one-sided reporting and reduced the press to little more than a nominally independent mouthpiece of the government, a stenographer to power. Especially on the White House beat, so-called objective reporting tended to produce news stories comprised largely of information reflecting the White House's own point of view—what (unnamed) official X thought about issue Y, what the President planned to tell foreign leader Z next week. Occasionally these views would be balanced by alternative voices, but in most cases, only marginally so. In the words of venerable *New York Times* Washington columnist James Reston: "What we do most of the time is, we really are a transmission belt." Nothing that the White House would "like us to be even more of a transmission belt than we already are," he added, "Probably we should be analyzing more than we do."

Or at least relying on a more politically diverse range of sources. "Serving as a stenographer to power isn't real objectivity," argued Robert Parry, a reporter who worked for the Associated Press and *Newsweek* during the Reagan years. "Real objectivity means listening to all sides of the debate. Many reporters won't deal with certain kinds of information because of where it comes from—say, from people who are sympathetic to the Sandinistas. I've been accused of being non-objective for that reason. But I think I'm being truly objective. I think you deal with *all* sides equally, evaluate their information, and if it checks out, you print it."

Former *Washington Post* assistant managing editor William Greider argued that the tendency of the press to serve as "more conduit than critic of the government" was due to an "ingrown quality of deference which makes the press unwilling to challenge presidential announcements. As a result, the press will print and broadcast reams and reams of rhetoric they themselves know to be wrong. Sure, they'll challenge him if he's got his facts 180 degrees wrong, but otherwise they're very reluctant."

"In the media at large there is no intellectual center of gravity," explained Robert Kaiser of the *Post*. "The practicing Washington press corps lacks intellectual self-confidence; [it] is most uncomfortable standing up and saying, 'Hey, naked, not so, stupid policy, dumb idea, whatever. If you talked to Lebanon experts about [the 1983 Reagan policy of] using U.S. marines as part of a peace-keeping mission, you knew it was a stupid policy from day one. But reporters don't do that. They cover it as a spectacle, as a political event: What are they saying up on the Hill?"

Presidential assistant Richard Darman told me that the so-called Teflon phenomenon—the fact that blame never seemed to stick to President Reagan, even after such disasters as the Beirut suicide bombing that claimed the lives of 241 marines—was directly related to journalists' tendency to emphasize personality over substance. "It doesn't ever say this explicitly," said Darman, "but what their [journalistic] culture tells them is: Your job, when a proposal is launched, is to talk about who did what to whom making it get launched, who's fighting with whom now that it has been launched, how is it being received here, there and such and such a place; in other words, what are its bureaucratic origins and what are its larger political prospects. The tendency is to concentrate on who did shoot John, who might shoot John, who wants to shoot John but doesn't have a gun.

"I don't think we consciously used [this tendency]," Darman continued, "[but] the President benefited [from it]. The Teflon phenomenon is a function of the fact that when there's a problem with substance, the press doesn't say there's something wrong with Reagan's policies. They say party A in the White House is fighting with party B *about* the policy. It tends to insulate the President from substantive criticism and convert it into personality stories about conflicts between individuals within the administration beneath the level of the President."

One other related but rarely acknowledged consequence of objective journalism's sourcing habits was to make the press in effect a hostage to the debate within the Washington political elite. Lesley Stahl, who covered the White House for CBS for the first six years of the Reagan presidency, alluded to this dynamic in a February 1987 interview on PBS's *MacNeil-Lehrer Newshour*. Conceding that the press had been slow to pick up on the Iran-contra scandal, Stahl laid part of the blame on the Congress, "which is often a source for these kinds of stories." Indeed, she added, one reason press coverage of Mr. Reagan had not been more aggressive throughout the course of his presidency was that the Congress "ha[d] not been a source for the press in the whole Reagan administration. They don't want to criticize this beloved man."

The press's overwhelming reliance on official sources meant that news coverage of Washington by and large reflected and reinforced the assumptions, opinions and general worldview of official Washington. Venturing beyond the boundaries of the Democrat-to-Republican spectrum was rare in the extreme. However valid a given political position might be on an intellectual level, if it was not forcefully articulated by a significant part of the Washington establishment, it received little or no attention from the mainstream press.

"It's a little harder for the boys in the White House to keep the troops in line than it is for the boys in the Kremlin," investigative reporter Seymour Hersh observed during a May 1987 seminar at the Institute for Policy Studies in Washington, "but it is true that *Pravda* and *The Washington Post* and *The New York Times* are alike in the sense that they don't report reality so much as what a small group of top leaders *tells* them is reality."

Thus did numerous journalists argue that if Ronald Reagan did get off easy, it was less the fault of the press than of the Democratic party. Not only did Democrats fail to project a compelling alternative to Reaganism, they often seemed either afraid or unwilling even to criticize it.

"Look at defense, it's the perfect example," exclaimed David Hoffman of *The Washington Post* in July 1985 interview. "Ronald Reagan will have doubled the defense budget in five years. *Doubled*. That's a lot of dollars every year they didn't have before. In *The Washington Post* as an editorial voice and even in our headlines and our stories in a certain sense, you see that the debate is now not over whether we should go back to half of what we have now. It's whether we should go back to zero growth. So Reagan has achieved a doubling of the defense budget, and as long as the public supports that [sic] and the public debate is over zero growth or 3 percent growth, that's where our debate is. Now, if next week every Democrat came out and said, 'We're going back to the Carter budget, back to half of what we have now,' we would start writing stories about that. But we're not going to write those until those politicians start to make those noises. We follow in that respect. . . . We fill the paper with stories on the margin of issues, not sweeping overviews. If you went through the paper and stamped every story whether it was 2 degrees, 5 degrees or 360 degrees [off the center of the debate], you would see a lot of 2-degree stories."

Hence the importance of the opposition party to Washington press coverage. The doctrine of objectivity meant that the press was, quite simply, only as adversarial as the opposition party allowed it to be. "I don't think the coverage has been terrible," remarked Jonathan Kwitney, author and investigative reporter for *The Wall Street Journal*. "There has been some good reporting. But there is no opposition within the political system, and that's partly why the stories don't keep running on page one."

Indeed, part of the reason Ronald Reagan was able to pull the political debate so far to the right during his presidency was that there was no countervailing presence on the left in the Washington political arena. In the United States, where anti-Communism had been injected into the collective consciousness so relentlessly for so many years, "soft on Communism" was the last thing any politician—or journalist, for that matter—could afford to have thought about him. Thus criticisms of the nuclear arms race had to be prefaced with declarations of not liking or trusting the Russians any more than the next fellow, and backed up by a voting record that looked favorably on at least some of the big-ticket weapons systems that the Pentagon and its nominally private sector allies ceaselessly put forward as additional necessary deterrence to the Soviet threat. Likewise, if a member of Congress disagreed with President Reagan's policy of making war on Nicaragua, that member invariably first made sure to emphasize that he detested the Sandinista government as much as Reagan did before voicing any preference for negotiations over bloodshed.

As *New York Times* correspondent R. W. "Johnny" Apple commented: "To come back from Europe [where Apple spent nearly ten years as London bureau chief]—where the parliamentary tradition is alive and the spectrum of acceptable political debate stretches from non-Communist Marxists and Trotskyists and Eurocommunists on the left to neo-fascists on the right—to Washington was striking. I had a broader range of opinion represented around my dinner table in London than you could find in official Washington. . . . My wife and I were sitting around thinking one night of who was the leading left-wing politician in Washington and we came up with Teddy [Kennedy]. Now, Teddy would feel very comfortable in the left wing of the [British] Tory party. He could be quite comfortably accommodated within the Christian Democratic party in West Germany. If he happened to be a socialist, he would be in the far, far right wing of the Socialist party in Spain. That says a lot."

"As a working journalist you have to talk to people and quote them," said Robert Parry. "Normally you go to the opposition party. But what we ran into during that period [of extreme Sandinista bashing from 1983 onward] was that no one would defend the Sandinistas, even to say they weren't the worst things on earth. No one would put them in perspective—by saying that this and this may be true about the Sandinistas, but this and this isn't—because even putting it in perspective was considered defending the Sandinistas. So it was very hard to write stories raising questions about Reagan's policy, because the Democrats weren't playing the role of an opposition party." Parry and his partner at the Associated Press, Brian Barger, responded by visiting Miami, where "the debate going on inside the Nicaraguan exile community was much more honest and broad-based than the debate going on in Washington. We were talking to people who were all anti-Sandinista . . . and they would talk about how artificial the contra movement was and about the corruption [within it]. They were very upset about it. . . . We got a lot more truth out of Miami than we did in Washington."*

But reporters like Parry and Barger were the exception. Most Washington journalists focused exclusively on doings in the capital, and thus tended to internalize, if only unconsciously, the basic premises underlying U.S. policy. In foreign policy, for example, the United States was presumed to act from an essentially defensive posture and with benevolent intent; recall, for example, Dean Reynolds's trust that the Reagan administration would not develop a first-strike nuclear weapon. And while the United States was by any historical definition an empire of extraordinary reach and power, with hundreds of overseas military bases and a long record of military and economic interventions aimed at toppling or propping up foreign governments, it was rarely referred to as an empire in mainstream news accounts, nor were its actions evaluated from such a perspective. Likewise, only official U.S. enemies practiced "terrorism"; U.S. allies like El Salvador that engaged in widespread and systematic violence against their civilians were called "democracies" and forgiven their excesses on the grounds that they were resisting "Communist subversion."

Human rights coverage provided perhaps the clearest illustration of the ideolog-

---

*A reporter covering the Middle East could have said the same thing about Jerusalem and Washington. The official debate was considerably broader in Jerusalem than it was in Washington, where, prior to the widespread Palestinian unrest of late 1987, administration and congressional officials alike rarely criticized the actions of the Israeli government.

ical double standard embraced by the U.S. press. While the media showered attention on physicist Andrei Sakharov and other dissidents living in the Soviet sphere
of influence, dissidents from the U.S. sphere were usually all but ignored.

Consider, for example, the parallel cases of Lech Walesa and Oscar Romero.
Both men suffered abuse at the hands of state authorities for leading struggles of
poor and working people for social justice, Walesa as the head of the Solidarity
movement in Poland, Romero as a Catholic archbishop in El Salvador. Walesa was
repeatedly harassed and imprisoned by the Soviet-backed regime in Poland; Romero was harassed and ultimately assassinated in March 1980 by death squads working for the U.S.-backed regime in El Salvador. Yet while Walesa became a virtual
household name in the United States, Archbishop Romero remained a stranger to
the American public. In the same manner, the U.S. news media lavished coverage
on the Solidarity uprising in December 1981, even as it completely ignored the
concurrent terror campaign then underway in Guatemala, where a U.S.-backed
military government was engaged in a repression of the civilian population that
was substantially more brutal than what was taking place in Poland.

"You're supposed to see El Salvador on one set of terms and Nicaragua on an
entirely different set of terms," charges Robert Parry. "I raised this once with Elliott
[Abrams] over dinner, and he said, 'I hope you're not going to get into this question
of moral equivalency.' . . . [Their] thinking is that when we invade a country, it's
okay, but when the Soviets invade a country, it's not." (Repeated attempts to interview Mr. Abrams were rebuffed.) Parry complained that government officials
applied a similar double standard to news coverage: "The difference is, if you're
writing a story the way they want you to, you could make as many mistakes as
you want and not be criticized for it. But if you're writing something that goes
against the grain, you had to be perfect. If you had the slightest error, they would
latch on to that and use it to come after you."

Journalists who refused to adopt the preferred double standard risked censure
not only from U.S. officials but from their colleagues in the press. Parry himself
was subjected to a "whisper campaign" in which administration officials, including
Elliott Abrams's press secretary, Gregory Lagana, attempted to discredit him as a
Sandinista sympathizer to at least two other reporters, according to interviews with
those reporters. One Reagan official even tried to convince Parry that his partner,
Barger, was politically suspect. "And if you don't succumb to all that," noted Parry,
"you get the line from your editors that maybe they should take you off the story,
since you seem to be pursuing a political agenda. When the government attacks
you, even your colleagues begin to doubt your credibility, when it should be just
the opposite."

Compared with the imprisonment and worse risked by journalists elsewhere in
the world who dared dissent from official orthodoxy, smearing of reputations and
derailing of careers was relatively tame stuff. But in the American context, such

tactics generally proved an effective form of coercion. The more a journalist strayed beyond acceptable bounds of discussion, the less likely he was to see his reporting printed or broadcast. As I. F. Stone explained: "There is a palpable range of discourse, and if you stray outside it—either to the right or to the left, but especially to the left—you're not in Siberia or *samizdat*, but you're in *The Nation*, or *In These Times*, or *The Progressive*, and not much read. A young journalist in the mainstream press doesn't have to be told this, he can see it all around him."

"It isn't very easy to try to respect the American tradition of journalistic fairness—'objectivity' is a strange word, I don't know exactly what it means, but 'fairness' is more operative—and it depends on your own perspective," acknowledged CBS News White House correspondent Bill Plante. "You can say it is all pablum, wire service straight down the middle, report the facts, serve as a conduit for the government, when you should be taking a point of view. I won't argue that it can't be bland, or that we are terribly successful in pointing out the inconsistencies, but I do think the American tradition of journalistic fairness is an important element in allowing freedom of opinion. It may also have helped homogenize thought."

Here Plante expressed the fundamental contradiction inherent in the reigning definition of journalistic fairness: although in theory it was supposed to encourage freedom of opinion, in practice it usually tended to limit the range of political discourse and encourage homogenized political thinking.

Plante's suggested solution to the problem? Teach courses on attribution in the nation's classrooms. Although he resisted the notion that television provided "a point of view that resembles the government's more than anything else," he did admit that "you have to read or listen very carefully to understand what's really being said." Asked to comment on *Boston Globe* political reporter Tom Oliphant's view that the press corps "conveyed Reagan's version of reality" in its 1984 campaign coverage, he replied, "Do you convey Reagan's version of reality, or do you convey what Reagan *says* is reality? We certainly conveyed what he *said* was reality. . . . Now, it may be true that most people don't make that distinction. They should. We ought to start off in grammar school, or junior high, with a course on reading the newspaper and watching television: how to understand attribution."

In the meantime, one alternative was for the press to devote as much time and space to White House critics as it did to the White House itself. The problem was, contradicting the President raised the issue of press neutrality. That did not mean it could never be done, but there were limits; one had to be fair about it. And what was fair? "I have the feeling, and we, meaning the establishment, have the feeling," explained ABC News senior vice president Richard Wald, "that you can say the President is wrong, and you can repeat it once, but after that it becomes a crusade. And television doesn't do crusades. Nor do newspapers."

This self-imposed restraint was the ideal definition of responsible journalism for the Reagan White House, for Ronald Reagan was nothing if not shameless about repeating statements and stories shown to be false or misleading. Since news organizations tended to consider almost anything a President said or did to be news, and since they were nowhere near as stingy about letting a President make his case as they were about correcting him, simple arithmetic meant that over time the public tended to get far more exposure to the President's than to competing versions of reality.

The political advantages for the White House in this were obvious. Especially during the first six years of his presidency Mr. Reagan time and again shifted the framework of debate simply by repeating the same dubious assertions over and over until they became accepted as political facts of life. On May 9, 1984, for example, Reagan delivered a nationally televised speech about Central America filled with enough accusations of Communist subversion to make one wonder if the White House had hired Joe McCarthy's ghost as a speechwriter. The President charged that "Sandinista rule is a Communist reign of terror" and that Nicaragua was engaged in an unjustified military buildup in order to "export terror to every other country in the region." All this was part of "a bold attempt by the Soviet Union, Cuba and Nicaragua to install Communism by force throughout the hemisphere." While the United States wanted only "to promote democracy and economic well-being" in Central America and would "never be the aggressor," the Communists were shipping tons of weapons to guerrillas in El Salvador who "want to shoot their way into power and establish totalitarian rule." If the United States did not act, quickly and resolutely, "our choice will be a Communist Central America with additional Communist military bases on the mainland of this hemisphere and Communist subversion spreading southward and northward."

Now, it would seem important for Americans to realize that many of the things their President had just told them were at best unproved assertions or one-sided interpretations and at worst demonstrably false statements. Yet not one of the network commentators pointed this out in their post-speech summaries. Neither did the next day's account in *The New York Times* or *The Washington Post*. To do so would have implied that the President was either a liar or a fool, hardly a politically neutral message. Instead, objectivity prevailed over accuracy, Reagan's statements were reported uncritically, just as Senator McCarthy's were, and the American people were left not merely uninformed but misinformed.

Had news stories given prominent if not equal weight to countervailing views, Reagan would not have been able to impose his often mistaken premises on the political debate so easily. It should have been a simple matter of standing up for truth and accuracy, but in the eyes of objective mainstream journalists such behavior smacked of partisanship and thus violated the sacred vow of neutrality.

James Reston, for example, though he lamented the press's tendency to serve as a "transmission belt" for the official government line of the moment, nonetheless argued that "it would be very dangerous, I think, for us to spend 50 percent of our reports announcing their statements and decisions and then using the other 50 percent to say what liars they are." And even Sam Donaldson, certainly one of the most aggressive reporters in Washington, made a similar point when he cautioned, "My mission is not to blow them out of the water every day. I think it would be very dangerous if I took that attitude."

All of which suggests the conclusion that during the Reagan years the Washington and especially the White House press corps functioned less as an independent than as a palace court press. Journalists were extremely adept at discovering and detailing the intrigues of palace politics—who were the powers behind the throne, what were the King and his men up to, what factions within court society opposed them and how strongly, what decisions were made and what effects they would have. This was valuable information, and often the press reported more of it than some, particularly the King and his men, would have liked. The press in this sense was the bad boy of palace court society. But the press tended to confine its naughtiness within relatively narrow limits. It was not inclined to step outside the mind-set of the authorities it covered, or to challenge in any fundamental way the policies they formulated or the assumptions and values that gave rise to those policies. As Robert Kaiser explained, journalists and news organizations "are members of this class, this governing, political class." As such, their coverage inevitably reflected the values, beliefs and interests of that class. Although formally independent, in practice the American press functioned more often than not as an arm of the American state.

ROBERT JENSEN

The Military's Media
(2003)

One of the first reports of the Iraq War from an embedded journalist has turned out to be remarkably prescient about the level of independence viewers could expect from U.S. television journalists. CBS News reporter Jim Axelrod, traveling with the Third Infantry, told viewers that he had just come from a military intelligence briefing, where "we've been given orders." Axelrod quickly corrected himself— "soldiers have been given orders"—but it was difficult not to notice his slip.

U.S. reporters weren't taking orders directly from the Pentagon, of course, but one could forgive television viewers for wondering, especially early on. U.S. commanders may have had a few problems on the battlefield, but they had little to worry about from the news media—especially on television.

If the first two weeks of coverage was any indication, this war will be a case study in the failure of success of U.S. journalism.

The success came in the technological sophistication and deployment of resources: the ability of journalists, demonstrating considerable skill and fortitude, to deliver words and pictures from halfway around the world with incredible speed under difficult conditions. The failure was in journalists' inability to offer an account of events that could help people come to the fullest possible understanding— not only of what was happening in the war, but why it was happening and what it meant.

First, clear criteria are needed to evaluate news media performance, based on what citizens in a democracy need from journalists: 1) an independent source of factual information; 2) the historical, political, and social context in which to make sense of those facts; and 3) exposure to the widest range of opinion available in the society.

News media failures on #2 and #3 are the most obvious. U.S. media provided woefully limited background and context, and the range of opinion tended to run, as the old joke goes, from A to B.

From *The Progressive*, May 2003.

On television, current military officers were "balanced" with retired military officers. (A recent study by Fairness and Accuracy in Reporting noted that 76 percent of the guests on network talk shows in late January and early February 2003 were current or former officials, and that anti-war sources accounted for less than 1 percent.) So for the week before and after Secretary of State Colin Powell's February 5, 2003, presentation to the United Nations—when a full and rich discussion about the war was crucial—there was no meaningful debate on the main news shows of CBS, ABC, NBC, or PBS. Studies of the op-ed pages of *The Washington Post*, often considered to be a liberal newspaper, showed that the pro-war opinions dominated—by a 3-to-1 ratio from December 1, 2002, through February 21, 2003, according to Todd Gitlin's analysis in *The American Prospect*.

The media didn't even provide the straight facts well. At the core of coverage of this war was the system of "embedding" reporters with troops, allowing reporters to travel with military units—so long as they followed the rules. Those rules said reporters could not travel independently (which meant they could not really report independently), interviews had to be on the record (which meant lower-level service members were less likely to say anything critical), and officers could censor copy and temporarily restrict electronic transmissions for "operational security" (which, in practice, could be defined as whatever field commanders want to censor). In the first two weeks of the war, two reporters—*Christian Science Monitor* freelancer Philip Smucker and Fox's Geraldo Rivera—were removed from the field for allegedly giving too much information about troop locations on television.

After being confined to press pools with heavy-handed censorship in the 1991 Gulf War, news organizations were understandably grateful for the embedded system, and about 600 journalists signed up (other journalists—called "unilaterals"— were covering the war without military approval). But most of the reports sent back by those embedded reporters in the first two weeks were either human-interest stories about the troops or boosterish narration of the advance of troops. Not surprisingly, the reporters ended up bonding with the service members with whom they shared the hardships and risks of life in the field. As NBC News correspondent David Bloom, who died tragically of a blood clot in his lung, put it: "[The soldiers] have done anything and everything that we could ask of them, and we in turn are trying to return the favor by doing anything and everything that they can ask of us."

Beyond this abandonment of even the pretense of independence, much of the coverage was devoid of useful information. Consider this exchange on March 20, 2003, between CNN anchor Aaron Brown and Walter Rodgers, embedded with the Seventh Cavalry.

Rodgers: "The pictures you're seeing are absolutely phenomenal. These are live pictures of the Seventh Cavalry racing across the deserts in southern

Iraq. . . . If you ride inside that tank, it is like riding in the bowels of a dragon. They roar. They screech. You can see them slowing now. We've got to be careful not to get in front of them. But what you're watching here. . . ."

Brown: "Wow, look at that shot."

Rodgers: ". . . is truly historic television and journalism."

Wow, we get it. Those are tanks: racing, roaring, screeching, firing shells. Historic. Wow, look at it. But what do we learn from it?

One way to judge the likely effects of the embedded system on the public is to pay attention to what military officials were saying. General Tommy Franks described the briefing podium at Central Command headquarters in Doha, Qatar, as a "platform for truth" (truth delivered on a set built by a Hollywood designer for a quarter of a million taxpayer dollars), but the goal of any military is not to distribute truth but to control the flow of information. Early on, U.S. officials judged the embedded system a success. "We're seeing most importantly how well equipped, well trained, and how well led U.S. forces are; we see how careful they are in carrying out their duty," said Bryan Whitman, a senior official at the Pentagon's public affairs department. British Defense Secretary Geoff Hoon declared, "The imagery they broadcast is at least partially responsible for the public's change in mood, with the majority of people now saying they back the coalition." To a large extent, the embedded system served the Pentagon well as propaganda. It conveyed the Pentagon's message, it touted the technological prowess of the U.S. military, and it fed the home audience a constant diet of U.S. bravery.

The other main sources of information for U.S. viewers were the statements of military officials. Televised briefings seem less central to the military's information strategy than in the 1991 war, but the media still relied heavily on what the high command dished out. Given the fast-moving nature of war, we should expect some inaccurate information, but we also should expect reporters to be skeptical. Among the most embarrassing incidents was when U.S. journalists reported as fact the military's claims that the people of Basra had risen up against Hussein's forces within days of the war's onset. Reporting of such "facts" was of great importance if the United States was going to convince the world that this was a war to liberate the Iraqi people—in which case it would help if the liberated appreciate their liberation and join in. But officials had to back off from that claim because, inconveniently, it wasn't true at the time.

Those reports eventually were corrected, but—as anyone who has ever been on the wrong end of a false media report knows—the initial lie usually travels further and with more effect on the public memory than subsequent corrections. These incidents also remind us that military officials don't always tell the truth (little shock, and no awe, on that count) and that, for all their talk about being skeptical, journalists are an easy mark for government disinformation, especially in wartime.

As the U.S. military discovered that the attack on Iraq wasn't going to be the "cakewalk" that some had predicted, journalists covered the debate among various politicians and generals about the wisdom of the war plan. But these debates over strategy and tactics don't get at crucial issues about the legitimacy of the war. While U.S. reporters did ask Secretary of Defense Donald Rumsfeld whether he had erred by not having more troops on the ground, they shied away from raising a question that gets at a fundamental U.S. hypocrisy. Rumsfeld condemned Iraq for videotaping interviews with captured American soldiers and airing them on state television, contending it was a violation of the Geneva Conventions. If U.S. military officials have such a commitment to those rules, why do they not do what they can to shield Iraqi prisoners from photographers, and why have they not called on the U.S. media to stop using such images? Perhaps more important, why does Rumsfeld refuse to even acknowledge the POW status of soldiers captured in the Afghanistan war? This incident jumped off the scale on the hypocrisy meter, yet the mainstream commercial press politely avoided or glossed over the questions.

Sometimes U.S. reporters seemed to be more hawkish than the generals. In the first two days of the war, TV journalists appeared overeager for the "Shock and Awe" bombing to start and even petulant that it hadn't. While waiting, reporters and anchors fed the public gushing stories about the marvelous destructive capacity of the weaponry. Three days into the war, CNN's Judy Woodruff ended a segment featuring an interview with an A-10 "Warthog" pilot with the comment, "We continue to marvel at what those planes can do." Once "Shock and Awe" began, some on-air reporters appeared jubilant—as if they were watching a fireworks display and not weapons that kill people.

For several days in news conferences, reporters had also pressed officials to explain why Iraqi television facilities had not been bombed. When U.S. planes finally hit the station on March 26, 2003, Pentagon spokeswoman Victoria Clarke was asked why the station was considered a legitimate target. "Command and control," she said tersely. Everyone realized the Hussein regime had used television to disseminate state-dictated propaganda (which raises an interesting question about the status of private television stations that are full of state-encouraged propaganda), but U.S. officials had not demonstrated that Iraq's TV facilities were being used for specifically military purposes. Amnesty International and the International Federation of Journalists have called the bombing a potential war crime, but the U.S. news media reported the attack matter-of-factly.

Probably one of the most surreal moments on television recently came when Alan Colmes—the "liberal" on Fox's *Hannity & Colmes* talk show—queried "elder statesman" Henry Kissinger about the TV station bombing. Colmes mentioned that Amnesty International had questioned the attack, and then asked Kissinger if that criticism was fair to the United States. Kissinger, with no hint of irony, replied that he had "never heard the argument that you can't bomb the television or radio stations in a war of the other side." Colmes explained that some thought the station was "a civilian object and thus protected under the [Geneva] accords." Kissinger, again with a straight face, answered, "I think it's extremely dangerous for outside groups to turn these things into a legal argument."

The firing of Peter Arnett, one of the most experienced war correspondents in the world, became a major media story. Arnett has an overblown sense of his own importance and lousy political judgment. That's been true ever since he became a television "personality," and he's hardly the only one with those traits.

But Arnett's pomposity and hubris were not what got him fired by NBC and MSNBC's *National Geographic Explorer* after giving a short interview to Iraqi state television. When the controversy first emerged, NBC issued a statement of support, which evaporated as soon as the political heat was turned up and questions about Arnett's patriotism got tossed around.

By going on Iraqi state television, which clearly was a propaganda vehicle for the regime, Arnett opened himself up to being used. That was a miscalculation.

Arnett compounded it by citing the "unfailing courtesy and cooperation" of the Iraqi people and the Ministry of Information. Certainly, Arnett knew that no foreign reporter could travel in the country without an Iraqi government minder and that the regime had kicked out some reporters.

Arnett likely was just being obliging. But his sin is one of degree; obsequiousness is common for reporters currying favor with sources.

If such criticism of Arnett was appropriate, we should also ask whether American journalists were overly deferential to U.S. officials. Consider George W. Bush's March 6, 2003, news conference, when journalists played along in a scripted television event and asked such softball questions as, "How is your faith guiding you?" Journalists that night were about as critical as Arnett was with the Iraqis.

Such performances left the rest of the world with the impression that American journalists—especially those on television—were sycophants, and Arnett's firing only reinforced that impression.

Every time the phrase "Operation Iraqi Freedom" appeared in the corner of the screen during an NBC report or journalists used it as their own, they were endorsing the Administration's claims about the motives for war. The same can be said for "coalition forces." Journalists' constant use of the term gives legitimacy to the Bush claim that a real coalition was fighting this war, when in fact it was a U.S. war with assistance from the British.

Reporting on Iraqi civilian deaths was notably skimpy or skewed. On the *CBS Evening News* one night, Dan Rather gave the death toll of U.S. and British soldiers, and then said the death toll of Iraqi soldiers and civilians was "uncertain." But reporting by non-U.S. media—especially Al-Jazeera and other Arab television networks—forced American reporters to mention the subject, though the images of the casualties were hard to find, and sympathy was often lacking.

On *Larry King Live* on March 29, 2003, CNN anchor Wolf Blitzer discussed the U.S. bombing of a Baghdad market that killed at least fifty people. His concern about the deaths seemed to be that "the pictures that are going to be seen on Al-Jazeera and Al-Arabia and all the Arab satellite channels are going to be further fodder for this anti-American attitude that is clearly escalating as this war continues." Blitzer said the United States would "have an enormous amount of work to do to . . . point out that if, in fact, it was an errant U.S. bomb or missile, that would be a mistake. It certainly wouldn't be deliberate."

Is this inevitable? Are we doomed to get home-team coverage of war from journalists at the dominant commercial media? A glance across the ocean suggests not. In Britain, some newspapers haven't performed any better than U.S. counterparts, but there are also many mainstream journalists doing excellent work. Every day, *The Guardian* and *The Independent* (both available on the web) offer sharp-edged reporting and critical commentary. In briefings, the British reporters consistently ask tougher questions of the generals. Brits are fighting alongside Americans, but these U.K. journalists don't shy away from describing the horrors of war.

Robert Fisk, whose gutsy Middle East reporting for *The Independent* has made him something of a celebrity in left/progressive circles in the United States, described American journalism in a lecture in early February 2003 as increasingly "vapid, hopeless, gutless, unchallenging" since 9/11.

It's hard to argue with him. When that U.S. bomb exploded in a Baghdad market, the U.S. military suggested it might have been the result of an aging Iraqi anti-aircraft missile. The reporter who found the remains of the bomb's serial number, identifying it as a U.S. weapon manufactured in Texas by Raytheon, was not an American reporter, but Fisk.

PERMISSIONS

The editors are grateful for permission to reprint the following copyrighted material.

"The House of Lords" by George Seldes. Reprinted by the permission of Russell & Volkening as agents for the author, copyright © 1935 by George Seldes, renewed in 1966 by George Seldes.

"Big Business and the Press" by George Seldes. Reprinted by the permission of Russell & Volkening as agents for the author, copyright © 1935 by George Seldes, renewed in 1966 by George Seldes.

"The Power of Advertising" by George Seldes. Reprinted by the permission of Russell & Volkening as agents for the author, copyright © 1935 by George Seldes, renewed in 1966 by George Seldes.

"Sex, Lies & Advertising" by Gloria Steinem. Copyright © 1990 by Gloria Steinem.

"Our Un-Free Press" by John Dewey. All quotations from works written by John Dewey are from *John Dewey: The Later Works, 1925–1953*, vol. 2, *1935–1937*, and are used by permission of the Center for Dewey Studies, Southern Illinois University Carbondale.

"Why a Review of Journalism?" by the editors of *Columbia Journalism Review*. Reprinted from *Columbia Journalism Review*, Spring 1962 © 1962 *Columbia Journalism Review*.

"Night Thoughts of a Media Watcher" by Gloria Steinem. Excerpt from "Night Thoughts of a Media Watcher" from *Outrageous Acts and Everyday Rebellions* by Gloria Steinem, copyright © 1983 by Gloria Steinem, copyright © 1984 by East Toledo Productions, Inc., copyright © 1995 by Gloria Steinem. Reprinted by permission of Henry Holt and Company, LLC.

"The Growing Gap" by Ben Bagdikian. From *The Media Monopoly* by Ben Bagdikian, copyright © 1983, 1987, 1992, 1997, 2000 by Ben Bagdikian. Reprinted by permission of Beacon Press, Boston.